RIGHT REASON

RIGHT REASON

William F. Buckley, Jr.

A Collection Selected by
Richard Brookhiser

LITTLE, BROWN AND COMPANY
BOSTON   TORONTO

FIRST PAPERBACK EDITION

Published by arrangement with
Doubleday & Co., Inc.

Library of Congress Cataloging-in-Publication Data
Buckley, William F. (William Frank), 1925–
Right reason.

Includes index.
1. United States—Politics and government—
1977–1981.   2. United States—Foreign relations—
1977–1981.   3. United States—Politics and government—
1981–   .   4. United States—Foreign relations—
1981–   .   I. Brookhiser, Richard.   II. Title.
E872.B83   1986   320.973   86-10328
ISBN 0-316-11444-8 (pbk.)

Drawing by Ed Arno © 1984 *The New Yorker* Magazine, Inc.

Doonesbury cartoons copyright 1974 G.B. Trudeau.
Reprinted with permission of Universal Press Syndicate.
All rights reserved.

"A Matter of Style" originally appeared in *Playboy*,
© 1983 by William F. Buckley, Jr.
"Queen of All Instruments" originally appeared in
The New York Times Magazine, © 1983 by William F. Buckley, Jr.

RRD-VA

*Published simultaneously in Canada
by Little, Brown & Company (Canada) Limited*

PRINTED IN THE UNITED STATES OF AMERICA

For Roger Milliken

ACKNOWLEDGMENTS

I am grateful to the proprietors of the enterprises in which the material in this book first appeared. They include *Dorm* Magazine, *Foreign Affairs*, Holt, Rinehart & Winston, *Life*, Little, Brown & Company, *National Catholic Reporter, National Review, The New Republic,* New York *Times Magazine, Penthouse, Playboy,* Regnery/Gateway, the Universal Press Syndicate, and the Washington Star Syndicate. Chaucy Bennetts is the finest copy editor I have ever experienced—my thanks to her. My thanks to Joseph Isola, yet again, for his fine proofreading; to Frances Bronson for her superintendence of the entire project; and to Dorothy McCartney for vital research.

I am above all grateful to my associate Richard Brookhiser who selected, arranged, and introduced the material for this book.

W.F.B.
Stamford, Connecticut
April 1, 1985

CONTENTS

INTRODUCTION

by Richard Brookhiser

I had been at *National Review,* the magazine Bill Buckley edits, for about a year when he called me into his office. There was an accumulated load, even heavier than usual, of ideas, projects, and assignments that had to be discussed, and he looked over his dense schedule for an opening while I consulted my considerably more spacious one. He frowned. "You'll have to go—" the usual place for office talk was Paone's, an Italian restaurant around the corner "—to Mexico." Sure, why not?

He had a speaking engagement in Mexico City, but before that he wanted to spend a day in Taxco, so as soon as we landed —the snow-capped volcanoes that loom over the capital gleamed in an unusually clear sky—he rented a car and was headed up over the mountains. Stalin, he noted, once murdered his ambassador to Mexico simply by recalling him and having an altitude-activated bomb planted in the plane. Past the city limits, he pulled over for a snack ("Don't be alarmed, I've eaten here since I was a teenager"). The john was the side of a rusty water tank out back and the towels were newspapers, but the tortillas were good and I am still alive. The proprietor served Dos Equis at a bar surmounted by a madonna, and we headed on.

It grew dark. He talked about Joe McCarthy; the Grateful

Dead; and about a former Mexican president with whom he had once broken the ice by confessing that he had worked for the CIA in Mexico during that president's tenure. "How amusing," was the reply. "Were you for me, or against me?" After a long, flat stretch the road began once again to rise and curl in switchbacks, and suddenly we were in Taxco.

The town is preserved from the seventeenth century. It looked as exotic as China, or the moon. The car crept up and down the gear-wrenching cobbles to the main square, where we parked and sat on the balcony of Bertha's, a bar overlooking the wrought-iron benches and the elephantine plane trees and the baroque churches sprayed with saints and doodads. Margaritas. More talk. It was very late, but we had farther still to go—and higher. Along the lightless road, the headlights picked out donkeys, cows. "I think it's here." He made a sharp turn into what looked like a thicket, but after a few rutted yards we came out to clear sky and the summit and the hotel. Shut tight.

Much knocking roused an Indian in a Black Watch cap who had been sleeping on a couch, waiting for late arrivals. He took a flashlight and led the way to the cottages. Faced with a sloping site, the builders had let their fancy run wild. The cottages were scattered around a central garden. The connecting paths ran over bridges and through arches; doorways looked down or peeked up unexpectedly. There was only one problem—Bill remembered a particular cottage where he and his son had stayed two years before, and the Indian didn't know where it was. So while the moon blazed and the shadows trembled, we scrambled back and forth across the slumbering grounds. At last, and reluctantly, Bill settled for a lesser perfection. A nightcap. Talk of harpsichord kits. He couldn't see actually building one. "I get bored winding my watch." He went off to his room, leaving me on my veranda, watching the strange stars and listening to the distant, braying beasts.

I didn't know, a year out of college, whether this version of a business lunch was the way of all editors; I suspected not. The truly unique thing about the episode, though, is that for Bill it isn't unique. Dozens of people who have crossed his path— colleagues and strangers, friends and antagonists—could tell kindred stories. Generous, curious, playful, orthodox—that's how he behaves. It is also how he writes.

This is the seventh collection of Buckley's articles and columns and the first edited by someone other than himself. It appears thirty-five years after he graduated from Yale (an education he memorialized in his first book); on the sixtieth year after his birth. A backward glance may be appropriate.

Buckley has been the acknowledged champion of American conservatism for three decades. But the conservative movement of the fifties was unrecognizably different from what it is today. It scarcely existed, and what existed was chaos. There were Marxists turned McCarthyites, and America Firsters turned globalists. There were free-marketeers and fans of Edmund Burke, defenders of business and bewailers of Appomattox. Toward the end of the decade there appeared Ayn Rand and Robert Welch who argued, respectively, that charity was criminal and that Eisenhower was a communist. And there were always, as on the margins of every movement, the trimmers, represented on the level of day-to-day politics by the prophets of Modern Republicanism, whose Sisyphean task it was to give coherence to the actions of the Eisenhower administration, and, on a somewhat higher plane, by Peter Viereck, who made a small career of explaining that the great modern conservative politicians were Adlai Stevenson and FDR.

National Review was crucial in bringing order out of this welter. The mainstream media treated nascent conservatism with indifference or hostility, and the right had had no journal of opinion of its own since *The Freeman* effectively self-destructed in 1953. Starting in 1955, and for more than a decade thereafter, *National Review* was the only place conservatives could talk to one another and yell at one another: a forum where the right relations between freedom and self-defense and transcendence could be hammered out.

And Bill Buckley was essential to *National Review*. He gathered a core of editors who covered the conservative gamut. They were brilliant and talented (and almost all a generation older than he). They were also frequently impossible. Willi Schlamm, a former confidant of Henry Luce, and Willmoore Kendall, a rebellious Yale professor ("every time I ask Yale for a leave of absence, I find it insultingly cooperative") ultimately departed. Frank Meyer, the fiery ex-Communist who became a premier book editor, hurled his thunderbolts from his mountaintop home in Woodstock, New York, a prudent distance. Russell Kirk, author of *The Conservative Mind,* contributed from an even greater distance—Mecosta, Michigan—which was just as well, since Meyer had anathematized him. James Burnham, the philosopher and strategist whose intellectual peregrinations had taken him from Aquinas to Trotsky to Machiavelli, worked selflessly for the common enterprise, but even he was not above mischief (his favorite method of igniting Meyer was to suggest that the book reviews be shortened). Buckley's achievement was to hold these and other talents together, using all his resources of charm (it works on fifty-year-olds too). In the words of William Rusher, *NR*'s publisher for twenty-eight years, "he kept all the bears in one cage doing their tricks."

If reason were all, this would have been enough. But the most exigent political motives are often irrational. Buckley, drawing on what depths of skepticism or wisdom I do not know, realized this very early on. In *God and Man at Yale* (1951) he defined liberalism's intellectual substance: its distrust of unmanaged economic transactions, its scorn for Christianity and religion generally. In *Up from Liberalism* (1959) he discovered the key to its success: that liberalism was a *fashion*—a collection of prejudices that governed the governors. Liberals, by the fifties, had stopped defending their ideas; they displayed them, like good clothes. Nonliberals, it followed, were worse than wrong; they were uncouth louts. This was Buckley's second achievement: to break the liberal monopoly on style—by writing as well, and by talking as fast, as any liberal pundit going. The effect was most startling on early segments of his television talk show, "Firing Line." Serene liberal guests left it sputtering; some avoided it altogether. (Why didn't Bobby Kennedy appear? Buckley was once asked. "Why does baloney reject the grinder?") The high point of this personal campaign came with his 1965 run on the Conservative Party ticket for mayor of New York City. Fate gave him the perfect opponent; John Lindsay—young, handsome, liberal, lumbering. Lindsay won, New York lost; Buckley, and derivatively conservatism, were on the stylistic map.

If the tasks for which historians are most likely to remember him were largely completed by the mid-sixties, then what has he been doing since? In part reacting to history, which is never as tidy as historians make it. Whittaker Chambers, another of *National Review*'s early editors, once quoted in the magazine's pages a letter of Trotsky: "Anybody looking for a quiet life has picked the wrong century to be born in." "The remark," Chambers added, "must be allowed a certain authority, since the century clinched the point by mauling with an ax the brain that framed it." American conservatives have been spared both the fate of Trotsky and the weariness that overtook Whittaker Chambers. They haven't enjoyed ease. The century of the monster state and the godless universe offers a continuing affront to their convictions.

The times, then, prod Buckley to write. But so do his convictions. Since you are about to read a hundred-odd expressions of them, I won't attempt to summarize them except to mention one that is relevant here: the conviction that all his other convictions can be applied in the modern world. Drugs in Harlem; defeat in Vietnam; the vernacular mass; the OPEC price gouge; Ronald Reagan's occasional losses of nerve, and Tip O'Neill's obstinate ignorance—these are not woes beneath our notice or beyond comprehension, but problems we can analyze, judge, and untangle. Not that we will act on our conclusions (the two colleagues whom Buckley perhaps most admired, Burnham and Chambers, agreed, despite vast differences in their minds and their temperaments, on one thing: a grim view of our prospects). The philosopher's phrase, *recta ratio*—right reason—suggests the possibilities; it denotes both the order of nature, and the order engendered in human thought and action when they conform to it. The conclusions are there to be drawn, and—who knows?—men have their free will.

Though this collection marks an anniversary, it is not conceived as a *Best of Bill Buckley*, covering his whole career. The man has thousands of columns and who knows how many books ahead of him, and there is plenty of time yet before we have to start worrying about chrestomathies.

Right Reason draws on the columns and articles that have been written in the seven years since *A Hymnal*, Buckley's last collection. So much has happened in that time—seven years ago, Karol Wojtyla was a Polish archbishop, Riza Pahlevi was the Light of the Aryans, and interest rates were kissing President Carter's popularity levels—that I thought it best to organize the material by tone rather than subject. "Assailing" shows Buckley dressed to kill; no time for thumb-sucking. "Commenting" collects solutions to a variety of problems, most of them quite specific. In "Analyzing" he tracks unfolding events. In "Reflecting" he steps back to get a larger perspective. (This is the longest section—it is what columnists spend most of their time doing, after all—and the most diffuse, but it offers the best sense of the sweep of the job.)

"Corresponding" gathers highlights of a regular feature of *National Review*, "Notes & Asides." In this biweekly page and a half, Buckley prints letters he has written, often controversial, as well as an extraordinary range of letters addressed to him. People write in to praise, to tease, to complain, to tell jokes, to air pedantries, and to make truly serious points. Sometimes Buckley responds; sometimes he is simply the sounding board. There is a piece to be written one day about the bulk of his correspondence: who are the best writers—prisoners, without question; who are the worst—those who sign themselves "Ph.D."; who are the most quarrelsome—Irish, Jews, Ukrainians, and Poles: you set off the Irish by saying anything nice about England; Jews, by saying anything nice about Arabs; Ukrainians, by saying Kiev is in Russia; Poles, by saying anything about anything.

"Appreciating," finally, draws together pieces that are called in journalistic parlance offbeat—profiles, eulogies, rhapsodies —though they are not, for that reason, less important. Here, released a bit from the baying and press of events, Bill Buckley turns his attention to friends, acquaintances, and things for which he has felt affection, admiration, or sorrow in this season of the wrong century.

Why, asked Yeats in his seventies, should not old men be mad? I cannot imagine Bill asking that question twelve years from now, or twenty. He knows the reasons for anger—and for pride, and for celebration. They are also reasons to write. I look forward to the next few collections.

RICHARD BROOKHISER

RIGHT REASON

I
ASSAILING

1
Introductory Epilogue

(What follows is an essay on the critical reaction to the publication of the hardcover edition of Overdrive. *It can be read before reading the book. Or after reading the book. Or not at all.)*

WHEN RAY ROBERTS, who is my editor for this paperback edition of *Overdrive*, asked if I would write an introduction to it I agreed right away to do so. I did this because I thought the reviews of it worth going over with some thought, hoping that such a study would interest readers, and knowing that it would interest me. There are over a hundred of these *(Overdrive* was handled intensively by the critical press) and they say something about the book but also about the culture in which they cropped up.

I begin, in search of focus, with a chronology. I reveal in the text of *Overdrive* when exactly it occurred to me (quite suddenly) to write this book, a journal of that particular week in my life. I had done such a book ten years earlier. It was here and there suggested by some critics that I had dreamed up a way to discharge an obligation to my publisher. Not so. In fact, the contrary is the case because when I decided to write this book I needed to get my publisher's agreement to postpone a commitment I had already made. I decided that I wished to write *this* book.

So I did: during the two months (in February and March), in Switzerland, when I have the time substantially to devote myself to book writing. It took me as many weeks to complete, almost exactly, as any of my other books, including my novels. It was suggested by one critic (you will see) that I more or less dictated scraps of this & that into a machine, presumably while skiing. Other critics, however (you will also see), did not challenge that the book was written with care.

When I returned to New York, the manuscript complete except for the fine-tuning I do in July, I sent a letter to the editor of *The New Yorker*, Mr. William Shawn. I told him I thought it unlikely he would want to see my new book, given that I used exactly the same formula I had used ten years before in writing *Cruising Speed*, which *The New Yorker* had excerpted. Mr. Shawn replied that he would like to read *Overdrive*, which he subsequently bought.

It happened that the task of editing *Cruising Speed*'s excerpts fell to Mr. Shawn, if it can be said that anything at *The New Yorker* "falls" to Mr. Shawn. In any event, I had the extraordinary experience of working with him, he going over every sentence. When we lunched together one day I remember that a substantial part of our meeting was concerned with my habit of placing commas in unconventional places. This finally drew from Mr. Shawn, over the telephone, what I take it must be the sharpest kind of reproach the gentleman ever permits himself: "I am afraid, Mr. Buckley, that you do not really know the proper use of the comma." If St. Peter had declared me unfit to enter the Kingdom of God, I could not have felt more searingly the reproach, delivered in Mr. Shawn's inimitable (meiotic) manner. I hardly intend to suggest that he is otherwise permissive, though he sticks firmly, after *The New Yorker* makes the first-draft selection, to his determination to let authors whose works are being excerpted signify what they wish included, what excluded. Merely that he is meticulous. "I want *you* to be pleased with what we publish," he said to me. I have had a wonderful relationship with *The New Yorker*, having submitted five book manuscripts to Mr. Shawn, and received five acceptances.

I did not again work directly with Mr. Shawn. My next editor, William Whitworth, also demanding, and thorough, and civil, is now the editor of *The Atlantic.* The succeeding editor was Patrick Crow, a genial, surefooted, relaxed and amusing man who does not for a moment attempt to conceal that Mr. Shawn is *the* editor of *The New Yorker,* who reviews every controversial decision made during the many hours spent between the author and his *New Yorker* editor. When the author especially pleads for inclusion of a passage to which Mr. Shawn unwaveringly objects, what happens is that Mr. Shawn calls the author up and patiently explains why he is opposed to the inclusion of that passage. This author has always relented. I would do anything for Mr. Shawn save join the Communist Party, and I am happy that it is unlikely he will ever ask me to do so.

All of this is by way of background, given that some critics a) concluded that I expanded by force-feeding into a book (about 75,000 words long) what I had written for *The New Yorker (The New Yorker*'s version ran about 45,000 words); while others b) pretended to flirt with the idea that Mr. Shawn had coaxed me into writing a self-parody, that he had acted as an editorial agent provocateur—a reading of Mr. Shawn wildly ignorant of the kind of person he is; leaving also c) a few critics who, though reviewing my book, obviously had not read it, having clearly read only the excerpts published in *The New Yorker.* One critic especially comes to mind, who warned, "Readers seeking the tart side of Mr. Buckley will be disappointed." The tart side of Mr. Buckley is well represented in the book, less so in the *New Yorker* excerpts because Mr. Shawn explained to me over the telephone, after I had pitched for the inclusion of one very tart episode, that *The New Yorker* does not have a letters column in which editorial targets can fire back, and that therefore he feels it morally important to avoid anything that might be thought of as hit-and-run.

In due course (January, February 1983), the *New Yorker* excerpts were published, and the reaction to them was, well, out of the ordinary. The Washington *Post*'s Curt Suplee reported joyously in his column, "That incessant scrunching noise you keep hearing to the north is Wm. F. Buckley Jr. attempting to squeeze his ego between the covers of *The New Yorker.* The

behemoth first half of his two-part personal journal makes
Proust looks positively laconic. Buckley maunders along like
Macaulay on Quaaludes about his house, limo, kids and friends,
gloating and quoting his snappiest ripostes . . . *And yet you
can't put the damn thing down!* Odd anecdotes bob up in the
verbal spew (e.g., the time a typo in his column made it seem as
if Pat Boone and his wife were wild about porno movies). The
rhythm becomes hypnotic and . . . is there such a thing as
smug-o-lepsy?"

I think I can only describe the reaction of *Newsweek* as
hysterical. Before *The New Yorker*'s ink was dry, Mr. Gene
Lyons published an excoriation in high tushery of indignation
("So who is this preposterous snob?"). Not satisfied with this,
Newsweek then published letters from readers for whom the
mere mention of my name is obviously emetic. And not content with *that*, *Newsweek* then published a piece speculating
on who might be the successor to William Shawn when he
retires as editor of *The New Yorker*, including reference to
unnamed critics' concern over Mr. Shawn's wilting powers, as
witness that he had published the "self-indulgent" journals of
Mr. Buckley. (The three assaults prompted me to write to
Newsweek to observe that I hoped their obsessive concern
over my self-indulgent journals had not got in the way of their
enjoyment of the two-million-dollar party *Newsweek* had
given itself in New York to celebrate its fiftieth anniversary.
The letter was published, but in bowdlerized form.)

Now, leading up to publication of the book and fired by *The
New Yorker*, came the parody makers. There was one by Jon
Carroll of the San Francisco *Chronicle* which was quite funny,
burlesquing among other things my occasional use of Latin
phrases. He had me referring to "Nihil Obstat, our Cuban-
American cook," summoning my "Honduran-American
driver, Pari Passu," sailing my "71-foot sloop, Malum In Sea,"
and using the services of my "ever efficient secretary, Gloria
Mundi." There was another treatment by Richard Cohen of
the Washington *Post*, good-natured and clever. Another in *The
New York Review of Books*, some of it very funny, and still
another in *The New Republic*.

I have elected to publish here in full the parody I thought
funniest. It was written for the University of Chicago daily, the

Chicago *Maroon*, by an undergraduate, David Brooks, the week before I went there as a visiting fellow. I put it all here in part because it is exuberantly readable but also because it communicates the nature of the irritation felt by some of the readers of the *New Yorker* articles. He touches, in the manner of the parodist, on themes that would be sustained by many of the critics when the book came out in August.

THE GREATEST STORY EVER TOLD

William Freemarket Buckley was born on December 25, 1935 in a little town called Bethlehem. He was baptized an Episcopalian on December 28 and admitted to Yale University on the 30th.

Buckley spent most of his infancy working on his memoirs. By the time he had learned how to talk he had finished three volumes: *The World Before Buckley,* which traced the history of the world prior to his conception; *The Seeds of Utopia,* which outlined his effect on world events during the nine months of his gestation; and *The Glorious Dawn,* which described the profound ramifications of his birth on the social order.

Buckley attended nursery school at the School of Soft Knocks, majoring in Art History. His thesis, "A Comparison of Michelangelo's David and My Own Mirror," won the Arthur C. Clarke award for Precocious Criticism and brought him to the attention of world luminaries.

His next bit of schooling was done at Exeter, where he majored in Pre-Yale.

Buckley's education was interrupted by World War II, during which he became the only six-year-old to fight in Guadalcanal and to land on the beaches of Normandy. Combat occupied much of his time during the period, but in between battles he was able to help out on the Manhattan Project, offer advice at Yalta, and design the Marshall Plan. His account of the war, *Buckley Versus Germany,* perched atop the New York *Times* Best Seller List for three years.

Upon his return to Exeter, Buckley found that schoolwork no longer challenged him. He transferred his energies to track, crew, polo, golf, tennis, mountain climbing, debate, stock brokerage, learning the world's languages, playing his harpsichord and, of course, writing his memoirs. By this time he had finished his ninth volume, *The Politics of Puberty,* which analyzed angst in the international arena and gave advice on how to pick up women. A friend at the time, Percy Rockefeller-Vanderbilt III remembered, "Everybody liked Bill at Exeter. His ability to change water into wine added to his popularity."

The years at Exeter were followed by the climax of his life, the Yale years. While at Yale he majored in everything and wrote the bestseller, *God and Me at Yale,* which was followed by *God and Me at Home,* and finally, *God and Me at the Movies.*

His extracurricular activities at Yale included editing the *Yale Daily News,* serving as President of the University, and chairing the committee to have Yale moved from New Haven to Mount Olympus. He also proved the existence of God by uttering the Cartesian formula, "I think, therefore I am."

While a senior, Buckley founded the publications which would become his life's work: one was a journal of politics entitled *The National Buckley,* and the other was a literary magazine called *The Buckley Review.* Later, he would merge the two publications into what is now known as *The Buckley Buckley.*

On the day of graduation, Buckley married Miss Honoria Haight-Ashbury and fathered a son and a daughter (Honoria helped) both of whom would be named Yale.

As any of you who read *The New Yorker* know, life for Mr. Buckley since then has been anything but dull. On any given morning he will consult with a handful of national leaders and the Pope, write another novel in the adventure series, "Bill Buckley, Private Eye," chat with a bevy of Academy Award winners, write a few syndicated columns, and tape an edition of his TV show, "Firing Pin." He also tames a wild horse, chops down trees to reduce U.S. oil imports, and descrambles some top secret Soviet spy transmissions.

In the afternoons he is in the habit of going into crowded rooms and making everybody else feel inferior. The evenings are reserved for extended bouts of name-dropping.

Last year, needing a break from his hectic fast lane life, Buckley sailed across the Atlantic in his yacht, the HMS *Armsrace,* and wrote a book entitled *Atlantic High.* In one particularly riveting scene, the *Armsrace* runs out of gas in the middle of the ocean and Buckley is forced to walk the rest of the way.

Buckley has received numerous honorary degrees, including an M.B.A., an Ll.D., a Ph.D., an M.D. and an L.H.D., all of them from Yale, of course.

During his two days at this university, Mr. Buckley will meet with students, attend classes, deliver a lecture and write four books.

So that as the countdown approached for the publication of *Overdrive*, one had the feeling that pens were being taken to the smithies to be sharpened. My son Christopher has a sensitive ear for these matters and advised me to batten down the hatches: I had seriously provoked, he warned me, substantial members of the critical community. And sure enough, his Farmer's Almanac proved reliable because the flak from the most conspicuous critical quarters (the New York *Times*, the Washington *Post*, *The New York Review of Books*, *The New Republic*, *The Nation*, *Atlantic*, and *Harper's*) was instantaneous, and heavy. These critics were uniformly—upset, might be the generic word to describe their emotions. They expressed themselves differently and at different lengths, ranging from the four-thousand-word review by John Gregory Dunne in *The New York Review of Books* to the two-sentence review in *The Atlantic*. They found the book variously boring, boorish, presumptuous, vain, arrogant, illiterate, solipsistic, and other things.

Kirkus Reviews, which is a prepublication bulletin designed for bookstores and libraries, summarized that "most readers will probably find this [book] tedious at best, sleekly loathsome at worst." The writing is "sloppy." An example of the kind of thing one finds in it is that at one point I ask myself why I labor, and answer, " 'the call of *recta ratio*,' and 'the fear of boredom.' He then goes on, patronizingly, to explain what *recta ratio* means." I think this means either that everybody already knows what *recta ratio* means, or that if not everybody knows what it means, an author should not explain the meaning, as to do so is patronizing. Writing for the New York *Times*, novelist Nora Ephron was oh so scornful. "He has written a book about money," was her principal finding. She imputed anti-Semitism (ever so deftly, but more readers would catch that than the meaning of *recta ratio*) and insensitivity to the suffering of my friends all in a single sentence: (". . . it's appalling that Mr. Buckley should mention Shylock when discussing *National Review*'s landlord or discourse so blithely on the physical infirmities of his friends"). And closed by suggesting that my affectations might best be understood by using a little ethnic imagination ("The English used to say, give an Irishman a horse and he'll vote Tory, but never mind").

So certain was Miss Ephron that much would be made of the fact that I get about in a chauffeur-driven limousine that she led off with it, quoting from my book at some length, to wit:

> I cannot imagine that anyone who reviews this book will fail to mention the part about the limousine, so I may as well begin with it. Only a few pages into *Overdrive*, WFB gets into his limousine . . . and the occasion inspires him to reveal the circumstances under which he had the car custom built. "What happened," he writes, "was that three years ago when it came time to turn in my previous car, which had done over 150,000 miles, the Cadillac people had come up with an austerity-model limousine, fit for two short people, preferably to ride to a funeral in. The dividing glass between the driver and driven was not automatic, there was no separate control for heat or air conditioning in the back, and the jump seats admitted only two. . . . This simply would not do: I use the car constantly, require the room, privacy, and my own temperature gauge. . . . There was, as usual, a market solution. You go out (this was in 1978) and buy a plain old Cadillac. You deliver it to a gentleman in Texarkana [I should have said Ft. Smith, Arkansas]. He chops it in two, and installs whatever you want. Cost? Interesting: within one thousand dollars of the regular limousine, and I actually don't remember which side."

Don't you see, Miss Ephron asks, "the story of the limousine is *emblematic"*? (My italics.)

My colleague Joe Sobran, on seeing Miss Ephron's review, sent me a memorandum: "Dear Bill, The critical reaction is interesting: Nora Ephron calls it 'a book about money,' when it's her *review* that's about money. I can't imagine you dwelling on the subject as she does; for that matter, I can't imagine you writing about your worst enemy as she writes about her ex-husband. Wonderful to hear such a woman lecture on poor taste, vulgarity, the nouveau riche. . . . My impression was that you can only be nouveau riche for the short-term; she seems to want to make you out as *second-generation* nouveau riche. She sees bigotry in a Shakespearean tag, then proceeds to make a crack about the Irish which the *Times* wouldn't tolerate about just *any* ethnic group."

Grace Lichtenstein, writing for the Washington *Post,* leaned heavily on the tease that William Shawn was pulling a fast one.

"When parts of this book first appeared in *The New Yorker,* I thought it was a joke, a Buckley parody of how some leftist might view Buckley's preoccupation with material possessions and his aristocratic lifestyle. Alas, it is not an intentional parody, although there are, swimming in this sea of trivia, some amusing anecdotes. . . ." Again, the business about my obsession with wealth, the slouchiness of my writing style; and then, to preserve her credentials as an even-minded critic, "Now let me tell you the most awful part of *Overdrive.* After plowing through a third of it I realized . . . I was also (deep breath here) [her deep breath] quite envious. I mean, who wouldn't want a stretch limo in which to dictate one's letters? [etc., extending to a cook and a chauffeur]—plebeian clod that I am," said Miss Lichtenstein, teasing us, because we are all supposed to know she is not *really* a plebeian clod.

Harper's took pretty much the same line, done by Rhoda Koenig, and *The Atlantic* saved space with a two-line review. "Mr. Buckley has assumed that a move-by-move record of one week in his bustling life, together with such recollections, reflections, and droppable names as occur to him en route, will be of benefit to the public. Ah, well, to err is human, and Mr. Buckley is not divine." There is a heavy burden, one can see, placed here on the word "benefit," as in "benefit to the public." Is Mr. Shawn, the revered longtime tutor of the editor of *The Atlantic,* engaged in "benefiting" mankind when he publishes *The New Yorker?* And if so, how do we measure these benefits (given that we are not divine)?

The San Francisco *Chronicle* also elected a short dismissal, by Patricia Holt, "Buckley has produced an overdone, overwritten, overblown 'personal documentary' whose preview in the *New Yorker* earlier this year provoked a brilliant sendup by Jon Carroll in these pages. Better to read that column than waste your time with this book." The revelation to the citizens of San Francisco that an editor of the San Francisco *Chronicle* was actually concerned about wasting their time was apparently met with such exuberant skepticism that *Overdrive* became, in that city, a modest bestseller.

The attack in *The New York Review of Books* was hefty and unexpected, this because its author, John Gregory Dunne, an acquaintance of long standing, had written to me after *The*

New Yorker articles had been published to say in a pleasant context that he had "inhaled" the *New Yorker* pieces and looked forward to the book treatment. Usually, if you hear that something you created had been "inhaled," you are likely to conclude something other than that your friend had been bowled over by a mephitic encounter. In any event, when Mr. Dunne's attack was published, the editor, Robert Silvers, punctiliously offered me space to reply. The gravamen of Mr. Dunne's objections was, really, my technicolored view of life. Unhappily, the discriminatory descriptions he gave of episodes touched on in the book justified his criticisms of them. If I were to write that Hamlet was a man who never could make up his mind and therefore manages to bore us to death I am, as a reviewer, fully protected—except against anybody who proceeds to read *Hamlet.* In my reply to *The New York Review of Books* I was concrete in the matter, excerpting exactly Dunne's description of one episode in the book (my quarrel with the Boston *Globe)* and then describing the episode itself. Mr. Dunne's version will live as a locus classicus of distortion (Locus Classicus, I should say for the benefit of Jon Carroll, is my Shangri-la).

A week after seeing Dunne's review I received a letter: "If they ever listen [to what you said in your book] (which must be a question) you will teach them not to take the sacred elixir of life and splash it all over the roadside, as they are too prone to do." That was the comment on *Overdrive* by Louis Auchincloss, whose profound advice is not heeded, even by writers some of whom can no longer blame their afflictions on youth. Lance Morrow (I anticipate my narrative) wrote, "I was just thinking about your book again, and about several exceptionally stupid reviews of it that I read. It seems to me that there was some massive point-missing going on there, but I can't quite account for it. Well, maybe I can at that."

Not easy. *People* magazine said of it, "Less self-confident men would be embarrassed to flaunt themselves so openly, but Buckley is obviously never shy." By contrast, Mr. Dunne was complaining: "[Buckley] is really not very giving of himself." *People* magazine would shrink to four pages if the editors suddenly found it "embarrassing" to express a curiosity about People ten times more inquisitive than any I would consent to satisfy. But Dunne was relentless in at once protesting the lack of profundity, while trivializing or ignoring what is there. Thus (in pursuit of the general vision of my hedonism), "[Buckley] spends every February and March skiing in Switzerland." That was on the order of my reporting, "Mr. Dunne spends every morning brushing his teeth." (My skiing occupies as much of my day in Switzerland as Mr. Dunne's stair-climbing does his days in Los Angeles.)

But oh how he worries about me!—as you would see if you read his entire review. I closed my letter to *The New York Review of Books* by quoting Dunne's final strictures, and my reaction to them:

"The show has been on the road too long," Dunne pronounced. "Mr. Buckley has spread himself so thin that he has begun to repeat himself, repeatedly. *Overdrive* is *Cruising Speed* redux as last year's *Atlantic High* is *Airborne* redux. As might be expected, Mr. Buckley is unrepentant." I answered, "As well complain that I edit a twenty-eight-year-old magazine which will celebrate the Fourth of July again on the Fourth of July. I have written a dozen nonfiction books, six novels, and a few books that are not routinely classified, though they are, by some, glibly dismissed. In 1985, I shall write a book called *Pacific High*, patterned after the first two. The literary technique explored in *Cruising Speed*—I think of it, occasionally, as on the order of the invention of the stage—is so majestically successful I intend to repeat it ten years hence, and ten years after that. At which point I shall be happy to review John Gregory Dunne's *True Confessions IV*, inasmuch as I am certain there will be great wit in it, as there was in its progenitor; as also in *True Confessions Redux*, published last year. [My reference was to *Dutch Shea Jr.]* I promise in my next book to scratch up a friend about whom I can say something truly unpleasant if Greg Dunne promises in *his* next book to come up with a murdered woman who doesn't have a votive candle protruding from her vagina."

But I shouldn't delay much longer in reporting that others viewed *Overdrive* very differently. Take, for instance, the question of snobbery. A number of critics came gleefully to the conclusion that *Overdrive* was the work of a snob. Mr. Charlie

Slack of the Chattanooga *Times* said it quaintly: "To call William F. Buckley Jr. a snob is to call the U.S.S. *Nimitz* a boat, the Sahara Desert a sandbox." The charge, widely if less picturesquely framed, struck the sensitive ear of *Time* essayist Lance Morrow. Now Morrow was himself disturbed by what he apparently deemed an unnecessary elongation in this book of hedonistic passages—at least that is what I think he is saying here: "Buckley luxuriates in his amenities a bit too much, and one hears [I wish he had written: "one hears, if one strains to do so"] in his prose the happy sigh of a man sinking into a hot bath." But he scotches conclusively, in a striking passage, the correlations so widely drawn about people who luxuriate in soapsuds. "So his enemies [note the *mot juste*] try to dismiss him as Marie Antoinette in a pimpmobile. They portray him as, among other things, a terrible, terminal snob. To make the accusation is to misunderstand both William F. Buckley Jr. and the nature of snobbery. Buckley is an expansive character who is almost indiscriminately democratic in the range of his friends and interests. He glows with intimidating self-assurance. The true snob sometimes has an air of pugnacious, overbearing self-satisfaction, but it is usually mere front. The snob is frequently a grand porch with no mansion attached, a Potemkin affair. The essence of snobbery is not real self-assurance but its opposite, a deep apprehension that the jungles of vulgarity are too close, that they will creep up and reclaim the soul and drag it back down into its native squalor, back to the Velveeta and the doubleknits."

Closely related to the charge of snobbishness was that of arrogance (egotism, vanity, what you will). The reporter for *Palm Beach Life*, who should be familiar with the phenomenon, wrote, "His book is outrageous in its egotism" (he concluded, "but amusing withal. Treat yourself to it"). Phillip Seib, writing in the Dallas *Morning News*, took arrogance for granted but ventured an explanation: "A certain arrogance is essential if one is to publish what Buckley calls 'a personal documentary.'" The trouble with that extenuation, as far as an author is concerned, is that it gives such comfort as you would get from reading, "Mr. Joseph Blackburn, who traverses Niagara Falls on a tightrope, is said to be a damned fool. But who else but a damned fool would be expected to traverse Niagara Falls on a tightrope?"

Thomas Fox of the Memphis *Commercial Appeal* evidently thought he caught it all when he pronounced *Overdrive* "nothing more than the product of a smug exhibitionist who likes to wave his ego in public," while Peter Richmond, writing for the Miami *Herald*, gritted his teeth: *Overdrive* "may be the most egregious example of the abuse of literary license since Jack Kerouac, well into fame, actually published 250 pages of his dreams." The publisher of *The New Republic*, James Glassman, wrote in *USA Today* that *Overdrive* was "an act of sheer gall" but he quickly gave an individuated explanation for it. "My theory is that Buckley wrote *Overdrive* as proof of his own security in social and literary matters. He must have known that the literati would make fun of the book, but he wrote it anyway, just to flout them." That is an interesting insight, but it fails to explain why I should go out of my way to slight so many critics in this special way, since I tend to do so routinely in so many other ways. And it is incorrect to say that I expected anything like the reaction *Overdrive* got, about which more in due course.

Pamela Marsh of *The Christian Science Monitor* said that, really, it was worse than sheer arrogance. "Add to that his obvious relish in what seems an overwhelming arrogance—he is in fact proud of his pride." That tends to ask for more thought than one is routinely prepared to give to such facile statements, unless they come in from philosophers. (Let's see: John is proud to be an American. John is proud of his pride in being an American. How about: John is proud of his pride in his pride in being an American. I wonder if Miss Marsh ever thought of that? Ever *worried* about that?)

Doug Fellman, a student writing for the *Hopkins Newsletter*, tried to be reasonable about the whole thing: "Naturally, some persons will complain that Buckley, in recording his life in such a journal, is committing an act of great egotism and conceit. Yet the autobiography is a common and accepted form of biography, and Buckley simply chooses to record his life in the present and as an excerpt." But untuned objections were everywhere. The Chicago *Booklist* said comprehensively that, for some readers, *Overdrive* would prove "a cross section of everything that is wrong with America, from elitism to Reaganomics." The Cleveland *Plain Dealer* found "the private Buckley who appears in this book . . . laced with pride, unflinchingly materialistic and self-centered—all in all, a popinjay."

I (happen to) prefer temperamental reactions to the lorgnetted sort of thing *Overdrive* drew from what one might call The Social Justice Set. I especially preferred Miss (Ms. would here be safer, I suppose) Carolyn See of the Los Angeles *Times,* who saw the author of *Overdrive* as "an American institution . . . lounging elegantly in his talk-show chair, driving Norman Mailer into a conniption fit, teasing and torturing Gore Vidal until he just can't take any more, driving at least 49 percent of the viewing audience into a state of mind that can't really be described in words, but it involves lurching up out of your chair, burying your hands in your hair and shrieking 'Yuuggh! Turn it off! Make him go away!' " There's no quiche in Ms. See's diet, 100 percent All Bran.*

The refrain on the matter of wealth was widespread, the popular corollary of which was to reason on to insouciance, with respect to poverty, as (Ann Morrissett Davidon, Philadelphia *Inquirer)* for instance: "But there is something rather beguiling and even enviable about this overdriven patrician and his way of life. Perhaps it is his apparently blithe blindness to most of the world's miseries." The patronizing explanation is both sweet and deadly. Jack the Ripper just didn't know it was wrong to strangle ladies, don't you see?

Two weighty voices, however distinct, came in from the Big Leagues.†

One of them Eliot Fremont-Smith of the *Village Voice,* the other Norman Podhoretz, the editor of *Commentary.* Fremont-Smith, in voicing qualified approval of the book and its

---

* Sometimes such wholesome antagonists go on to blush. Ms. See concluded her colorful review, "Buckley shows us a brittle, acerbic, duty-bound, 'silly,' 'conservative' semi-fudd, with a heart as vast and varicolored and wonderful to watch as a 1930s jukebox."

† I am grateful to a score of critics whose reviews, appearing in newspapers and magazines that seldom penetrate the Eastern Seaboard Establishment's switchboard, were understanding in every case, in some cases even encouraging, in a few even affectionate.

author, is a prominent liberal who found himself teeming with things to say.*

He began with the novel point that those who harp on the theme of the privileged life of the author of *Overdrive* tend to neglect a not insignificant point. "I think of *his* dilemma. No public figure I know of has been so chided by people he likes or is willing to admire or takes it with such aplomb." He insisted that *Overdrive* (a point made by several other reviewers) was ultimately a book about friendship. "Friends are more important, indeed all important. *Overdrive* is a record and celebration of connection, of how association (memories, locales, daily working intercourse, surprise, pleasure) improves the soul and perhaps the cause of civilization and bestows grace on all and sundry, by no means least of all" on the author. Fremont-Smith, unlike the automatons who approached the book with floodlights in search of Social Justice and a hemorrhaging psyche, had eyes for *detail* (of which, in many reviews, there was a total absence). "He . . . discourses on Bach and Scarlatti with the likes of . . . Fernando Valenti and Rosalyn Tureck, and also mediates between them (the sections on music and the ego requirements of great performers are among the funniest, most scrupulous, and moving in the book)."

Fremont-Smith finally declines to accept my implied proposition that the literary form I adopted (one week in the life of X) is generally viable. He rejects the notion that the form is widely useful. Rather, he insists that it must be taken as a singular phenomenon. "Two questions [in fact] arise: a) How is all this activity possible? b) Can we stand it? Particularly, can we stand Buckley's glorying in it? . . . basically *Overdrive* is a log—not a how-to-do-it but how-has-it-been-done in a particular frame of time by one particular energy."

I come now to Norman Podhoretz, who in November led the Book Review section of *Commentary* with an answer to the critics of *Overdrive,* interrupting a long silence as an active book reviewer. I am moved by the self-pride abundantly so designated in quotes already cited—but above all by feelings of

---

* His task was concededly complicated by a personal friendship, recently formed.

gratitude most readers in my position would, I think, understand—to quote from this review. Podhoretz began, no less:

"The first thing to say about *Overdrive* is that it is a dazzling book." And then, of course: "The second thing to say is that it has generally been greeted with extreme hostility."

Podhoretz went on to examine the causes of such hostility, discarding routine ideological antagonism as a satisfactory answer. "I do not believe that the injustice done to *Overdrive* can be explained in strictly political terms. Something deeper and more interesting is at work here." What that is is not easily distilled, though I will have a few thoughts on the subject at the end of this essay.

To those who declaimed first against the insubstantiality of *Overdrive* and then against the craftsmanship in *Overdrive*, like the lady who thought it should have been subtitled "Dictated but not read," Podhoretz replied: "The material is fascinating in itself and all Buckley's virtues as a writer are called forth in the recording of it. The prose flows smoothly and elegantly, its formality tempered with colloquial touches that somehow never jar, its mischievous wit coexisting in surprisingly comfortable congruence with its high rhetorical solemnities, its narrative pace sure-footed enough to accommodate detours and flashbacks without losing the necessary forward momentum." (Compare Grace Lichtenstein in the Washington *Post:* "What Buckley needed was a snappy rewrite by an experienced *People* hand. . . .") Podhoretz, who does not like to give ground, dealt defiantly with the matter of Money: "I for one do not doubt that the delight Buckley takes in his privileges is an exemplary spiritual virtue. If I do have a doubt, it concerns the extent of this delight. I mean, is he always so cheerful? Does he never suffer from anxiety?" (Eliot Fremont-Smith was more direct on this point: "In the book, Buckley has exquisite sandwiches but never takes a pee." (I wrote to Mr. F-S that I had trained myself never to pee, but he has not answered this letter, nor publicly celebrated my achievement.) (". . . What I was most struck by were the parts in which you tell us what you have to be sober about," my colleague Richard Brookhiser wrote me.)

To Mr. Podhoretz, I take the opportunity to say that I thought the shadows were there, in *Overdrive*, and that if they were not discernible to him, I do not know what is the appropriate reaction. Angst, in this volume, would not work.

Well, then. I have before me page after page of excerpts from reviews that make interesting observations. But economy requires that I put aside these notes and conclude. I do so by probing two questions, one concrete, and in its own way heuristic, the second general and critical.

The first is the matter of the limousine and the prominence it was given.

There was remarkably less fuss about my limousine when it figured in *Cruising Speed*. What, then, was the provocative difference between my *1970* limousine and my *1981* limousine? Hard scrutiny of the reviews suggests that the second *having been custom-made* caused it to be marginally insufferable. This is very interesting, especially so since the offended reviewers did not (many of them) hesitate to quote my narrative, in which, as Miss Ephron has reminded us, I revealed that, in 1978, a limousine with roughly the same features as the traditional, i.e., pre-austerity, limousine, cost approximately the same as the regular commercial limousine now being offered by the Cadillac company.

What then was it about the customizing that so inflamed?— that caused the New York *Times Book Review* critic to begin her review by concluding that *everyone* would focus on the limousine, whereafter she proceeded to devote almost one-third of her review to it?

Is it—I explore the question again—simply the economic point? That a limousine is expensive? If so, isn't it odd to weigh in so heavily on this, given that a limousine costs only about twice what a Ford sedan costs? It does not require that one belittle the figure to ask: Why is it, when other finery of affluence is there to choose from, that a limousine is so conspicuous? I explain, in *Overdrive*, how I spend my days; and it quickly becomes obvious that it would no more be feasible to spend my days as they are spent in the absence of a car and driver than it would be to run a taxi service without taxis. Without going over a time sheet, in the week I recorded I would guess that eight hours of work resulted from being driven rather than driving. What is it that especially affects so many about this particular auxiliary to one's commercial life? The cost of it?

But that is hardly rational. Well then, is it the point that one ought not to expect rationality in a review of how one American (this American) leads his life if his *modus vivendi* is judged obnoxious? I say it is irrational because hardly anyone bothered, in reviewing *Overdrive,* to dilate on his objections to extravagances even when clearly unrelated to productivity. E.g., owning and maintaining a 36-foot sailing auxiliary which (by the way) costs three times what a limousine costs (ask any of the hundred thousand Americans who have one). I own a grand piano worth more than my limo; used less, and mutilated more. Or consider articles of unquestioned and unmitigated professional uselessness, like a thirty-three-year accumulation of one's wife's jewelry. . . . What *is* it about a limousine?

Sometime after the first dozen reviews appeared, I lunched with Sam Vaughan of Doubleday and told him I was astonished by the intensity of the concentration on the matter of my limousine, which at this point I was tempted to paint khaki. Sam observed that typical luxuries go largely unobserved, but that a chauffeur-driven car is the single most provocative possession of the modern urban American. "Everyone," he expanded, "no matter who, has in New York been caught on a street-corner in the rain, waiting for a bus, or trying to hail a taxi. And inevitably they will see a limousine slide by, with the lumpen-bourgeois figure in the back seat, maybe smoking a cigar; maybe even reading *The Wall Street Journal.* That is the generically offensive act in the big cities." A good point, if the idea is to explain the spastic hostility toward limousine owners. Not, I think, a sufficient point to understand the peculiar emphasis put on the limo in some of the reviews of *Overdrive.*

I think that of the several points raised in opposing the book, this concrete point puzzled me the most. I dwell on it because American culture has tended to be guided—not finally, but substantially—by utilitarian criteria. Does John Appleseed produce more using a tractor than a horse-drawn plow? Does Tom Wicker perform more efficiently using a typewriter and going on to a word processor, than with a pencil? Why isn't the utilitarian coefficient dispositive in the matter of a limousine? Is it because the critic cannot distinguish between the limou-

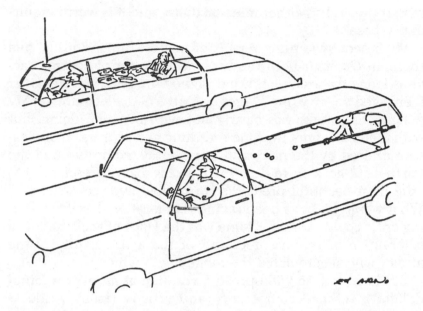

sine *qua* limousine—i.e., a luxury vehicle associated with inau-
gurations, weddings, and funerals—and the limousine as mobile office? If so there are two problems, the first the failure of
the critical intelligence. The second, whether the envious
view, transformed to resentment on that rainy day, on the
sidewalks of New York, of the man comfortable in his limousine
isn't, to use Miss Ephron's freighted word, "emblematic" of a
public, rather than a private, disorder?

The second point touches on the corrosive use of the word
"gleeful" to describe a reaction to one's material situation. I
have especially in mind, because it was so frequently adduced
by reviewers, my reference to a swimming pool. What I said
about it parenthetically—words if I may say so, gleefully reproduced—was that it is "the most beautiful indoor swimming
pool this side of Pompeii."

Now I found it odd that several reviewers of obvious intelligence bridled at this. (They might, at one level, have passed it
by, as "I saw the best movie last night since *Birth of a Nation*"
would presumably have been passed by.) In doing so it seems
to me, on hard reflection, that they must have understood me
to be saying something different from what I intended to say,

so that the fault is either mine or theirs, and it is worth inquiring: Whose?

My indoor swimming pool is of modest dimensions (I give them, in *Overdrive*). In the book, as a matter of course, I acknowledge the architect who designed the pool, and the artist I engaged to give me a mosaic pattern to decorate it. My delight, therefore, was clearly not with my own doing, but with theirs. I cannot imagine resenting any expression of pleasure uttered by the man who, having, say, commissioned the Parthenon, goes on to describe it in his diary (presciently) as "the most beautiful pre-Christian temple ever constructed." What would he have been saying that a rational, self-respecting critic could object to? Mine was the voice of acclamation: a celebration of the architect and of the artist; hardly of the author who accumulated the money with which to pay them.

But how odd, so widespread a reaction at an expression of delight at others' competence and artistry (many made as much of my reference to an "exquisite" sandwich made by our cook). Isn't it the job of the critic to distinguish between a compliment slyly paid ostensibly to someone else, actually to oneself, and a genuine compliment? Or are the critics reading self-congratulations by the man who had the wit to commission the pool, and the taste to appreciate the singularly well-made sandwich? That surely is reaching, isn't it? Would a reviewer single out a diarist's encomium on the performance of a visiting artist as an effort to draw attention to the author's piano? Or to his leverage on the artist?

I focus, finally, on what appears to have been a highly provocative literary proposition, namely my contention that a scrupulous journal of a week in an individual's life is at least a literary form worth thinking about, at best a literary idea worth celebrating. Many years ago the editor of the humor quarterly *Monocle* (it was Victor Navasky, now editor of *The Nation*) asked me to do a review of the work of the columnist Murray Kempton. I replied that he was asking me for the equivalent of a review of the work of Walter Lippmann, never mind that it would be more fun. Was I supposed to go back and read, or rather reread, fifteen years of Murray Kempton in order to write three thousand words?

I came up with a formula that satisfied Navasky, satisfied me, and planted, I think, the idea that blossomed, if that word is not too tendentious, in *Cruising Speed* and, now, *Overdrive*. Why not take a week of columns by Murray Kempton—next week's columns, say—and talk your way through them? He was writing five times a week back then, so that the chances were on your side that you would catch Murray Kempton reacting to a satisfactory range of challenges, phenomena, provocations, scandals, whatever. Enough to acquaint the reader with the moods (penetrating), style (incomparable), and thought (unreliable) of Murray Kempton.

It worked, in my judgment.

And so does it work, again in my judgment, on a larger scale in *Overdrive*.

To ask and quickly answer the most sensitive question, let me simply blurt it out:

Not everyone can write such a book. Or, if it goes down more smoothly to put it so, not everyone would read such a book if written by anyone.

William Murchison, the columnist from Dallas, Texas, wrote, "Few indeed are the authors who could bring off such an enterprise as this. A week, literally speaking, with Ralph Nader; or Walter Mondale; or Phil Donahue; or General Westmoreland! To think of it is to weep."

Now Mr. Murchison has a point here, but not of the kind that should cause the egalitarian furies to howl.

We seem to concede, without any problem, that only people who are technically qualified can satisfactorily perform on the piano before an audience. So we concede, again without any apparent problem, that unless one deftly uses paint and canvas, one ought not to expect to be able to merchandise one's art. I do not see why there should be so much difficulty in applying the same implicit criteria in order to distinguish what one might call the "performing writer." Perhaps the problem exists at all only because very few people without the technique to bring it off would undertake to play the "Flight of the Bumblebee" on the piano. Not many weekend painters would expect to sell their canvases even to the very little galleries.

By contrast, everybody—writes. And, in writing, there is

progressive fluency that approaches artistry. No one can say exactly where the line is, but it is to comply with the requirements to the full disclosure laws to admit: it would probably separate those who, using this standard, could, and could not, publish their journals, only the former being "performing writers." Okay. So why should it be difficult to accept the proposition that, from a writer, one expects work of a distinctive quality, even as one would from a painter or musician or plumber? If one managed that problem, one would cope with the preliminary objection: to write a journal based on a single week in a person's life, the person needs to be a writer.

But if the writer *is* qualified, what besides that does the reader, in order to be satisfied, require?

The reader would want an interesting sensibility. What is in process, in such an undertaking, is a literary self-portrait. I say "literary" only because the author's reactions are sometimes limned with operative emphasis on *the way* in which the reactions are expressed: and what then happens is that you collect, one by one, the little colored dots which, when they are, however chaotically, assembled, leave you with a mosaic, at best a pointillist portrait of—one human being.

Why should you care to have a self-portrait, as done, for instance, by William F. Buckley, Jr.—or by Groucho Marx? Or by Kay Graham?

Because, I think, self-portraits of many people can be interesting. If they work, they amuse. Enlighten. Explain. They provoke. And—I cling to the point—although the formal autobiography lets the actor stage his life and thought with more regard for conventional architectural prominences, the week's journal has complementary advantages. If I were offered today the alternative of reading an autobiography of Walter Lippmann, tracking his career, with which I am routinely familiar, or another comprehending his activity and his thought hour by hour during a single week, I *think*—I'm not sure—I might not lose by choosing the latter. Remember that the supplementary alternative isn't necessarily excluded.

A book like *Overdrive* written by Ralph Nader? Well—who knows? He has not, true, achieved a reputation as a writer. Indeed one might go further and say that the authors' oligopoly is one he has not cracked. On the other hand, if he had the training to carry it off, would I be interested in reading a journal of a week in Ralph Nader's life? My own answer is, Yes: I would. So would I—I mean it—a week in the life of Phil Donahue. In fact, I would sleep outside the bookstore, waiting to put my hands on such a book; if there were such a book. It would take only one or two other explorers to set the form in concrete. Murray Kempton comes to mind as ideal. Or Patrick Moynihan. Or how about Jesse Jackson? If he would speak Honest Injun, as I do.

I regret many things about the reception of *Overdrive*, though I am obliged to record here two qualifiers. The first is that the book has been a solid, if not spectacular, entrepreneurial success. The second is that the book has generated an extraordinary amount of mail from strangers, strangers who, after reading it, thought to write to me, their motives varied. The volume of that mail I was unprepared for—the reach of *The New Yorker* always astonishes me—but I think no book I have written (with one exception) has got such a response, overwhelmingly grateful—for what I take to be the sense communicated of a common and joyful search for serenity, in which the readers appear to have been helped. (One wrote, "Rambling, idiosyncratic, amused, cranky, occasionally flamboyant—your observations and recollections were most enjoyable testaments to a vital life. You actually believe *something:* Something old, something blue, with flecks of tweed, patches on the elbows, old Nantucket and Martha's Vineyard before everyone else came, in short: the right way of doing things." Another: "In a confusing world, I must express my gratitude. . . .") For that reason, among others already given, I regret the facile dismissal of the literary form by some reviewers (there were exceptions: *Time*'s Roger Rosenblatt wrote me, "I think you've invented a genre. Pepys on speed, but better") who, in their haste to disparage, did not give sufficient thought to the potential uses of such a form by people whose thought and careers they would read about with less resistance. I hope, before I die, to see others using this form. In my reply to Greg Dunne of *The New York Review of Books* I said airily that in ten years I intended to write a sequel to *Cruising Speed* and *Overdrive*, and ten years after *that*, a fourth journal. The prospect of this will cause a disturbing number of people to wish me . . . retired sooner, rather than later. But I caution them against strategic optimism in these matters. My limousine has miles to go before I sleep.

2

Meanwhile, at the Zoo

October 7, 1978

For every good reason in the world, the doings of the United Nations are not widely reported. For one thing they are mostly meaningless. But mostly the reason is that there is an inherent offensiveness in hypocrisy, particularly if it is studied. Every now and again one comes upon such a person as Daniel Patrick Moynihan who, at the UN, told the little creeps they could not get away with it in *his* presence, and for a few glorious weeks he drowned them out. But the assertion of reason, in a chamber given over to surrealism, creates an intolerable stridency, so Moynihan soon left, and the UN resumed its war on moral understanding. Still, as a gesture, every now and then, one should report a UN venture, just in case anything changes, and I have elected for this reason to report on the deliberations of the UN's Decolonization Committee in the matter of Puerto Rico.

That committee has passed by a vote of 10 (in favor) 0 (opposed) and 12 (abstaining) enjoining a course of action on the United States government.

We are directed to put an end to "the persecutions, harassments and repressive measures to which the organizations and persons struggling for independence have been continuously subjected, constituting violations of the national rights of the

Puerto Rican people to self-determination and independence."

We are further directed to "unconditionally release the four
Puerto Rican political personalities who have been incarcerated for more than twenty-four years."

We are further advised that if Puerto Rico continues to vote
for its present commonwealth status, that will not do. Nor
would it do if Puerto Rico voted to ask for statehood. No vote
by the Puerto Ricans that would continue the existing relationship, or that would take them to statehood, would be tolerable
to the UN. *First* they have to be given independence. Then,
and *only then*, may they vote a different relationship. Obviously, we are to infer, Hawaii and Alaska are illegitimately
states of the Union, since there was no intervening period of
sovereignty.

Now: If there is persecution, harassment and repression of
those who seek independence in Puerto Rico, it is extraordi-
narily subtle. A champion of the independence movement
recently appeared on television in San Juan using the government's television facilities.

Not only did he come in and out without being frisked, the
personal office of the governor was turned over to his use.

The "political personalities" who have been "incarcerated
for more than twenty-four years" expressed their personality
by sneaking into the visitors' gallery of the House of Representatives in 1954, pulling out pistols, and shooting at our elected
representatives, wounding five. They were given life sentences. In most of the countries that voted the resolution in
question they'd have been shot.

Now, who voted for the resolution denouncing political harassments in Puerto Rico and asserting "the inalienable right
to self-determination and independence"?

The Soviet Union, China, Bulgaria, Czechoslovakia, Cuba,
Ethiopia, Iraq, Syria, Tanzania and Afghanistan. The Soviet
Union's respect for the territorial integrity of Bulgaria and
Czechoslovakia is legendary. China's respect for the territorial
integrity of Tibet is one of those matters we do not mention at
the United Nations. Ethiopia's government is maintained in
power by Cuba, as Cuba's is maintained in power by the Soviet
Union. Syria and Tanzania are one-party dictatorships where

the will of the people is consulted as regularly as Scottish hunters consult grouse.

So what else is new? What (while serving in the UN) I once dubbed "the Pontius Pilate vote." Not so new—they have been doing it for years—but always inexcusable. Consider Australia. Why should it go along with the sham? Australia's ambassador did attempt to soften the resolution, as did Sweden's—to make the condemnation of repression hypothetical rather than historical. These resolutions failed.

Why then did Australia and Sweden abstain? China owes us very little. On the other hand, Chile's complaints against UN hypocrisy sound a little tinny when Chile goes on to acquiesce in it.

The explanation, if that is the word for it, is that there are fewer and fewer countries prepared to stand up against the Third World and the communist bloc. They muster only enough courage to wash their hands of the question of right and wrong. Fortunately, as I say, nobody listens, except the occasional few who wander about the zoo sections of the planet's parliaments. But high in the spheres the dissonance is caught, and the conscience of civility and reason is stained.

3

Infield Practice
with the BBC

September 29, 1979

A COUPLE of chaps from the BBC have been over here on the
nether side of the pond doing a radio documentary on the
awful effects of McCarthyism on America's China policy, and
at the interview they came directly to the point:

"Looking back to the fifties, Mr. Buckley, what do you have
to say about the disastrous effects on your China policy brought
about by McCarthyism?"

I asked: What disastrous effects?

After they had composed themselves, they informed me
that, among other people, they had interviewed the great Professor Owen Lattimore, and that he agreed that the effects of
McCarthyism had been disastrous. Lattimore, they pointed
out, was one of the principal victims of Senator Joseph McCarthy.

I had handy—I travel with a copy of it, even when I swim—
the book *McCarthy and His Enemies*, which I wrote with
Brent Bozell back in 1954. On page 158 is reproduced the
jacket copy from a book called *Solution in Asia*, which was
Owen Lattimore's handbook published in the late forties, for
China policy.

Quote: "He [Lattimore] shows that all the Asiatic people are
more interested in actual democratic practices such as the
ones they can see in action across the Russian border, than they

are in the fine theories of Anglo-Saxon democracies which
come coupled with ruthless imperialism . . . He inclines to
support American newspapermen who report that the only
real democracy in China is found in Communist areas." I announced that I found objectionable then, as I find now, thirty
years later, the suggestion that Stalin was a practitioner of
democracy, that Mao Tse-tung was leading a democratic
movement, and false the prophecy that all would go well in
China (Lattimore's "Solution") if we backed Mao instead of
Chiang Kai-shek.

Well, the BBC said, didn't I find it inexcusable that Henry
Luce refused to publish in *Time* magazine certain dispatches
from Theodore White during that period?

No, I said, not "inexcusable." Because as Theodore White
himself reveals in his latest book, he had going there for a while
a considerable romance with the Maoists, and Luce distrusted
the objectivity of Mr. White's reporting on the subject.

Isn't it typical of the damage done to reputations, what happened to Theodore White?

Theodore White, I said, happens to be one of my favorite
people. But I think he too would agree that it is institutionally
hazardous to side with an unpopular cause. For instance,
Teddy White probably suffered more for writing evenhand-
edly about Senator Goldwater in 1965 and about Richard
Nixon in 1969 than he ever did at the hands of Henry Luce. So
badly was he treated for his Republican heresies that by the
time 1975 came around, he was instructing his publisher not to
send advance copies of his books to *The New York Review of
Books*, which can cut off a writer's head much more effectively
than McCarthy ever did.

"Well, isn't it fair to say that Henry Luce had become an
agent of Chiang Kai-shek?"

Only, I said, in the sense that it would be fair to say that a
decade earlier Luce had become an agent of the British government in urging U.S. involvement in the struggle against
Hitler. Another way to put it is that in 1939 Henry Luce espied
an identity of interest between the American people and the
British people in opposing Hitler, and in 1949 an identity between the American people and the Chinese people in opposing Mao Tse-tung.

Well, didn't McCarthyism delay our current reconciliation with China?

No. What made possible our current "reconciliation" with China was the dispute that began, three or four years after McCarthy was dead, between China and the Soviet Union. Stalin was a hero of Mao Tse-tung. And remains a hero of Mao Tse-tung's successors. You cannot walk through a public square in China without staring at a huge picture of Stalin, as secure in the Chinese communist pantheon as Babe Ruth is in Cooperstown. Joe McCarthy had nothing to do with the estrangement of the Soviet Union from Red China in the sixties—unless Joe is up there showing God a photostatic copy of Solzhenitsyn's *Gulag Archipelago* and Simon Leys's *Chinese Shadows* and making the pitch that two such countries are better off opposing each other than acting in unison.

Well, they concluded, does that mean I approve of McCarthy's demagoguery?

No, I said, I don't approve of anybody's demagoguery, but I find it less objectionable when used to the disadvantage of Communist tyrants than when I find it used to their advantage: which, roughly, was the difference between Lattimore and McCarthy.

At which point we ran out of time, the BBC kindly advised me that my fly was open, we shook hands, and here I am.

4

Fun and Games

Los Angeles.—It is Merv Griffin time, and guess who is scheduled on?—routine, no fuss; just another guest. We have already had Mr. and Mrs. Arthur Murray, who although they may have taught us dancing in a hurry, didn't do so because *they* were in any particular hurry: they are in splendid shape, having recently celebrated their fifty-third wedding anniversary. A second guest is a ballad singer, envelopingly warm, talented, who sings songs about father-son relationships. There is a smart-aleck author type there to sell his new book. And . . . and . . .

What's her line? Well, she produces and directs porno flicks. The hard stuff. She looks rather like Kay Kendall. How old are you, dear? Twenty-three. What religion were you brought up in? Catholic. Still practice your religion? Well—tee hee—no, not really, don't go to church much. Did you go to college? Yes, Michigan State. Graduate? Yes. Major? Phys. Ed. What made you go into—porn movies? Wanted to get into the business, and worked for a while as a cashier at a movie house that featured X-rated movies, so got interested in the business, asked around, and went to Hollywood. Do you make . . . all . . . kinds of . . . films? No, we don't go into, well, bestiality, sadomasochism, that sort of thing. Just, you know, the regular stuff, only, in a way, you know, we try to experiment, new positions, that sort of thing.

The singer came in and said he thought it was all a pretty good idea. He and his wife had an X-rated film which they showed regularly on their home videocassette system, and he thought it was very healthy, after all we're part animal, and we have animal instincts, and what's wrong with recognizing anything that obvious?

The author mumbled something about its also being an animal instinct to eat other animals, but we don't make movies about people eating other people, but the audience didn't like that. And Merv said to the author: Have you ever seen a pornographic film? Sure, the author said, I've done a lot of reprehensible things.

Well, that did it—what was so reprehensible about it: I mean, here's a sweet young thing, twenty-three, Phys. Ed. from Michigan State, making the kind of movies that the singer and his wife showed in the privacy of their living room, so what's so bad about that?

At this point the author tried to take the offensive, but he sounded awfully stuffy. He said that the whole situation reminded him of the point Irving Kristol had made in one of his essays for *The Wall Street Journal,* that such was the inversion of values in America that an eighteen-year-old-girl could legally have intercourse live on a stage in New York provided she was paid the minimum wage. Are you—he directed his question to the singer—in favor of permitting people to make snuff films?

What are snuff films?

Well, snuff films are where a guy (or gal) is actually killed in the film, the victim being a masochist inclined to go all the way, and the executioner being a masochist inclined ditto. It is reputed that there are in fact some snuff films, is that okay?

The porno-director shook her head, as did Mr. and Mrs. Arthur Murray, as did the singer, as did Merv Griffin.

Merv asked the lady how much she had spent on her current porn movie and she said about $116,000. How much money have you grossed from it? So far this year? Oh, about a million dollars. But we can go on and on selling it, it will last for years, she reassured Merv. What happens, the author asked, when you run out of positions? The lady laughed, Merv laughed, Mr. and Mrs. Arthur Murray laughed, the singer laughed, and the time was up and everybody went home, just as if they had heard from someone who had made a success starting up a chain of doughnut shops.

On the way home the author tried to remember a couple of lines from Hilaire Belloc, but couldn't. The next day he found them. "We sit by and watch the Barbarian, we tolerate him; in the long stretches of peace we are not afraid. We are tickled by his irreverence, his comic inversion of our old certitudes and our fixed creeds refreshes us; we laugh. But as we laugh we are watched by large and awful faces from beyond; and on these faces there is no smile."

5

An Anarchist's Progress

November 3, 1979

OVER THE COURSE of a single fortnight one is reminded of the kind of thing that brought H. L. Mencken to write that "government is the enemy of all well-disposed, decent and industrious men." Grant that man is inherently flawed and capable of evil. Still, we do aspire to codify rules of conduct, so that when an individual violates a code he excites retaliatory mechanisms, whether criminal or social. On the other hand, there is no end to what one can do if one acts as a collectivity or on behalf of a collectivity. Five items:

—The Shah of Iran is admitted into a New York hospital on the assumption that he has cancer. The Ayatollah Khomeini gives out to the press his commentary: "I hope he does have cancer." The Ayatollah, whose profession is that of a holy man, will not accept minimal restraints on his appetite for vengeance. There is something more barbarous about saying one wishes one's political enemy would contract a terrible disease than saying one wishes he would be brought to trial for his crimes. It is the appalling rupture of basic standards of civil discourse that catches the eye, indeed the breath.

—The Queen of England goes all the way downstairs at Buckingham Palace (these gestures, though requiring so little physical energy, mean a great deal in British protocol) for the purpose of displaying a special warmth toward Hua Guofeng.

He is the traveling chairman of the world's largest totalitarian power, who left his country at about the time a diffident dissenter who asked for a few civil liberties in the accents of Oliver Twist asking for "more" was tried and sentenced to fifteen years in prison. The crimes of the regime with which Hua is associated, the mutilation of the spirit under the Cultural Revolution, the increasingly perceived lunacy of Mao Tse-tung's tyranny, are appalling. The queen is instructed by her ministers to go the extra mile to receive Chairman Hua more warmly than, probably, she would receive Mother Teresa.

—Elsewhere in London, Robert Mugabe and Joshua Nkomo are treated with the deference owed to respectable representatives of a contending position. Always the realist, perhaps the day will come when the British government entertains the assassins of Lord Mountbatten at Claridge's, and discusses with them, joking where necessary, the terms by which, in pursuit of peers, they might be persuaded to stop disemboweling women and children.

—At the United Nations, which perversely prime ministers, kings and popes regularly address as though it were the gathering place of the birds of paradise, Fidel Castro gives his usual speech, denouncing the usual people, applauding the usual people. He has emerged as the leader of the nonaligned world, thanks to an ideological semantics entirely controlled by the left. When he is through, he is given a rousing ovation. His appearance is roughly contemporaneous with the release, after twenty years' imprisonment, of Huber Matos. A description of those twenty years as Castro's guest in Castro's prison makes one wonder over the stamina of human sadism. Year after year after year in solitary confinement, wallowing in his own ordure, not seeing light of any sort; a former companion-in-arms of Castro himself, whose heart was stone when successive appeals reached him for mercy; which heart, however, now weeps copiously at the General Assembly of the United Nations for the poor and afflicted of this world. The greatest boon Castro could make to aid the poor and afflicted would be to disappear. The Ayatollah would put it: to contract cancer.

—And finally, there is Cambodia. Much of the suffering from hunger and disease in this world is something of a Malthusian scourge, which asymptotic efforts can and must be made to alleviate. But in Cambodia, between the time these words are written and read, as many as 10,000 people will die, and several millions will wish they were dead rather than endure their awful hunger. Listen: There are five "government" bodies involved. 1) The Chinese; 2) Pol Pot's; 3) the Soviet Union's; 4) Cambodia's puppet government; and 5) the Vietnamese. All five of these "forces" have subordinated the survival of the Cambodian people to their factionalist ends. There has never been a more striking example of the utter irrelevance of the human being when the politics of totalism is involved.

But you can count on it: whoever prevails, the leaders will in due course appear in the United Nations, even as Pol Pot's representative already has, and be greeted there as, what, a peer? One fears that that is exactly what these men are. Peers. Peers of all those who exercise powers. These are the anarchic thoughts of this morning.

6

The Brit in Washington

August 9, 1980

THERE'S a character in Washington who writes for the Washington *Post* and should be slipped a tranquilizer, though these are said not to mix happily with booze. His name is Henry Fairlie and, to the great relief of Great Britain, he is an expatriate, devoting himself to advising Americans how to behave.

Somewhere along the line he picked up the designation "conservative." The etiology here eludes the memory, but it is true that he defended U.S. participation in the Vietnam war of resistance. One suspects, after enduring a few short hundredweight of Mr. Fairlie's homilies, that he really came out for the Vietnam war in order to create a certain rhetorical commotion about himself. And, then, every now and again he will drop the word "aristocratic," or will quote from Cato the Elder, or whomever, to maintain the minimal flying time necessary to guard his license as a "conservative." What he is, is an undisciplined Catherine's wheel, whose columns read like an angry and disordered reflection of the previous night's dissipations. He must have disported heavily on the evening that Reagan was nominated.

Would you care to know how our British friend characterizes the men and women who voted for Reagan? They are "narrow minded, book banning, truth censoring, mean spirited; ungenerous, envious, intolerant, afraid; chicken, bullying; trivially moral, falsely patriotic; family cheapening, flag cheapening, God cheapening; the common man, shallow, small, sanctimonious." So much for the 60 percent of the American voters who, when last heard from, prefer Reagan over any named alternative.

But isn't this image inconsistent with the reputation—at least—of the (largely Jewish) intellectuals who make up the neoconservative movement? I mean, such folk as Norman Podhoretz? Irving Kristol? Daniel Bell? Midge Decter? Seymour Lipset?—those highly educated, highly idealistic men and women who have had the courage to measure the shortcomings of schematic liberalism? "These men," says Mr. Fairlie, "are not evil. They are not even reactionary. They simply are vulgar ['are simply vulgar' would be less vulgar]." No one with nostrils less flared than Henry Fairlie's can imagine the pain of having to breathe the same air as Irving Kristol.

You see, although he elected to leave Europe, Fairlie simply has to say it for our own good. America is less *cosmopolitan* than Europe. Poor Europe. "Europe shudders today," Mr. Fairlie tells the readers of the Washington *Post.* "The America which Europe fears is the America of the Reaganites . . . The Reaganites on the floor [in Detroit at the convention] were exactly those who in Germany gave the Nazis their main strength and who in France collaborated with them and sustained Vichy."

Waal, Henry, over here in America, though less cosmopolitan than across the pond among the folks you came from, we never have elected a Hitler to power. Strange. And we never had a Vichy government—strange. And we never swore we'd refuse to fight for king and country, at a moment in history that made possible the rise of Hitler. And we didn't fashion the diplomacy that created two world wars, thirty million killed; and an Eastern Empire ruled by Josef Stalin. Perhaps it requires a little provincialism to contrive a diplomacy of a kind that doesn't depend on the United States, every generation or so, to send the Yanks over to bail out the cosmopolitans.

Mr. Fairlie begins his lovesong to America by denouncing the tiresomeness and vulgarity of Henry Mencken, who himself railed against the philistines. "Mencken could in his writing be as much a boor as them," pronounces Henry Fairlie, who should study grammar before graduating to the study of manners.

7

Come Undressed

September 6, 1980

IT IS axiomatic that the village underworlder will seek the approval of the same community he systematically despoils by ostentatious public benefactions. Joe Bananas supporting the local church. Billy Sol Estes hosting a Boy Scout picnic. Louis B. Mayer contributing to an institute of higher learning. No one has practiced the art of civic diversion more prodigiously than Hugh Hefner, the founder of *Playboy* magazine and godfather of the sexual revolution. His formula was as straightforward as the advertisements in *Playboy* for sexually stimulating paraphernalia: make a lot of money by pandering to the sexual appetite, elevating it to primacy—then spend part of that money co-seducing critics or potential critics.

It was years ago that Harvard theologian Harvey Cox wrote an essay on *Playboy*, denominating it the single most brazen assault on the human female in general circulation. What seemed like moments later, the same scholar found himself writing earnest essays for *Playboy;* and before long he forgot all about his mission to identify *Playboy* for what it essentially is: an organ that seeks to justify the superordination of sex over all other considerations—loyalty to family, any principle of self-discipline, any respect for privacy, or for chastity or modesty: sex *omnia vincit,* Hugh Hefner's magazine told us, issue after issue. But the genius of Hugh Hefner lay in the embellishments. Walking down his massage parlors, you find the hallways decorated with facsimiles of the Bill of Rights, illuminated scrolls from Milton's *Areopagitica*, earnest rebukes of any impositions on our privacy if committed by the Central Intelligence Agency. The passageway to the brothel takes you through the vaulted cathedrals of piety and self-mortification, sacrifice and social concern.

Really, I wonder if anyone in the future can ever again take seriously the Anti-Defamation League. Here is an organization "dedicated to the combating of prejudice and discrimination against Jews and other minorities, and to the protection and extension of our democratic system for the benefit of all Americans." "The League" the brochure continues, "works with the various institutions of our society, public and private, religious and secular, to achieve these ends." And it is celebrating later this month its First Amendment Freedoms Award by giving a dinner-dance in honor of—Hugh M. Hefner. About the honoree the ADL says, with an apparently straight face, that he "began with little more than a unique idea for a magazine" (nude women, jokes about copulation, and advice on how to seduce young girls) "and a philosophy of social change." (The "philosophy," quite simply, that the gratification of the male sexual impulse is to be achieved without any second thought to the possible effect on a) the girl, b) her family, c) your family, d) any code of self restraint.) "The empire he founded has had a far-reaching impact, not only on the publishing industry, but on the mores of American society as well." That is correct. Any serious disciple of Hugh Hefner would not hesitate to purr anti-Semitic lovelies into the ears of his bunny, if that was what was required to effect seduction.

The Anti-Defamation League has, in the past, surrendered to temptations alien to its splendidly commendable purpose, namely to focus public attention on, and bring obloquy to, acts of racial discrimination. It meddled actively in the presidential campaign of 1964, endeavoring to scare its clientele into believing that Senator Goldwater was an ogre of sorts, backed by fanatics and atavists. Its current director, Mr. Nathan Perlmutter, is a man of high sensibility, gentle, firm, discriminating, a scholarly man long associated with Brandeis University. One notes that he is charging $250 a plate to guests who seek the privilege of joining with him to honor Hugh Hefner. The tawdriness of the symbolism is driven home. Even as Hugh Hefner sells pictures of parted pudenda in order to make the dollar, a nickel of which he donates to institutions devoted to the rights of Nazis to march in Skokie and of fellow pornographers to hawk their wares, the ADL raises money to combat discrimination by honoring the principal agent of the kind of selflessness that deprives racial toleration of the ultimate sanction. This sanction rests on a profound belief in the sanctity of the individual—yes, even that of the nubile girl.

Take away from the struggle for racial toleration the profound spiritual commitment to the idea of a higher law, and the code against anti-Semitism becomes a mere matter of social convenience, the kind of upwardly mobile patter one is taught in the pages of *Playboy* to imitate, on the order of wearing Dior handkerchiefs or Gucci loafers. Racial toleration draws its principal strength from the proposition that we are all brothers, created equal by God. The *Playboy* philosophy measures human worth by bust line and genital energy. The affair will be celebrated, appropriately enough, in Hollywood, at the Century Plaza Hotel. The invitation specifies "black tie." Well, if the guests arrive wearing only black ties, that will be more than some of the guests wear at Hef's other parties.

8

Beware Varig

November 13, 1980

MY FAST and abstinence on the subject of airline travel, which I had resolved to make last for one whole year, was broken in Mexico City under extreme provocation. It is unlikely that your immediate plans call for flying on Varig Airlines (Brazil's) from Mexico to Rio, but should they do so, change these plans instantly. In fact, if you plan to travel with something more than one set of underwear and a paperback copy of *Gone With The Wind*, bring lots of money, because lots of money is what Varig desperately wants.

A little history. With the development of jet travel, the airlines inherited a loophole: namely, an excess-baggage rate fashioned years earlier with reference to the tiny little marsupial cavities associated with propeller flight. For 110 pounds of excess baggage, the airlines took to charging you one-half of the *first-class* fare. Now this meant that if you were traveling tourist to, say, Rome, and you had 220 pounds of extra luggage, you were paying the airline one full first-class fare, in addition to your tourist fare. If it happened that you yourself weighed 220 pounds you ended in the paradoxical situation of paying about twice as much for your excess luggage as for yourself, notwithstanding that your luggage received no free champagne, saw no movie on the flight, and ate no meals whatever.

The hero in this situation is a young activist lawyer from

Miami, Florida, Mr. Donald Pevsner, who brought suit with the Civil Aeronautics Board charging that the "reasonable surtax" on overweight permitted by the relevant conventions was not reasonable at all. After furious litigation stretching over a half-dozen years, Pevsner and the people of America triumphed over the airlines—and the CAB issued a ruling that passengers would be allowed two suitcases, no matter how heavy, free of charge; for each extra suitcase they would be charged a flat rate, once again per article, not per pound, because a jet airline is relatively blasé about weight.

But then the question arose: how to make foreign airlines comply with the American rules? A tricky diplomatic business, but the CAB recognized a responsibility to protect American consumers, and therefore acted favorably on a suit the effect of which could be to deny landing rights to foreign carriers that continued to extort from passengers the usurious rate. Okay, easy enough when the question is foreign carrier X traveling from Rome to New York. But what about foreign carrier X traveling from Cairo to Rome to New York? Is it to be allowed to swindle you on the Cairo–Rome leg? Or, for that matter, if you got off in Cairo, and were swindled on overweight, would that carrier forfeit the right to land in the United States? That matter is in negotiation. Enter Varig Airlines.

We (wife and I) arrived with seven heavy suitcases for the Mexico–Rio leg of a business journey. We expected to pay $60 or so for each of the three surplus suitcases. The lady behind the desk did a little calculating and informed me that I would need to pay Varig $1,295. I thought perhaps I was being sold some shares in Varig Airlines, and having none such in my little portfolio, I was rather attracted by the idea, however unorthodox the approach; but of course it turned out that she desired over $400 per bag for the nine-hour trip.

I was convinced she had made a mistake, and the manager, Mr. Ranato Rocha, was summoned. Mr. Rocha is of that young breed of bureaucrats trained in the letter of the law and in the sweet fragrance of dissimulation. He told me that the government of Mexico by law forbade charging less than the old excess rate. The laws of the government of Mexico are sacred on no other subject, I suggested, appealing the objectively unreasonable suggestion that three bags containing mostly books and papers should each have to pay $400 to hitch a ride to a friendly country down south. Mr. Rocha was adamant, so I crossed the aisle, spent ten minutes with a most amiable lady from Eastern Airlines, which flew us to Miami, connecting with Pan American to Rio, where we arrived at the pleasant hour of 8 A.M., only two hours after Varig's flight, which arrived with two empty seats Mexico–Rio; and two canceled seats from various points in Latin America to other points in Latin America over the ensuing fortnight.

So: If you have any overweight, check; and avoid Varig, or any airline that continues the old gouge. And don't forget, every now and then, to think gratefully about that energetic young lawyer in Miami.

9

St. Giamatti and the Moral Majority

September 5, 1981

Well, that was a close one. The 1,267 members of the freshman class of Yale University have been warned against the Moral Majority by President A. Bartlett Giamatti. And what a speech it was: Jerry Falwell, head of the Moral Majority, is said to be quite a fulminator himself. He should go to Yale. To study under Bart Giamatti. Learn a thing or two about how one fulminates in the big leagues.

What's going on? To be lectured against the perils of the Moral Majority on entering Yale is on the order of being lectured on the danger of bedbugs on entering a brothel. What is it that exercised Mr. Giamatti, a man of great urbanity who has some lovely and incisive things to say about many issues, as witness his forthcoming book of essays?

Well, he says the Moral Majority are "peddlers of coercion" and that they have made "a radical assault" on pluralism, civil rights, and religious and political freedoms in the United States. How so?

Because they are "angry at change, rigid in the application of chauvinistic slogans, absolutist in morality." Thus, "they threaten through political pressure or public denunciation whoever dares to disagree with their authoritarian positions." Moreover, "they presume to know what God alone knows, which is when human life begins."

Enough.

On the latter point: How is it that the president of a distinguished and cosmopolitan university tells us that God alone knows when human life begins? If you penetrate this rhetorical formulation, you have a dimly obscured invitation to nescience. "God-alone-knows" is the safest way to say, "That-is-unknowable." Inasmuch as God is not invited to teach a regular course at Yale, Mr. Giamatti is saying in effect that the search for the answer to "When does life begin?" should be abandoned—because no one can tell.

Why not? If you grant the metaphorical extravagancies (Life Begins at Forty) you can indeed ask scientists to make sound judgments on when life begins. Or moralists. Or theologians. And in any case, the question is ultimately decided by civic action. But civic action is regularly informed by theological insights. Thus we've had for many years a group known as Clergy and Laity Concerned. They used to be Concerned About Vietnam, but lately they are just Concerned. That concern regularly focuses on the sins of everyone who wants America to be strong militarily, or wants to develop nuclear energy. These people are very big on denunciation, and it is interesting that Mr. Giamatti hasn't gone after them. Is it really his position that people reading the Bible are not free to enjoin its messages? Its messages as they read them?

Mr. Giamatti said he had no quarrel with the values of the Moral Majority, defined in the paraphrase by the New York *Times* as "love of country, a regard for the sanctity of life, the importance of the family, and high standards of personal conduct." But "the point is," said the president of Yale, "the rest of us hold to ideas of family, country, belief in God, in different ways. The right to differ, and to see things differently, is our concern." Well, so is it the concern of the Moral Majority, isn't it? They are saying that certain values should govern Americans. Aren't we free to disagree? And why should they not say so, believing such values to be true? It is quaintly interesting that there isn't a single tenet of the Moral Majority (so far as I know) that hasn't officially been held by Yale University over a century or more of its life, and more or less unofficially since then. So what on earth is exciting Mr. Giamatti?

That the Moral Majority are "angry at change"? But anger was officially cultivated, by Yale among other institutions, quite recently in the matter of such things as civil rights and the Vietnam war. "And God said to Jonah, 'Doest thou well to be angry?' And he said, 'I do well to be angry, even unto death.' " Mr. Giamatti should lecture the kids against the dangers of gonorrhea and gnosticism, and let the Moral Majority alone.

10

Hollywood Piety

(Review of *True Confessions* in *National Review*, September 18, 1981)

LET ME be done with it and say that the movie *True Confessions* is (in an opinion with which men may with impunity differ) awful; whereas the book of the same title from which it is taken is (an opinion with which no man may safely differ) rich as Rabelais, haunting, evocative, synaesthetically sensational. In the movie, Robert De Niro is badly miscast. He is never entirely convincing, and words are put in his mouth ("I've packed up my bags," when he announces he has cancer) that one wouldn't think wild horses could have dragged from the typewriters of the talented screenwriters. The scenes are one cliché mounted joylessly on another, so that the unfolding of each reminds you progressively of the weakness of the predecessor. But I am not here to criticize the movie—rather to remark the ease with which Hollywood now handles the theme of the thoroughly disreputable priest, though the priest in *True Confessions* isn't actually all that hateful, no more is his boss the cardinal; nor, for that matter, is his brother Tom, the driven, cynical policeman.

Monsignor Desmond Spellacy is ambitious. In his dealings with the cardinal he is somewhere between docile and servile.

He is bright enough to know what's really going on, and that what's really going on shouldn't really go on, because Mother Church in Los Angeles has no business giving one of those annual medals ("Catholic Citizen of the Year," or whatever) to a big, beefy, repulsive character, no matter how much money he has given for the construction of parochial schools, if it is known among the cognoscenti (1949 was before Vatican II outlawed Latin) that said character had got rich by pimping, is probably still connected with organized crime, and regularly devotes himself to the easier part of that biblical injunction to go out and multiply. What fascinates—or is supposed to do so— is the cultural departure in protocol.

It used to be that Hollywood priests were Bing Crosby, going his way and making ours lighter; or Spencer Tracy, telling the Dead-End kid he was a good boy after all, with transmutational effect; or Ingrid Bergman, raising money for the bells of St. Mary's and, while at it, tingling the chimes within the human spirit. Most people, I should think, knew that this was romance; that in real life Bing Crosby neglected his children, Spencer Tracy kept a mistress, and Ingrid Bergman not only looked after orphans, but produced them.

But the theatrical convention was there: that all priests be- have in such a way as to dare emulation. Between the fifties and the seventies no professional class (save possibly investiga- tive journalists) was presumptively supposed to be engaged in altruistic activity. Ben Stein wrote a book *(The View from Sunset Boulevard)* about a year in Hollywood during which he had come upon not a single "good" businessman, or "good" military officer in the pulp forests he had seen produced for television and the movies. If John Gregory Dunne had sat down to write a book about a priest who behaved like Mother Teresa, not even with the aid of his talented wife, Joan Didion, would he have been invited to make a movie based on his discovery. The priestly calling is a theatrical victim of an age of skepticism; and it isn't entirely unreasonable that the theater- goer should take this in stride. For one thing there are all those thousands of priests and nuns who have been "laicized," a desertion no man may judge harshly whose own faith, whether in God, marriage, country, or politics, has ever been shaken. But desertion it was: i.e., one pledged one's life to a calling, most spiritual in aspect—and after a while the public recognized you as the fellow drinking beer with the wife or girlfriend while watching Monday night football, waiting your turn at the bowling alley. The stereotype of tenacious Franciscan asceticism is irretrievably gone.

And then, too, there was the ideologization of religion. It's easier, among Catholic clergy, to pick a fight over whether to send arms to the rebels in Nicaragua than over whether the Shroud of Turin bears the marks of an extraworldly implosion.

So that John Gregory Dunne's colorful story about priests who have one eye on ambition, and cardinals who leave it to God to forgive the means by which the local philanthropists accumulated their money in the first place, isn't likely to disrupt the rhythm of the movie audience munching its popcorn. The book, by the way, is infinitely more shocking than the movie: but this was so not because the clergy were proved human, but because the language, particularly of the cop and his sidekick, is textured with a blend of profanity and obscenity which almost everywhere (I think of one or two lapses) transports the imagination to a delight unsullied by the ultimate moral corruption. True corruption is what happens when you are asked to believe that as between right and wrong, there really aren't any differences. It is one thing to discover that the pious priest was really Elmer Gantry all over again. Something else to read in the Playboy Philosophy that philandering is good because anything that *feels* good *is* good—except maybe lynching uppity niggers. *(Playboy*—and Hollywood—feel they have to draw the line somewhere.) The book *True Confessions* shocks by color and an irreverence that knows itself to be that. You could fit every Christian martyr in the chasm between *True Confessions* and *Last Exit from Brooklyn.*

The cultural difference is worth noting, however. Thirty years ago there was plenty of sin going on. In the Eurasian continent more people were killed probably than in three millennia of recorded history. Even so, for a period, however brief, in popular culture benign presumptions were indulged. Just as rabbis were "wise," priests were "benevolent." Drank a little too much, like Barry Fitzgerald maybe; but good fellows, professionally devoted to philanthropy of sorts. The viewer was only occasionally teased into examining the underlying dogmatic solemnity of it all.

The Spanish, twenty-five years ago, brought out a discreet little venture in evangelism, as charming as *The Hobbit*. A little orphan boy, living in the monastery, whisked away bread and an occasional apple to feed the disconsolate figure on the crucifix in the attic, where, at mealtime, before the dazed stare of the child, the incarnation was reenacted, day after day at 6 P.M.—till the monks, counting lost apples, broke the reverie (*Marcelino, Pan y Vino*).

At the hot end of the electric theological prod, the viewer could see a dazzling blend of faith triumphant over sacrilege (*Le Défroqué*). Without faith there cannot, of course, be sacrilege: and here we had the sometime priest, become agnostic professor of philosophy, dining with his young protégé who had stayed true to their once-common faith and was now freshly ordained in the priesthood. In the noisy, bibulous tavern crowded with hedonists, three violinists carry about the huge five-liter tankard of wine, playing noisily and *accelerando* gypsy-rhythmed catalysts to frenzy, while one at a time guests chug-a-lug, the leader so far having emptied only a fifth of the seemingly bottomless barrel.

It is now routinely refilled, and the violinists place it on the next table down, where the earnest young priest is talking affectionately with his apostate mentor. The audience is distracted—and at just that moment the ex-priest, driven to black-mass exhibitionism, quietly intones, within the hearing only of his young, freshly consecrated friend, the transubstantiating incantation: *Hic est enim Calix Sanguinis mei . . . For this is the Chalice of my Blood . . .* The violinists, unaware, resume the routine. The young priest, dazed by his knowledge that apostate priests are not shorn of their sacramental powers, lifts the tankard—the blood of Christ—to his lips. He begins to drink . . . the crowd goes wilder . . . the violinists sweat . . . the professor is alarmed . . . Now he has emptied the tankard; the crowd is delirious with admiration. . . . The young priest, stumbling outdoors to the cheers of the crowd, succumbs and dies. Flash forward to the funeral. It is being conducted by the professor. Dressed in clerical garb. Returned to the faith. Nobody who saw *Le Défroqué* will forget it.

True Confessions (the movie, not the book) is unlikely to be denounced even by the Legion of Decency. Catholics don't have an Anti-Defamation League, for one thing; for another, there isn't anything there that is truly sacrilegious. Some priests will visit brothels as long as lust is given a fighting chance on earth, and it is an organizing Christian proposition that even Christ was tempted. The Catholic Church is the inspiration for great utterances, even as it has provoked resonant denunciations. G. K. Chesterton, face to face with his time's version of Hollywood agnosticism, concluded a major book by writing that "there are an infinity of angles at which one falls, only one at which one stands. . . . To have avoided them all has been one whirling adventure; and in my vision, the heavenly chariot flies thundering through the ages, the dull heresies sprawling and prostrate, the wild truth reeling but erect."

Those who will be shocked by *True Confessions* may—or may not—achieve perspective by reminding themselves that a century ago Charles Kingsley was writing such witty stuff as, "The Roman religion . . . for some time past, [has] been making men not better men, but worse. We must face, we must conceive honestly for ourselves, the deep demoralization which had been brought on in Europe by the dogma that the Pope of Rome had the power of creating right and wrong; that not only truth and falsehood, but morality and immorality, depended on his setting his seal to a bit of parchment."

Now that's the kind of anti-Papist stuff that makes Hollywood's *True Confessions* taste like a no-cal popsicle. But—a note to all those who seek to offend, or to be offended: Caution! Kingsley, above, brought forth Newman's *Apologia pro Vita Sua*, the crushing masterpiece that British newspaper readers lined up to buy when it was serialized, a book that devastated Kingsley, leaving that urbane, witty skeptic to sound like the village atheist. Impiety breeds piety. I don't know what the movie version of *True Confessions* will bring on, but pending that dreadnought, you are vouchsafed these little words, good for just enough life-sufficiency to keep you afloat until the genuine article comes along.

11

Do You Need to Know
What Joe Says?

April 5, 1983

THE INVITATION—by Mr. Ted Koppel, ABC's very bright young man—was to discuss President Reagan's press conference on Wednesday, at which he signified his willingness to take an interim position on the matter of intermediate missile deployment in Europe. Who else would be on? Zbigniew Brzezinski, said the producer, and Joe Adamov. Who's he? Joe Adamov, she said, is a radio-TV commentator for Radio Moscow.

On the way home, a couple of hours before studio time, I went over the day's mail and found a letter from a hot-blooded classmate who pronounced himself just about ready to give up on America. Why? Because, he said, he had watched "Nightline" the week before, where comment had been made on Reagan's missile defense speech. And one of the commentators was Vladimir Posner, Soviet radio and television commentator. And then—my friend's indignation caused the type to tremble—the following morning, the "Today" show featured commentary on the President's speech by Georgi Arbatov, the head of the U.S.–Canada think tank in Moscow. And in case you thought CBS was above that kind of thing, one of its programs had featured one Gernnandi Gerassimov, also of Radio Moscow.

When asked by Mr. Koppel what I thought of the President's

declaration, I replied that more interesting, really, than to devote my three and one-half minutes to saying the routine things about Mr. Reagan's anticipated compromise was to remark the extraordinary appearance on ABC television of a certified Soviet propagandist, Mr. Adamov, who if he did not say what he was told to say about Mr. Reagan's press conference would never again be heard on Radio Moscow, or for that matter anywhere else, save by fellow inmates in a psychiatric institution or fellow prisoners in Gulag.

Mr. Adamov replied with great wit that during World War II, whereas Americans had lost only 1,000 casualties per day, the Russians had lost 14,000 casualties per day. Whereupon I said that that meant Stalin needed to kill 14,000 fewer people per day, so put that down as a Russian contribution to the economy. Whereupon Joe said that Gulag was back in Stalin's day, there wasn't any of that kind of thing left, and Ted broke in and said that thanks very much, but he thought there was still Gulag there. So it went.

But then Koppel said to me that, after all, wasn't it the business of American newscasters to find out what the Soviet people were thinking? To which the answer of course is that you don't find out what the Soviet people are thinking by asking a Soviet propagandist. And you don't find out what the government is thinking by finding out what the government is saying.

The seven o'clock news had reported that not a single Soviet broadcaster had made any mention of Reagan's press conference—just as if it hadn't happened. Why? Because the Kremlin had not yet decided on what line to take. When it did decide, the word was passed along to Joe Adamov, among others, and he passed it on to the American television audience, via "Nightline."

It occurs to me that the Soviet Union must feel an enormous contempt for Americans who are playing horse to its Lady Godiva. If one of Dr. Goebbels' henchmen had got on U.S. radio to explain what great efforts were being made in Nazi Germany to further interracial amity, Goebbels would have been pleased by his success in using up American air time to broadcast his baloney, and utterly contemptuous of the Americans who let him get away with it.

It is something else for a news commentator to say, "Tonight, the Soviet press denounced President Reagan, calling him a liar, a hypocrite and a warmonger." That's ho-hum stuff. But to put on, live, someone who because he is a human being involves others in situations in which the social conventions are appropriate, where one has to nod one's head and affect to deliberate the Soviet's declarations, is to impose very heavy strains on other commentators, let alone listeners who have to sit there and gnash their teeth. If Mr. Joe Adamov had said what he truly thinks, he'd be the late Mr. Joe Adamov. If he actually believed what he said, he has no business lecturing to ten people, let alone ten million. It's a rough world, but why do we need to make it rougher?

12

Exit Andropov

February 12, 1984

On the whole, I favor frequent rather than infrequent changes of tenure by Soviet leaders. Moreover, it must be assumed that they pass on into a better world or, if not that, to a world not very much different from the one they had got used to. But the trouble with the periodic deaths of Soviet leaders is that they fertilize the most awful rash of commentary by scholars and pundits, which commentary, no matter how it gets there, always, but always, ends by saying one thing, namely that the United States has got to improve its ways.

Consider Mr. Seweryn Bialer of Columbia University. He was recently in the Soviet Union and was terribly distressed by what he calls the "incessant, agitated, and strident vilification of the United States." Terribly put off because he fears that the Soviet Union may very well go on to indulge itself by being obstreperous. What went wrong? Reagan is what went wrong, Professor Bialer says. Because Mr. Reagan's rhetoric "has badly shaken the self-esteem and patriotic pride of the Soviet political elites."

And Professor Stephen Cohen of Princeton argues that the next leader of the Soviet Union may come in committed to the cold war. Because the cold-war lobby will "finally prevail, if it has not already, largely because Soviet pro-détente arguments are in shambles." And why is that? Right. Because "Ronald

Reagan, not Richard Nixon, is the real face of America. And thus, for the Soviet Union, cold war is both political virtue and eternal necessity."

Henry Kissinger has frequently warned that we have time and again permitted the Soviet Union to treat the bargaining table as a psychopolitical venture. The Soviet Union generally comes to the bargaining table not to bargain, but to manipulate Western policy. For instance: The United States announces it is prepared to bargain. It goes to Geneva. The Soviet Union makes proposals that add up to unilateral Western disarmament. We reject those proposals. They call back their ambassadors to Moscow and pout. But their pout is transformed into such instruments as Professors Bialer and Cohen and the great legions of those who feel that failure at the bargaining table is a failure of the West to comply.

It is true that Reagan speaks about the Soviet Union much as Winston Churchill used to speak about the Nazis. That is to say, he tells the truth. This is not merely self-indulgence. It is, for the leader of a democracy who is asking for almost $300 billion per year for defense, a necessity. You see, such sacrifices as American taxpayers are asked to make do not make sense in the absence of a clear vision of what an alternative way of life, dominated by the Gulag tenders, would be like. If the Soviet Union were simply a matter of a different way of life, a different culture, we would not need to bank all that firepower.

What is generally not recognized about Ronald Reagan is that other than the increased military budget and the disposition to say the truth about the Soviet Union in retaliation for the Soviet Union's telling falsehoods about the United States, Mr. Reagan has been a remarkably unprovocative President. He gave up on the pipeline issue. He ended the agricultural boycott. He is abiding by the SALT II treaty he denounced. He has yet to deploy the MX, to come up with the B-1, to give us the neutron bomb. He made four successive conciliatory gestures at Geneva, traveling a long way from the Zero Option, itself an enormously risky concept. He has not held the Soviet Union accountable for Syrian military extremism or for Cuban Central American expansionism, or for martial law in Poland.

Just how is it expected that the next Soviet leader will "renew the cold war"? By making more weapons? Deploying more weapons? But even the Soviet Union recognizes that at some point there is redundancy. By staying away from the negotiating table? But the purpose of the negotiating table has always been to seek out common interests, not merely Western interests. How is a legitimate Soviet interest served in a cold war by ignoring it? Will they—what? Try to overrun West Germany? But don't you see, that is what we have attempted to prevent, via the deployment of the new missiles.

This is not to say that it doesn't matter who is the successor to the KGB head. Merely to say that honeyed Western talk is designed, really, not for Soviet ears, but for Western ears; and that if we hear such talk, we are hearing evidence of the continued success of the Soviet Union in manipulating the Western will.

13

Run Jesse Run

Penthouse, July 1984

INTEGRAL—but absolutely integral—to the success of the Reverend Jesse Jackson is his idiom. Without it his heroic up-from-slavery posture simply evaporates. H. L. Mencken once wrote that the Latin recited by the priest was essential to the apparent sublimation of the liturgical process. Unless the priest is incanting in an exotic tongue, uttering strange and progressively hypnotic sounds, the mind of the communicant inevitably focuses on a middle-aged man, his armpits asweat under the encumbering vestments, who if he had not elected to receive Holy Orders would probably be clerking at a grocery store or tending bar. The image is Mencken's who lost few opportunities to make sport of religion. But the insight is universal: The style is very often the man, is another way of putting it.

Listen, *"We're movin' on up!"*—uttered slowly, just a hint of mounting excitement.

"At the '72 convention, George McGovern was the nominee . . . Reubin Askew was the keynoter . . . I was just fightin' for a seat in the hall. And I beat 'em in New Hampshire!"

Pause for a moment.

Suppose that he had said, "We're moving up," instead of, "We're movin' on up." Why, the whole image drains. As if Gary Cooper, having peered over the boulder and viewed the ap-

proaching Indians, had reported back to his beleaguered colleagues, "I estimate there are two dozen of them, armed with
rifles, and that the probability is they will charge us some time
before sundown." No, no, no!

*"There's a lot of them out there, I figure, maybe twenny,
twenny-five. Got guns. They'll pro'bly come on in befoh the
sun sets."* That's more like it.

"Movin' on up." The anaphora. The rhetorical device whose
effect is achieved by repeating the initial phrase of a sequence.
For maximum effect, it is run quickly after the termination of
the preceding sentence, as in:

"I have a dream today. I have a dream that one day the state
of Alabama, whose governor's lips are presently dripping with
the words of interposition and nullification, will be transformed. . . .

"I have a dream today.

"I have a dream that one day every valley shall be exalted.
. . . *I have a dream."*

*"Movin' on up. Alan Cranston, a powerful senator from
California, and I beat him!*

"Fritz Hollings." [Long pause.] *"When he was governor of
South Carolina, I couldn't use the bathroom in the state capitol. I beat Fritz Hollings! We're movin' on up.*

*"John Glenn was up there orbiting the earth when I was
scufflin' for dimes down here. Now he is gone,* and I'm still in
the race. *We're movin' on up."*

And then the triumphant bugles sound. The gates of paradise open. . . . *"I am at the apex of the triangle.* And that is
the very opposite of blacks being taken for granted by the
Democrats or written off by the Republicans!"

Ratiocination is subversive in revival meetings. If the American people were tomorrow given the choice of McGovern
versus Jackson, Askew versus Jackson, Cranston versus Jackson, Hollings versus Jackson, or Glenn versus Jackson, the score
would be Jackson, 0. So that Jackson is left, really, without a
point to make. And certainly without any claim to having
advanced the evolution of Martin Luther King's dream, which
was that white and black Americans would in due course mix
as though differences in the color of their skins were irrelevant.

Jesse Jackson is engaged in attempting to do quite the opposite. His success is measured precisely by the extent to which
he can persuade the black community that just as he, Jackson,
is primarily a black man, they are primarily black men and
black women, and that therefore their ethnic bond is the chain
that binds them together above all other kinships, attenuated,
that they share with their neighbors.

This exuberant tribalism makes for flash-flood victories (27
percent of the vote in Virginia, that kind of thing). But the
flash-flood victories (remember, George Wallace actually won
the primaries in Maryland and North Carolina in 1972) don't
really add up to very much, not if such victories tug against
orderly inertial thought. And that is a good thing, because we
should not wish any political movement to succeed that says of
a Jew or of a Protestant or of an Italian or of a Hispanic that he
is primarily that, secondarily other things. When John F. Kennedy became the first Catholic elected President, he managed
this by persuading the American people that his being a Catholic affected not at all his qualifications to serve as disinterested
chief executive. If Jack Kennedy's bellowed stand had been
that he stood at the apex of a triangle in which he represented
Catholic interests in America, he would not have gone on to
carry Boston.

Jesse Jackson is a remarkable figure. But his strengths are
primarily theatrical. He strains, for the most part, athwart the
American tradition of progress. That tradition is extraracial.
The tradition does not enjoin Jews from helping other Jews,
Italians from helping other Italians. In *Beyond the Melting Pot,*
sociologists Nathan Glazer and Daniel Patrick Moynihan remarked that 95 percent of the commercial business done by
Chinese Americans in New York went to other Chinese Americans. Now here they remarked an interesting disparity: Negro
Americans (as they were then called) patronized primarily
white businessmen (the exceptions: beauticians and morti-
cians). If Jesse Jackson were aiming at cultivating pride in the
black American of the kind that results in fraternal commercial camaraderie—in creating a demand for more black businessmen, more black professionals—Jesse would be moving
with tradition. And this he began to do a dozen years ago with
Operation PUSH. That was when he was speaking out about

how black Americans need not stand out as athletes: Let them
stand out also as mathematicians and as doctors; but lo, this
requires homework, and great, extraathletic application. In
recent years, however, Jesse Jackson has sold out to the old
political dream. The dream that suggests that the state is the
witch doctor with the keys to prosperity.

Up to a point, the state can be the effective ally of the oppressed. A convulsive effort, enlisting the police powers of the
state, was required to liberate black people from slavery; another statist effort, 100 years later, to give the black people the
vote and spare them the humiliation of Jim Crow. But now,
even though there are residual prejudices, of course—as there
are against Catholics and Jews, Italians and Mexicans—there is
no Fortress America, calculated to exclude blacks from any
position of prominence. To suggest otherwise—which is exactly what Jesse Jackson continually suggests (the Reagan administration is "racist")—is to mobilize an army behind an
objective that is either unclear (What, assuming President
Jackson were inaugurated, would he do for blacks?) or, where
it is clear, un-American (Blacks cannot, by virtue of being
black, deprive nonblacks of their own rights and opportunities).

Jesse Jackson is a man of transient fixations. For a while he
seemed to be concerned exclusively over 1.6 million Palestin-
ian refugees. This at a time when there were 2 million refugees
in Africa. He never acknowledged the 350,000 Ethiopians in
the Sudan, the 125,000 Angolans in Zaire, the 134,000 Burun-
dians in Tanzania, the 200,000 Ethiopians in Somalia, the refugees in Cyprus, or Pakistan, the Cambodians in Thailand, the
Burmese in Bangladesh.

No, it was the Palestinians, even as now it is South African
black victims he wishes to organize our foreign policy around,
not Nicaraguan victims, or Chinese victims, or Afghan victims,
let alone Russian victims. "Let's build houses, not bombs," he
says, which is flower-child cant, like saying let's have fiddlers
on the streets, not policemen. He is given to the most grating
verbal rhetorical disjunctions in contemporary language.
("We're going from the outhouse to the White House."
"They've got dope in their veins rather than hope in their

brains.") But he knows how he can turn them on. He is the biggest political aphrodisiac since Martin Luther King, Jr.

He will, of course, be a major production in San Francisco. The Democratic professionals desire only this, that he not lead a third party. If he decides to do so, it will be ostensibly for the sake of showing how massive the black vote can be, and how critical in critical states. But in order to document this, it will be necessary to document that the black vote is an instrument at the disposal of a "black leader," and this is unhealthy. I so referred to him once, in a public exchange, and was rebuked. "Do you refer to Ronald Reagan as a white leader?" No, I said. "Because Reagan does not seek to be a white leader." But though Jesse Jackson talks about rainbows and extraracial brotherhood, he is in the business of consolidating black America, and that isn't good, not for blacks, not for America. It is good only for Jesse, who is primarily engaged in kingpinmanship.

What else is he engaged in? He was asked this recently. He replied: "We . . . found this widespread dissatisfaction among members of the rainbow—women, Hispanics, blacks, Asians, young people, handicapped people, peace activists, environmentalists. We determined that the way to institutionalize the concerns of the rejected people was to forge an alliance."

Well, women, to the extent that they are dissatisfied, aren't going to look to Jesse for relief. Hispanics, by order of U.S. courts, are receiving free schooling even if they are illegally in the country. Asians who are mad at America are mad over our failure to abide by commitments in Vietnam that Jesse deplores were ever made. Young people, if they have complaints beyond those that young people organically have, can complain about the high overhead of life, much of it owing to Social Security payments to their retired grandparents. Handicapped people are literally causing the streets to be repaved. Peace activists are free to hawk their wares everywhere except in those countries that threaten the peace, and the environmentalists not long ago succeeded in getting the Secretary of the Interior fired.

What Jesse Jackson needs is what he is bound in due course to get: a dose of realism, after all the noise subsides.

Jesse run! Jesse run!

Where?

He's movin' on up—and one day he will scale the mountain and there have a view of reality. Reality is progress achieved by hard work, faith, self-reliance. Not by camp-following with political medicine men.

II
ANALYZING

1

Iran

REFLECTIONS ON THE DEPARTURE
OF THE SHAH

January 27, 1979

THE SHAH'S ejection from Iran is certainly the great event, as advertised. Nothing, as the saying goes, will be the same again. In the perspective of a fortnight, a few thoughts come to mind.

The first is that it was a grand event viewed purely as testimony to the human spirit. The thought of dislodging a despot who superintends the whole modern apparatus of suppression is—*en ipso*—exciting. The very thought of its being doable seems almost reactionary. We are trained to believe that totalist governments cannot be overthrown by the people, only by coups d'état. Here was a single individual who, playing the role of the prophet and leader, found that his words had electric effect a thousand miles away among millions of people who did exactly as he bade them to do. Electronic communications, which are the century's gift to totalitarian states, played paradoxically into the hands of the insurgents. If ever in the history of the world there was a popular revolt, the one against the Shah was it. Which teaches us a great deal about the limited vision of popular revolts.

Two generations ago it happened in the Soviet Union, only there it began as a popular revolt, and ended as a coup. Still, those were days that shook the world. But Lenin had working for him not only the excitement of throwing over a dynasty, but of remaking a state around an ideological paradigm that excited everyone by its call to equality.

The Ayatollah's revolt is more negative in nature. The people knew what they did *not* want, which was a continuation of the rule by the Shah. They do not really know exactly what it is that they do want. "An Islamic republic" conjures up a departure from secular concerns, from that modernization of which the Shah was the symbol. Those Iranians whose enthusiasm is for the return of orthodoxy will presumably get what they want. But after the return of orthodoxy, what else will they be looking for? It was insufficiently stressed during the upheavals that the Shah's violations of Islamic practices were on the order of allowing commerce on Sundays in a Christian country. The Shah himself worshipped at Islam's altar.

But the state was not run as a theocracy, and one wonders therefore exactly what it is that the Ayatollah has in mind when he speaks of an Islam republic. Probably he bothers to use the word "republic" only in the symbolic sense of assuring his followers that the dynasty will be overthrown. But to depose a king is not to institute a republic. A republic—the kind of thing coughed up in Philadelphia two hundred years ago—is far from what is in the mind of the Ayatollah, however inscrutable his pronouncements.

The people of Iran are, therefore, almost certainly in for great disillusions. Not, one hopes, on the scale of the disillusions practiced on the wretched Russians by the wretched Lenin. But the people of Iran have seen Paree, and monasticism almost by definition appeals only to the very few. The notion of imposing it on an entire state is the stuff of dreams, of ideology. The Iranians, after they have done with the rituals of execration, are going to want that which is universally popular. Cars, rock music, Bloomingdale's. This is not in prospect.

There was talk, during the convulsive days of riots and demonstrations, of dismantling the military. The problem isn't dismantling the military, the problem is dismantling the threat. If the Soviet Union turned its army into sheep grazers and threw its missiles into the sea, the Iranians could concentrate entirely on the good life, spiritual and material. But Iran presents the most tempting contiguous country on the borders of the most avaricious superpower in history. To disarm is, in effect, to sue for annexation. In the event matters take that turn, Iranians will discover that the new Soviet rulers are, on the whole, unmarked by the dictates of Islam. There were plenty of Russians who, early into Leninism, dreamed about life under the czars. Perhaps the destiny of the emperor will be to lead a guerrilla war for the return of his country's sovereignty.

Still, there is no denying the sheer thrill of the experience viewed discreetly. Imagine if there were ayatollahs around, one each for Bulgaria, Romania, Czechoslovakia, Poland, the Baltics. For the republics within the Soviet Union. A general strike in Moscow! The raising of the portcullis in Gulag! The Ayatollah has demonstrated the strength of the people, even if he is unlikely to demonstrate the superiority of the alternative.

GEORGE KENNAN WOULD DECLARE WAR

March 11, 1980

TUCKED DEEP in a story that features one part of George Kennan's testimony before the Senate Foreign Relations Committee is an account of what he thinks we should have done when the Iranians seized our hostages. To reproduce the effect the testimony must have had on the senators, the context is necessary. Mr. Kennan had been talking about Afghanistan: we overreacted most awfully. The author of the Doctrine of Containment believes that the military conquest of Afghanistan by the Soviet Union, though of course deplorable, is not to be interpreted as a first salient toward the Persian Gulf; we should not have retaliated as we did, exhausting our nonmilitary resources; we shouldn't aid the resistance movement with arms; and so on. Mr. Kennan in late years has had a vision concerning the vector of Soviet leadership, and if he turns out to be correct, I would give him the Nobel Prize, make him emperor of Siam, turn over the keys to Fort Knox, and—perhaps the greatest gift of all—resign my profession as a political commentator. So much for Afghanistan, and picture now the smiles of contentment on the faces of those senators who, whenever they hear the warbling of a dove, will coo along with delight.

Then somebody raised the question of Iran. Ah well, said Professor Kennan, the United States should have declared war against Iran.

The United States should have *what?*

Declared war against Iran, said Professor Kennan.

I wasn't there, but I can imagine that the senators stared at him as if he had just been entered by an incubus. Dr. Strangelove.

Professor Kennan continued with his characteristic calm. Yes, we should have declared war, and then instantly interned all Iranians living in this country, holding them hostage against the safe return of our own citizens. We should, moreover, have prepared to take such military measures as might seem advisable in the event our hostages were harmed.

Holy caterpillar! To declare war in this country would require a researcher to inform the President and Congress on just how to go about doing it. Declaring war is totally out of style, the post-Hiroshima assumption being that the declaration of war brings with it the tacit determination to use every weapon necessary in order to win that war. Thus we didn't go to war against North Korea, North Vietnam, or Cuba.

But George Kennan made a striking point, namely that a declaration of war invoked the correct relationship between a power whose citizens have been officially detained and a country which has refused petitions for their release. A call by the President for a declaration of war last November would have passed Congress overwhelmingly and, you betcha, with Senator Kennedy voting in favor. The declaration having passed, the juridical house is now in order. Not only the impounding of funds, which the President managed under an old law, but much more. Specifically, the internment of the Iranian population, most of them students. It is never pleasant to punish those who are personally guiltless, but that happens necessarily when reason and diplomacy break down. Our hostages are innocent too. Fifty thousand interned Iranians, held in a revivified army fort, and the Commander-in-Chief licensed by the Congress of the United States to pursue the war against Iran by

any means he thought applicable would have had some influence not only on Iran, but on other fractious members of the
world community, not excluding the Soviet Union.

How would the Soviet Union have reacted? No doubt by
contriving some means of siding with Iran. But at huge risk.
Except for the Communist bloc and Grenada, if we can any
longer distinguish between the two, the United Nations registered their protest against Iran, denouncing an action which at
any time in the history of warfare would have been accepted as
a *casus belli.* To declare war is not necessarily to dispatch
troops, let alone atom bombs. It is to recognize a juridically
altered relationship and to license such action as is deemed
appropriate. It is a wonderful demystifier, sucking up the
smoke from the room, so that you are left there with your
objective in very plain view. That such a recommendation
should have been made by a man once dubbed one of the
principal ambiguists among the American intelligentsia reminds us that purposeful thought is still possible; and causes us
to wonder, wonder, why our leaders, surrounded by all those
expensively trained brains, can't come up with something that
now appears so obvious.

THE QUESTION OF THE HOSTAGES

April 1, 1980

THE SALIENT ASSET of television showman Phil Donahue is
probably his personal amiability, but his usefulness is as a remarkably reliable index of what it is that people are concerned
about. It would be useful to politicians and journalists alike to
be able to read a daily Donahue Index giving the weight he
attached to the problems of the day. Last week Phil Donahue
was lecturing me about the hostages in Iran before an absorbed audience of several thousand women (and several million listeners); and, as I went on to three successive encounters
the next day with business and academic audiences, verily it
transpires that the hostages continue as a major preoccupation
of the public. Which is why the time is overdue for the Presi-

dent of the United States to say that from this moment on, the survival of the hostages will cease to be the coordinating aim of American foreign policy.

Mr. Carter, to be sure, is not anxious to take on Phil Donahue. But Mr. Carter is the President of the United States, not the chairman of a Committee to Free the Hostages. The freedom of the hostages should be an incidental effect of our foreign policy, not its engine. The difference between the two positions is both central and comprehensive.

Very early on—indeed two days after the hostages were taken—Henry Kissinger in a private conversation warned against putting their release as the first aim of our foreign policy. It is easier to make this point by bringing in the relevant context. Although the United States has not bothered with the clerical bookkeeping, we are—or should think of ourselves as being—at war with the state of Iran. Iran has violated American territory, done so without contrition, and holds fifty American citizens in bondage. They are, then, properly viewed as prisoners of war.

Now, wars are waged in a variety of ways, ranging from the dropping of atom bombs to vigilant supervision of a post-hostility period (the state of war between Germany and the United States lasted seven years after the death of Hitler). Wars of whatever kind are not successfully waged by assigning top priority to the return of the POWs. In point of fact, as a psychological matter a country tends to be weakened by such an assignment of priorities. When in the summer of 1972 Senator McGovern, running for President, announced that he would crawl on his knees if necessary to bring home our POWs from North Vietnam, he almost certainly prolonged their detention. Anything the enemy understands to be that supremely valuable, it is less likely to give up. (The hostages are one thousand times more valuable to the Iranian desperadoes for the attention that has been paid them.) The dutiful Mr. Walter Cronkite closes his broadcast every night by citing the number of days the hostages have been imprisoned. The television cameras seldom miss a day in the infinitely prolonged negotiations having as their objective the hostages' release. The result of this kind of thing over a period of five months is that we are not one step closer to manumission than we were on the fifth of last November.

Phil Donahue made several proposals to an audience at least half of which was with him. The President of the United States should swallow his pride, turn to Iran, and say, "I'm sorry." (Such a gesture, its moral objectionability for the moment aside, would put an instant world premium on the seizure of other American citizens in any country that holds a brief against America, and that list is long.) Or—Phil Donahue came up with an alternative that also commended itself to his audience—the Shah should undertake to return to Iran to face the punishment. (This magnanimous willingness to bring martyrdom to someone else recalls the wisecrack of 1939 to the effect that the British were prepared to fight to the last Frenchman.)

We need to "forget" the hostages. A simple declaration to the effect that the state of Iran will suffer greatly if any harm comes to the hostages, and will suffer here and now for its unlawfulness, is required. Our policy should aim at reparations (legislation could be devised to confiscate, rather than merely impound, Iranian assets). Iranian students should, in progressive numbers, be interned. An inventory of Iranian needs, economic and other, should be carefully studied, with a view to frustrating their satisfactions to the extent possible. The pressure should be relentless. But above all things, these pressures should not be influenced by any threats made on the hostages themselves, any more than wars are fought for the purpose of releasing POWs. It is providential that the right philosophical approach to the hostages—which is to subordinate their safety to higher policy—is the likeliest to effect their safety.

MR. CARTER'S RESCUE MISSION

May 1, 1980

I HAVE SPENT seventy-two hours uninterruptedly meditating the question: Why should any Iranian resent Mr. Carter's military adventure? No Iranian that I have heard of, not even the chief madman, has contended that the Americans in the embassy are there voluntarily. None adduces any Iranian law that justifies their detention, nor any international covenant, nor—most interesting of all—any Islamic code. Quite the contrary: the legal, diplomatic and theological illegality of the detention of our diplomats is unchallenged. What rights, then, inure to the country whose responsibility it is to safeguard the lives of its citizens? At the very least those rights exercised by Mr. Carter last Thursday.

And what's this about U.S. "violation" of the sovereignty of Iran? Our venture into Iran was for the purpose of rescuing fifty Americans. It isn't possible to reach Tehran without traversing Iranian territory, so the Iranian government's formal protests are simply inexplicable.

What then about our allies in Europe?

We sent ninety Americans into Iran to rescue fifty Americans. Not long ago we sent five million Americans into Europe to rescue several hundred million Europeans from the legal government of Germany. The Europeans have muted their criticism of our latest rescue effort; not so the Japanese, who speak as though military efforts should not be undertaken on a scale less than Pearl Harbor. There are no grounds for any allied resentment of any efforts by the United States to rescue its own citizens.

And domestically, some of Mr. Carter's critics are acting as though the very idea of a military intervention is outlawry. "In a parliamentary regime," Professor Arthur Schlesinger, Jr., writes in the New York *Times*, "Mr. Carter would be finished. Responsible leadership, if any survives in Washington, would throw out the team that conceived this misbegotten adventure and bring in people whose experience and record would command the confidence of Congress, the American people and the NATO allies." Mr. Schlesinger is engagingly unpredictable in these matters. He did not, for instance, recommend wholesale resignations after the Bay of Pigs fiasco, nor did he demand that the name of John Kennedy be stricken from the honor rolls for having begot the Vietnam war. As for Teddy Kennedy, Mr. Schlesinger has very nearly talked himself into the position that the American people should elect him president not in spite of Chappaquiddick, but because of Chappaquiddick, but Carter, if he followed parliamentary principles, should resign because of one failed helicopter. Such confusion—all very discouraging.

What—as they say—are the lessons of our current tribulation?

1. If Iran is being "driven into the arms of the Soviet Union," as our rhetoricians increasingly put it, then we must seize the occasion to remind ourselves that it is the Soviet Union we really have cause to worry about. If Iran were being driven into the arms of Switzerland, that would not be a tragic international development. So, then, what is it that we are doing to protect ourselves against the eventuality of an increasingly strong Soviet Union? Nothing. On the Iranian desert, we were short one helicopter. In the area of the Persian Gulf, we are short approximately two battleships, one military base, thirty minesweepers, 100 A-6's and about $10 billion worth of miscellaneous hardware. To this need, General Schlesinger has contributed only the proferred services of Field Marshal Kennedy.

2. The military raid was obviously unsuccessful, and we need better-trained guerrilla forces, and perhaps one or two different generals. But secret rescue missions are not designed by Swiss clockmakers. Fort Douaumont at Verdun was one hundred times as impregnable as the American Embassy in Tehran. Several hundred thousand lives were spent in trying to take it in 1917. In the end it was captured in the predawn hours by a dozen German soldiers. Thus might it have gone in Tehran.

One can have no objections whatever to President Carter's mission, restricting our criticism to the maladroitness of its execution and the insufficiency of contingency planning. The replacement of Mr. Carter is certainly a national imperative, but he did much more damage on May 22, 1977, when he repudiated what he saw as our inordinate fear of communism, than he did on April 24, 1980.

2

Reaganomics

December 6, 1980

THE REAGAN ADMINISTRATION should make a fundamental decision, philosophical in nature. We are poised in America for only a very short period of time, measured in historical stretches, when the opposition is at once weak, and curious. The managing editor of *The New Republic*, the principal tablet-keeper of orthodox liberalism, said the other day, in effect, that conservatives have been saying this-and-that for ever so long, why not go ahead and let them run the country for a while, and see what happens?

That empirical spirit is interesting both because it is organically American ("if it works, it's good"; "nothing succeeds like success"), and because pride is a hugely important factor in the operation of governments, which after all are run by human beings. The Catholic Church asks of converts something called "internal assent"—i.e., belief in the Christian credo utterly uncoerced. Religion cannot, really, ask for less, but politics can. It is one thing to say to John Kenneth Galbraith: I want you to *applaud* the abolition of the minimum wage because its abolition will result in a diminution of unemployment and in generally improved economic circumstances. It is something entirely different to say to John Kenneth Galbraith: We're going to go without minimum wage for a stretch. Go ahead and

ventilate your skepticism. But please try not to be obstruction-
ist. Give us a chance—and four years from now we'll have a
look at the situation, and see if there is any improvement. Fair
enough?

Ronald Reagan, in his first State of the Union address, can ask
Congress to experiment with deep therapy. He can do so most
persuasively not by asking for internal assent, but by asking for
a renewal of the pragmatic spirit. Unlike Franklin Delano Roosevelt, who confronted a Congress he entirely dominated, Reagan confronts a House of Representatives organized by the
Democratic opposition; and, in the Senate, there are a great
many single players. The courts, moreover, are less malleable
than they were even for Roosevelt. The Supreme Court gave
him problems, and he tried to pack it, a piece of constitutional
tinkering some people compare with Nixon's Watergate, to the
disadvantage of FDR; and, eventually, got himself a court that
would go along. Reagan will have to deal with the courts in
order to effect some of the reforms most greatly needed. But
the key to the projected operation is, "Let's try it"—not, "We
were right all along."

Milton Friedman stakes his considerable reputation on the
proposition that if all taxes were reduced to a top level of 25
percent, the revenues of the government would in fact increase. Not two, three years down the line, which is what
Kemp-Roth promises us in the form of "flowback": instantly.
Because, says Friedman, there are 31 million Americans paying more than 25 percent tax on their top dollar, and these
Americans are busily engaged in activity whose only motivation is to seek tax relief. Some work less; some invest in tax
shelters; some engage busily in the growing underground
economy, avoiding the IRS altogether.

Why not ask Congress, in the spirit of experimentation, to
try this? Because it will help only the well-to-do? No: because it
will help America. Assuming Professor Friedman is entirely
wrong, which is entirely inconceivable, you are risking only 13
percent of existing revenues, which is approximately the same
as a typical Carter-year deficit. But if Friedman is right, and
logic is on his side, the reform could have wonderful repercus-
sions.

Remember Great Britain, Argentina, Chile. Mrs. Thatcher's

tax reforms have been insufficient to generate the kind of economic motion needed. Argentina's gifted economic czar has moved so slowly, inflation continues; in Chile, by contrast, it is very nearly arrested.

And if, in four years, the economic climate is not dramatically improved, why, the taxes can be reintroduced, can they not? We are not asking Congress to shift the axis on which the planet rotates. This (about which more in due course) should be the line: Reagan the Pragmatist.

ON BALANCING THE BUDGET

December 16, 1980

W E HAVE BEEN prompting the idea of Reagan the Pragmatist, having advanced recommendations he might make to Congress in the way of tax reform and antidiscrimination reforms by the courts.

By the same token, President Reagan could face, pragmatically, the apparently uncontrollable problem of financial restraint. The dilemma is as simple as that an expense that costs every American a mere penny or two—i.e., discretely viewed, insignificant pain—brings intense pleasure to the constituency of a congressman who receives all those pennies. Yesterday, in the general rush to get things done, Congress passed a bill authorizing the expenditure of $2 million for beetle inspection in the town of Baltimore. Of all the people I know, with all their passions, crotchets, velleities and hostilities, I don't know a single person who is unfriendly toward the city of Baltimore. And, no doubt, the congressman sponsoring the bill represented it as not only of potential national importance (what if we woke up tomorrow and found we were surrounded by Baltimore beetles?), but also very dear to his heart. The Senate and the House are made up of nice people and who wants to ruin the spirit of Christmas?

The trouble, of course, is that the spirit of Christmas extends throughout the congressional season, and that a penny here, a penny there, results in $100 billion per year deficits. There is a lot of academic infighting going on between the classicists ("cut the budget, don't cut the taxes"), and the supply-siders, ("cut taxes whatever else you do, but try hard to cut the budget"). But both sides, represented by Mr. Regan as Treasury chief and Mr. Stockman as budget chief, agree that cutting expenses is indispensable.

Recognizing the dilemma—best described in James Dale Davidson's *The Squeeze*—a number of serious men and women have in the past few years decided that only a constitutional amendment to limit spending would relieve Congress of the unendurable stress of balancing a budget, over against satisfying their constituents. There are several versions of the constitutional amendment but the idea is a) to limit spending to a percentage of the GNP, and b) to make the arrangements flexible enough to permit Congress—by vote of, say, two thirds —to override them.

Mr. Reagan might profitably select one version of the amendment and address Congress as follows:

Ladies and gentlemen: The common argument against the constitutional amendment to limit spending is that it is unnecessary—Congress is capable of exercising the necessary restraints without having its hands bound with the chains of the Constitution.

Let us be pragmatic. I urge you to pass the Spending Limitation Amendment. Like most constitutional amendments, it will require several years to get action on it from the states. During those years Congress can consider that it is, so to speak, on probation. If it should manage the self-discipline required by balancing—or nearly balancing—the budget, then the state legislatures will conclude that it is not, after all, necessary to go into constitutional overdrive. If on the other hand—notwithstanding my own determination to exercise the veto as vigorously as President Ford exercised it in an effort to contain spending—the budgets are swollen, the state legislatures will have the opportunity to act, imposing on Congress that discipline it is incapable of imposing on itself.

Again, the model is that of the pragmatic administration. The mood is *a priori*—i.e., Reagan is reasoning from principle; but the experiment is *a posteriori*—i.e., he reasons from actuality. The combination is healthy. It does the least in the way of antagonizing. The proposal is one of my housewarming gifts to President Reagan.

THE FAILURE OF RONALD REAGAN

February 10, 1981

M R. REAGAN'S proposals—an across-the-board 10 percent per year tax cut going over a period of three years—came as partial relief after persistent news stories to the effect that he would not propose to Congress reduced taxes at the highest brackets. To do any such thing, his advisers are quoted as having finally persuaded him, would be to bring on political damage and jeopardize tax cuts altogether.

But President Reagan was true to his commitment to endorse the Kemp-Roth principle. Unhappily, what he did not do was to stress the critical point, the thing primarily to remember about the Laffer curve and the point made with such comprehensive brilliance in George Gilder's new book *Wealth and Poverty:* It is that relief is most important at the higher tax rates. What is the marginal rate of taxation? is the single most relevant question to ask if you are an economic physician probing an anemic patient. The pity is that the greatest living political communicator did not take the opportunity to confront such arguments as those Senator Kennedy and Mr. Mondale used to bring down the house at Madison Square Garden last summer during the Democratic Convention. There must have been fifty references to "rich men's" tax bills. There were none directed at the question: Is it sound public policy to overtax the rich if by doing so a) you reduce the prospects of the nonrich, and b) you reduce total revenues?

Because that is what has been happening, and Mr. Reagan should take an early opportunity to spread those figures before the public. *The Wall Street Journal* recently poked about various studies of the effect of the reduced 1979 capital gains tax (the law reducing the tax from 49 to 28 percent). Opponents of the proposed reduction did everything except commit satyagraha to stop Congress. Among other things they claimed that the measure would cost the government, in lost revenues, $1.7 billion.

What in fact happened? The Treasury collected $1.1 billion *more* in taxes under the lower rate than under the higher rate.

But that isn't all. In 1969, the last year of an earlier lower capital gains tax rate, 698 new stock offerings went out, issued by companies whose net worth is less than $5 billion. Five years later a total of four new issues were floated. In 1977, the figure was thirteen; 1979—the year of the substantial decrease in the capital gains tax—forty-six; in the first ten months of 1980, eighty-nine. In other words, although we are a long way from the level of entrepreneurial activity by small business we were at in 1969, we are pointed in the right direction. The importance of such activity is merely suggested by the following data, drawn together by the economist for the W. R. Grace Company. Between 1969 and 1976, over 80 percent of all new jobs were created by companies with fewer than one hundred employees. So that the approximately eleven million Americans added to the work force during the past decade owe their jobs to the disposition of fellow Americans to take risks. Will they, under Reagan's plan, do so at a more intensive level?

Kemp-Roth is good stuff, though it would be sounder if the lesser rates held and the top rates were instantly reduced. But consider: the average security is now held for 7.2 years. Assuming the current maximum rate of taxation on capital gains and 14 percent inflation, this means that if during that period you doubled your money, you would pocket after paying taxes 67 percent of your original investment. Reduce the inflation rate to 10 percent: that means that an apparent 200 percent return translates to a real return of 87 percent—or less than you had seven years earlier.

"Probably no one in the current Administration," writes a *Wall Street Journal* editorial writer, "disputes the economic rationale" for an instant reduction of the maximum rate on unearned income to 50 percent—the maximum rate on earned income. "The problem is purely political"—notwithstanding that history shows the "rich" would actually be paying more, appearances suggest they are being favored. But surely Mr. Reagan's skill is in demonstrating the fallacy of so many populist assumptions. Why not use that skill for that purpose?

THE MEDIA AND MR. REAGAN

March 4, 1982

IF YOU HAVE BEEN out of the country for a few weeks, you will have forgotten that some of the media proceed as though their national sponsor were the Democratic National Committee. Certainly, judging from a single broadcast, one would guess that the Democrats have secretly purchased NBC, if Jessica Savitch, the anchorlady last Saturday night, is an example. There cannot have been a higher congestion of implausibilities and distortions than those she relayed in two or three minutes devoted to the theme of how, under Reagan, the rich are exploiting the poor.

NBC gave us some nice lines there to choose from, but my favorite was the one about how people earning $10,000 per year are going to endure a greater diminution of benefits than those earning $80,000 a year. How much more? Three times.

An outrage.

Sometimes one has the feeling that it is unconstitutional to think when one listens to the evening news, but at the risk of committing that offense, one might ask: Why isn't it not 3 to 1, but 100 to 1? Or 1,000 to 1? Because we should, really, Democrats and Republicans alike, agree on the proposition that people making $80,000 per year shouldn't receive any welfare measures from the taxpayer.

As to the reduction in welfare aid to the $10,000 family, one would need to know just what form it took before becoming indignant. If, for instance, that loss were $100 worth of food stamps, but were offset by an increase of $350 in purchasing power due to a slowdown on inflation, why that should be OK, shouldn't it?

Then Miss Savitch announced that tax breaks for a family earning $10,000 amounted to $120, while tax breaks for a person earning $80,000 came to $15,000. If you stare at those figures for a mere thirty seconds or so, you find, don't you, that it's as though someone had dropped a cake of mud in your inbuilt little computer (we all have these, and they come in very handy). Surely that can't be exactly right?

So the next morning you look at the entire report, and does it tell you that you will receive $15,000 tax relief at $80,000? No, it doesn't. It says that the *average* tax relief to be received by everyone receiving $80,000 or more will come to $15,000. Well, forget what the tax relief would be to Nelson Rockefeller or H. L. Hunt, how much would it be to someone who earns $80,000? Answer: $4,500. Already this year? Well, no. Next year? No. The third year.

What would a single person earning $80,000 be paying in taxes? Answer: $23,470. So what is his net relief? Answer: About 15 percent. Is that scandalous? I don't think so, which doesn't matter. What does matter is that probably NBC's listeners wouldn't think so either if they were given a chance to have the facts, other than as distorted by Miss Savitch and NBC's news department.

But so it goes. I was in Kansas City the other day and read a report by one Michael Kilian of the Knight-Ridder newspapers, and I thought for a while he was writing about Mussolini; but no, it was of course Reagan, the man who carried forty-four states of the Union at the last election by saying he would do what he is now doing—except for balancing the budget; which if he did balance it, by reducing federal expenditures, the gentlepersons of Kansas City would be reading from Mr. Kilian not a description of Mussolini, but of Hitler.

Here is his lead: "The Republican Party must come to realize that it faces a threat in the Reagan Revolution far greater than the Watergate debacles and possibly as devastating as 'the Hoover Depression.' The radical changes and assaults upon institutions, the hard economic times, perceived cruelty and ideological thuggery that have come to characterize this nominally Republican and supposedly conservative administration have alienated, offended or frightened Americans by the millions. The prospect is for a sound GOP thrashing this November and a Republican catastrophe in 1984."

Perceived cruelty and ideological thuggery, wow. The last time a major political party faced a catastrophe was the Democrats in 1980. One wonders what Mr. Kilian or Miss Savitch diagnosed as the cause of it? There's a lot of bad news in the world, but the good news is that, by and large, for all their lapses and infidelities, the American people are so very much smarter than the hysterical types who try to tell them what to think.

EXIT REAGANOMICS?

July 24, 1982

THE COLLAPSE of Reaganomics (as the event is accurately being described) is testimony to a failure of both nerve and understanding. Sen. Robert Dole, R-Kan., the chairman of the Finance Committee, who mobilized all eleven Republican senators to vote for the highest single peacetime tax increase in U.S. history (in round figures, $100 billion), is suddenly being greeted as a hero—by the Democrats. And with good reason.

In the first place he has thrown in with voodoo redistributionism, by coming in with a tax bill substantially aimed at higher income taxpayers and corporations. And he has baptized that bill as a Republican measure (all the Democratic senators voted against it); so that Republicans running for re-election will have the choice of explaining to their constituents that either a) Americans are undertaxed; or b) Reagan made an awful ass of himself in 1981 by asking for more tax reductions than he should have. I suppose a finished politician will come up with a third way of saying it, but if I were his Democratic opponent, I wouldn't let him get away with it.

Senator Dole and his Republican colleagues appear incapable of making one or two very simple declarations.

The first of these is that the progressive rate of taxation is too steep. Americans who work, who earn income, who provide jobs by investing that income or who provide markets by spending that income have been penalized. Taxed too much. Moreover, taxed without the explicit consent of their representatives in Congress. The tax on $10,000 in 1972 was 7.5 percent. In 1980 it had grown to 10 percent. Up one third. The tax in 1972 on $30,000 was 14.7 percent. In 1980, it had grown to 21 percent. Up almost 50 percent. The idea, then, was to flatten the progressive curve because its steepness had begun to choke economic enterprise. We are scheduled to spend 23 percent of every dollar on government this year. Twenty years ago that figure stood at 13 percent.

The original idea (Kemp-Roth) was to reduce taxes even-handedly. Since everyone knows that 10 percent of $100,000 is more than 10 percent of $10,000, the Reaganites should have been prepared for all that rhetoric about favoring the rich. But not having stressed the risks of excessive progressivity, they proved unready for it. Came the big media ululations about the rich. So along comes Dole with a complicated 24-point tax increase, aimed primarily at depressing exactly those people and enterprises we need at this moment to energize. Why increase taxes on corporations, when corporations are earning at the lowest rate in years and are going bankrupt in the greatest number since the Depression? Why are we so concerned to get more money from General Motors, when General Motors is already losing money?

And we are going now to tax dividends and savings at the source. The same President who as governor of California denounced the withholding tax would preside over its extension to bank accounts. Why? To feed more money, more quickly, to the government. Which means the banks will need to charge more interest to pay for the paperwork. Oh yes, and if they work longer hours they'll smoke more cigarettes and, paying higher taxes, will swell government revenues. So will you when you telephone, or travel by airplane. The airlines are losing money, so tax air travel.

The philosophical basis of Reaganomics was in part that people overtaxed don't do as much. And in part that government does too much. Senator Dole has capitulated on both fronts. One must hope that the President's tacit approval of Dole's bill was wrung from him in the middle of a coughing fit, during which Mr. Reagan could not collect his senses. Or that he will now regroup his forces, fight it out in the House and veto the bloody thing on the grounds that when he said he wanted to reduce taxes and reduce government, he didn't mean the opposite of that.

IS THERE A CASE FOR THE DOLE TAX BILL?

August 12, 1982

Having written with some heat in opposition to the Dole tax bill, I feel obliged to relay the reasoning of Mr. Reagan in the matter, so here goes, faithful to the old injunction that a polemicist is obliged to make as forcefully as possible the case for the arguments he opposes.

Mr. Reagan, in 1981, declared that his policy would include cracking down on people who, in defiance of the law, were simply not paying the taxes they owed. Reasoning backward, we are aware that economists calculate that $100 billion or more in taxes is not being paid in—by people who have discovered the means of avoiding it.

One is trained automatically to think of the rich man in this connection, who takes advantage of a tax loophole. But this is not what we have in mind here, not at all. Tax loopholes, for instance investments in tax-free municipal bonds, are thoroughly legal.

This is not to say that there aren't rich people who illegally evade taxes. Of course there are. It is to say that the bulk of the so-called underground economy is not the business of rich people, not by any means. Middle- and lower-income earners are likelier to find themselves situated to avoid taxes. Most obviously in this category are those who realize a substantial amount of their income from tips.

Now, says a prominent member of the Reagan camp, we estimate that about 80 percent of the $100 billion in taxes over the next three years is to be realized first from this category of noncompliant taxpayers, and second by taking back from the business community certain accidental breaks it received as a result of the omnibus legislation of 1981.

Inevitably, when you pass a detailed and complicated measure, there are elements that creep in which subsequently need to be fine-tuned out. For instance—the Reagan people say—it wasn't seriously contemplated that certain benefits of

ANALYZING 91

leasing one corporation's tax breaks on over to another corporation should have been countenanced, and 7.7 percent of that
$100 billion will come from putting an end to that. Ditto to
some of the reinsurance provisions which were an unpremedi-
tated bonanza to the insurance companies. The investment tax
credit was too high, and lowering it will bring in 5.2 percent.
Requiring corporations to come in more quickly with taxes due
will mean 4.5 percent.

So where are we?

In round figures, one half of what the 1981 bill gave in breaks
to American business is taken back by the bill.

There is no way in which fresh taxes on cigarettes, on tele-
phones and on air travel can be held to be a venture in compliance. These are, pure and simple, fresh taxes.

The bottom line? Approximately 75 percent of the taxes
directly paid by individuals can be held to be tax enforcement,
or—in the case of dividend payments and interest payments—
an imposition on one category of income of the same liabilities
sustained by another class of income. A taxpayer is entitled to
ask why, if his salary tax is withheld, his neighbor's bank earnings are not also taxed at the source.

Are we finished?

Comment No. 1: Why did the tax package mix categories?
One that was directed exclusively at compliance would have
been philosophically easier to handle. But what we have is a
great huge blur, an omnibus bill that goes everywhere from
collecting taxes on tips at hamburger stands, to one that clips
you extra on a phone call, to one that immobilizes one or
another business merger because of changes in tax scheduling.
When such blurs happen, the public tends to lose sight of
distinctions, however clearly they were intended. That is why
very bright people are saying: Mr. Reagan in 1981 came out for
lowering taxes, and in 1982 for raising them, which shows that
he was wrong in the first instance.

He wasn't wrong.

Comment No. 2: The implicit deal was that for every dollar
in extra taxation, government expenses would reduce by three
dollars. But the ratio is not being kept. This is in part due to Mr.
Reagan's entirely commendable concern for our derelict defense system; but in part also because his commitment to the

so-called safety net protects 70 percent of public spending from any pruning. The resulting blur inhibits the view of what Mr. Reagan is seeking to accomplish. And his vision is not only correct, but incorruptibly correct.

DON'T FORGET: BLAME REAGAN

January 13, 1983

IF YOU will lift your head just a little, you will sniff political compulsion. It is definitely in the air to go after Ronald Reagan very hard. When Walter Mondale declares his race for President, which effrontery is now scheduled for mid-February, he will hit Reagan very hard. In doing so he follows, of course, the popular fashion, which is to assume that we live in a society in which all that happens is the doing of the President of the United States. In the unlikely event that Mr. Mondale becomes the President, he might someday regret this tendency.

But for the time being, Blame Reagan is the signal. The lead editorial in the Sunday edition of the New York *Times,* once labeled, properly, the Big Bertha of Eastern Seaboard Liberalism, gives us not only the tune but the full orchestration: "The stench of failure hangs over Ronald Reagan's White House." Missing is only an exclamation point. There follows a list of most of the things that are wrong in this world. Deaths from cancer are the only thing Mr. Reagan is not held responsible for.

Now, most of the talk has to do with the economy. And indeed it is not too early to ask: Whose fault is it?

If we want to talk defense, then it is half correct to say it is the fault of Ronald Reagan, because indeed he came to power after four years that can be likened to the years of Defense Secretary Louis Johnson in the sleepiest days of the Eisenhower presidency. Reagan said we needed to rearm.

Now the money voted for rearmament is of course voted by Congress, and indeed money measures must, specifically, originate in the House of Representatives. Which is run by Democrats. So that it is a little bit glib to say that Ronald Reagan gave us high defense expenditures. But the responsibility is clearly his to face the country and to ask whether we do really intend to economize at the expense of a military judged to have been dilapidated by the end of Mr. Carter's term of office.

Two things have laid waste economic projections of Mr. Reagan. One is his fault, the other isn't. Unemployment has risen by about four points, and every percentage point of unemployment represents $25 billion in cost to the government, a figure arrived at by adding lost tax revenue to increased welfare expenditure.

Laying the blame for that increase on the shoulders of Ronald Reagan is not easy to do. If the cause of the unemployment was high interest rates, we need only note that when he was inaugurated, interest was at 21 percent; now it is at 13 percent. So we are to blame what? Tax relief? But tax relief is, by almost every economic school of thought, held to be the proper thing in times of recession.

For what is Mr. Reagan himself to blame? For permitting the country to assume that the great tax bill of 1981 solved, or came close to solving, the great problem. That problem is runaway government spending and prohibitive taxation. Mr. Reagan's two grave mistakes were first to encourage the notion that the so-called safety net meant immunity for all entitlement programs. It was obvious well before Mr. Stockman adopted *The Atlantic* as his confessor that you cannot reduce federal spending from 23 percent of GNP to 19 percent of GNP by attacking food stamps and the half-dozen other little programs that account for only 30 percent of federal spending.

Mr. Reagan's second mistake was in failing to get to the root of the tax problem, which is, very simply, high marginal rates of taxation. Kemp-Roth envisioned a reduction, over three years, to 37.5 percent top tax rate. After three years, Mr. Reagan's top tax rate will continue at 50 percent. The reason these figures are important is that the country continues to suffer from massive neglect of savings and investment. And the redirection of sleeping capital is what is needed to bring on the rejuvenation Mr. Reagan proclaimed. It is by no means possible to say that had he confronted Congress with a suitable program, Congress would have granted it to him. But it is possible to say that Reagan's failure to finger the difference between what he got and what he might have asked for accounts for the residual sluggishness.

So how do we make the final adjudication? Why not use a Democratic measurement of the Misery Index? Remember? You add the unemployment figure to the inflation figure. Under Mr. Carter, the Misery Index stood at 19.8. Under Mr. Reagan, at this moment, when the stench of failure hangs over us, it is 15.8.

3

Korean Airlines Flight 007

THE INITIAL SHOCK

September 6, 1983

THE SHOCK has been instructive both to Americans and to Russians. On the scales on which crimes are abstractly measured, the figure of 269 people killed is negligible. If that were the total number of violent deaths caused by the Soviet empire on a single day, September 1, 1983, would go down as evidence of the greening of communism. We do not have such figures and probably never will, but between midnight the last day in August and midnight the first day in September, there were violent deaths effected in many parts of Russia and in territory controlled by communists. In Afghanistan. In Cuba. In El Salvador, Nicaragua, China, Vietnam, Laos, Cambodia. How many times 269? Ten times? One hundred times?

But—and not without reason—this was the act of violence that inflamed the public imagination. It is worth asking why.

1. Most Americans have now experienced air flight. And many Americans have experienced air flight over foreign territory. The loneliness of flight is not entirely overwhelmed by cabin movies, the drinks, the food and the *Gemütlichkeit* of shoulder-to-shoulder life. Outside there is cold and blackness. And below there is, at 25,000 feet, a distance equal to approximately 25 times the height of the Empire State Building. To go suddenly from the safety of a serene flight through the air to what happened to those 269 passengers is to feel, empathi-

cally, what it would be like to be dropped into the sea from a height 25 times that of the Empire State Building.

2. The psychological imagination continues to agitate. The actor-dancer Gene Kelly once told me about his experience. It had been the maiden flight of our proud Boeing 707, west-bound, London to New York: America's big entry into the jet age, England having failed when its Comet jets exploded mysteriously in the early fifties. Both the captain and the copilot on that historic Pan American flight had ambled aft to chat with the passengers when it happened. The plane began a nosedive toward the earth.

Gene Kelly recalled that as the captain struggled to reach the cockpit—it was like climbing a vertical pole, such was the g-pressure against which he was working, given the plane's diving posture—every passenger in that plane knew that death was moments away. But very long moments. Because, you see, it takes a long time for even a stone to drop 35,000 feet. There are two or three or four minutes of sheer torture.

We do not know whether the Soviet missile exploded inside the Boeing 747. If it did, then mercifully the passengers were instantly dead. More likely it did not, so death came to them only several minutes later when the mortally wounded airplane struck the Sea of Japan. In the case of the Pan American plane, the captain succeeded in reaching the cockpit and unscrambling the frozen autopilot only hundreds of feet before disaster. The experience, Gene Kelly reports, will wake those passengers up in the middle of the night for as long as they live.

3. Add to this that the passengers were as innocent as one can be of malevolent intent against the Soviet Union. Sure, Representative Larry McDonald was on board, and he wished, as most thoughtful people do, for the earliest possible end to the vermin who preside from the Kremlin over the vast and aggressive slave empire. But flying over the Sakhalin Peninsula in an unarmed Boeing 747, Congressman McDonald was about as dangerous to the Soviet Union as Shirley Temple. Is it, therefore, the innocence of the passengers that has caused the international outcry? Well, it is a factor, but hardly conclusive. To be innocent has never earned anybody immunity from communist sadism. For every human being tortured and killed because he conspired against the Soviet state, there must be fifty

whose crime consisted of the Soviet equivalent of double parking.

It was something that combined all these factors that has caused a wave of indignation almost unparalleled in recent years.

When the Poles declared martial law and a country of forty million people found itself without the vestigial liberties it had been exercising, there was an outcry. But less passionate than this one. Because we learn from life what art teaches us. It is that, to use the fancy words of English professors, "we generalize by particularization." The awful death of 269 people in a single airplane reminds us, more starkly than an old-fashioned purge of a million or so faceless men and women whose lives we never share, what it is like to be at the mercy of the new barbarians, who have hold of the electricity Lenin coveted.

THE DAY AFTER

September 8, 1983

AFTER the first flush of horror American leaders began asking themselves: What were we going to do about the execution of 269 passengers, including thirty Americans, one a congressman? Some of the relevant data:

1. From the beginning, there had been from the Soviet Union nothing but a succession of lies. The Korean aircraft had not responded to signals, the Soviets said (false). The aircraft had not obeyed instructions (false). The aircraft was obstinately headed deeper and deeper into Soviet territory (false). The Soviet plane hadn't in fact knocked it down (false). If a Soviet plane had done so, it was not acting under instructions (false).

As late as twenty-four hours after the incident, Soviet citizens had not heard over their own radio and television that the plane had been knocked out. And to cap off a day of lies, the Soviet Union came up with the invention that no foreigners could use Soviet satellites for their usual network transmissions on Thursday night because they were considered overloaded. Oh yes, the Soviet ambassador in Japan said that the West was engaged in attempting to create anti-Soviet hysteria. He found it a little difficult to get through his line of reasoning, because at that point the Soviet Union was not even admitting that the aircraft had been downed.

2. A number of congressmen and senators were heard from, and the usual words were used, from awful to woeful. New York Senator Daniel P. Moynihan stood out, in part because when he gets on a head of belligerent steam, he fairly sizzles, and it is a joy to watch, particularly if you are not the object of his anger.

What he said was that a) the United States should instantly summon the UN Security Council into emergency session; b) the President should reconvene Congress to decide on emergency action; c) the United States should sue before the World Court asking for maximum indemnity, "pending," he said, a note of caution entering in, "a truthful statement by the Kremlin of why it happened."

Two Soviet specialists suggested that if indeed there are frontiers of the Soviet Union the crossing of which means instant attack by fighter planes, these frontiers should be advertised. And Harold Brown, former Secretary of Defense, who can be presumed to know about such matters, flatly declared that since the aircraft had been tracked over a period of two and one-half hours, it was simply inconceivable that the order to shoot it down emanated other than from the Kremlin.

3. These words are written before President Reagan has been heard from directly, to make any concrete recommendation. One can assume that there is pressure on the Kremlin, by Western diplomats but also by Soviet insiders, to repudiate the act. The trouble here is that surrounding circumstances put the Soviet Union in the position of a drunkard being asked to repudiate his liver. It is extremely difficult to do. It would have been blissful for them if they could have said that a hot-tempered pilot had lost hold of himself, that he is being sent to a rehabilitation center, that maximum efforts will be made to compensate the families of the victims. Andropov could show up at a funeral of one of the victims.

But that is not the Soviet mode. When they get around to apologizing for actions taken by Soviet officials, it is usually after many years have passed and quite a few million have died, as when Khrushchev apologized for the excesses of Stalin, whose excesses Khrushchev zestfully performed during the thirty years he served Stalin. It is more likely that the Soviet Union will nestle some fiction or other about a mystery airplane that might have been carrying lethal cargo—that kind of thing, leaving it to Mr. Reagan to take the initiative.

What should happen is what should have happened when martial law was declared in Poland: a total economic, social and cultural ostracism of the Soviet Union. No trade, no cultural exchange, no nothing. But if that plane had been carrying the President of the United States, the Queen of England, the President of France, and the prime ministers of West Germany, Japan and Italy, plus Jackie Onassis and the Rolling Stones, we would not do that which should be done. Because the Western spirit is weak. If it hadn't been, the plane would not have been shot down in the first place.

THE AMERICAN RESPONSE

September 10, 1983

We SHOULD face it that understanding the Russians isn't something we are ever likely to master. James Reston struggles valiantly in his column and says perhaps they shot down the Korean airliner because they were invaded by Napoleon. That is as good a guess as any. Even concentrated Soviet-watchers are surprised by the voluminous lies being told. The Soviet Union is now suggesting that the tape that plays the exchanges between the fighter pilots and their command base is "perhaps two years old." How do you deal with people like that?

And what satisfaction are we supposed to get out of the Soviet explanation that a) they didn't shoot down the plane; that b) on the other hand they did shoot it down because c) it was really an American spy plane; which d) actually it was not, but the Korean airliner was engaged in a spy mission; and e) the Soviet pilot in fact mistook the Boeing 747 for the Air Force RC-135. Since the RC-135 was on land 1,000 miles away from the shooting, and since it does not look like the Boeing

747, the effect of the Soviets' reassurance is on the order of saying that they thought it was the Eniwetok Atoll, and all along it proved to be Detroit they dropped the bomb on, and that's Detroit's fault.

New York Senator Daniel Patrick Moynihan is profoundly correct in saying that last week the Soviet Union was guilty of two atrocities: the first, the shooting down of the airliner; the second, their behavior after shooting it down. No one since Charles Manson gloated over the blood he and his groupies shed in Hollywood that night has cackled more grotesquely than the Soviet Union in flaunting its insouciance over the death of men, women and children innocent even of the knowledge that it is dangerous to fly in a commercial liner across the borders of the Soviet Union.

There has been some dissatisfaction over the President's speech. Hardly surprising. It was a magnificent forensic performance. For that reason, it was emotionally frustrating. If Winston Churchill had declaimed that the British had nothing to gain but blood, toil, sweat and tears and therefore he would go to the Commons and to the House of Lords and ask for a joint declaration against Adolf Hitler, his speech too would have bred frustration.

On the other hand, we don't—do we?—know what to do. War is excluded these days, and everything short of war runs into a vested interest: the wheat farmer, the Pepsi-Cola people, the gas pipeline manufacturers, the truck people, the bankers.

True, we could draw strategic inferences from Soviet behavior, one of them that a treaty is not really worth the trouble of devising, because it is violated whenever it suits the Soviet interest to violate it, and meanwhile the Soviet Union profiteers from the sense of security that emanates from such a treaty. We have a treaty against the use of chemical warfare, which the Soviet Union is regularly violating in Cambodia and in Afghanistan. We have a covenant on human rights grandly ratified by the Soviet Union in 1973, reaffirmed in Helsinki two years later, reaffirmed in Madrid a few months ago, and now our Secretary of State is in Madrid where he gives us the consolation of promising that he will devote the entire first session to the question of the downed Korean airliner.

We have a covenant (the United Nations charter) against the use of military aggression, which did not deter the Soviet Union in Hungary or in Czechoslovakia or, now, in Afghanistan. History will probably record that the most severe anti-Soviet measures undertaken as a result of the downed Korean airliner is the reaffirmed resolution of the citizens of Glen Cove, Long Island, not to permit Soviet personnel living in their dacha on the North Shore the use of the beach facilities of Long Island Sound, inasmuch as they are not paying their share of taxes.

If, on the other hand, the critics of President Reagan are saying that he ought not to pay any attention to the wheat farmers, the Pepsi-Cola makers, the gas pipeline makers and the bankers, then those critics are absolutely right, the only trouble being that he would not then be President Reagan, he would be Governor Reagan, or Ronald Reagan, or just a speechwriter or anticommunist orator, like thee and me. Sometimes leaders can bring an entire people around, and sometimes Abraham Lincoln is President.

ONCE AGAIN: NOTHING

September 13, 1983

THERE ARE those who said the "crisis" in Soviet-American relations would not last. We were right. It is substantially over. Concerning the episode, a few observations:

1. The struggle to disbelieve is eternal. Usually what one struggles to disbelieve is that which is unpalatable to one's predispositions.

The dominant impulse in what one legitimately designates as the "appeasers"—i.e., those who are simply not disposed to make strenuous efforts to resist Soviet imperialism—was first to doubt, then to belittle the Soviet incident. The term "appeaser" is used here not merely as a lazy pejorative. The appeaser tends to oppose a national draft, to oppose any increase in defense spending, to oppose economic boycotts, cultural boycotts, boycotts of athletic events.

It is undeniably true that the Soviet Union holds sway over Eastern Europe, is actively engaged in a war against Afghan independence, in consolidating victories in Southeast Asia, and in fomenting revolution in Central and South America. And it is as undeniably true that the American appeaser is found everywhere opposing any realistic brake on such Soviet enterprises.

The relevant questions, after the shooting down of the Korean airliner, were: 1) How does one punish a punishable act? (Answer: By demanding reparations.) 2) How does one take reasonable steps to see to it that such an act is not committed again? (Answer: By getting assurances from the tort-feasor.) The appeasement community in America has not demanded reparations in any meaningful way. To ask the Soviet Union kindly to pay money to the families of survivors is not to be confused with "demanding" reparations.

And on the matter of getting assurances from the Soviet Union that nothing of the sort will happen again, the appeasers have come much closer to getting from the Soviet Union assurances that precisely the same kind of thing will happen again to any airplane detected over Soviet territory.

2. Then there is the school, not unrelated to the appeasers but distinct from them, that says we vastly overestimate the power of the Soviet Union and in doing so merely betray two things: our paranoia and our disposition to serve those whose interest in defense is purely commercial.

One gentleman wrote to me during the crisis to say: How would America like it if the Soviet Union had nuclear weapons in Mexico and in Canada? My answer: It would bother me not at all provided the Soviet Union were Switzerland. But until that happens, it would bother me very much, though not all that much more than I am already bothered by the existence of weapons whose arrival time between Russia, where they now sit, and Detroit is only fifteen or twenty minutes more than if they were buried in the plains of Manitoba or in the Sierra Madres.

The school goes on to say, Hell, the Soviet Union is a military mess! It took them two and a half hours to shoot down that lousy airliner, and they probably didn't in fact know it was an airliner, so rudimentary is their equipment, and anyway, all you people care about is cranking up American fear so that you can have MX missiles and more profits for defense. To which an appropriate answer is that the Soviet Union discovered the wheel a long time ago, that it was the first country to orbit the earth, and now has the undisputed resources to blow the United States to kingdom come. And it is about as convincing to say that Americans favor free speech because we profit from it. In short: Yes. We all profit from an effective defense. And finally:

3. Diplomats show yet again how insular is their world. Dr. Zbigniew Brzezinski consoled us all the way from Ottawa that the West will have achieved a "significant" boycott, thereby robbing the word "significant" of any significance.

We felt it triumphant to have lined up thirteen countries in the UN Security Council to back us in complaining of the lost airliner. Canada's sixty-day suspension of reloading facilities for Aeroflot is less punishment than a Quebec magistrate would give a kid for merchandising a joint. The only thing we know for absolute sure that has come out of this is that never again will a Korean airliner carelessly overfly Russian territory. And that, ladies and gentlemen, was the point the Soviet Union sought to make. It has made it.

4

Invading Grenada

HOW IT WAS BEFORE D-DAY

October 27, 1979

THEY ARE the last places. Sun-soaked, unpolluted, pin-clean.
A crescent of hundreds of islands, islets, and cays stretches
enticingly down from Puerto Rico and the Virgins to the South
American continent. It is a sailor's paradise. Green seas beat at
rust-colored reefs, leggy palms fringe legendary beaches. Uni-
formed children make their way to school, the boys in knee-
pants and cricket caps, the girls' skirts immaculately pleated.
Where there is cricket, can there be Castro? Not many are
noticing, but the ex-British Caribbean is in turmoil, weather-
ing the first wintry blasts of communism.

It began in March. On the twelfth of that month, Grenada's
elected Prime Minister, Sir Eric Gairy, left his sunny satrapy
for New York to consult with his UN mission (Grenada is the
second smallest member of the UN, but by no means the least
talkative). Before leaving, he had impounded a boat labeled
Grease which, however, was gun-laden, courtesy of Cuba. He
was apparently confident that by taking the boat he had
aborted a coup d'état; but other arms had been infiltrated into
the country, and on the thirteenth the so-called Jewel movement announced over the radio that its new People's Revolutionary Army had taken possession of the island, that the
"criminal dictator" Gairy was abroad, his ministers in jail, the
state's barracks burnt to the ground.

Within weeks, heavy armament from Castro was on its way to Grenada (population about 100,000): artillery, antiaircraft weaponry—pretty sophisticated stuff. The militia consists primarily of fifteen-year-olds, who alone are permitted to bear arms and, in their exuberance, have been known to kill or castrate themselves endeavoring to master the loading techniques of Czechoslovakian rifles. The official propaganda is resolutely anti-American specifically, and antiwhite in general, a social tragedy in an island that has been racially integrated for generations.

Were there protests? Yes, St. Lucia (about a hundred miles north) fired off a cable to the queen, just as in the good old days, asking that her government not recognize the revolutionaries. The reply was as expected: Her Majesty's government need neither recognize nor not recognize the new government.

The fact of it is that Great Britain is now tired of the West Indies, which for a generation have cultivated anti-English sentiment, have achieved independence, and have made economic demands on the most straitened country in Europe. The last whiff of British imperial grapeshot was fired a dozen years ago in an *opéra bouffe* military operation against Anguilla which very nearly got Harold Wilson laughed out of office. Count Great Britain out.

Meanwhile, of course, there is chaos in Guyana, where Kleenex sells (on the black market) for $6 a box and a Marxist government proceeds chaotically to destroy the country. In Dominica, another palace coup (pronounced "coop" in the area). And on July 2, St. Lucia's prime minister lost in the polls to an ex-judge who talks hysterically on the podium, terminating his speeches with *"Viva la Revolución!"* The three revolutionary prime ministers scheduled a summit in Grenada, where they congratulated each other extensively and sported placards reading "CATO NEXT," the reference being to the stable government of Premier Minton Cato in St. Vincent's. Since the communists already have Cuba, and have all but satellized Jamaica and Guyana, the question arises how long Barbados and Trinidad can hold out and, to the far north, Antigua.

And here is the awful demographic center of gravity. The area we describe contains five to seven million people. In some islands, as many as 60 percent of the population are under nineteen. Where will they find work, with the tightening of the borders? One speculation is that these young people are valuable as the newest export: ideological mercenaries. The Soviet Union is not disposed to use its own troops in the various wars of liberation. We have seen what thirty thousand professionally trained soldiers can do to bring stability to Africa, in the felicitous phrasing of Andy Young. Why not another thirty —or one hundred—thousand West Indian communist mercenaries, otherwise jobless, to help the Soviet Union get on with exporting misery to the world?

U.S. policy in the matter, when last heard from, was incoherent.

ON HEARING THE NEWS

October 29, 1983

THE AZORES—Circumstances have placed me two thousand miles away from the good old U.S.A., more or less at sea—in fact, at sea, the victim of radio communications so erratic that an entire week has gone by without the news. Then suddenly the airwaves open up and a flash comes in: The United States, in company with four Caribbean nations, none of which can remotely be thought of as a satellite of the United States, has invaded Grenada. The purpose, according to the BBC announcer, is to safeguard foreigners living in Grenada and apparently endangered by the communists who overthrew, and killed, the antecedent communist, who had brought misery to the little island of Grenada and opened it up to Soviet and Cuban military plunderers who were busily engaged to try to do to Grenada what the Soviet Union tried to do to Egypt until, on that bright day in 1972, Sadat kicked them out. The strategic objective of the Soviet Union was plain: to convert little Grenada, with a population of 80,000 people, into a little Gibraltar, guarding the eastern channel into the Caribbean through which the vital foreign oil passes to sustain the United States with necessary energy.

Without knowing the details of the military operation, or of events immediately antecedent, how does one spontaneously react on hearing such news?

This Rip Van Winkle declared it to be champagne time. Not because Grenadians are presumably being killed as these words are written, and conceivably also Americans, and some soldiers from other eastern Caribbean nations, but because the United States has finally acted decisively in its self-evident interest. The point of having Marines is to use them when necessary. It is always depressing when the use of force becomes necessary, diplomacy having been exhausted. But it is even more depressing when force, though appropriate, is not used, putting off the day when the choice becomes to use greater force or give up. In the memory of most living Americans, as many Marines as have currently landed in Grenada might have landed in Havana and done a humanitarian service to the Cuban people while guarding our geopolitical frontiers that do not end in Key West simply because our flag is not hoisted beyond that point.

Without knowing details of the engagement, it is predictable that the usual people will deplore this "resort to the military." It is at such moments that the Rip Van Winkles need to remember that the military arm of a free nation has got to be sheltered from the prevalent bias that assumes that any use of the military is intrinsically evil. The failure to use the military when the situation calls for its use in the international arena is as inexcusable as the failure to use the police when the domestic peace is threatened.

There are those who accuse the President of a return to chauvinism and imperialism. But to suggest that the United States has secretly coveted Grenada requires the accuser to assume a most astounding and prolonged American continence. If our objective all along was to take over Grenada, it beggars the imagination why we didn't do so earlier—say, in 1920. Or even a decade ago, when Grenada was given its independence by Great Britain. The search for evil American motives will stretch the resources of the most adamant critics of America. Not that they aren't up to the challenge: They were up to it in their criticism of Lyndon Johnson when, in 1965, he sent the Marines to the Dominican Republic. When you ask them exactly what imperialistic or other heinous objectives the Marines could serve in 1965, they will change the subject. For some people it suffices to accuse America of cruel and atavistic motivations.

The Rip Van Winkles aboard this little vessel, even in the absence of more specific news than you can get from a two-minute shortwave broadcast, were heard to say, God bless America. Even as so many British, when tested in the South Atlantic a few months ago, found themselves saying, with special meaning, God save the Queen.

MISSING THE POINT OF GRENADA

November 5, 1983

THERE IS an upwardly mobile cliché going the rounds, to wit that we should not resort to force except as the last resort.

The trouble with that doctrine, if strictly applied, is that it can lead to a call for action at a moment when the objective has become very nearly impregnable. At that point either you proceed or you do not proceed. If you do, the cost can be very great. If you do not, then you end up accepting that which you began by assuming its unacceptability.

Consider, for instance, Cuba. It is, quite simply, the one great strategic foothold of the Soviet enterprise in this hemisphere. It is a 700-mile-long staging base for Soviet operations in Latin America. But for Cuba, there would not now be the problem of Nicaragua, let alone Grenada. So when does it become relevant to take Cuba out by force? Twenty-two years ago we made a halfhearted attempt to move, and even then it was too late. Too late for the effort we were willing to put into it. To take out Cuba today, a senior military strategist reports, "would be on the order of taking out Okinawa in World War II." Assuming, of course, no nuclear interference.

The New York *Times*, which would have argued against using force to take Bunker Hill, expresses its dismay over the rationale for moving against Cuban-dominated Grenada by saying, "What, in any case, could Cubans have done from Grenada that they cannot do better from Cuba?" Quite apart from the military fatuity of the observation ("What, in fact, can Americans do from Guantánamo that they cannot do better from Miami?" "What in fact can the Russians do from Afghanistan that they cannot do better from Russia?"), what is precisely left unanswered is what we are going to do about Cuba. Unanswered because the answer is unanimously affirmed.

What we are going to do about Cuba is nothing. Why? Because we waited until a resort to force would have required too much of it, and when that happens the will to use force has a way of atrophying.

Notice also that critics of the Grenada operation are telling us that there was no indication that our students in Grenada were going to be detained. Well, there was no indication that our embassy staff in Iran was going to be detained. The suggestion that the detention of American personnel was a step Grenada's General Austin was too civilized to resort to requires us to say that the same man who shot in cold blood his predecessor and most members of his cabinet would have been too squeamish to take 500 Americans hostage. Thanks, but most of us prefer a commander in chief who doesn't run risks of that sort. We know that there were arms enough in Grenada to equip five divisions. Those arms were presumably designed to aim at people other than the Cubans who brought them in.

Why are they so appalled when the United States makes an intelligent move on the world scene? Would you believe the Harvard law professors who cabled the White House their protest against the rescue operation on the grounds that "it seems one more incident in the history of American suppression of progressive movements"? You tell me that it is progressive to stage a military coup, imprison, torture and execute the opposition, turn the island into an armed fortress, and I'll send you to Harvard to teach law.

If we reflect on it, it is discouraging that so many voices are raised to say the most irrelevant things. Rather like asking whether the lifeguard who rescued the drowning swimmer was correctly attired. Yes, it is true that on the whole we want the press to cover our military operations. Yes, it is true that there is a presumption against the landing of the Marines to straighten out local messes. Yes, it is true that our students were not yet hostages. But surely the salient point is that with minimum loss of life we have rescued a little island in the Caribbean from a monstrous tyranny whose script was being written in Moscow and Havana, that we obliged that island's neighbors who were obviously targeted for subversion, and that we have the manifest gratitude not only of the American students, but of the population of Grenada. Isn't that, really, the point?

5

Dubois Memorial Lecture

Address Delivered at Mount St. Mary's, Emmitsburg,
Maryland, May 6, 1983

I AM HONORED to be associated with your 175th anniversary
and of course honored to have been asked to inaugurate the
Dubois Lecture series. I should reveal to you that I have received a most intimidating letter from your president, Dr.
Wickenheiser, in which he suggested that my remarks here
today might serve as a model for future speakers. I am normally reluctant to contradict college presidents. But it is not
only unlikely that I shall serve up a precedent, it is also undesir-
able. I have always assumed that I had things to say that were
worth listening to. To claim otherwise, given the life I lead,
would be to engage in imposture on a very grand scale. But I
have incurable stylistic and intellectual mannerisms I wouldn't
want others to imitate—assuming the inconceivable, namely
that anyone would be tempted to do so. I am attracted to
varieties of anomalous thought which, expressed by more prudent men, would be taken as contumacious. I wish that all the
world were of my opinion about most things, but it makes me
nervous to be set up as a paradigm of anything at all. So then
with some formality, speaking *mutatis mutandis ex cathedra*, I
hereby liberate all successor speakers on this august series

from any obligation, explicit or implicit, a) to sound like me, b) to behave like me, c) to speak like me, d) to reason like me. To be sure, the residual problem of those speakers who avail themselves of all these licenses is how to make their way into the Heavenly Kingdom.

I am going to devote my time today to setting forth one or two propositions, some of which I tender asseveratively, others —well, inquisitively.

The first of these is, How, in modern circumstances, does one go about defining, in the vocabulary of full-scale war, an "innocent party"?

You will correctly have supposed that I am vexed by the thinking that substantially undergirded the conclusions arrived at by the bishops at their plenary session in Chicago. Much time had been given in the attempt to translate into public policy the protectiveness Christian thought is expected to extend to innocent parties—so to speak, to bystanders in a hostile confrontation.

A simple statement of the obvious distinction is given by imagining an escaped murderer who disposes of a hostage. It is clearly immoral to proceed against the murderer without taking care for the survival of the hostage.

We tend, though only by slighting analytical precision, to graduate the isolation of the innocent bystander to situations in which, on thoughtful reconsideration, it is not easy to hold fast to the progenitive distinctions. Consider, for instance, the distinction, especially pressed since the Second World War and the advent of nuclear weaponry, between "counterforce" and "counter-value" weapons and objectives.

By counterforce we mean American weapons aimed at aggressively postured military installations. In the imagination of moral man it is accepted that those men who garrison such concentrations are, in wartime, fit objects of our retaliatory, defensive or preemptive war machines.

Now it is one thing to comprehend that in order to prevent a rifle from continuing its fire it is necessary to aim a bullet at the man whose trigger finger is firing that rifle. That is instrumental knowledge. If the man firing that rifle is a social outlaw—a criminal, a murderer—one can with moral confidence return fire aimed at this inner-directed aggressor.

But I think the proposition highly doubtful that military men who are members of the armed services of aggressive political regimes are in any clear sense of the word themselves "aggressors." We have spent a lot of time in recent years, it is worth noting, attempting to denature sex. For instance, to the point of sending women to Annapolis and to West Point, in order to drive home the point that those human properties generally associated with successful soldiery are not monopolized by men. The assumption here, just to begin with, is that there is no such thing as the gentler sex in war-making when one makes basic taxonomic calculations.

I think that finding is probably correct. There is the *physically weaker* sex—women. But women, we are informed, are capable of acting as ferociously as men. So that in an age when technological proficiency rather than brute strength is the critical qualification, efficient fighting creatures are judged as such primarily with reference to skills unattached to gender. We conclude that women as well as men can be thought of as aggressive agents, and therefore fit objects of our retaliation.

Thus already one of our more venerable traditions weakens, but we are still left with by far the most formidable tradition to contend with. Let's take it on:

Dmitri and Valerian are twin brothers. Both are interested in the arts, particularly in ballet. They turn eighteen, and Valerian fails his physical—he has a disqualifying heart murmur. Dmitri, however, is drafted, and in due course finds himself attached to a missile silo battery. His brother Valerian meanwhile goes to the ballet at night, but during the day he works at a factory that manufactures missiles.

Dmitri, in standing by the trigger of his SS-20, is doing what he is told to do. Valerian, standing by the assembly line pouring whatever it is you pour into missiles to enable them to destroy Paris and Detroit, is doing what *he* is told to do.

Well, some people are at this point willing to give you earnest money on their flexibility: We will concede, they say, that missile factories fall under roughly the same category as missile launchers. Therefore it is morally acceptable to include Valerian's factory as a counterforce target.

But the organic porosity of that factory tends to overwhelm the search for logical moral boundaries. You see, their cousin,

Nikita, is engaged in mining the special metals required to manufacture that mortal missile, and he works out there in the Urals, and in fact as recently as last year he got a medal, along with his co-workers, in acknowledgment of the national dependence of the Union of Soviet Socialist Republics on his work.

I do not need to draw it out that the exercise I have done involving Nikita can as easily be done to demonstrate the dependence of the front-line soldier on the farmer who grows the wheat without which Nikita the miner could not continue to forward to Valerian the missile maker the metals necessary to forward to Dmitri the finished missiles that aim at Paris and Detroit. It may be that the next war, if there is to be another war—God forbid—will be over, so to speak, after a single volley, rendering subsequent support from the farmers to Nikita, from Nikita to Valerian, and from Valerian to Dmitri a routine logistical problem, transacted without the umbilical urgency of war-making (the assumption here is that the enemy was disposed of in a first strike). But of course that might not happen. The missile silo, or its sister silo, may be needed again. And of course if the war goes forward with tactical weapons, then all the farmers and all the Nikitas and all the Valerians will be working day and night, causing the moralists to chew their nails over the question: Are these, indeed, innocent parties?

Well, then, if the mutual interdependence of the war-making world is such that you cannot successfully distinguish between the soldier who fires the rifle and—at the extreme and ostensibly pacific end of the spectrum—the farmer who feeds that soldier, is it easier to distinguish between counterforce and counter value by inquiring into motives? The soldier knows that he is engaged in an act designed to kill people. The farmer has no such direct knowledge. He does not know whether the wheat he is tilling will reanimate the soldier who mans the nuclear missile silo, or whether that wheat is destined to be consumed by a ballerina who that night will find the strength to leap to record highs in her *pas de deux* in *Don Quixote.*

But does this observation liberate us? If we are prepared to say that Dmitri as a missile firer is *eo ipso* an aggressor, then we would need to assume that his experience in basic training with the Soviet military transmogrified him so that now he has become by nature an aggressor, sharply to be distinguished from Valerian, by nature a balletomane. The trouble with this is that a) it isn't so, and b) we know it isn't so.

During the last few months of my military career as a second lieutenant in the infantry I was in charge of what they call a Casual Department—about one thousand transients who arrived at Fort Sam Houston in San Antonio, Texas, in order to be discharged but were for unusual reasons not yet fully qualified for a discharge. About half of them had venereal diseases; the other half, pending court-martial charges. So they had to while away their time, substantially at my direction, pending their formal return to civilian status. About the lot of them the single generality could safely be made that these were Americans who yearned to return to civilian life, to abandon careers in which the use of guns was intrinsic. Fifteen million Americans served during the Second World War. It is not the finding of any sociologist I know of that these men evolved as a *lumpen-aggressive* body which, on reintegration into the civilian community, coarsened it, bringing on a deterioration in the prevailing gentility—a general contamination brought on by the absorption of alien bodies into the civic bloodstream.

Do we have any reason for supposing that it is different in the Soviet Union, if there is a temperamental difference between Sergeant Dmitri and factory worker Valerian, such that we would feel justified in prescribing the destruction of the one and the survival of the other? Who ever said that Dmitri was happy doing what he is told to do? Who ever demonstrated that he harbored ill feeling toward the French in Paris, or Americans in Detroit? When he vacations with his twin brother, is there visible any aggressiveness in the soldier, distinguishable from that of the mechanic? No. The differences between them are rather a formal convenience for foreign moralists than a reality.

If moral retribution were ruthlessly pursued, surely we would enter into the vocabulary of war the term "counter-authority." Because it is those who instruct Dmitri to fire his weapons at Paris and Detroit against whom we have the truly legitimate claim. Except for them—and we are speaking of a half-dozen men, associated with the Kremlin—Dmitri's silo might as well hold soybeans as intercontinental nuclear missiles. Theirs are the true hands at the trigger of war. And although they do not always escape punishment, not since the Nuremberg and Tokyo trials, more often than not, of course, they do. Hitler died at his own hand, not ours. The Kaiser, leaving fifteen million dead, lived out a long life in Holland. And corresponding chiefs of state, if memory serves, mostly wrote memoirs.

But of course the difficulty with a counter-authority strategy is that just as authority has the power to begin a war, so it has, one must assume, the power to end it. And in the absence of authority, we do not know what are the contingent instructions left with Dmitri. If he picks up the telephone and nobody answers, is he supposed to fire off his missile or let it dawdle there, pending the resurrection of Comrade Andropov—not, we pray, on the third day. So that while there is no apparent moral case against counter-authority weapons, there is a prudential case against them.

From all of which I emerge doubting the relevance of moral pedagogy based on traditional distinctions that have sought to discriminate, for a relatively short period in history (remember that during the Middle Ages the siege of whole towns was the convention; and in the Old Testament, entire regions were made to suffer for the sins of the few), between the guilty and the innocent, the activists and the bystanders, the combatants and the noncombatants.

I ask, then: Does the proposition that it is no longer possible morally to distinguish between the military and the civilian populations in any way help us to advance our strategic thinking along moral lines? I think it does; but in between, it becomes necessary to linger over a second proposition.

It is that the most important endeavor of man is to seek to distinguish between right and wrong. Hardly a new proposition; but one which, in my own judgment, we tend to view, these days, without a secure sense of what it is we value more, what less. Our apparent attachments would certainly have confused, among others, Father Dubois.

My proposition is that the love of life is a holy sanctified impulse, while the veneration of life is idolatry.

The meaning of this is hardly perplexing to a Christian audi-

ence. It may well be that the future will judge the commotions
of the sixties, which revolved about Vietnam, and the ongoing
minicommotion of the eighties, which revolves around the
question whether young men should register simply because
Congress tells them that that is what they should do, as an
incipient struggle between free men and democratically
elected governments over the exact locus of power over the
individual's life. For generations, Western tradition has accepted the convention that soldiers, whether volunteers or
conscripts, go where they are told to go. If they die, they may
have died in order to make a morally transcendent point that
will resonate through the ages, for as long as we admire hero-
ism—so are the men remembered who fought the Battle of
Britain. Or they may die among the six hundred in the Light
Brigade, proving nothing more than that British officers can
exercise command over life and death even if they are quite
stupid.

Now during the protests of the sixties, there crept into view
something called selective conscientious objection. Father
John Courtney Murray, shortly before his death, acknowledged that the idea was less than entirely frivolous. That is to
say, a young man cannot automatically be condemned for having acted frivolously if he sets out to weigh the demands of
loyalty to his country's government against the cogency of the
military objective he is being conscripted to risk his life for.
What Fr. Murray did not conclude, perhaps because it cannot
be schematically concluded, is whether the challenge posed to
democratic authority by the very idea of selective conscientious objection is lethal. We don't know. We don't know because the moment has never come to America when at once its
life was blatantly challenged and it found itself short of men
willing to serve, whether as volunteers or as conscripts.

But the impact of the scientific developments that have absorbed the moral energies of our bishops and of the American
clerisy in general prompts questions more basic than the question of selective conscientious objection. By "basic" here I
mean questions that touch on assumptions so axiomatic for the
Christian that life for centuries has proceeded on their tacit
acceptance, so that suddenly to question them is on the socially
disruptive order of suddenly asking your son, whose teeth are

separated to break into a hamburger, "By the way, Johnny, do you really think it moral to kill an animal?"

Many people today are beginning, as I see it, to blur the distinction between loving life and venerating it. To love life is wholesome. To venerate it is, surely, to violate the second Commandment, which permits the veneration only of God. To venerate life is to attach to it first importance. Surely if we were all to do that, any talk of war, just or unjust, prudent or imprudent, limited or unlimited, provoked or unprovoked, would be an exercise in moral atavism, it having been decided that the taking of life, because life is venerated, was a comprehensively prohibited act.

If we love life, then we are forced to ask, *Why* do we love it? To answer merely by giving biological explanations—for instance that sensual pleasures ensue on breathing when suffocation threatens, on eating when one is hungry, resting when one is weary, defecating when the stomach is cramped—is morally uncivilized. That is to say, it is to give answers that are incomplete, for those who understand man as more than merely a biological composition.

We cherish life mostly because it permits us to love, and to be loved. And we cherish it in a dimension wholly other from that which gives pleasure by satisfying biological appetites. We love life because there is a range of experience given to us in life that regularly pleases, sometimes excites, occasionally elates. I have mentioned, preeminently, the joys of loving and being loved. And there are the delights rendered by poetry and music. But all these are overwhelmed by God. And so it is at this point that I intrude the distinction between love and veneration. We venerate Him, we love one another. It is my suspicion that the evolution of the idea of selective conscientious objection, whatever its sophisticated rationale, is in fact leading in the direction not so much of a discriminating love of life, against which a blind patriotism is definitely measured, as a sophisticated means of more discriminatingly sharing political power. I think it augurs a move toward the veneration of life such that all other considerations are as quickly subordinated as a computer nowadays reorders all derivative calculations, once you have altered the value of the prime figure.

I think that that is the direction in which many of our moralists are mistakenly headed. To help themselves, they begin by making false assumptions, such as those that distinguish, or rather seek to do so, between combatant and noncombatant members of an aggressive community. Then they find themselves speaking about prudent and imprudent uses of deterrent weapons, and finally we have the sense—or at least some of us do—that what is going on is a creeping philosophical reconciliation with that definition of life that does not stop short—ask Bukovsky, ask Mendeleev, ask Solzhenitsyn, ask Shcharansky—of transforming life, the life we properly love, into mere biological life. And when, the challenge having confronted us, we choose mere biological life over the *risk* of death in pursuit of Christian life, we come perilously close to worshipping false gods.

Or so it would appear to me.

It is most awfully strange for a man of my age, approaching senior citizenship, born to Catholic parents who loved God, each other, and their ten children, with joy, with curiosity, with respect, to find myself, after three quarters of a lifetime in the faith, almost everywhere assaulted by arguments emanating alike from agnostics, Christian laymen, and churchmen of all faiths, that seem to pay in most cases literally no attention whatever to Christian teaching, which speaks of the end of the world quite fatalistically; or, where attention is given to apocalypse, it is done with the kind of mythological detachment that characterizes quaint literary references to Eve and the serpent, or Jonah and the whale. I am hardly here to celebrate the one hundred and seventy-fifth anniversary of Mount St. Mary's for the purpose of suggesting that your two hundredth anniversary may be postlapsarian in a new sense of the word.

But I am here—and this is my final proposition—to say that no biblical paradox can be more relevant today than Christ's, which said that His Kingdom is not of this world. As a child, I simply interpreted this as that Christ had a different address from my own, and perhaps could be reached only by air mail. As a young man, I interpreted this as an injunction to care about Christlike things rather than about things of this world; but in due course I smelled Manichaeism in this, which a natural hedonism helped me to overcome.

As an older man, though no doubt one who has yet to reach

full maturity, I understand Christ to have told us that although his Kingdom was not of this world, it is a Kingdom he will one day share, leaving it to us, inhabiting our own city, to be counseled by the lessons Christ taught us, and inspired by the example he set of his love for us, by coming to us. It can never be suspected of the man who died on the Cross that he venerated the life which, to be sure, he loved.

Does this reduce to strategic formulas? Only negatively. Yes, I would resist any philosophical usurpation that sought to put biological life on the throne. No, I do not deduce from this any concrete arrangements for facing the most awful threat of this century, animated by a fetid materialism. How blessed we are that the Bolsheviks so specifically reject God! How unbearable it would be if they committed their workaday horrors under the putative guidance of the Cross!

But I would deduce this much, namely that any deceits we practice—for instance in inviting the disability of our deterrent powers by seeking to distinguish between combatant and noncombatant—that any stratagems we follow ostensibly in pursuit of morality, when what we are really pursuing are false idols, are not becoming to a country as blessed as our own has been. How much America, and Americans, do suffer; but we suffer mostly as human beings living in natural conditions. How can we deny the horrors of the human condition when, as recently as two days ago, four children were uprooted and killed in California by a stochastic typhoon?

But how much range has been given to us, given to you at Mount St. Mary's, finding yourselves a few steps from a library where you can read what you wish, a few miles from bus and railroad and airplane stations where you are free to travel as far as your savings will take you. A few miles from political offices to which you have a constitutional right of access. And a few steps from a chapel in which you can pause to venerate that which alone is venerable.

6

Nicaragua

THE MESS

April 11, 1984

As THESE WORDS are written, officials from Executive agencies will be appearing before a Senate committee, and then a House committee, in closed session, there to answer questions concerning Nicaragua. Not easy, because what the Administration is up to in Nicaragua is both confused and confusing, and very very messy.

The general situation is as follows. The bad guys (the Soviet Union and Cuba, primarily) are continuing to send in arms shipments to Nicaragua to be used for two purposes, both deplorable. On the one hand, as the totalitarianization of Nicaragua continues, more arms are needed to keep Nicaraguans docile. There are two species of Nicaraguan dissidents: those actively engaged as guerrillas seeking to overthrow the despotic successors to the despot Somoza; and inactive Nicaraguans who nevertheless look for opportunities to assert themselves. To cope with the former you need things like tanks and machine guns. To cope with the latter you need things like rifles and hangman's nooses.

The other major enterprise of the Sandinista government in Nicaragua is expansionist communism. Just as Cuba receives arms from the Soviet Union and exports them to Nicaragua, so Nicaragua receives arms and exports them to the rebels in El Salvador. United States policy, in respect of what is going on, seeks to be comprehensive. We would like to see the communization of Nicaragua by Nicaraguans ended; as also the communist-led guerrilla movement against El Salvador.

So how have we gone about interdicting the flow of arms into Nicaragua? Apparently by mining Nicaraguan harbors. The idea is to discourage ships coming into Puerto Corinto and Puerto Sandino on the Pacific Ocean, and into El Bluff on the Atlantic side. The resulting attrition would have two effects: denying arms to the Sandinistas, and precipitating an economic crisis of a kind that would destabilize the government.

Enter the World Court controversy. The Nicaraguans take the position that they can appeal to the International Court of Justice in The Hague to denounce U.S. interference with Nicaraguan ports. We take the position that it is up to us to decide whether to accept jurisdiction by the World Court. The Connally Reservation, remember, gives us the right in domestic affairs to grant or not to grant jurisdiction to the World Court. Whether it gives us the identical right in affairs involving other countries is the subject currently in dispute. Nicaragua has hired itself some fancy lawyers, including Abram Chayes of Harvard, to contend that the U.S. has no such right.

Meanwhile, the United States is being denounced on a number of fronts as engaged in terrorist activities (mining harbors) of the kind we criticize when done by others.

Running one's fingers lightly over the profile of the Administration's case leaves one utterly lacking in enthusiasm for it. On the one hand the objectives are thoroughly desirable. But the means by which we seek to realize these objectives are both questionable as means, and problematic as instruments for the effectuation of the ends desired. It is true that we caused one refinery in Nicaragua to shut down for a while because oil wasn't getting through. But the likelihood that we can cause the Sandinista government of Nicaragua to come to its knees by mining its harbors is slight. And meanwhile, by engaging in what began as covert activity on so melodramatic a scale, we outrage people we really do care about, for instance our European allies.

Now all of this is being done to avoid the obvious alternative, which is to quarantine Nicaragua selectively. That alternative has no doubt been considered and rejected. It would involve using the American Navy to detain ships headed for Nicaraguan ports, examining the contents of those ships, and letting them pass or not pass depending on whether they carried bombs or bananas. Granted, if we permitted all economic traffic to get through—for instance, oil—there would be no prospect of crippling Nicaragua economically. All we would stop is the flow of arms. We would need to supplement that naval blockade by an aerial blockade. Which reminds one that so far we have not trained antiaircraft ordnance to shoot down planes headed for Nicaragua. That would be the aerial equivalent of mining Nicaraguan harbors.

Nasty business. But far better, surely, publicly to order the Navy to do its business discriminatingly, than covertly to order the CIA to do its business wantonly. And the overarching danger is that the Administration, by such actions, might forfeit general American support for resistance in Central America to communist aggression.

ONCE AGAIN

May 9, 1984

If YOU ARE looking for a handy way to curb the population explosion, try the death penalty for anyone who says: "Do you believe that the end justifies the means?" I was a schoolboy when a professor of philosophy, overhearing this logical barbarism, announced that he would leave the room if ever he heard it again. The proper formulation, he told us, is: "Do you believe that the end justifies any means?" It is just this simple: Ordinarily, you would not push violently an old lady, steal a piece of bread, or fire a gun into the face of a human being. But each of these things you would do if a) the old lady would otherwise be hit by a bus; b) your child would die of hunger; c) the human being would plunge his knife into your heart. What you would not do, if you agree that the end does not justify any means, is fire a gun at the bus driver as the alternative to pushing the old lady out of the way; shoot the baker for putting a price on a loaf of bread; trigger fusillade fire at a row of people knowing that one of the bullets will nail your assailant.

But sure enough, there was Sam Donaldson of ABC, who unhappily had had no contact with the professor in question and did not learn the distinction osmotically, saying to Henry Kissinger on the David Brinkley show: So you believe that the end justifies the means?

Henry Kissinger spent half his life teaching, and he was under some strain to remember that he should not deal with Sam Donaldson as he would have dealt with a freshman at Harvard. So he tried to say it all coolly, and he did a pretty good job, although additional exasperation would have been understandable.

Look, he said, it makes sense, in considering the question of Central America, to start from the other end. The other end is: What do we desire to see *not* happen? Presumably, the communization of Nicaragua as an expansionist, aggressive Soviet base. If we desire an end, then we desire the means appropriate to that end's realization, fair enough? If the baby is starving, first you go out and buy food. If you have no money, you beg for food. If no one responds to your supplications, then you steal it. If someone is there to keep you from stealing it surreptitiously, then you use force to steal it. Always the objective is to keep the child from starving.

Now, in international affairs the security of the state is the end, the realization of which is paramount. That is why when Jeane Kirkpatrick came on the same program she had so little difficulty in disposing of silly questions involving the World Court. Someone proposed that the World Court rule whether the mining of the harbors of Nicaragua was "legal." Mrs. Kirkpatrick countered that there is no body of law that governs legality when the matter of protection against aggression is raised. That, after all, is why we have a Security Council. It is that body that weighs threats to the peace. And, of course, that body was constituted with reality in mind, namely that no major power is going to permit a dozen judicial savants in Holland—some of them nominated by Soviet antinomians—to prescribe that which is lawful when the survival of the state is in question.

Now Daniel Patrick Moynihan has made a colossal fuss over

the question of "legality," and he has not given satisfactory public attention to the question of legality up against illegality. In brief, how is one expected to act when an aggressor, observing no law, no codes, is dreadnoughting his way into your garden of liberty? But once we have pointed out this delinquency in Senator Moynihan, it remains true that although the mining of the harbors in Nicaragua could be said to be "legal" in the sense that self-preservation is legal, it was a miserably mistaken, maladroit thing to do. Precisely because it enhances the illusion that we need to act covertly to defend our vital interest, whereas we simply do not need to do so. That is why the alternative—a declaration of war—is so much more appealing. It is a superstition to suppose that a declaration of war requires instant mobilization, with atom bombs dropped on Monday and paratroopers on Tuesday. What the declaration of war says is that a power has become a hostile entity, and that the rules that govern relations between countries at peace with one another no longer apply.

WHO WAS RIGHT?

June 27, 1984

IT IS worthwhile, before the controversy crystallizes in the memory as one in which we (the United States) were wrong, and they (the World Court) were right, to shake up the set pieces a little and see where they reassemble under the prodding of a little thought.

The United Nations was set up to bring about world peace, as I guess most of us remember. Complicated instruments were baptized with that imperative in mind. The crucial provision in the United Nations Charter is Article 24, and what it says is: "In order to ensure prompt and effective action by the United Nations, its members confer on the Security Council primary responsibility for the maintenance of international peace and security . . ." That means that when there is a dispute between Nicaragua and El Salvador in which the UN is involved, the Security Council has "primary responsibility" on how to dispose of it.

Well, what about secondary responsibility? Here we consult Article 33, which provides, in part, that "the parties to any dispute, the continuance of which is likely to endanger the maintenance of international peace and security, shall, first of all, seek a solution by negotiation, inquiry, mediation, conciliation, arbitration, judicial settlement, resort to regional agencies or arrangements, or other peaceful means of their own choice."

But what if a party in contention does not seek to avail itself of the secondary means of proceeding? When the United States ratified its own membership in the World Court, it reserved the right to determine the court's jurisdiction as it might be said to apply to the United States. This reservation was, of course, philosophically compatible with the idea of the veto in the Security Council.

Ask yourself, then, whether the dispute between Nicaragua and the United States is a political or a factual dispute, on the understanding that factual disputes are more properly the business of courts to decide, while political disputes are more properly the concern of the Security Council.

If there are factual questions to be solved, how will the World Court solve them? By subpoenaing the KGB records of the Kremlin and the CIA records of the United States? Will Mr. Chernenko's attorney disclose the volume of military hardware shipped into El Salvador to aid the revolution there? Will the United States Solicitor General reveal how we have ascertained that Nicaragua is pressing its revolution by force of arms?

Triple fiddlesticks. Professor Abram Chayes of the Harvard Law School, who was counselor to the State Department during Mr. Carter's regime and is now counsel to Nicaragua, contending all the silly things professors of law get paid to contend when rich clients are out on a limb, wrote a *Harvard Law Review* article in 1965 ("A Common Lawyer Looks at International Law") in which he acknowledged that "most great disputes between states, even when they involve important legal elements, are not justiciable." Lloyd Cutler, who was counsel to President Carter, said to the American Society of International Law on April 14: ". . . the [World] Court has never before determined that an act of aggression or an unlawful use of armed force has occurred or that a threat to the peace exists, nor has it ever before been asked to grant an interim or a final remedy for such an event."

So? Senator Moynihan and Anthony Lewis charge that Ambassador Jeane Kirkpatrick and her legal adviser, Allan Gerson, are ignorant of the law. Moynihan adds the homily that even though the Soviet Union does not abide by the law, that doesn't mean we shouldn't. It's true that just because the Soviet Union shoots people and uses poison gas, we shouldn't. But we are not here talking about abstract imperatives to good conduct. We are talking about points of contention between great powers. If the United States and the Soviet Union conclude a treaty not to engage in antisatellite technology, it makes all the difference whether the Soviet Union abides by the treaty: because the United States' pledge to do so is precisely contingent on Soviet compliance.

The Soviets desire to rule the world, and en route to doing so is Central America. They push there, we properly resist there. The notion that a World Court should assume the authority to tell the Soviet Union to go ahead, and us to cease and desist, is the kind of squishy-soft eristic cuckoo-talk that used to cause Daniel Patrick Moynihan to weep in despair, back when he was in the United Nations, back when he was fighting the good fight.

III
COMMENTING

1

Unendurable Bureaucratic Pain

January 10, 1978

NOT MANY years ago, arriving home from the city, I discovered the normally imperturbable lady who has cooked for my family for a quarter-century far gone in weeping. She is an elderly and hardy Cuban black who early in life suffered a lifetime's ration of sorrow and pain, and for that reason her tears were not treated as though caused by a collapsed soufflé. I got the story from her in spurts. A message, through an intermediary in Miami. Her sister. Dying of cancer in Havana. Miserable pain. No morphine, because Castro's supply was available only to the army.

I called my favorite doctor. Out of town on a fishing trip, unreachable. I asked another doctor a hypothetical question: What would a doctor's prescription look like authorizing enough morphine for daily doses for sixty days to a dying patient? I scratched out the hieroglyphics on a doctored pad, approached the pharmacist, who whistled at the size of the order but got out the stuff, which I drove to Pan American at Kennedy and put in the hands of a pilot. In Madrid, my brother had arranged to meet the pilot, to take the package, and give it to an Iberia pilot bound for Havana. Twenty-four hours later the dying woman had her short lifetime's supply of morphine. Back from his fishing trip, the doctor telephoned me. Easygoing type, in his conversational style, but steel in his system. "I note from records that have come in from the pharmacy that I authorized you to pick up morphine worth about $50,000 on the black market. Are you enjoying it?" I explained. He sighed, executed papers that designated the dosage as designed for a case of terminal illness, and somehow the irregularity of the transaction never attracted official attention.

What does attract official attention has become the object of a crusade led by Mrs. Judith Quattlebaum of Potomac, Maryland. She is the head of something called the Committee on the Treatment of Intractable Pain, and her objective is to sweep the bureaucratic cobwebs that prefer human agony to medical improvisation. There are a number of objectives endorsed by Mrs. Quattlebaum's committee, but that which has received the most attention is the licensing, for patients who suffer from terminal cancer, of the heroin drug.

Mrs. Quattlebaum had a personal experience during the Second World War, observing the agonizing death of her grandmother. Then she watched Stewart Alsop on the Dick Cavett show, describing the death throes of a patient occupying an adjacent room. She launched the committee. And people began to send her case histories, which she has compiled. One example will do (one example is almost too much): "I have lost my mother with incurable uterine cancer. Her pain was so horrid that she lost her mind and ate her bottom lip completely off from clenching her top teeth so tightly. My thirteen-year-old sister and I watched this for six weeks. We would enter the small hospital and hear her screams as soon as we closed the door. The nurses had no way to quiet her. She was immune to conventional pain-killers."

It is not safe to say that such torment as this would simply cease to be if the United States were to change its laws in order to permit the manufacture and administration of heroin under carefully controlled circumstances. But doctors seem to agree that heroin will do more than morphine for several reasons. One is that it is capable of producing a higher degree of euphoria. Another is that the hydrochloride content makes it more soluble, so that a small dose inserted into the flesh can do more than larger doses of morphine. In Great Britain, where much experimentation goes on, there is something widely known as the "Brompton Cocktail," discovered at the Brompton Hospital. This may sound like a sick joke, but is not received as such by patients who, upon taking it, are ushered out of this vale of tears less tearfully than the woman with uterine cancer. The Brompton Cocktail consists of heroin, cocaine, and phenophiacine (an anti-emetic). Administered before the probable onset of spasms of pain, it tends to abort them, or to help to neutralize them.

Thus it goes. But the committee, which has acquired some distinguished sponsors including the active patronage of Congressman Newton Steers of Maryland, is up against the conventional unbudgeability of the law which in effect authorizes the use of heroin only for teenagers in ghettos, who have relatively little trouble in acquiring it while their grandmothers die in pain under the hygienic auspices of the law. The Committee on the Treatment of Intractable Pain can be reached at 9300 River Road, Potomac, Maryland 20854.

2

Coping with
South African Investments

April 25, 1978

T HE COLLEGE STUDENTS, here and there, have discovered—
or more properly rediscovered—the cause of South African
Economic Disengagement. At a number of colleges, trustees
are gathering under student pressure to consider whether to
empty their portfolios of securities in companies with economic ties to South Africa. Right away there is the problem of
making a distinction. If the trustees are mandated to sell securities in any company doing business *in* South Africa, they will
have to sell any securities they own in 350 major U.S. companies. This is the rough equivalent of coming to Manhattan for a
visit and boycotting the area bounded by the Hudson River,
the East River, 35th Street and 57th Street.

But the problem only begins. The totalists also want the
trustees to refuse to buy securities in any U.S. companies doing
business *with* South Africa. All that this mandate would require is divesting oneself of shares in 6,000 U.S. companies. It is
difficult to know exactly what would be left for the trustees of
U.S. colleges to invest in, but if you see your local drugstore rise
to the height of the Empire State Building, you will know that
the idealists triumphed. To be sure, the following year scholar-
ships at U.S. colleges might be reduced by 20 or 30 percent.

Leaving aside for the moment the demands of the totalists,
the so-called Sullivan principles should be more widely adver-

tised. The Reverend Leon Sullivan of Philadelphia, a black Baptist, is a director of General Motors. He does not believe in economic withdrawal from South Africa. He does believe, however, in activist antiapartheid policies by U.S. firms doing business in South Africa. He has laid down six principles, and as of a week ago eighty-five U.S. companies in South Africa have subscribed to these six principles. The idea is that a U.S. company will insist on subscribing in practice to these principles, on the threat of closing down if the South African government denies them permission. They are:

—Nonsegregation of the races in all eating, comfort and work facilities.

—Equal and fair employment practices for all employees.

—Equal pay for all employees doing equal or comparable work for the same period of time.

—Initiation and development of training programs that will prepare in substantial numbers blacks and other nonwhites for supervisory, administrative, clerical and technical jobs.

—An increase in the number of blacks and other nonwhites in management and supervisory positions.

—Improvement in the quality of employees' lives outside the work environment in such areas as housing, transportation, schooling, recreation and health facilities.

Now these strictures, like some of those laid down by HEW and OSHA, are as a matter of plain fact almost impossible to interpret with any consistency. Moreover, like the UN Declaration of Human and Social Rights, it suffers from excessive specificity. One wonders whether the board of General Motors is going to have to set up courts to hear complaints by an individual worker in an individual plant complaining that his recreational facilities are inadequate, or that his house is inconveniently located.

Still, the thrust of the Six Principles is admirable. One wishes one might mobilize American idealism to insist on complementary principles to govern U.S. investment, or U.S. economic credits, in the Soviet Union. It would be interesting to observe the reaction of the Soviet Union if U.S. companies and banks involved in subsidizing, say, the Kama River Trucking Plant were to announce Six Principles as follows: All Russians employed by U.S. capital must be given:

—Freedom of speech.
—Freedom of assembly.
—Freedom of religion.
—Freedom of travel.
—The right of habeas corpus.
—The right of public trial by a jury of their peers.

Fortunately—for all its faults—South Africa isn't the Soviet Union. Unfortunately—for all their virtues—American idealists are not impartial in their hunger for justice.

Still, to repeat, the promulgation of the Six Principles is encouraging, and they should be accepted by American opinion as a desirable substitute for the draconian alternatives recommended by the extremists. The Vice President of Brown University in charge of financial affairs has remarked dryly that if the demands of the students were met everywhere in the United States, the South African government would have no alternative than to embargo the repatriation of capital.

This would mean that instead of automobile plants in South Africa being run by General Motors, and computer plants run by IBM, they would be run, having been nationalized, by the government of South Africa without benefit of one, let alone six, of the Reverend Sullivan's principles. The U.S. would be left with several billion dollars' worth of South African bonds. Presumably we would not take great moral satisfaction from being the largest South African bondholder in the world.

3

The Pope I Want

August 26/September 2, 1978

ON THE UNDERSTANDING that I am neither theologian nor close observer of Vatican politics, I write as a lay Catholic about the events precipitated by the death of Pope Paul. So to speak, I write as a consumer of Catholicism; or as one shareholder in the enterprise, always with the understanding that the Pope has all the voting stock. These metaphors, I confidently believe, will not upset the Holy Spirit.

What do we—or, better, I—desire? Chesterton, almost everyone recalls, described his circumnavigation in search of something which, when finally he came upon it, he discovered to be—orthodoxy. The Pope as Theological Swinger is not what one wants. People who think of themselves as modernists usually ask one of two things. Either they want the Catholic religion to adopt reforms so convincing as to render the denomination indistinguishable from other Christian denominations, or they want the Church to throw itself into the problems of mankind, which they almost always describe in materialist terms. The Reverend William Sloane Coffin repeatedly uses the metaphor of the floating crap game. Where the action is, this is where the churchman should be, he says, wiping his brow of the sweat from the most recent anti-Vietnam demonstration. Even though the proposition that the Pope should qualify for Pulitzer prizes in investigative theology is not by any means universally accepted, most of the anticipatory journalism about who will be the next Pope consists of good guy/bad guy polarization based on these sorts of standards.

I think, for example, of a recent catalogue of mini-biographies of all the cardinals, *The Inner Elite: Dossiers of Papal Candidates*, by Gary MacEoin and the Committee for the Responsible Election of the Pope (Sheed, Andrews and McMeel). The authors rate the cardinals more or less by ADA standards. Each cardinal is asked whether he is "committed to guiding the church into the mainstream of the world's search for justice and dignity." Cardinal Cody of Chicago, the book says, would "undoubtedly line up with the most reactionary United States and Roman cardinals." Cardinal Krol of Philadelphia would be "a leader of the reactionaries." Cardinal Siri of Genoa "will be a powerful leader of the most reactionary elements," Cardinal Seper of Zagreb "would form part of the hard-core curial conservative bloc." Apparently there are those who want a Pope who seeks economic redistribution among the haves and the have-nots, and dogmatical redistribution among believers and nonbelievers.

The Pope, on the one hand, must unmistakably be the Pope of the Church of the Poor, who feels the whiplash of hunger and pain and cold, and reminds his flock encephalophonically that what we do to the least of God's creatures we do to Him. But in doing so he must also emphasize the Church's primary mission on earth, which is to minister to the spiritual needs of man rather than to his corporal needs. Men are destined to suffer the vicissitudes of life, but the Pope is there to preside over an institution whose principal relevance is its irrelevance to terrestrial, if not mundane, problems. The Pope must stand out as the principal symbol of the transfiguring dimension of life. The Church is built on that rock. If men do not live by bread alone, they do not live for bread alone. The Pope's capacity persuasively to superordinate the spiritual over the material is the highest skill his community can demand from him. For this reason the philosophical Christian resists the tendency of the ideologues to describe candidates for the office as "conservative" or "liberal." These terms are associated with a penchant for modes of social organization that are of subordinate concern to organized Christianity, which is not to say they are of no concern.

The new Pope has got to be strong enough to acknowledge past mistakes, among them the excesses of Vatican II. What were the accomplishments of Vatican II? This question reminds one of President Eisenhower's famous response when asked to catalogue the contributions of Vice President Nixon during their eight years together: "Give me a week, and I'll think of one." The Church is far less powerful than it was in the days of Pius XII, far less magnetic: and, for that reason, far less offensive to members of other communions. If, as we are told in *The Devil's Dictionary*, admiration is the recognition of other people's similarity to oneself, then the road traveled by the Catholic Church after Vatican II made it more popular among Protestants, to be sure.

It is not absolutely safe to say that the 10,000 American priests who abandoned their vocations and the 40 percent of American Catholics who ceased regular attendance at mass did so because of the dilutions of Vatican II. There were other pressures. The Playboy Philosopher was the most spirited evangelizer of the 1960s; the iconoclastic imperative showed itself triumphant. It has been an age when churchgoing became, as Bernard Iddings Bell complained even a generation ago, "a pastime, preferred by a few to golf or canasta" and, if Peter Berger is correct, we began facing up to the possibility that religious faith might be all but extinct by the end of the century.

Vatican II cannot be blamed for all of this. Nevertheless, the symbols of Vatican II, for the communicant, were a Uriah Heepishness in all matters save those that touched on sex. The showplace of the Church is the liturgy, and here the reforms proved disastrous: a disfiguration of what was venerable and beautiful into a vulgar collegiality that is artificial, distracting and appropriately celebrated by the worst abuses against the English language in the history of syntax. The lifting of the ban against eating meat on Fridays was a huge error in psychology, the equivalent of sending free valentines every week of the year. ("If all the year were playing holidays,/To sport would be as tedious as to work.")

The new Pope, facing a shortage of clergy caused by the dilution of spiritual vitality, will face yet again the question of whether a noncelibate order should be permitted. (Paul VI ruled on the matter administratively, not theologically.) I think it is reasonable to say that if he were to permit such an order of priests, he would not undermine the vitality of the institution of the priesthood or the faith of those who believe that priests are a distinctive spiritual caste. A more difficult corollary is the question, bound to return to the Pope's attention, of contraceptives. That they are widely, if not universally, used by the Catholic community is not an argument for repealing the arguments of the encyclical *Humanae vitae.* The case for repealing those arguments, or amending them, was made by the *periti* designated by the Pope to inquire into the theological question in a report recommending, by a substantial majority, such a repeal. The new Pope is likely to look again at these arguments, and it is likely that, in a fresh allocution, he will modify *Humanae vitae* at least to the point of making it paradigmatic as distinct from binding. To say that the supreme point of sexual union is the continuation of life is to say that and not necessarily more than that. A retreat from a strict-constructionist reading of *Humanae vitae* probably would be welcome in the long run without being held up as evidence of theological demagogy. Concerning sex in general, the new Pope cannot, surely, damage his Church by stressing yet again that the sins of the spirit are more awful than the sins of the flesh, sinful though these latter continue to be.

The new Pope should be cautious to avoid the lure of ideological identification. The pull from the third world, to which Pope Paul was by no means immune, need not be resisted completely. But the next Pope must sharply distinguish between explicit sympathy for the wretched of this earth, and apparent support for a doctrinal redistribution based on primitive economic credenda which reduce Christianity to socialist cant. The Pope cannot increase his prestige among thinking men by uttering pieties whose structure rests on economic fatuities.

Having said all of this, it is proper to call to the attention of the non-Catholic community that the reverence Catholics feel for their Popes rests in considerable part on the conviction that through them, the Holy Spirit is sometimes at work. This means that there is an obligation in conscience to consider a statement by the Pope at least as deferentially as we are nowadays trained to consider decisions of the Supreme Court. The next Pope will need to catch the flagging attention of a world much caught up with Mammon. The reason why Catholics pray for divine guidance in the Sistine Chapel during this period is that they hope for a vehicle sensitive to the rendering of Christian intelligence to a headstrong world absorbed in the lesser pursuits of the human imagination.

4

Enough Is Enough

July 3, 1979

IT IS all very well for President Carter to be apoplectic with rage against the OPEC powers. What is he going to do about it? What has he brought forth from his visit to Tokyo in the way of ideas to protect the American economy from being satellized by the Persian Gulf?

The official estimate is now entered: the increase in the price of oil—60 percent over the beginning of the year—will account for 2.5 percent of U.S. inflation. Very well, so we blame that 2.5 percent inflation on the OPEC powers. On whom do we blame the other 10 percent? The estimate, come the end of the year, was inflation at 7.5 percent.

Mr. Blumenthal, in the spring, revised the figure. More like 8.5 percent, he said. Now Mr. Kahn, who should have stayed in the airline business, says 10 percent. We are running in fact at the rate of 13 percent.

If Mr. Carter wanted to punish the man principally responsible for this, he would commit suicide. He has been President for two and one-half years. He took over the presidency at a time when inflation was down to 4 percent, pledging to reduce it further. He submits the budget to Congress. He appointed the head of the Federal Reserve Board.

Although Carter's own policies, along with those of Congress and of the Fed, will result in five times as much damage to the

American consumer as all of OPEC's depredations, Mr. Carter correctly perceives that something must be done to stop the gouging.

Herewith a plan:

1. The United States will contract with Saudi Arabia and, one would expect, with the United Arab Emirates and Kuwait to purchase all the oil we want at $12.50 cash per barrel, the figure to be increased once per year to reflect any inflation in the value of the dollar.

2. The difference between the figure of $12.50 and the "world price" actually fetched by OPEC on other markets would be calculated at the end of the year, and a bond in that amount issued, payable twenty-five years later—i.e., the first bond would be redeemable in the year 2004, the second bond in 2005, etc.

3. These bonds would bear no interest. In lieu of paying interest, the United States would guarantee the defense of the Persian Gulf against aggression by any superpower. Since we are paying well over $100 billion per year to contain the Soviet Union, which long since would have invaded the Persian Gulf but for U.S. military might, there is an instant sense of justice in the exchange.

4. The bonds payable beginning in twenty-five years would be paid only to nonrevolutionary successor governments. That is to say, if Saudi Arabia's government were toppled by a coup d'état, the bond would instantly become forfeit.

The United States would instantly decontrol its own oil and gas enterprises. No increase in taxation would be imposed provided the increased profit was devoted to the search for energy in any form. The increase in tax revenues to the federal government from a continuation of the present tax would be consigned to a crash program of exploration of alternative means of energy development of such a nature as private capital would not be likely to subsidize because of the exorbitant economic risk.

What we cannot do simultaneously is control inflation, develop new sources of energy, and pay out an additional $20 or $30 billion more every year to the OPEC powers.

Ah, you will say, a splendid idea. All we need to do is get Saudi Arabia to agree.

That is the job of the United States government. Here is what we have working for us: 1) The most formidable military technology in the world. 2) The only military machine capable of staying the Soviet Union. 3) $35 billion of Arab-owned assets. 4) $50 billion per year of revenues to OPEC oil countries even at the lower price. 5) A navy which can be made to control all access to Arab oil. And finally, 6) A superpower, a few miles north of the Arabs, with which we once upon a time joined hands to consummate an imperative common enterprise in Europe.

An unpleasant thought, that; but unpleasant thoughts include going bankrupt, which the administration's Barry Bosworth now talks of as a possibility. What do we have our sovereignty for, if in fact the future of our economy is going to be decided by a few sheiks meeting occasionally in Geneva?

5

Bring Back Linkage

July 27, 1979

THE LINKAGE THEORY is in intellectual disrepute, from which it should be rescued. Under linkage, you punish the Soviet Union for sending Cuban troops to Africa by curtailing the export of U.S. grain—pick your own combination. So long as it's asymmetrical, it's linkage.

The only existing pressure we are exerting now on the Soviet Union is a negative pressure. We have denied it, under the terms of the Jackson Amendment, the status of most favored nation, which is to say that the Soviet Union does not qualify to export to the United States at the lowest prevailing tariff rates. Inasmuch as Soviet exports to the U.S. are relatively small, $540 million, this is a pressure hardly unendurable. Otherwise it would be difficult to come up with evidence of hostility to the Soviet Union. I suppose that an inspection of the targeting mechanisms inside the Minutemen missiles in North Dakota would show that they are set to land at Minsk or Pinsk, and in this sense our posture is latently anti-Soviet. But how else?

Any American citizen who can get a Soviet visa can travel there. Any American firm that wants to export to the Soviet Union can do so, barring a few proscribed items. Soviet citizens can almost without exception travel here. Our great credit institutions can and do lend money to the Soviet Union. Our

Voice of America has become practically oleaginous in its handling of Soviet news.

We are preparing, one year from now, to participate in the great Olympic Games in Moscow, as routinely as if the Games were being held in Switzerland. The President of the United States departs from his meeting with the leader of the Soviet state by embracing him, a gesture of affection he would deny to members of his own Cabinet. Meanwhile, the Soviet Union continues in its struggle for the world.

Mr. Brian Crozier, director of London's Institute for the Study of Conflict, writes about a major Soviet industry, which is the production and subsidy of world terrorism. He reminds us that two wars in Indochina were for the most part fought by acts of terrorism: i.e., the use of violence for political ends.

No venture in terrorism is too small to escape patronage by the Soviet Union, which scatters about funds for terrorists like HEW in search of welfare clients. It was the Soviets who secretly subsidized the Baader-Meinhof gang: a quarter-million dollars, channeled by East Germany to the magazine *Konkret,* run by Ulrike Meinhof's sometime husband, Klaus Rainer Rohl. It was the Soviet Union that sent arms to the IRA provisionals in 1971, using Czechoslovakia as middleman. In 1973, IRA officials received arms through the Soviets' North African protégé, Libya.

It is generally believed that Libya's Qaddafi gave refuge to the world's most wanted terrorist, Carlos ("The Jackal"). Crozier reports that Carlos was given $2 million as reward money for kidnapping the OPEC oil ministers in Vienna. Carlos was recruited by the KGB in Venezuela, trained in Cuba and "brought to his fine pitch of murderous efficiency in Moscow" before being turned loose in the world.

Yasir Arafat, for whom terrorism is a way of life, was invited to Moscow to open an office there in August 1974. Ten years earlier, the Vietcong's political wing (the NFLSV) was issued a similar invitation, and that augured the Soviet commitment to the final drive against the noncommunist Vietnamese.

The insurrections in Mozambique and in Angola began with terrorism, backed by the Soviet Union, even as the Soviet Union is now backing Mugabe against Rhodesia. The U.S.S.R. is, as Crozier summarizes it, "deep in the 'educational' side of terrorism, training terrorists, saboteurs, assassins and (yes) guerrillas by the thousands through Moscow's Lenin Institute and the exquisitely named Patrice Lumumba People's Friendship University."

The United States representative in the United Nations will now and again speak out against terrorism. But if there is one thing that terrifies U.S. representatives more than terrorists, it is the prospect of irritating the Soviet Union. The direct response to anti-Western terrorism should be anti-Soviet terrorism.

There is something in our tradition that shrinks from sending sticks of dynamite for use against boulevardiers in Leningrad. The alternative is linkage. An end to tourist travel to the Soviet Union. Cancellation of the Olympics. A shot of testosterone in the Voice of America. A running polemic against Soviet terrorism in the United Nations, at Geneva, Vienna, Helsinki— wherever we meet. Boycott of Libya. You are into linkage now, and that's good.

6

What to Do?

August 26, 1980

IT IS the dream of every man who dreams that one day, over the rainbow, one incident in the Soviet empire will prove to be the cordite that will bring down the House of Lenin. It is the nightmare of the slavemasters of the House of Lenin that one day, one incident in the Soviet empire will be the cordite that will bring the emancipation of the dead souls they collect so avariciously. That is the reason why a mere labor-union strike in a remote corner of Poland causes the world to hold its breath. The chances that we have come to the end of the rainbow are infinitesimally small. Far greater that we have come to another of those periodic tests of will at which the Soviet Union excels even as we flounder.

At the same moment when the prospective next Vice President of the United States, George Bush, is more or less assuring the largest totalitarian nation in the world that if elected the Reagan administration will do nothing to formalize our commitment to Taiwan's freedom, the Soviet Union, through its puppet Gierek, is telling the Polish strikers that if they persist in their demands for economic and political freedom, what goes by the name of the Polish border will disappear—i.e., direct control by the Soviet Union, versus indirect.

Those who think this makes little difference have not experienced that difference. Ten years ago, after a week in the Soviet

Union followed by a day in Warsaw, I wrote that after you leave Russia, everyone in Poland sounds like Lenny Bruce. It requires a special map to find in Poland anyone who approves of the current bondage, or of those in Moscow who make it so. But the Poles, as a people, are realists, and know that they are better off than they would be under a more fastidious domination by the Russians, which is why the explosion of frustration at Gdansk is a possible flashpoint.

What to do?

The autopsists still rage against each other, endeavoring to answer the question of whether United States policy was responsible for the bloodbath in Budapest in 1956. The position of the United States Government is that there is nowhere traceable any official suggestion that the United States would intervene to protect a Hungary that sought to detach itself from the Soviet empire. Still, in those days there were idealists who spoke occasionally about liberation; indeed, that galvanizing word was uttered by John Dulles during the 1952 campaign that ended in his installation as Secretary of State. And, in 1968, the gleeful international reception given to the Prague Spring unquestionably influenced the Russians in the direction of their massive suppression—which (again, an excruciating historical symbol) tended to coincide with the massive dissolution of our will in Southeast Asia.

What hurts is that there is always a suspicion that the State Department—yes, even one headed by a Polish-American [Edmund Muskie]—rather wishes the crisis had not occurred. We are wallowing about in something that (fairly or unfairly) goes by the name of the Sonnenfeldt Doctrine, and what it says, essentially, is that we must avoid destabilization. Destabilization is a fancy word for: "Don't do anything that might upset the Soviet Union, either by taking from it something it already has, or by acquiring for your own account something you didn't use to have." Destabilization was written into the Helsinki accords, which—a juridical sleight of hand—suggested that that over which the Soviet Union has control, it shall continue to have control over. The great compensator was the provision signed by the Soviet Union guaranteeing all kinds of freedoms which went by the name of Basket III, and was instantly celebrated by the Soviet Union by putting into jail anyone who uttered the word "Helsinki."

So, again, what do we do? Well, Radio Free Europe and the VOA are faithfully reporting events over their facilities—but, careful, all opinions are those of other entities; nothing provocative. Mr. Carter is likely to express his deep, deep concern, especially to Polish audiences, before whom he is unlikely to recall his glowing words about the goals of the Polish communist leadership, uttered in Warsaw early in his presidency.

Ronald Reagan? Let us see.

There is always the United Nations. It is a) a moral mess; and b) primarily an anti-Israel lobby. But when last heard from, we did occupy a seat on the Security Council, and we might just bestir ourselves to call a session in order to condemn Soviet violations of Articles 18, 19, 20, 21, and 23 of the Universal Declaration of Human Rights, Principle Seven of Basket I of the Helsinki accords, and all of Basket III. That won't do very much for the Polish heroes, but it will do something for our own self-esteem.

7

Meanwhile, Over at Cardinal Hayes

December 5, 1981

WHEN Monsignor Thomas J. McCormack announced that, inflation being what it was, he would most regretfully need to charge a tuition of $90 per month, nearly 10 percent of the parents of the 1,250 students who attend Cardinal Hayes High School in New York wrote in to complain. "Complain" may not exactly reflect the emotions of parents who had, after all, been paying $85 per month. Everyone knows the impartial ravages of inflation, and any parents who desired to look into the matter at Cardinal Hayes would see that it was running at an annual deficit of $200,000. Moreover, the school's budget is only $1.5 million.

Just two years ago, a total of fourteen teachers approached the monsignor and said, in effect, Look, I love this school, and the job it is doing for inner-city students is remarkable, but I can't get along with a salary differential as exaggerated as that paid me by Cardinal Hayes, compared with that available to me in the public high schools. In other words, the parents recognized that nobody was getting any richer from the five extra dollars per month being asked of them. So their representations to the authorities were more in the way of an invitation to consider the pain that an extra $5 per month causes the very poor in New York, many of them one-parent households supporting four, five, six children.

So what does Cardinal Hayes do? Well, it does everything. There is an Inner City Scholarship Fund (its chairman is Jewish). There is the annual money-raising dinner for the benefit of the thirty-five schools run by the Archdiocese of New York, which last year raised $1 million. The rest has to be got from the archdiocese, which comes up with the money to the extent it can. To the extent it can't, the boys at Cardinal Hayes whose parents can't make it are detached; and go to the public schools, which are free. And which cost the New York taxpayers not $90 per month, but three to four times that figure.

Those who oppose the notion of tuition tax credits are enemies of education. The idea of public education is first to promote education. The word "public" is an adjective adorning the word "education" which, being public, is advertised as free. Inasmuch as we should all by now know that there is no such thing as a free lunch, we acknowledge that even the very poor in the inner city in New York, as elsewhere in inner cities, are paying for their public schools, through taxation direct and indirect. But many of them are not getting an education, certainly not of the sort that causes parents to sacrifice to send their children to Cardinal Hayes.

The students are there promptly—at the entrance is one of the thirty-six laymen (there are also sixteen priests and six brothers), clapping his hands, urging them to run in to be punctual. They come dressed in tie and coat. There is no such creature as a security guard. The fourteen-year-old freshmen often need a little decompression, and 5 percent of them will flunk out for failure to meet academic standards; another five percent for failure to meet behavioral standards. After making it through sophomore year, there are few disciplinary problems, none at all of the kind one reads of as regularly tormenting the life of children in many of the public schools. It is hardly a matter of race—at Cardinal Hayes 53 percent are Hispanics, 35 percent blacks, zero percent are troublemakers. Eighty-five percent of the seniors go on to higher education.

Not surprising. Father Walsh teaches a history class for advanced placement students and today he is talking about the rough syllogism attempted by Alexander Hamilton when he said: a) Good government is in the national interest; b) The "rich" and "wellborn" serve the national interest; therefore c)

The "rich" and "wellborn" (by such terms, Hamilton meant the eighteenth-century squirearchy) serve good government. "That isn't necessarily true," said Father Walsh. "But that was Hamilton's position." Later he told the visitor that he teaches only historical episodes in which controversy figures.

Much of what goes by the name of social tragedy it is not easy to do anything about: for instance, drug abuse, illegitimacy, crime. When one comes upon such an institution as Cardinal Hayes—serving the cause of education, of racial integration, of good manners—and reflects that a few adamant ideologues, pleading a construction of the First Amendment that would have baffled the men who wrote that amendment, threaten its survival by blocking tuition tax credits, one despairs over the noxious lengths to which ideology taxes us.

8

Hunger and the Feds

August 20, 1983

FOR THE FIRST TIME in many years, we are hearing the dread word hunger.

It is a dread word because it describes the most primitive of our needs. Everyone alive, if deprived of food for twenty-four hours, will begin to feel a sensation that evolves into physical pain obsessive in its demands over the sufferer, and the end is: death. Hunger is the first concern of organized and disorganized societies. Any concern for welfare begins with the fact of human hunger.

Now in the United States, during the sixties, it gradually transpired that there was real hunger in the land. The causes of that hunger were complicated, but unquestionably in many cases people were going hungry not out of ignorance of diet, or for reasons tangential to a short change of money. They were simply hungry because they could not get food to eat.

At about that time, in 1969, an economist, Dr. Ruth Logue, retired now from the Federal Reserve Board, published a fascinating essay in the Washington *Post.* Dr. Logue had had training in agricultural economics on the basis of which she was able, with authority, to single out four basic foods that could satisfy 99 percent of our biological requirements. They are bulgur wheat, dried skimmed milk, dried beans and lard.

(Later she withdrew the recommendation that lard be included, on the grounds that it was only marginally necessary.)

Dr. Logue had a modest proposal to make. It was this: that unlimited supplies of these foods should be made available to anyone who wanted them. There would be, in other words, no eligibility requirements. She used the term "lifeline foods." Under her plan, every grocery store in the United States would have been furnished with as much of the four foods as there was any call for. Anyone short of sustenance could, by use of these foods, maintain perfect health, however uninteresting the diet. She reminded us that in fact most people in the world cling naturally to a narrow diet, for instance the Chinese and their rice, Mexicans and their beans, even Americans and their hamburgers.

What about the factor of cost? Extremely interesting. Dr. Logue estimated that the cost of implementing her program would be about $1 billion. Translated into the inflated dollars of 1983, that figure would rise to about $3 billion. In other words, biological hunger (as distinguished from, say, gourmet hunger) would have been abolished by an expenditure on that scale. As things now stand, we are spending $312 billion in social welfare. In 1968 we were spending (I am using constant dollars) just over $100 billion. The cost of our food stamp program is not $3 billion, but over three times that sum, $11.2 billion. It is as though we have built a 30-story hospital but hadn't yet got around to taking care of childbirth.

To eliminate technical hunger by spending $3 billion per year gives society a perfectly defensible sense of moral composure. "How can you leave spaghetti on your plate when you know there is someone in town who is hungry?" is something we hear at age five, and something that rests in the inner ear at age fifty-five. What appalls is the sagging inefficiency of corporate welfare. To spend $300 billion a year while hunger, abatable at $3 billion, survives, is an example of the muddled mind at work, spending, spending, spending and accomplishing so very little.

Dr. Logue was not making an argument against welfare unrelated to hunger. Nor is this such an argument. There are still schools that are needed, shelter, medical care. But the first of these is, acknowledgedly, hunger. And given that we have a huge agricultural surplus, the existence of hunger in a country groaning with excess food makes keener the paradox. It is unhappily true that people are pointing to the survival of hunger as evidence of the parsimony of federal interest in human welfare. It is something else: one more indication of the failure intelligently to regulate priorities, and sensibly to approach the need to cope with them.

If one looks at the problem of hunger and asks the questions that come to mind, they would surely include: How much of the cost of food stamps goes into ascertaining the eligibility of users? How much goes into administration? We cannot give free housing to the homeless, or free medicine to all who wish medicine at no cost. Dr. Logue did not come out for the nationalization of agriculture. But her intuition is of general interest.

9

Human Rights and
Foreign Policy: A Proposal

The Soviets in Geneva [to negotiate SALT II] never even hinted
at the Kremlin's resentment of the Carter human rights policy,
and the Americans were equally careful not to echo their Government's criticism of Soviet human rights abuses. Unaware of
this rule, a newcomer to the U.S. team brought up the dissidents
in an informal tête-à-tête with his Russian opposite number.
When he reported the exchange later in a 'memcon,' his superi-
ors told him never again to mix business with displeasure.
                              —*Time* magazine, May 21, 1979, a
                              Special Report on the history of
                              the negotiation of the SALT II
                              treaty.

A GREAT DEAL has been written about human rights and
foreign policy in the recent past.[1] With much of what I propose

[1] The curious should read *American Dream/Global Nightmare: The Di-
lemma of U.S. Human Rights Policy*, by Sandra Vogelgesang, published in
1980 by Norton. I read the manuscript, courtesy of Ms. Vogelgesang. Daniel
Patrick Moynihan and I both wrote books about service with the Third
Committee (Human Rights) of the General Assembly of the United Nations,
and his book is also an account of his tenure as U.S. Ambassador to the UN.
The books are, respectively, *A Dangerous Place*, Boston: Little Brown &
Company, 1978; and *United Nations Journal: A Delegate's Odyssey*, New
York: Putnam's, 1974. *Freedom in the World, Political Rights and Civil Lib-
erties 1978* is a Freedom House book edited by Raymond D. Gastil, New

to discuss below, before arriving at a policy proposal, I expect there will not be substantial disagreement; with some of it inevitably there will be. We are all agreed that the movement for human rights, politically expressed, is quite new; that U.S. involvement in that movement has been uneven; that the advent of the United Nations Covenant on Human Rights slightly altered the juridical international picture; that the Soviet Union came recently to a policy of manipulating the West's campaign for human rights; that the Vietnam war brought on a general disillusionment with American idealism; that the Realpolitik of Nixon-Kissinger generated first congressional resistance and then, through candidate and later President Jimmy Carter, executive resistance to adjourning official U.S. concern for human rights. And, of course, everyone knows that Mr. Carter's human rights policy is now in a shambles. This is the case, in my judgment, not because of executive ineptitude but because of morphological problems that can't be met without an organic division of responsibility.

II

Although the very idea of human "rights" is firmly rooted in biblical injunction, which asserts a metaphysical equality ("Thou shalt love thy neighbor as thyself") and enjoins altruism ("Inasmuch as ye have done it unto one of the least of these my brethren, ye have done it unto me"), biblical insights made little political progress over the centuries in which church and state joined in accepting, and even underwriting, civil class distinctions at the extreme of which were self-assured kings and self-abnegating slaves, never mind that the political phenomenon never challenged, let alone diluted, the theological conviction that both kings and slaves would eventually answer to the same divine tribunal.

Human rights, including a measure of political rights, were

York, G.K. Hall and Company. I found four articles particularly helpful. They are, in chronological order of their publication, "A Reporter at Large—Human Rights," by Elizabeth Drew, *The New Yorker,* July 18, 1977; "The Politics of Human Rights," by Daniel Patrick Moynihan, *Commentary,* August 1977; "Human Rights and the American Tradition," by Arthur Schlesinger, Jr., *Foreign Affairs: America and the World 1978;* and "Human Rights Muddle," by Irving Kristol, *The Wall Street Journal,* June 27, 1978.

asserted, and to a degree explicated, in the documents that led to, and flowered from, the American and French revolutions. The Bill of Rights and the Declaration of the Rights of Man enumerated individual rights which the state might not impinge upon, save by due process. The respect paid to these rights by sponsoring governments varied with the vicissitudes of the historical season, an ambivalence by no means outdated. Negro slaves in America coexisted with the Bill of Rights; the Reign of Terror in France with the Declaration of the Rights of Man; Gulag with Helsinki. There are few surviving commentators, let alone historians, who are inclined to defend the proposition that the articulation of a human right leads to its realization.

In short, though inchoately an ancient idea, human rights are a relatively new political objective, and as often as not, only a nominal political objective.

The United States has had cyclical romances with the notion of responsibility for the rights of extranationals, an insight also biblical in origin ("Am I my brother's keeper?" asked Cain, who, having drawn the wrong conclusion, slew Abel), cosmopolitanized by John Donne's resonant assertion that we are, as individuals, involved in mankind. Professor Schlesinger nicely summarizes the episode involving Louis Kossuth, driven from Hungary by the Austrians during the repression following the convulsions of 1848.[2] There were those in Congress who came close to advocating a punitive expedition against Austria; others considered lesser sanctions, but all in all, Congress engaged in a feisty bout of moral indignation. The prevailing voice, however, was Henry Clay's. His argument was in two parts: the first, that the United States, with its fitful record, uneasily judged the delinquencies of other nations; the other, that condemning Austria while ignoring such conspicuous transgressors on human rights as Turkey, Spain, Great Britain (yes, Great Britain!) and Russia, was simply—eccentric.

Several years before Professor Schlesinger reminded us of it, George Kennan, in his exasperation over the Vietnam war, had called attention to the tranquilization of rambunctious Ameri-

[2] Schlesinger, op. cit.

can idealism by Secretary of State John Quincy Adams, delivered, appropriately enough, on the Fourth of July (in 1821). "Wherever the standard of freedom and independence has been or shall be unfurled," Adams said, "there will be America's heart, her benedictions, and her prayers. But she goes not abroad in search of monsters to destroy. She is the well-wisher to the freedom and independence of all. She is the champion and vindicator only of her own."[3]

The rhetorical exaltation of what is still known as Wilsonianism reached its apogee in the inaugural address of President John F. Kennedy. It is painful to repeat those ingenuous strophes, so dissonant to the ear after the Vietnam war, but a narrative of U.S. attitudes toward human rights abroad is simply incomplete without them. We will, declared the freshly anointed President, "pay any price, bear any burden, meet any hardship, support any friend, oppose any foe, to assure the survival and the success of liberty."

Did Mr. Kennedy, in uttering those words, recognize the *weight* of the responsibility he was assuming on behalf of the United States? The answer is that he *gloried* in that responsibility: "In the long history of the world, only a few generations have been granted the role of defending freedom in its hour of maximum danger. I do not shrink from this responsibility—I welcome it."

Was this pure bombast? Or was the listener entitled to assume that the new President had actually given thought to the practical consequences of his words? "The energy, the faith, the devotion which we bring to this endeavor will light our country and all who serve it—and the glow from that fire can truly light the world." A few months later that glow lit up the Bay of Pigs, but by no means the world, or even the Capitol steps from which these quixotic—pot-valiant?—words had been spoken.

In short, U.S. involvement in the movement to universalize human rights has been episodic, but even early on, it evi-

[3] George Kennan, Testimony before the Senate Foreign Relations Committee, February 10, 1966. *Supplemental Foreign Assistance Fiscal Year 1966— Vietnam.* Hearings before the Senate Foreign Relations Committee, 89th Cong., 2nd Sess., Washington: GPO, 1966, p. 336.

denced an inchoate disjunction between the power to affirm and the power to dispose.

Yet the scaffolding on which President Kennedy had spoken was not insubstantial. There were the Fourteen Points of Woodrow Wilson, which he coupled to his antecedent crusade to make the world "safe for democracy." There came then, in 1941, Franklin D. Roosevelt's Four Freedoms. These—in passing—were significant for transmuting human rights into something much more than the negative injunctions on government activity conveyed in the Bill of Rights. FDR did not exactly discover, but he and Winston Churchill gave declamatory voice to positive, but not readily achievable, obligations of government: something called Freedom from Want, which seven years later gave birth to about thirty importunate children (e.g., "Everyone has the right . . . to free choice of employment") in the Universal Declaration and related documents—children who, for the most part, have lived unhappily ever since.[4] But while Woodrow Wilson and Franklin Roosevelt and John F. Kennedy were merely American Presidents, giving voice to an erratic, yet progressively universalist statement of American idealism, the birth of the United Nations and the subscription by member states to its Charter gave near-universal codification to the notion of the obligation of the state to acknowledge the human rights of its own citizens, and hinted at the mutual obligation of states to ensure each other's fidelity to these obligations. Because the Charter itself —and this before the ensuing elaboration in the Universal Declaration and other comments—committed its members to "reaffirm faith in fundamental human rights."

In short, the United Nations transformed human rights into something of an official international paradigm, and began to suggest an obligation by member states to modify their foreign policy accordingly.

[4] For convenience' sake I group together the following instruments: the Universal Declaration of Human Rights, the Convention on the Prevention and Punishment of the Crime of Genocide, the International Convention on the Elimination of All Forms of Racial Discrimination, the International Convention on Economic, Social and Cultural Rights, the International Covenant on Civil and Political Rights, and the Optional Protocol.

The Universal Declaration's International Covenant on Civil and Political Rights, and on Economic, Social and Political Rights, were announced on September 26, 1973, as having been ratified by the Presidium of the Supreme Soviet and thus under the Soviet Constitution became the supreme law of the land. The Soviet ratification aroused little popular notice. To this day there is no universally accepted explanation for Soviet timing. Probably it had to do with the Soviet Union's efforts to ingratiate itself with those European countries with which, two years later, it concluded the Final Act of the Conference on Security and Cooperation in Europe (Helsinki Accords). "Basket Three" of this pact became the most emphatic juridical validation of certain individual rights in Soviet history. The Universal Declaration, after twenty-five years of desuetude, had become, for most nations, mere liturgy; safe, therefore, to ratify without giving rise to international expectations. Basket Three was widely held to be the indispensable moral quid pro quo by the Soviet Union to the Helsinki Accords, which gave the Soviet Union what it had wanted for so long—namely, de jure recognition of the postwar frontiers.[5] To have accepted Basket Three while ignoring the Universal Declaration would have posed problems for Soviet negotiators.

As it happened, most of the Soviet citizens who undertook actively to monitor compliance by the Soviet Union with the terms of Basket Three are in jail, psychiatric hospitals, exile; or mute. Their Czechoslovakian counterparts have been tried, convicted, and sent to jail.

In short, the Soviet Union in due course recognized the necessity to cope with, and therefore manipulate, the human rights dimension as an aspect of its own foreign policy.

[5] Two months before the announcement of Soviet ratification of the Universal Declaration, Lord Home had spoken at one of the opening sessions at Helsinki with these words: "If your conference is essentially about people and about trust, then it is essential that we should do something to remove the barriers which inhibit the movement of people, the exchange of information and ideas." And on September 26, addressing the General Assembly of the United Nations as British Foreign Secretary, Lord Home spoke hopefully, "I trust that the communist countries will be able to prove that they are for the basic freedom of people everywhere."

III

Nobody knows exactly what impelled Jimmy Carter to seize on human rights as the touchstone of U.S. foreign policy. Mr. Carter's opposition to the Vietnam war could be classified as ritualistic: i.e., he was not one of its early critics. Now the U.S. venture in Vietnam has been disgraced by most moralists, which is to say less than that it has been disgraced by history. Its relevance here is that Jimmy Carter on several occasions spoke ill of it. In his acceptance speech at Madison Square Garden upon being nominated for President, he spoke of it as an "immoral" war. At Notre Dame University in 1977, he stated that our "inordinate fear of communism" led us to the "intellectual and moral poverty" of the Vietnam war. Senator Daniel Patrick Moynihan's comment is here relevant not merely for the job it does of effective contention, but in shedding light on the confused provenance of Jimmy Carter's stated redirection of U.S. foreign policy with emphasis on human rights. Moynihan said, "This causal connection can . . . be challenged. Some of us said at the time that the enterprise was doomed because it was misconceived and mismanaged. Are we to say now—in this, echoing what our enemies say of us —that it was also wrong or immoral to wish to resist the advance of totalitarian communism?"[6]

Carter's reference to Vietnam, together with Moynihan's demurral, catapults us into the awful complication posed by the Vietnam war, coming on the heels of the attempted liberation of Cuba. The *moral* disavowal of the Vietnam war took us a long way toward the Platonization of the spirit of our concern for human rights. Elizabeth Drew reminds us that Jimmy Carter came to the whole subject of human-rights-as-an-integral-part-of-foreign-policy in a haphazard way—not to be compared, say, with the evolution of Lincoln's structured approach to slavery.[7] In an address to the Foreign Policy Association in New York in 1976, Carter said that "we . . . can take the lead

[6] Moynihan, op. cit.
[7] Drew, op. cit.

in . . . promoting basic global standards of human rights"[8]—a statement that might have been made, and has been, by an orator in the United Nations. But by the time he reached his Inaugural Address he was speaking of his commitment to human rights as "absolute."

The opposition to the war in Vietnam did more than implicitly disavow any generic responsibility by the United States to resist totalitarian aggression in such terms as had been advanced by President Kennedy. So bitter was the opposition to the war that it was transmuted in some quarters into a tacit disavowal of the modus operandi of American culture, recalling Henry Clay's arguments against U.S. moral effrontery. The process began by stressing the imperfections of our ally Ngo Dinh Diem; went on to the immorality of our military procedures (napalm, bombing); and ended by concluding that the United States was so tainted that there was nothing really to say about the superiority of our own society over that against which we had set out to defend the South Vietnamese.[9]

The effect of this self-denigration must be supposed to have had a great impact on the perception of the People's Republic of China. Barbara Tuchman, for instance, came back from China to write a paean on Mao Zedong, conceding only perfunctorily that, to be sure, there were certain "negative aspects," which, however, "fade in relative importance" alongside the accomplishments of the regime.[10] John Kenneth Galbraith managed an entire book about the new China in which he could find to criticize only the excessive use of tobacco, though, to be sure, he made it clear that Maoism wouldn't work over here.[11] Others—for example, James Reston, Seymour Topping and Ross Terrill—wrote in a similar

[8] Jimmy Carter, Address to the Foreign Policy Association, New York, June 23, 1976.

[9] There is a vast body of literature to sustain this statement. A heavy concentration of it may be found in *Authors Take Sides on Vietnam*, Cecil Woolf and John Bagguley, eds., New York: Simon & Schuster, 1967. See especially the entry by Herbert Read.

[10] The New York *Times*, September 4, 1972.

[11] John Kenneth Galbraith, *A China Passage*, New York: Houghton Mifflin Co., 1973.

vein.[12] One must conclude that the hectic enthusiasm for a society that observed not a single provision of the U.S. Bill of Rights must have reflected the low opinion of the United States, its paraphernalia of rights notwithstanding, that prevailed among the most intense critics of the Vietnam war.

In brief: the retreat from Vietnam was not merely a disavowal of Wilsonianism as a foreign policy, but a disavowal of Wilsonianism as metaphor. Who is to say that the society that grants such liberties as we grant, and is nevertheless so rotten, is necessarily to be preferred over such a society as Ho Chi Minh and Mao Zedong created, without human rights, to be sure, but otherwise so wholesome? Surely utopia lies somewhere beyond the rights of Coca-Cola to operate—or even of the Bill of Rights to guarantee individual inviolability in the face of social *force majeure?* Although the intellectual community is retreating from its position on Mao Zedong ever so slowly, indeed one might say *pari passu* with the retreat of the present rulers of China from idolization of Mao, it *is* doing so. The events in Cambodia and the phenomenon of the boat people have likewise injured the perception of North Vietnam as a kind of godfatherly presence in Indochina. The prominence given to Carter's position on human rights was a reaction to the radical ideological egalitarianism brought on by the Vietnam war—the criticism whose base was, in effect, "Who says we-all are better off than them-all?"

During these years (1969–76) our foreign policy was given over to the balance-of-power politics of Nixon, Kissinger and Ford. Critics of the war became hard investigators of executive military and paramilitary procedures. Of all things, the CIA under Kennedy (leave aside the tangentially relevant question whether at his instructions) apparently expressed a velleity (it cannot have been more than that) to assassinate Cuba's Fidel Castro; failing which, to make his beard fall off; failing which, to contrive to give him laughing gas or whatever, which would activate in the middle of one of his speeches (one wonders, what would be the resulting difference?). The investigators

[12] James Reston, the New York *Times*, July 8, 1971; Seymour Topping, the New York *Times*, June 25, 1971; Ross Terrill, "The 800,000,000," *The Atlantic*, November 1971.

learned that the U.S. government had intervened, however indirectly, to help those in Chile who resisted President Salvador Allende. And, of course, we continued our alliances with random dictators, in South Korea, in the Philippines, in Iran and Pakistan; all over. President Carter, joining the critics even as he plunged headlong into his crusade for human rights, summed it all up at Notre Dame a few months into his presidency by saying that "our inordinate fear of communism" had driven us (the President at this point was referring to preceding administrations) "to embrace any dictator who joined us in our fear."

The political right, meanwhile, staggered from a succession of shocks absorbable only because their longtime attachment to Richard Nixon appeased their strategic misgivings (how could *he* betray the cause?). The first of these was the triumphant opening to Beijing. Whatever its usefulness as strategy, a public that had been brought up to believe that Mao Zedong combined the vices of the theoretician Lenin and the executioner Stalin saw their champion on television toasting the health of Mao in the Great Hall of the People and returning to Washington to give personal testimony to "the total belief" of the Chinese leaders in "their system of government." A few months later Nixon was off to Moscow where he participated openly, indeed effusively, in the apparent *Gemütlichkeit,* with leaders who were simultaneously provisioning the North Vietnamese who were continuing their workaday slaughter of American soldiers in Vietnam.

Then, in the summer of 1975, Solzhenitsyn came to Washington—and President Gerald Ford, on the advice of Henry Kissinger, declined to receive him.[13] The impurity of that gesture resonated in the consciousness of those who felt that morality had at least a symbolic role to play in foreign policy.

Two events give historic importance to the second of the three debates between President Gerald Ford and candidate Jimmy Carter. The subject was foreign policy, and the Carter entourage were anxious that their candidate not give the impression of being too soft to cope with the Soviet Union, too

[13] Kissinger acknowledges the mistake (personal conversation).

good-natured, too manipulable. It is reported that Zbigniew Brzezinski advised the candidate to revise his position on the Helsinki Accords, which he had theretofore merely criticized as giving the Soviet Union legal standing in Eastern Europe. Why not go soft on the treaty, which was popular in Europe and in much of the United States, and bring up the Soviet Union's failure to live up to its obligations under Basket Three? "According to a number of witnesses, it was in San Francisco that Carter first heard of Basket Three—a term that in the course of the debate he dropped on what must have been a puzzled nation, as if he had been familiar with it for some time."[14] On the same program in which Candidate Carter showed a deft familiarity with an outstanding, if already forlorn, mechanism designed to protect certain rights of citizens living under Soviet domination, the President of the United States announced that Eastern Europe was free of "Soviet domination." The questioner, Max Frankel of the New York *Times*, could no more believe his ears than the millions of listeners, and thought it a slip of the tongue, asking the question one more time: "I'm sorry, could I just follow—did I understand you to say, sir, that the Russians are not using Eastern Europe as their own sphere of influence in occupying most of the countries there and making sure with their troops that it is a communist zone?" President Ford answered emphatically, "I don't believe, Mr. Frankel . . . that the Poles consider themselves dominated by the Soviet Union."[15]

In a single broadcast, Jimmy Carter had shown himself sensitive to human rights and to Soviet infidelity to a treaty commitment, while his opponent gave the impression that he was not even aware that a whole people were being routinely deprived

[14] Drew, op. cit.

[15] One viewer (it was I) expressed the general sense of disillusion: "There is a television series running that features someone called a Bionic Man. He is reconstructed from an airplane wreck, or something of the sort, and after umpteen operations by ambitious doctors, runs now faster than a gazelle, lifts weights heavier than a crane could lift, sees further than a telescope—a miracle of scientific reconstruction. It is as if, somewhere along the way, the Bionic Man, sitting by the fireside, discussing poetry with his staff, suddenly reached down, picked up the cocker spaniel, and ate it. "Curses!" the scientists say. "We forgot to program him not to eat dogs!" (Syndicated column, "Mr. Ford's Polish Joke," October 14, 1976.)

of their rights. It is a subjective judgment that Gerald Ford's gaffe, alongside Carter's thrust, affected the outcome of the election. In any event, Carter did win and human rights, as U.S. policy, were back in the saddle, though reconciliations that were to prove impossible lay ahead.

In short, realpolitik crowded out human rights during the Kissinger years, but the momentum of the criticism of the Vietnam war drove critics to superordinate the right of the sovereign nation (e.g., Chile, Cuba) over any responsibility by the United States to frustrate totalitarianization. Jimmy Carter detected, in his random emphasis on human rights, a popular political response that issued from (a) conservatives affronted by the collapse of the social face of diplomatic anticommunism, and (b) liberals who felt that the denigration of human rights in the tidal wave of anti-Americanism required reconsideration.

IV

Another reason for Executive assertiveness in the matter of human rights was the mounting activity of Congress, motivated once again by the momentum that had been generated against Executive unaccountability during the Vietnam war. Inevitably, a branch of government losing power to other branches of government attempts to redress the balance. The lesion of power to Congress during 1969–76, expressed in such legislation as the Cooper-Church Amendment and the War Powers Act (measures designed to limit the power of the Executive to take the country into protracted military engagements like Vietnam), had the effect on the Executive that daily calisthenics by a contender would have on a prospective competitor. Professor Schlesinger quotes Deputy Secretary of State Robert Ingersoll, warning Kissinger in 1974, "If the Department did not place itself ahead of the curve on this issue [human rights], Congress would take the matter out of the Department's hands."[16]

Indeed Congress had been busy. A profusion of human rights legislation began with the passage of the Amendment to

[16] Schlesinger, op. cit.

the Foreign Assistance Act of 1973,[17] multiplying enormously the scattered bits of law enacted previously.

The showcase legislation is the amendment passed in 1976 to the Foreign Assistance Act, and for this reason I quote extensively from the language of the Act, to give an indication of the temper of Congress before President Carter was inaugurated.

Section 502B provides flatly that: "The United States shall, in

[17] For convenience, I shall refer to "U.S. human rights legislation" without singling out the relevant act. The acts are in several categories: (1) Economic Assistance—Section 116 of the Foreign Assistance Act of 1961, as amended, (FAA) (22 U.S.C. 2151n) (1975); development assistance—Sections 101 and 102 of the FAA (22 U.S.C. 2151) (1961) and (2151-1) (1978); agricultural assistance—Section 112 of the Agricultural Trade Development and Assistance Act of 1954 as amended—(ATDA) (7 U.S.C. 1711) (1977); International Financial Institutions (the International Bank for Reconstruction and Development, International Development Association, International Finance Corporation, Inter-American Development Bank, African Development Fund, Asian Development Bank)—Title VII of PL 95-118 (22 U.S.C. 262g) (1977) and (262c note) (1977); Overseas Private Investment Corporation (OPIC)—Sections 239 (1) of the FAA (22 U.S.C. 2199) (1969); Section 240 A of the FAA (22 U.S.C. 2200a) (1969); Export–Import Bank—Section 2 (b) (1) (B) of the Export–Import Bank Act, as amended, (12 U.S.C. 635 (b)(1)(B)) (1977); Section 2 (b) (8) as amended (12 U.S.C. 635 (b) (8)) (1978); Section 402 of PL 93-618 (19 U.S.C. 2432) (1975) (the Jackson-Vanik Amendment); Security Assistance—Section 502B of the FAA (22 U.S.C. 2304) (1974); Section 543 (3) of the FAA (22 U.S.C. 2347b) (1976); Country-Specific Restrictions—Section 4 (m) of the Export Administration Act of 1969 as amended, (50 U.S.C. App. 2403) (1969); Section 5 of PL 95-435, 1978 Amendments to the Bretton Woods Agreements Act, (22 U.S.C. 2151 note); Section 602 of PL 95-424, International Development and Food Assistance Act of 1978 (22 U.S.C. 2151 note) (1978), Section 610 of PL 95 426, the Foreign Relations Authorization Act, Fiscal Year 1979, (22 U.S.C. 2151 note); Section 406 of PL 94-329, International Security Assistance and Arms Export Control Act of 1976 (22 U.S.C. 2370 note) (1976); Section 35 of PL 93-189, Foreign Assistance Act of 1973 (22 U.S.C. 2151 note); Section 620B of the FAA (22 U.S.C. 2372) (1977). Anti-Discrimination Provisions—Section 666 of the FAA (22 U.S.C. 2426) (1975); Section 505 (g) of the FAA (22 U.S.C. 2314 (g)) (1976); Section 5 of the Arms Export Control Act as amended (22 U.S.C. 2755) (1976); Section 5 of the Arms Export Control Act as amended (22 U.S.C. 2755) (1976); Section 121 of the Foreign Relations Authorization Act for Fiscal Year 1977 (22 U.S.C. 2661a) (1976); Section 113 of the FAA (22 U.S.C. 2151k) (1973); Miscellaneous —Section 624 (f) of the FAA (22 U.S.C. 2384 (f)) (1976); Section 408 of PL 94-329, International Security Assistance and Arms Export Control Act of 1976 (22 U.S.C. 2291 note) (1976); Section 32 of PL 93-189, Foreign Assistance Act of 1973 (22 U.S.C. 2151 note) (1973).

accordance with its international obligations as set forth in the Charter of the United Nations [note the obvious effort by Congress to suggest that it is about to do something in no sense different from what every member of the United Nations is implicitly bound to do] and in keeping with the constitutional heritage and traditions of the United States, promote and encourage increased respect for human rights and fundamental freedoms throughout the world without distinction as to race, sex, language, or religion. Accordingly, a principal goal of the foreign policy of the United States shall be to promote the increased observance of internationally recognized human rights by all countries." (The operative de-energizer of that sentence is the phrase "a principal goal." There cannot be "a" principal goal. The word principal denotes primacy. Since in foreign policy there can only be the principal goal of securing the safety of the state, other goals are by logical requirement secondary, or even tertiary.)

With respect to security assistance, the President of the United States is, by Section 502B, "directed to formulate and conduct international security assistance programs of the United States in a manner which will promote and advance human rights and avoid identification of the United States, through such programs, with governments which deny to their people internationally recognized human rights and fundamental freedoms, in violation of international law or in contravention of the policy of the United States as expressed in this section or otherwise." Security assistance is to go forward only as restricted by this mandate, and crime control and detection equipment cannot be exported, nor can security assistance to the police or any military education and training assistance be provided, to a country "which engages in a consistent pattern of gross violations of internationally recognized human rights" —unless (you guessed it)—the President "certifies in writing that extraordinary circumstances exist."

Ensuing provisions require the Secretary of State to furnish Congress with a report on U.S. assistance to any country, giving details of that country's behavior in respect of human rights. Congress may then, if it disagrees with the Executive, by joint resolution suspend further security assistance to the country concerned. The Act also establishes an Assistant Secretary for Human Rights and Humanitarian Affairs. The incumbent, Patricia Derian, has a staff of ten which helps to prepare the annual reports for Congress.

Now all this legislation is at once a comprehensive assertion of U.S. interest in human rights, and an invitation to philosophical and diplomatic chaos. It reflects most of the weaknesses of our public policy in its practical deviousness and in the selective indignation it encourages. Congress had ruled that no economic assistance may be extended to any country engaged in gross violations of "internationally recognized" human rights—"unless such assistance will directly benefit the needy people in such country." It is difficult to imagine a situation in which economic assistance, particularly in kind, would not in fact help needy people, or fail so to represent itself. The act goes on to require of the State Department a yearly report, one that would take into account the probings of relevant international organizations on the status of human rights within all countries receiving assistance.

The legislation is interesting in that there isn't (to my knowledge) any record of any congressional review of assistance given to a delinquent country which actually led to the official congressional conclusion that such assistance was illegal on the grounds that (a) the country was a gross violator of human rights, while (b) U.S. aid did not in fact help needy people. The impact of the yearly reports is, then—assuming the President elects not to act on them—purely psychological: to hold in obloquy those nations that are gross violators of human rights. To let them, so to speak, twist slowly, slowly in the wind of moral displeasure, even if their stomachs are full. All this figures substantially in the conclusions to which I have been drawn, below. A second, and perverse, feature of the annual report is that it tends to highlight the villainies of countries to which we routinely give aid. Since we do not give aid to the communist countries they are officially exempted from the annual pathological examinations—an interesting means of achieving immunity.

Congress, moreover, directs U.S. representatives in the international financial institutions to "seek to channel assistance" toward countries other than those that are gross violators of human rights; but—again—unless such credits serve "basic human needs."

The Overseas Private Investment Corporation is not supposed to insure (against confiscation) U.S. investments in any country that grossly violates human rights—again with the standard exception that the needs of the needy shall be the primary consideration. With respect to the Export-Import Bank, the President is required to determine that favorable consideration by U.S. officials to applicants be conditioned on advancing U.S. policy "in such areas as international terrorism, nuclear proliferation, environmental protection and human rights." The President hasn't existed who couldn't get around that one.

On the other hand, we saw in the legislative season before Carter's inauguration the beginning of a so-called country-specific procedure. South Africa—by name—may not receive credits except under extraordinary circumstances; and purchasers, in order to qualify for economic advantage, must prove, in South Africa, that fair employment principles are practiced. In addition to South Africa, action has been taken (whether by the Executive or by "country-specific" restrictions set by Congress itself) against Uganda, Vietnam, Cambodia, Cuba, Chile, Argentina and Brazil.

The Jackson-Vanik Amendment—denying most-favored-nation treatment to countries that deny their citizens the right or opportunity to emigrate—is the most celebrated of the congressional human rights enactments. Although clearly aimed at one country (the Soviet Union) for the benefit of one class of aspirant emigrés (Jews), the language is generically drawn. The amendment, by the way, preserves the usual waiver granted to the President under specified circumstances. The Soviet Union objected violently to its passage, canceled a trade negotiation and, after the bill's passage, retaliated by reducing the number of Jews to whom it issued exit visas. Henry Kissinger and Richard Nixon have on more than one occasion cited the Jackson-Vanik Amendment and its consequences as clear evidence that "quiet diplomacy" works better than legislation when the objective is an actual change in policy rather than moral rodomontade.[18]

[18] Henry Kissinger, *White House Years*, Boston: Little, Brown and Co., 1979, pp. 1271–72. Richard Nixon, *RN: The Memoirs of Richard Nixon*, New York: Grosset and Dunlap, 1978, p. 876.

In brief: the encyclopedic intervention by Congress into the international human rights market has by practical necessity needed to provide for Executive waiver. But the residual effect is to encourage specific pressures against (a) countries of less than critical strategic importance; and (b) countries without U.S. constituencies sufficient to exert effective influence on the U.S. government. The resulting mix is ineffective in respect of the enhancement of human rights, and unedifying in respect of a consistent regard for human rights.

v

Although President Carter, as we have seen, had been generally bland on the subject of human rights, he was a tiger by the time of his inaugural address: "Our commitment to human rights must be absolute." The real problem, of course, is where to fix our commitment to human rights on this side of absoluteness.[19] President Carter's inaugural address presaged the ensuing chaos. For a while there was great excitement. However short-lived, it was breathcatching. In a few days Jimmy Carter actually answered a letter addressed to him by Andrei Sakharov. A few weeks after that he contrived to meet and shake hands (no photographs) with the valiant Vladimir Bukovsky, among the most illustrious of Soviet dissidents. The Soviet Union exploded. Within a year, the United States ambassador to the United Nations Human Rights Commission in Geneva was being privately instructed by President Carter's Secretary of State *under no circumstances* even to mention the name of Yuri Orlov, who had just been packed off to jail for the crime of monitoring Soviet noncompliance with the provisions of the Helsinki Accords' Basket Three, which candidate Carter had castigated the Soviet Union for failure to live up to. Jimmy Carter was crestfallen, the great Human Rights Band laid down its instruments, and everyone has been struggling ever

[19] The President is plagued by verbal imprecision. It does not really mean anything at all to say that one's commitment to human rights "must be absolute." Since it *cannot* be absolute (an absolute commitment would require us to declare war against China and the Soviet Union, just to begin with), then it has to be something less than absolute.

since plausibly to give the theme of our policy on human rights.

An attempt to say what is operative U.S. policy in respect of human rights requires a survey of the behavior of the principal Executive of U.S. foreign policy. President Carter's position is best attempted not by reasoning *a priori* from his general commitment ("absolute") to human rights, but *a posteriori* from his actions. Almost immediately it transpired that the State Department bureaucracy was apprehensive about the impact of Carter's human rights declarations on concrete questions being negotiated or prospectively in negotiation.[20] The military, in pursuit of its own concerns for U.S. security, was similarly troubled. The State Department and the disarmament folk feared that an antagonized Soviet Union would behave more militantly at the bargaining table. The military was quite unwilling to trade Subic Bay in the Philippines for a moral boycott of President Marcos. An opportunity arose for President Carter to begin to make critical distinctions. Fogbound, he did not do so.

In a speech delivered March 25, 1964, in the Senate, Senator William Fulbright, at the time Chairman of the Senate Foreign Relations Committee, made a useful distinction, even if he went too far with it: "Insofar as a nation is content to practice its doctrines within its own frontiers, that nation, however repugnant its ideology, is one with which we have no proper quarrel." That distinction is geopolitically appealing. Thus in 1965, to guard against what President Johnson perceived as the threat of a communization of the Dominican Republic (it is immaterial whether the threat was real or fancied), we landed armed forces in the Dominican Republic. The western half of Hispaniola had been for eight years under the domination of a murderous Haitian doctor who routinely practiced all the conventional barbarities on his people, and not a few unconventional ones. It did not occur to us to send the marines (as once we had done during this century, though our motives were eclectic) to put down Papa Doc—tacit recognition of the intuitive cogency of Fulbright's doctrine. At its most menacing, Franco's Spain threatened nothing more than Gibraltar, which

[20] See Drew, op. cit.

was in any event a nostalgic fantasy in irredentism, and excusable, if you like, under the various anticolonialist covenants, save for the disconcerting fact that inhabitants of Gibraltar preferred to remain a crown colony. As it happened, Franco satisfied himself to lay economic siege to Gibraltar, and however persistent the criticism of his regime from its inception at the end of the civil war, no U.S. administration—from Roosevelt's forward—ever proposed collective action against Spain. By contrast, we very nearly went to war to protest the communization of Cuba, less because Castro's doctrines were inherently repugnant than because a Soviet salient deep within the womb of territory putatively protected by the Monroe Doctrine was deemed intolerable.

But President Carter not only failed to remark Fulbright's distinction, he agitated to blur it. "I have never had an inclination to single out the Soviet Union as the only place where human rights are being abridged," he said at his press conference of February 23, 1977. And again on March 24 at a press conference, "I've tried to make sure that the world knows that we're not singling out the Soviet Union for abuse or criticism." By June, he was sounding defensive.[21] Not only had the phrase become formulaic ("We've not singled out the Soviet Union for criticism"), he went on to say exactly the opposite of what all his rhetoric required: "and I've never tried to inject myself into the internal affairs of the Soviet Union. I've never made the first comment that personally criticized General Secretary Brezhnev."

Human rights everywhere was the President's theoretical objective. And so it remained, even if there were to be no more letters to Sakharovs or visits with Bukovskys. He clung tenaciously to his theoretical position: "I've worked day and night to make sure that a concern for human rights is woven through everything our Government does, both at home and abroad," he said at a press conference at the end of his first year in office (December 15, 1977); and one year later, commemorating the thirtieth anniversary of the adoption of the Universal Declaration of Human Rights (December 6, 1978), he pronounced, "As long as I am President, the Government of the

[21] Press conference, June 13, 1977.

United States will continue, throughout the world, to enhance human rights. No force on Earth can separate us from that commitment."

It became clear, as time went on, that specific as distinguished from omnidirectional, censorious presidential declarations would become scarce, indeed might end altogether, leaving to the State Department the clerical duties Congress had legislated before Carter came to office. In due course, Chile, Argentina, Brazil and Paraguay were singled out for criticism, based on the annual reports by the State Department required in the 1976 law: economic credits and military assistance, in varying forms, were withheld. In other countries, notably South Korea and the Philippines, the President invoked the authority given him by Congress to subordinate the concern for human rights to a concern for security interests, and aid continued uninterrupted.

But the President, although he summoned the necessary discipline to restrain himself from criticism, found it difficult to avoid diplomatic hyperbole. Arriving in Warsaw on December 30, 1977, he greeted the communist proconsul Gierek with the astonishing news that Poland was a "partner in a common effort against war and deprivation." He recalled that at the end of World War I Herbert Hoover ("a great American") "came to Poland to help you ease the suffering of an independent Poland. Circumstances were different and the struggle was long, but Hoover said, and I quote, 'If history teaches us anything, it is that from the unquenchable vitality of the Polish race, Poland will rise again from these ashes.' And," said Carter—jubilantly?—"his prediction came true." These words were perfectly congruent with the picture of Poland described during the famous debate by Gerald Ford. They would not have needed changing if it had happened that during the week before Carter's touchdown in Warsaw, Poland had suddenly wrested its independence from the Soviet Union. The press did not have long to wait. Later in the day:

Q. During the presidential debates, in a celebrated exchange, President Ford claimed that Eastern Europe was not under Soviet domination. And you replied, 'Tell it to the Poles.' Well, now that you're here, is it your view that this domination will continue almost into perpetuity, or do you see a day when Poland may be actually free?

The President replied that "our nation is committed to the proposition that all countries would be autonomous . . . and . . . free of unwanted interference and entanglements with other nations. . . . I think . . . it's a deep commitment of the vast majority of the Polish people, a desire and a commitment not to be dominated."[22]

Q. You don't deny that they are dominated here?
A. I think I've commented all I wish on that subject.

Four months later, on April 12, 1978, President Carter welcomed President Ceausescu of Romania to the White House. At the ceremony, Carter announced that "the people of the United States are honored by having as our guest a great leader of a great country." And he went on to say, "Our goals are also the same, to have a just system of economics and politics, to let the people of the world share in growth, in peace, in personal freedom." In Civil Liberties, Freedom House gives a rating of six to Romania (seven is the lowest rating). In its Ranking of Nations by Political Rights, it gives Romania a seven.

In greeting Yugoslav President Tito (March 7, 1978), Carter said: "Perhaps as much as any other person, he exemplifies in Yugoslavia the eagerness for freedom, independence, and liberty that exists throughout Eastern Europe and indeed throughout the world." Freedom House on Yugoslavia: Civil Liberties, five; Political Rights, six.

It was not until April 21, 1978, that Carter got around to criticizing Cambodia. When he did, he called it the world's "worst" violator of human rights. "America," he said, "cannot avoid the responsibility to speak out in condemnation of the Cambodian Government, the worst violator of human rights in the world today." America, through its President, precisely *had* avoided the responsibility to speak out in condemnation of the Cambodian government about whose practices as much was known by the end of 1975 as by the spring of 1978.[23]

[22] Press conference, December 30, 1977.
[23] Richard C. Holbrooke, Assistant Secretary of State for East Asian and Pacific Affairs, denounced Cambodia on September 5, 1977.

In brief: by his own example as President, and by the let-down that followed his exalted rhetoric on the subject, Mr. Carter, with some help from the 93rd Congress, has reduced the claims of human rights in U.S. foreign policy to an almost unparalleled state of confusion.

VI

My proposal is to separate two questions. The first is: How do human rights fare in a given country? The second: What should the United States do about it? It is the commingling of the two that has brought forth existing confusions and distortions. The question whether we collaborate with the Soviet Union in order to avoid a world war is unrelated to any commitment a civilized nation ought to feel to human rights. Although the avoidance of a world war and the safety of the American state are primary objectives, the ethical imperative requires us as a nation journeying through history regularly to remark the brutality of the Soviet system—even if we make no commitment, thereby, to do anything concrete to mitigate those conditions.

On the whole we are better off stating, at all those international conferences, what it is we believe sovereign states owe to their citizens in the way of recognizing individual rights, and let it go at that, than to collaborate in rituals of efficacy which we know will be without operative meaning. By the same token a constant encephalophonic reading, uninfluenced by distractions of diplomatic concern, of the condition of human rights in a given country, to the extent that this can be accomplished (the difficulty in ascertaining these conditions obviously varies), gives a gyroscopic steadiness of judgment which is the enemy of hypocrisy, dissimulation, and such other inventions as have disfigured the idealism of the human rights movements.

Congress should repeal existing legislation on the question of human rights (although, because of the loopholes, it would not really need to do so in order to promulgate the commission described below). It should then establish a Commission on Human Rights composed of a chairman and four members, with provisions for a staff of a dozen persons (approximately the size of the staff of the Assistant Secretary of State for Human Rights and Humanitarian Affairs). For symbolic reasons primarily, but also for practical reasons, the commission should not be affiliated with the Department of State. It might plausibly be affiliated with the judiciary, or perhaps even with the Department of Justice. What matters most is that its mandate should be distinctive, unrelated to policymaking, whether by the executive or the legislative branch of government.

The commissioners should be appointed by the President and confirmed by the Senate. The Act should recommend to the President that the commissioners be selected from a roster of candidates nominated by existing agencies devoted to the internationalization of human rights including—but not restricted to—the International Commission of Jurists, Freedom House, Amnesty International, the Anti-Defamation League, the several religious committees and the Red Cross.

The mandate would most severely restrict the commission's public role to the reporting of factual conditions: never to the recommendation of policy. Policy would continue to issue from Congress and the Executive. The commission would report publicly, once a year, to the President and to Congress—in the nature of the event, to the world—on the condition of human freedom in every country, using the Universal Declaration of the United Nations as the paradigm. For administrative purposes, much as in the annual reports of Freedom House, these freedoms might be grouped together—e.g., in such a way as to distinguish usefully between the right (Number 5) not to be tortured, and the right (Number 24) to "rest and leisure."

The commission would be available to the Executive, or to Congress, for such questioning as the government chose to direct to it—e.g., on any special knowledge acquired about human rights in any given country, movements within that country to improve conditions, whatever. However, the tradition should vigorously be nurtured that no policy of the Executive or of Congress would flow from any initiative of the commission, even if that policy resulted from legislative or executive reaction to data collected by the commission.

The chairman of the commission, or any other commissioner designated by him, would represent the United States government in several relevant posts within the United Nations, occupying there the chair in the Third Committee of the General Assembly. The commission's restrictions would carry over: i.e., the representative would make the case for human rights, answer questions about human rights in the United States, and describe their findings, insofar as they were relevant. He would leave to the representative of the regular U.S. delegation the exercise of the vote (in favor, against, or abstaining) on any concrete proposal concerning, e.g., the treatment of terrorists, hijackers and so forth. This division of duties would not be so difficult as the reader might suppose. Most of the argumentation before the Third Committee is over trivial points, forgotten the day after they engage the delegates' attention; and in any event, recommendations of the committees are subject to acceptance or rejection by the General Assembly, where the permanent representative of the United States votes on instructions from the Department of State.

By the same token the Commissioner (or his representative) would sit at the Geneva sessions of the standing United Nations Commission on Human Rights. Once again, his role would be to report on the condition of human rights in any country under discussion; once again, he would decline to vote on recommendations that called for policy decisions. A vote condemning, let us say, racial discrimination, or a condemnation of bondage, or of sex discrimination, or religious persecution is not a vote on U.S. policy toward those countries guilty of such misconduct. The commissioners would, clearly, be permitted to express themselves in favor of the human rights the very existence of the committee ostensibly seeks to augment.

The commission would have the right of access to a fixed number of broadcast hours per country per year, for the purpose of factual reporting of its findings. These reports—again, without policy recommendations—would go out over the Voice of America, and affiliated broadcasters in Europe, Asia, Africa and Latin America. Such reports, though unaccompanied by policy recommendations, would not need to go out as dry-as-dust statistics. They could, indeed should, engage the dramatic attention of the listener by, for instance, permitting refugees to tell their own stories. An appropriate term of office for the commissioners, and for the chairman, might be seven years.

VII

It should be unnecessary to explain that the existence of a United States Commission on Human Rights could not constitutionally deprive either Congress or the Executive of powers that inhere in those institutions. No one has the power to tell the President he should not make a fool of himself on landing in Warsaw—he would still be free to do so. But the silent, yet ominipresent, countenance of the Commission on Human Rights, with its lapidary findings on the condition of human rights in Poland, would make it less likely that the President, in pursuit of diplomacy, would traduce idealism. Congress can vote to deny arms or soybeans or *Saturday Night Fever* to any country Congress chooses to punish or victimize or bully or wheedle; but the existence of the commission, with its findings, would provide certain coordinates that might guard against such caprice as nowadays tends to disfigure country-specific legislation.

And—viewed from the other end—for the wretched of the earth in their prisons, with or without walls, in the torture chambers, in the loneliness they feel as they weigh the distortions of diplomacy, there would be something like: a constant. A commission mute while the United States collaborates with Stalin in pursuit of Hitler, or Mao in pursuit of Brezhnev, but resolutely unwilling to falsify the records of Josef Stalin and Mao Zedong in their treatment of their own people.

"The great enemy of clear language is insincerity," Orwell wrote, in the same essay in which he lamented that "in our time, political speech and writing are largely the defense of the indefensible."[24] To say the truth—says Solzhenitsyn—is the single most important thing of all. Politicians cannot always say the truth and pursue policies organic to their profession. But the saying of the truth about human rights, as distinguished from the superordination of human rights over all

[24] George Orwell, "Politics and the English Language," in *A Collection of Essays*, New York: Harcourt Brace Jovanovich, 1953.

other concerns, is not incompatible with the mechanics of foreign policy.

Finally the question is asked: Would such a commission, with its yearly findings, its reports to the nation, its testimony before Congress, its international broadcasts of its findings—would it enhance human rights? It is quite impossible to assert that it would do so—or that it would not do so. With the best will in the world, Wilsonianism succeeded in making the world most awfully unsafe for democracy. But, as mentioned earlier, there is an encouraging survival, through it all, of the idea of the inviolable individual, and that idea needs watering, not only by the practice of human rights at home, but by the recognition of their neglect abroad. It is a waste of time to argue the inefficacy of telling the truth, the telling of which is useful for its own sake.

IV
REFLECTING

1

Back to Prison

In the summer of 1965 I wrote a piece about a convicted murderer in New Jersey who had been in prison for eight years under sentence of death in the electric chair. "The Approaching End of Edgar H. Smith Jr.," published in Esquire *in November of that year, launched Smith as a national figure. A fund to help him with his legal expenses was organized, which I initiated by contributing the fee for my article. In the ensuing years Smith was frequently in the news, losing one appeal after another, twice approaching the chair, saved on one occasion by high-wire judicial tactics at the eleventh hour. I continued to write about and work for Smith's defense, enlisting the aid of New Jersey and Washington lawyers. In 1968 Edgar Smith published his own account of what he called his mistrial, a book that became a bestseller and was widely translated. When the Supreme Court ruled in 1971 that Smith would have to be retried or released, the news was reported throughout the country.*

I had first learned of Smith's existence on receiving a clipping that noted the impending departure from the state prison in Trenton, New Jersey, of the Catholic chaplain, who was a subscriber to National Review. *The chaplain's leaving meant that one of the occupants of the death house would no longer be able to borrow the chaplain's copy of the magazine. I wrote to offer a "lifetime" subscription to the magazine to Smith, and a correspondence was struck up. After a few exchanges, Smith asked whether I would be willing to spend an hour with a private eye who had followed the case. I did—and was hooked. Before writing my initial article, I read the court record and traveled to the places in New Jersey that had figured in the top crime story of that state for 1957. By the time I had completed my investigations, I was convinced that at the very least there was reasonable doubt as to Smith's guilt, and eventually I became persuaded that Smith was innocent. I was not alone.*

So when Smith walked out of prison on December 6, 1971, he was a national celebrity, notwithstanding a confession of guilt that was universally understood as having been wrenched from him by the State of New Jersey. For a brief period he remained prominent. And then, in October of 1976, once again he was in the news. The story that follows tells what happened.

FOLLOWING on his triumph with *In Cold Blood* in the late 1960s, Truman Capote emerged as something of a lay criminologist, appearing on the talk shows, writing and directing an hour's documentary on the death houses of America, explaining such terms as "sociopath," "psychopath" and other arcana of penological psychology; so that when, in 1968, I gave him Edgar Smith's book, *Brief Against Death*, I was particularly anxious for his opinion.

"Well," I said after he finished it, "what do you think? Was he guilty?"

"Oh yes," Capote giggled.

"What makes you say so?" (I was clearly defensive about my protégé.)

"I never met one yet who wasn't."

That was a nice line, and while expressing myself at a number of forums arguing the probable innocence of Edgar Smith, I would occasionally drop Capote's wisecrack, intending to caricature the *Côte-Basque* cynicism of that class of people who accept dogmatically the guilt of anyone convicted by a court of law—unless ideology gets into the act. Sacco and Vanzetti could have strangled Barbara Walters on the "Today" show and we'd have books and magazine articles proclaiming their innocence. But Edgar Smith had no politics, although *National Review* appealed to him. If they had asked him what was his political faith—that night in March 1957 when the police came to his trailer and led him away to question him for seventeen hours about Vickie Zielinski, whose scattered remains had been discovered that morning near a sandpit in Mahwah, New Jersey—he would probably have lied, because that was what he did instinctively. Then he'd have calculated what was the answer that might best advance his interests, and try that out. But he had no interest in politics, none in philosophy; none, really, in anything at all, except a biological interest of sorts in bumming his way through life with the least personal invest-ment and highest sensual returns: a life as close as possible to the saloons and poolrooms of his neighborhood, dodging amia-bly the ministrations and remonstrances of his exigent, de-voted but frustrated mother, who had never given up on him, starting when he was put on probation as a teenager for mo-lesting an eleven-year-old girl (Edgar denied it). Nor had his mother given up when he left the private Catholic day school she sacrificed to send him to, nor when he quit high school two years early to join the Marines, nor when he was discharged from the Marines with vaguely unflattering references on his record to schizophrenic and antisocial problems but, formally, because he had slightly defective hearing in one ear.

A certain aura attaches to any man sent off to be executed. In the 1950s, at the death house in Trenton, such a man would customarily stay around a year or so during the routine appeals before being led down the corridor to the room behind the steel doors where the electric chair sits that dispatched Bruno Hauptmann, the kidnapper of Lindbergh's baby. (Was Haupt-mann guilty? Ask Capote.) As it happened, Edgar Smith occu-pied the same end cell from which Hauptmann had only a few yards to walk to the chair. Smith had no lobby trying to keep him alive, unlike Sacco and Vanzetti, the Scottsboro Boys or Caryl Chessman. What did come along, and just in time, was the Warren Court, which had begun to scatter a trail of drag-ons' teeth that slowed the juggernaut of justice. Edgar Smith turned, in the course of a few years, from a semiliterate to an accomplished practitioner of criminal law, after a while even writing his own briefs. During that long, tense period when his appeals succeeded in keeping the bulkhead between his cell and the chair sealed—even as several of his less resourceful fellow prisoners walked by him into the death chamber—he began to win an audience.

I was one of the earliest and certainly the noisiest of converts, though the far reaches of his notoriety were achieved primarily by himself, by means of his bestselling book that didn't convince Truman Capote but *did* convince others. Ross MacDonald, reviewing it for the New York *Times Book Review*, had written: "If Eddie didn't kill Vickie Zielinski—and I find myself seriously doubting that he could have—he has been cruelly mistreated." And Christopher Lehmann-Haupt, writing for the daily *Times*, concluded that Smith "achieved his major purpose in writing his book—'to leave the reader with an abiding sense of doubt' as to his guilt."

The Smith case reminds one of the difficulty of persuading people who review the identical evidence that a single conclusion is required. The circumstantial case against Smith was very persuasive, and indeed the jury delayed only two and one half hours, including a lunch break, in finding him guilty of murder in the first degree; finding, in effect, that beyond a reasonable doubt, Edgar Smith had at 8:45 P.M. on March 4, 1957, stopped his car to offer a ride to fifteen-year-old Vickie on a lonely country road (she was walking back to her parents' house after doing homework with a friend); that he had driven her off to the local lovers' lane; that, having attempted unsuccessfully to seduce her, he had chased her down a hill with a baseball bat, clobbered her and dragged her, still alive, back up the hill to an obscure corner of the sandpit—where he crushed out her brains with a forty-four-pound rock.

However, there were anomalies, and judicial irregularities.

Pleading one such irregularity, after having failed in nineteen consecutive appeals in state and federal courts (coming twice to within a few hours of execution), Edgar Smith finally, triumphantly, won. The Supreme Court of the United States ordered a hearing on the question of whether the alleged "confession" had been legally obtained. John J. Gibbons, a circuit court judge in Newark, thereupon conducted an extensive hearing to ascertain whether rules of procedure had been violated; whether the prosecutor's manifesto—Smith's ambig-

uous confession—had been coercively extracted, and whether
he had been advised of his legal rights. Judge Gibbons, finding
for Smith on all points, pronounced the verdict of the trial
court null and void. The State of New Jersey could either retry
Smith within sixty days, said the learned, unflappable young
judge—or set him free. That ruling on May 14, 1971, was front-
page news in the New York *Times*. Because Edgar Smith had
become, in the acidulous words subsequently used by one commentator, "the most honored murderer of his generation." But
Smith didn't become the prisoner for whom thousands
cheered simply because a federal court had come around to
discovering procedural irregularities of reversible gravity.
Quite the contrary: many of Smith's boosters were predisposed
against the very same rulings from which Smith benefited.

Smith's special appeal drew its strength from two sources.
The first was an educated doubt about his guilt.

John Selser, the highly respected lawyer who defended
Smith at trial, remained articulately convinced of his client's
innocence. Andy Nicol, the private investigator retained by
Smith's mother to assemble evidence contradictory to the
prosecutor's, had been formally dismissed after only a few
weeks when Smith's mother ran out of money; but, at no
charge to his client, Nicol persisted, pursuing a hunch as to the
true identity of the murderer that he cautiously communicated to those few who seriously interested themselves in the
case. And the State's narrative of the crime was inherently
implausible. It required Smith, in an interval of twenty-five
minutes, to have been active beyond the rhythm one is readily
prepared to associate with seduction attempted, resisted, followed by chase, followed by murder, followed by attempts at
concealment. Smith, according to the prosecution, 1) picked
Vickie up and drove two miles to the lovers' lane, 2) chatted
with her in the front seat of the car, 3) made sexual advances to
her, 4) progressed far enough to leave tooth marks on one of
her breasts, 5) frightened her into leaving the car, 6) pursued
her 334 feet down the road, 7) bruised her head with a baseball
bat, 8) tossed the bat away a distance of 160 feet, 9) carried her
364 feet back to the sandpit, 10) dragged her up to the top of a
mound 60 feet away, 11) killed her with a blow from a heavy
boulder, and 12) drove home a mile to his trailer. In less than a

half hour. Then there was the testimony of the coroner that Vickie had died at midnight, give or take one hour. But Smith was back at the trailer at 9:15 P.M.

Those facts, provocatively organized, raised doubts. But it was the character of Edgar Smith—or, more precisely, the personality of Edgar Smith—that got him his ardent supporters. Here was a romantically engaging vision of a young man, occupying a cell eight feet by eight feet in solitary confinement, who had now set the United States record for time served in a death house, writing in longhand briefs that kept a seemingly inexhaustible trickle of sand clogging the terminal gear of justice. The raw facts caught the attention of the public. But through it all Smith had managed (and this is the key) to put forward his case in an almost disinterested perspective. He was by turns mordant, judicious, inquisitive, impudent, amused. He even had a thesis about what the New Jersey death penalty abolitionists had in mind. They would tolerate his execution—then stir up a backlash of revulsion that would eventuate in the repeal of the capital punishment law. He commented coolly, "I am not a candidate for martyrdom; if nominated I shall not run, and if elected I shall decline to serve."

That is the way he came across. In the seven years we corresponded while he was in the death house at Trenton, he wrote me 2,900 pages of letters, most of them in longhand until, toward the end, the New Jersey authorities finally relented and let him have a typewriter. He expressed himself in many moods in that correspondence, but what was distinctive was his sense of detachment, which he combined with a kind of gallows wit, that left some readers mysteriously but deeply moved. In the article I did on Edgar Smith in 1965, when it appeared that the State would finally overcome him, I gave out great doses of Smith the correspondent. In the same letter in which he fatalistically advised me that his most recent petition for a review of his case had been denied by the U.S. Supreme Court, he had gone on to write that his long campaign to achieve for me the right to visit him had been won. "Well, I'm not a total failure. Judge O'Dea has granted the request for the court order allowing visitation. The dungeons have been thrown open for your inspection."

I had from the beginning been struck by his apparent imperturbability, a word I used twice in my correspondence with him, twice turning out to be once too often. But occasionally the breathlessness of his struggle throbbed through his clinical reports on legal machinations. The State of New Jersey at one point adopted the strategy of waiting until the very last moment to reply to Smith's petitions. The idea was to catch him up in a chronological bind in which New Jersey would say no at the end of the countdown, leaving Smith only a few, insufficient hours to draft an appeal to the federal courts. Before the feds could act, the State would execute him. "[This time,]" he wrote in April 1965, "I wrote to the Court and the Attorney General, telling them I'd wait three more days before asking [Justice Brennan representing] the Federal Court to again take jurisdiction. Mirabile dictu, I received a decision the following day. Frankly, my friend, things were a bit close for a while: I had the suspicion I was batting a sticky wicket. You can bet your best ski boots that the State isn't going to throw any parties for Justice Brennan *this* month."

Although at the time I had become something of an authority on the factual disputes in the Smith case and theoretically had earned the right to pass judgment in the matter, I finished one letter, in the summer of 1964, by blurting out impulsively, "My God, I wish I could be absolutely certain you didn't kill that girl!" Smith replied with wonderful aplomb, "My God, *I* wish you could be absolutely certain I didn't kill that girl." But then, characteristically, he situated the question in the appropriate judicial perspective. "I think, for now, that I am satisfied that you aren't *certain* that I did kill her." As a conservative (he reproached me) I was bound to translate a reasonable doubt into a verdict of "not guilty." "Besides, do you really think it would do any good for me to tell you I didn't? Would that convince you? Disclaimers of guilt are a dime a dozen around this place."

I remember only one time, during those years crowded with letters from Trenton, when his impatience was entirely explicit. I had written him that God had apparently recently visited the subways, to judge from graffiti I had come upon that morning. "GOD IS DEAD—NIETZSCHE," someone had written in chalk. Under which had been scrawled in block letters,

"NIETZSCHE IS DEAD—GOD." I then made a second allusion, coming apparently too close on the heels of the first, to his imperturbability.

"I had not intended to write again so soon," he began glacially, "but I am quite frankly somewhat disturbed by your very apparent misapprehensions as to my state of mind. Your references to my serenity, imperturbability, etc., impute [sic] that I am some Buddha-like anachronism, fast approaching Nirvana. Tell me—does the fact that I am in the Death House mean to you that I should be perpetually atop a soapbox, shouting my protestations to a cold, cruel, unhearing world? I assure you, my friend, if I thought soapbox oratory would serve me any good purpose, I would climb onto the closest box handy and put George Wallace to shame. The fact is that what you mistake for serenity, or an air of detachment, is nothing more or less than the realization on my part of the fact that my situation is not going to be improved by breast-beating and lamentations, however loud or sustained—it can only be changed by and in a court of law. Perhaps my letters should be appropriately tear-stained when they arrive at your office, giving them a more pathetically desperate quality. Again, if it would do me any good, I would cry you a river—à la Julie London." Then, with only the break of a new paragraph, the pulse normalized; Queen Victoria remounted her throne. "I trust you will not misinterpret the tone of this letter. I was not especially unhappy that you failed to understand my feelings, but I did think it was worth clearing up."

In the autumn of 1971 the Supreme Court of the United States unanimously affirmed the decision of the circuit court mandating a fresh trial. The congratulatory mail was very heavy, but Edgar confided to me only a single communication, from a stranger: a telegram. "JUST RETURNED FROM VIETNAM. READ BUCKLEY PIECE. HAVE TIRED OF STRUGGLES BUT PLEASED TO HEAR TONIGHT OF YOUR VICTORY. I HOPE THE CHANGES BROUGHT ON BY THE YEARS OF FRUSTRATION ARE ENOUGH TO GUIDE YOU AND OTHERS TO FURTHER PATIENCE AND ULTIMATE PEACE. CONGRATULATIONS. PETER GILLETTE, LEXINGTON, KENTUCKY."

The great day came on December 6, but the conditions

imposed by the State of New Jersey were harsh. At a meeting the preceding week, early in the morning, Edgar, his lawyer Steve Umin and I met in a tiny room in the prison, and the decision was made: he would abide by the terms, though he had sworn as recently as a month earlier that he would not. The terms were that Smith would plead guilty to the murder of Vickie Zielinski, that the judge would then rule that it was murder in the second degree and would hand down a sentence of twenty-five to thirty years, giving him credit for the time already served with good behavior and suspending the balance —so that one hour after the proceedings he would be free on probation. What, he had asked Steve Umin, were the odds of winning if he took the alternative and insisted on a new trial? Umin put them at 70 percent on a first-degree charge, 50 percent on a second-degree charge. That posed the burden of yet more time in jail, preparing for trial, the great cost of the trial and the risk of defeat. What finally persuaded him was his own analysis. If he were exonerated, most of those who thought him guilty would nevertheless continue to think him guilty, reasoning that he had escaped by a technicality, courtesy of the Supreme Court. If he were reconvicted, most of those who thought him innocent would continue to think him innocent.

The hunger for judicial self-justification was very pronounced, so that when he addressed the defendant in a Hackensack courtroom crowded with reporters, Judge Morris Pashman savored Smith's prerehearsed replies to all the questions:

The Court: Mr. Smith, did you and you alone kill Victoria Zielinski?

A: I did.

The Court: Was anyone else there, Mr. Smith, when you killed her?

A: No.

The Court: Did you see anyone else in the area during the time you were in the sandpit with Victoria Zielinski?

A: No.

The Court: After arriving at the sandpit, Mr. Smith, and a space of time thereafter, did you strike Victoria Zielinski?

A: I did.

But the counteroffensive had been carefully planned, and

we put it into immediate execution. He had first to return 100 miles to Trenton, there to produce the court order releasing him. I waited for him in a limousine. The glass partition between front and back raised, Edgar and I and Jack Carley—who as a law student at Yale had volunteered to do legal research for Edgar, and had done so patiently over the years—ate roast beef sandwiches, drank, moderately, rosé wine and agreed on a formulation that would communicate the message, yet keep him out of the striking range of the probation officer. We were headed for a television studio and there, effecting his entry with great difficulty through the mob of photographers and reporters, Edgar Smith sat for two hours on television, discussing with me and others all kinds of things, but the message was loud and clear: he was innocent of the slaying of Victoria Zielinski. He had gone through a necessary ritual for the sake of the judicial pride of the State of New Jersey.

Edgar's very first year out of prison was dreamlike. He was a considerable celebrity. He earned a thousand dollars at a clip lecturing at colleges. Lecturing, even, to a law enforcement association in Pennsylvania. Appearing on the "Mike Douglas Show," the "Merv Griffin Show," on hundreds of local television and radio shows. A qualified expert on prison, and prison reform, and criminal law. He wrote an article or two for the New York *Times* and for *Playboy* magazine.

But the message had gotten thinner and thinner. He had no thesis, really, to ply. His final book, *Getting Out*, dedicated to me, was anemic stuff, larded with Spiro Agnew jokes, and—I was for the first time alarmed—conspicuous for signs of ingratitude verging on coarseness, vouchsafing only perfunctory credit to the work of the brave, tenacious, erudite Sophie Wilkins, Edgar's book editor, who had attempted to do more for Edgar than anyone alive. One of his editorial contributions to the *Times* on prison reform had come out embarrassingly jejune. His stuff was being rejected by the same press that had made him famous when he wrote from the death house. It wasn't merely that it is more exciting to publish copy by someone writing a few yards from the electric chair. He had lost the discipline, the tautness, the harnessing energy. He had walked out of Trenton into the more incapacitating bonds of anomie. He became, slowly, bored—and then boring. And so he began drinking, and did so for an entire year, before resolving to try again out West, with a new bride.

When last had I seen him? I lectured in San Diego in the spring of 1976, and, after it was over, I had a drink with Edgar and his wife, Paige (I met her then for the first time), at the fancy bar of the fancy hotel where I was staying. Seated at the adjoining table with friends was my adversary during the evening's debate, former Mayor Joseph Alioto of San Francisco. I introduced him to "Mr. and Mrs. Smith," and when Edgar went off for cigarettes and Paige to the ladies' room, I leaned over and whispered to Alioto that this was the notorious Edgar Smith who had spent more time in the death house than any other American, and who had written the bestsellers. The moment I did this, I remember feeling ashamed. That sort of thing must have happened to Edgar every day, everywhere.

Edgar made something of a ceremony of paying for the drinks, having written to me on learning of my forthcoming appearance in San Diego to tell me, in the emphatic language he sometimes used, that though to be sure he was down and out, *he* would pay for the drinks while *I* was at San Diego. Since he had long since defaulted on a debt of several thousand dollars, I let him pay. He was in no position to repay the principal, and his pride was slightly restored by treating me to two scotches and soda. I noticed he put them on a credit card. Noticed because when he had come to me, two years earlier, to ask for the loan, he confessed that he had misspent a whole year. "The worst thing ever invented was the credit card. I've just burned them. The whole lot." He was going west, and needed to pay off his debts. There he would make headway, find a good job, use his talents.

On the last day of September 1976, Edgar had conferred with Gerald Warren, editor of the San Diego *Union*, about the possibility of a full-time job. He was unemployed. Warren, at a previous meeting, had given him an assignment, an essay for the op-ed page on an ongoing Nebraska trial at which the judge had put a clamp on the press. Edgar's contribution was judged inadequate, and Warren, exercising the tact he learned during six and a half years as deputy press secretary for Presi-

dents Nixon and Ford, told him to go to the library, do some
more research and try again. As for a full-time job, there were
no openings. Edgar Smith was ill disposed to routine jobs.
Paige had urged him to drive a taxi pending a better job opening. He disdained this, preferring, while at the same time resenting, the job of de facto housekeeper for his young wife,
who worked a full day at the Bank of America and then attended nursing school. Still, no one detected on the last day in
September—though Warren said Smith had appeared more
nervous than on the previous visit—that Edgar was on the
brink of anything save, perhaps, one more lost day.

Lefteriya Lisa Ozbun, thirty-three, was an immigrant seam-
stress who was working for the Ratner Corporation, clothing
manufacturers, on L Street in Chula Vista, California, near San
Diego. On Friday October 1, 1976, she was pleased by the
coincidence of two events in an otherwise uneventful season.
Her husband had recently been put on the day shift, so that
their working hours would coincide for a change. And then, at
2:30, she had been told there was nothing left to do; she could
go home. As she later told the story: "I left work but I'm not
going to wait until my husband pick me up. I was going to go to
the shopping center and look in the stores and then I'm going
to take the bus back." There followed two hours of un-
scheduled strolling through the streets, timed to effect the
rendezvous with her husband at five exactly. After her touring
she took the bus back to the Ratner factory and began to walk
in toward the parking lot. She was distracted by something. "I
heard the car. And I was walking in the side, you know . . . so
I don't get runned over, and then the car was going real slow."
A stranger accosted her and told her to enter his Pontiac. "I
realized he had a knife. He put it at my throat and he squeezed
it real tight, and he said, 'Don't make a move and don't scream
or I'm going to cut your throat right here!' "
Mrs. Ozbun got into the car. The driver thrust her arms
behind her, taped her wrists together and headed off toward
the freeway.
"I said, 'What are you going to do with me?' you know, and
he told me to shut up." After the car was in motion she said,
"Where are you taking me? What are you going to do to me?"

He said, "I'm going to take your damn money and I'm going to stick that knife in you." And she said, "What do you want to stick the knife in me? Why do you want to kill me? I have three kids in the house. If you want the money, take it and just let me go." He said, "Don't be stupid."

The ensuing three or four minutes have few rivals in the annals of resistance. As the car drove up the freeway, Mrs. Ozbun, who weighs about 100 pounds, thrust her feet into the windshield, breaking it. The driver grabbed her head and sat on it, with one hand trying to control the movements of the car, with the other to maneuver the knife. She writhed in resistance, having freed herself of the binding tape, and he plunged a six-inch blade into her, from the back, up toward, but barely missing, her heart. She reached with one foot to apply pressure on the brake, and lunged at the wheel, struggling with the other foot to open the door. When her left hand was dislodged from the wheel, she applied it to the horn. The car reeled about the freeway toward an exit ramp, where the driver narrowly escaped hurtling over a steep embankment and thrust his foot on the brake. Mrs. Ozbun, succeeding in opening the door latch, rolled out of the car and fell on the grass, the knife handle protruding from her back. She fell near a young man who was "hauling flowers." Lying face down she muttered to the boy, "Will you please get my purse?" The young man walked over to the stunned driver and asked, politely, might he remove the purse from the floorboard? The driver dumbly nodded his assent and, remobilized, roared off down the freeway, passing several cars that had stopped on the ramp to observe the excitement. Several of the witnesses, including a drug enforcement official who had a radio in his car and ordered an ambulance, noted the license number, and the California authorities had it within minutes, leaving it a mystery why there was no one there at his apartment to greet Edgar Smith when he drove in to perform the identical ablutions of nineteen years earlier—an effort to remove the blood from his person and clothing. His wife, Paige, was at work, and although no plan of action came immediately to mind, he took thought to feed the cats, surmising he would not soon again inhabit the apartment. Then he took off aimlessly, awaiting his

wife's release from work, at which time they joined a friend
and drank scotch into the evening.

He told them he had been involved in an attempted robbery. Three days later, on Monday, a friend of long standing,
Barbara Fenity, drove him to the airport in Los Angeles, from
which he flew, by circuitous route, to Philadelphia, then went
by train to New York. Incredibly, it was not until six days after
the kidnapping—on October 7—that a general alarm was sent
out and the identity of the alleged kidnapper revealed. The
following night Edgar called Barbara Fenity and instructed
her to call him back on a pay phone, giving her the area code
and telephone number.

"And could you please tell us," the prosecutor at the subsequent trial asked Mrs. Fenity, "did you confront him with what
you had learned?"

A: That was the first time I had the opportunity to do so, yes.

Q: Tell us how it was that you confronted him.

A: I screamed and yelled and cussed my head off at him.

Q: And what exactly—I know it's difficult to say the words,
but I think you're going to have to give us some idea what you
said.

A: An "idea" or "exactly?"

Q: Exactly.

A: "Jesus f——— Christ, Edgar, what did you do?"

The words nicely framed the thoughts of his friends in the
East. The word had flashed through the Old Boy network
within thirty minutes of a telephone call from the New Jersey
prosecutor to Edgar's former lawyer, Steve Umin, who called
me. I was staggered. But—for some reason—I did not doubt. It
did not cross my mind to say, "It's got to be *another* Edgar
Smith. It's got to be a mistake." The first person I notified was
Sophie Wilkins, Edgar's editor at Alfred Knopf, who over a
three-year period had visited Smith frequently in prison and
written him hundreds of letters, seeking to educate, encourage
and entertain him. It was she who undertook the awful task of
telephoning Edgar's mother, with whom she had developed a
warm friendship. His mother, retired in Florida, took the next
bus to her sister's house in New Jersey, to avoid the neighbors'
learning about her wayward son from anticipated visits to her
home by policemen. I then called Jack Carley, the young law-

yer. Each of the Old Boys telephoned two or three friends and rooters, giving out the incredible news, which made the next day's headlines. There was no doubting that it was Smith. The victim was in the intensive-care ward of a hospital, and it was not known whether she would recover, but she had nodded when shown a photograph. Several bystanders had identified Smith from pictures. The car was indisputably his.

Ten days later all of New York was wired to trip him up—local police, FBI, California sheriffs. His picture appeared in all the newspapers and on television. In the interval, Edgar undertook a hegira. He went down deep into Pennsylvania in search, he later said, of a cemetery, at which he meditated. Then up through New Jersey to New York, sleeping in the car, eating at McDonald's, telephoning from time to time to Barbara and to an attorney in San Diego. He was desperately short of money when he telephoned his aunt in New Jersey, who, against the advice of her embittered sister, Edgar's mother, agreed to meet Edgar at a rendezvous at the World Trade Center. There, on the unconditional understanding that he would take the next flight to San Diego and give himself up, she gave him $1,000, sufficient for the air fare and for a small deposit to his attorney. Edgar's mother communicated this information to Frances Bronson, my secretary, who passed the word on to me in Albuquerque, where I was lecturing. The next morning at ten Miss Bronson's telephone rang. It was Edgar. "How are you, Frances?" (Frances Bronson had served as something of a message center and coordinator for Edgar while he was at Trenton and for several months after, and, like all of us, had been caught up in the drama.) "Where's Bill?"

"He's in Albuquerque."

"Can you tell me where to reach him?"

"No"—Frances thinks quickly—"but I know how to track down his hotel . . . where can he reach you?"

She expected evasion. Not at all.

"I'm at a hotel in Las Vegas." He recited the telephone and room numbers.

I had the data a minute later, and a minute after that, the New York FBI hot line assigned to Edgar Smith, Wanted, had it from me. Exactly twenty minutes later FBI agents, having made routine inquiries at the desk, entered his room, to find

Edgar sound asleep. He dressed, and they replaced the hand-
cuffs from which he had been relieved four years and ten
months earlier.

At 11 A.M. on Wednesday March 30, 1977, Judge Gilbert
Harelson called the San Diego court to order. The trial of
Smith for his attack on Mrs. Ozbun had lasted five days, during
which testimony was taken from twenty witnesses. Now it was
over and, a jury having been waived, the time had come for
the judge to pronounce his verdict. But the question instantly
arose whether the defendant was in a position to receive a
verdict. He had been helped into the chamber by guards. He
was wearing, at his insistence, the same bloody clothes he had
had on when, hearing a great racket in the large cell shared by
Smith with thirty-eight other prisoners, the guards had found
him the night before and had taken him to the hospital, where
he was treated for broken ribs and a broken nose.

The word went out that, on hearing over the evening news a
recital of the testimony Edgar Smith had given during the day,
his fellow inmates had been outraged at the final confirmation
—from Smith's own lips—that he had, indeed, murdered a
fifteen-year-old girl in 1957 by smashing her skull to pieces
with a huge rock. There is a code, we hear it said often, among
criminals; and one of the crimes not tolerated is a crime against
children. Accordingly, they there and then administered a
thorough beating to the child-killer.

That was the story generally accepted. But the motivation
for the beating, prison-wise officials will tell you, was in fact
quite different. Sure, Smith's companions thought the murder
of a fifteen-year-old a repellent form of crime; but these nice
discriminations, among men who mug and rape and kill, are
whimsical. Young Vickie was a nubile teenager, and if she had
been the kind of girl willing to run away to New York, not
many of the men who now kept company with Edgar in that
cell would have hesitated to pimp for her or, if she held back
on her earnings, to beat her up savagely—stopping, to be sure,
this side of squandering a capital asset. Edgar Smith's crime, in
their eyes, was that he had confessed guilt to a murder after
maintaining his innocence so brazenly, so tenaciously, so effectively for twenty years. Edgar Smith had been the most cele-

brated American convict concerning whose guilt there had been substantial doubt in the mind of a great public. By his confession, he had discredited a whole criminal class whose prospects depended on the continuing plausibility of the whole notion of justice miscarried. So the beating.

What, actually, did Smith say in court when he elected to take the stand?

In *Brief Against Death*, Smith had related, with great scorn, what the New Jersey prosecutor had told the jury, step by step, that Edgar had surely done to Vickie Zielinski. Now, addressing the San Diego court, Smith revealed that, step by step, *exactly* what the New Jersey prosecutor had charged years before, he had in fact done.

Prosecutor Richard Neely, clearly astonished by this unexpected narrative, asked him:

Q: Have you ever [previously] admitted the truth to anybody?

A: Not even to myself.

Q: Why not to yourself, Mr. Smith?

A: Because I didn't want to believe that I am what I am.

Q: Why are you testifying now as to . . .

A: Because—because on a Saturday afternoon in October I stood in the cemetery in Pennsylvania and for the first time in my life I recognized that the devil I had been looking at in the mirror for forty-three years was me.

Q: Why did you go to that cemetery?

A: The cemetery is where Victoria Zielinski was buried. I was looking for her grave but I didn't find it.

Q: Was it at that time that you decided to return to San Diego?

A: No, it was at that time I recognized that my life had reached a point at which I had a choice of doing two things: I could kill myself or I could return to San Diego and face what I was.

Neely at this point intuited what Smith's strategy was. Accordingly, Neely attempted to determine whether Smith was in fact telling the truth "for the first time." Because this representation conflicted with a curious but obstinately held position by Smith that he had never *actually* lied.

Q: You did, as a matter of fact, represent to a number of

people who came to your aid that you did not in fact kill
Victoria Zielinski?

A: No, I did not.

Q: You did not tell them that you were innocent of the
charge?

A: I never denied the crime. I was asked to and I did not deny
it.

Q: These individuals that were aiding you, you didn't tell
them that you had not committed the crime?

A: No, the individuals—the only person I really talked to was
—about the crime—was William Buckley.

Q: Okay. You informed Mr. Buckley that you did not commit
the crime?

A: Mr. Buckley wrote me a letter and asked me. His exact
words were, "My God, Edgar, I wish you'd tell me you didn't
do it."

Q: And you did?

A: And I wrote back and told Mr. Buckley, "My God, Bill, I
wish you wouldn't ask me that." And that was the only answer I
ever gave him.

Neely persisted.

Q: . . . you were [finally] allowed to plead guilty in 1971
and then were released forthwith?

A: That's correct.

Q: And then you recanted that particular judicial confession
by telling people on national TV, etc., that it was a lie, that you
did not in fact kill Victoria Zielinski?

A: That's correct.

What was going on was both perverse and exalting. At one
and the same time Smith was appealing to the judge to believe
that he had lied all of his life and was only now telling the
whole truth. But, rather pathetically, he was recalling (to himself, mostly—inasmuch as very few of his old friends would
ever read the transcript) that he had taken great, circumlocu-
tory pains never actually to deny his guilt directly to those who
had most intimately befriended him. A matter of honor.
Whether the distinction was caught by the judge is not clear.
Neely, who had studied Smith carefully, detected it. It was an
act of pride, yes; but also part of a grand strategy. The judge
was to believe that Smith would not lie to *him.* About what?

Smith's strategy—believe it or not—was to convince the judge that Smith was a congenital sex pervert. His own attorney elicited from Smith, by careful prearrangement, the story of the eleven-year-old girl. Had he in fact sexually molested her? Yes. What had he attempted on Vickie Zielinski? Coitus. What had been his motive in kidnapping Mrs. Ozbun? Rape.

Smith spoke at considerable length about his determination to rape somebody. *Anybody?* In a way, yes; for a while he had considered raping the assistant to a local veterinarian, but the opportunity was never quite right. He had located, in the outskirts of Chula Vista, a sandpit—yes, a *sandpit*—that was consistently deserted. He knew, because he had parked his car there for hours at a stretch and had never seen another car come in. There he would take the rapee.

But why Mrs. Ozbun? Had he ever laid eyes on her before the afternoon he kidnapped her?

Never. But that happened to be the moment when the impulse overtook him.

Then why had he told her he wanted her money and told others—his friend Barbara, his wife Paige—that it was all about robbery?

To lessen their concern for the gravity of his offense.

It was all an intricate judicial game. Because, as of March 1977, the law in the State of California was more severe on kidnapping and inflicting bodily harm with intent to rob than on kidnapping and inflicting bodily harm with intent to rape, and let us not pause here to explore the history of the anomaly.

The next day the judge, after taking explicit pains to verify that Smith and Smith's attorney desired that the proceedings should continue notwithstanding Smith's battered physical condition, summarized the testimony:

"As you know, the Court must judge the credibility of the witnesses who have testified. In determining the credibility of a witness, I may consider any matter that has a tendency, in reason, to prove or disprove the truthfulness of their testimony, including but not limited to, their demeanor while testifying and the manner in which they testify, the existence or nonexistence of a bias, interest or other motive, a statement previously made that is inconsistent with his or her testimony and his or her admission of untruthfulness.

"It appears to the Court that the defendant is the only one who would have a motive to testify untruthfully—kidnapping to commit robbery with bodily harm is punishable by life imprisonment without possibility of parole, while kidnapping [even with intent to rape] is punishable in the state prison for not less than one nor more than twenty-five years. The defendant is also the only witness who made statements previously that are inconsistent with his testimony at trial and the only one who has admitted untruthfulness.

"After an entire comparison and consideration of all the evidence I am convinced beyond a reasonable doubt that the defendant did commit the crimes charged against him in Counts One through Four of the Information.

"I therefore find the defendant Edgar Herbert Smith, Jr., guilty . . ."

The ball game?
Not yet.
Sentencing was set for three weeks later, April 21.
Edgar Smith moved for a new trial—on the grounds that on the day the verdict was given he was not, because of his injuries, "competent" under California law. Neely, recalling Smith's and his lawyer's waivers, and pointing out that Smith had conducted interviews with the press after the verdict, charged that his petition was "frivolous."

"I suppose, your honor"—Smith had insisted on taking the stand to argue his own motion—"it's somewhat incongruous that a person who has had the experience with the criminal justice system that I have had would harbor a respect for the system. I do. I have throughout my life held respect for criminal justice in this country. I haven't always agreed with everything that was done, but I haven't played games, except within the rules. I haven't exercised anything that I do not believe to be my right. I never in my life in any court, going as far back as a wooden-floored, folding-chair municipal courtroom on top of a rickety firehouse in Municipal Court in a small town in New Jersey, as far as the United States Supreme Court, ever filed a single motion, a single petition, or a single application for the purpose of delay. . . ."

(I thought back. February 3, 1965. The Supreme Court had

turned down Edgar's latest appeal. *"Throw me a parachute,"* he wrote to me in Switzerland. *"I've been shot down by the Warren Escadrille. It may take a few weeks to determine which way, legally speaking, I will go next. It appears that my best bet will be to hang up my appeal in some manner"*—he meant delaying action, for the sake of delay—*"in order to give the Supreme Court time to reach its* [other, possibly relevant] *decisions. Of course, delaying actions aren't ethical—but, then again, I'm not a lawyer, am I? Perhaps this would be a good time to ask the County Court to correct some of these minor errors in the record. . . ."*)

The judge denied the motion based on Smith's claims of incompetence on the day of judgment.

Edgar then made another request.

"I am a Mentally Disordered Sex Offender, your honor. I know it. I have probably known it all of my life. I didn't know what it was called, but I knew what it was.

"I have never in my life begged. I've never in my life pleaded, but today, your honor, I am going to beg and I am going to plead and I am going to appeal to the Court's compassion. I don't know whether I deserve the Court's compassion. I don't know whether I deserve anyone's; I certainly have very little for myself."

(March 28, 1965: *"I hate like hell to put you to a lot of trouble on my account, but I have to plan ahead. Quite frankly, Counsellor Smith is in somewhat of a quandary. Do I compromise my not too abundant principles and prepare the abject, bowing and fawning type of brief the State Courts have come to expect from indigent lay appellants? Or do I stand by what I know is right? . . . If it would do me any good, I would cry you a river—à la Julie London."*)

It did him no good.

Edgar's last tack was to raise the question of rehabilitation:

"I'm sure it's the People's position that I be sent to the penitentiary. If, your honor, I am in fact a Mentally Disordered Sex Offender, [and] I am sent to the penitentiary and I spend I don't know how many years, ten, fifteen, twenty, perhaps making license plates with cute little nicknames on them, when I'm released I'm *still* going to be a Mentally Disordered Sex Offender. The People will have gained nothing. The People will not have been protected. Now, I don't sit here, your honor, as an advocate of the People, but I do think it is in the People's interest that if there is some way that Edgar Smith, through treatment or through therapy, through whatever it is that they do in places like Atascadero, if there's any possibility that I can be turned into a human being, then, your honor, then the interest of the People would be served. . . . I need the chance, your honor. I know I have very little to recommend me. I've hurt people. I regret that. But, your honor, I can't change without help."

(December 6, 1971, in answer to a question put to him on television the night he left Trenton: *"I don't think you rehabilitate anybody. I don't think you can, even with all of the doctors and all of the sociologists and all of everyone. Put them in there, and they cannot rehabilitate anyone. A person has to rehabilitate himself. The best they can do is help him. Some men need education, some men need guidance, some men, like myself, need to be left alone."*)

Neely was ready again. "This defendant," he addressed the Court, "wants a chance to get up to the hospital and to manipulate so bad that he can taste it. If there's one thread that has run through everything that I have seen and your honor has seen, it is the statement by Dr. Goldzband: 'The problem is that [Smith] is using all of this knowledge not for any real insightful change but rather for manipulative purposes. This is a man with extraordinary intelligence, sensitivity and perceptive capacity, and he uses all of this to get around people.' "

The judge sentenced Edgar Smith to life, without possibility of parole. A year later, while upholding the conviction, the Supreme Court of California struck the parole provision to conform, retroactively, with fresh legislation on the question. Edgar Smith is now eligible for parole in October 1983.

Edgar Smith's conviction of the crime against Mrs. Ozbun was routinely treated by the press; not so his testimony that in fact he had killed Vickie Zielinski. Although that testimony came at trial six months after Mrs. Ozbun's victimization, and although Edgar's friends had unanimously concluded that he must have been guilty of the first crime, his actually saying so created a sensation of sorts. In particular, the New Jersey press was inflamed. In some of the commentary there was positive, indeed, voluptuary satisfaction. The former assistant prosecutor Edward Fitzpatrick did not suppress his glee, giving statements to the press and addressing an open letter to me all but accusing me of knifing Mrs. Ozbun myself. Reading over the clippings and the mail, one comes to the rueful conclusion that many people would have preferred reading a headline that Edgar Smith had killed another girl, to one announcing he had won a Nobel Prize.

The salient lesson to be learned from the public reaction is, really, that no *solutions* to the human predicament suggest themselves from the experience. Fitzpatrick told the Ridgewood *News* that now we must turn our attention to "what forces were at work" to put Edgar Smith back on the street. "It was as tight a case as I have ever seen, but there were powerful forces at work." What powerful forces? He can only have meant the Supreme Court. Impeach Warren? Or did he mean an author's right to champion a cause in the press? Repeal the First Amendment?

John Selser, Smith's original lawyer, who believed so profoundly in Smith's innocence, was quoted by the Associated Press: "He made a damned fool out of me." Selser now wished Smith had been executed. Since Selser hadn't believed Smith should be executed after he had been tried and convicted, he can only be understood to be saying that Smith should have been executed lest the risk be run that he live to make a fool out of John Selser.

Judge Pashman had ruled in Hackensack on December 6, 1971, that the case against Smith was properly murder in the second degree. Has anyone in recent U.S. history served longer than fourteen years for second-degree murder? After the San Diego conviction, the Bergen *Record* wrote editorially: "Edgar Smith is a bad man—a murderer, a psychopath, call him what you will. He is, in the antique phrase of prosecutors, a menace to society. He ought to be locked up for the rest of his life. We trust he will be." Yes—but does that illuminate the question of whether Judge Pashman was right to let him out? What are we to make of the expert psychiatric testimony that Edgar Smith was no longer a menace to society? Why did Fitzpatrick not stand up in court and object to the release of

Smith? Why—in fact—did he say in open court: "If your honor please . . . the State will recommend a sentence for Mr. Smith as would provide for his immediate release from incarceration . . . [The State is] motivated to this recommendation [by] the rehabilitation of this defendant as evidenced by the psychiatric reports which I know your honor is familiar with. And finally, it was the considered judgment of all those involved from the State's point of view that this plea would be a just disposition of this case at this time considering not only fairness to this defendant but also to our society."

Ideological opportunism is a full-time sport. The Paterson *News* pronounced: "Edgar H. Smith Jr., once the darling of the do-gooders, has finally confessed that he is a murderer. And by doing so he has advanced a strong argument in favor of capital punishment." Are we to execute second-degree murderers? Or only those second-degree murderers who, in the opinion of the New Jersey press, are clearly a menace to society? Much of the public was expressing the general frustration over the high crime rate and turnstile justice. It is common to personalize one's feelings. Joe Piscione of the Trenton *Times* conceded that "maybe the evidence I'd heard had helped cause my feeling. But I didn't like Edgar Smith one bit. I didn't like the way he leaned against the wall [at the courthouse in Newark] looking smug and flicking ashes on the polished floor."

The New York *Daily News* writer took satisfaction in the pain of Smith's advocates. "Buckley's satisfaction lasted for some time. It finally vanished five years later when he learned that he had been manipulated as if he was a country bumpkin." Guy W. Calissi, Jr., who originally prosecuted Smith, contributed the view that only those naïve few who believed the court-selected psychiatrist had any reason for "expressing any surprise"—suggesting what? That the particular psychiatrist tapped by Judge Pashman was incompetent? Or that psychiatry is incompetent? Calissi's son, who had written a privately published book in reply to Smith's book, reasserting Smith's guilt, suggested that "notables" should get out of the way. "There are hundreds of criminals out there ready and able to con, fool, and convince notables like Buckley."

The Philadelphia *Inquirer* editorialized: "Nobody quite knows what happened to the mind of Edgar Herbert Smith,

perhaps the most honored murderer of his generation, between the gold Cadillac days of 1972 and the clumsy, vicious
kidnapping and assault of a California woman last fall." Nobody quite knows. But are we to reason from the experience, a)
that in the future no one should listen to any claim made by
someone who insists he was unfairly prosecuted or unjustly
convicted? ("I never met one yet who wasn't . . .") or b) is it
merely "notables" who should get out of the way? Should
Arthur Miller have disdained to protest the conviction of the
Reilly boy—whose confession and conviction were subsequently upset, to the general satisfaction of the community?
and c) which of the specific decisions of the Warren Court
should be overturned? *Escobedo? Mapp?* I could be persuaded
—but why don't the high-dudgeon Smith people come out and
say it? Other than that I and Smith's other supporters were
wrong, which is obvious—without its being obvious that we
acted wrongly—what has come of it all? It is a pity that *nothing*
that is generally useful has been written as a result of the Smith
experience.

Or is he unique?

In a letter she wrote to me early last year, Paige Smith said,
"Did you read in the paper where he said, 'Big deal, I've only
been in jail twice,' or something to that effect? He is obviously
sick but has no way to get help. He told my mother that he is
bitter against me because I didn't stick by him. I thought I had
done a good job of sticking by him until I came to my senses.
Do you think I was wrong?" The letter referred to a quite
extraordinary interview with Edgar Smith. It was published in
the Bergen *Record* on February 19, 1978, under the by-line of
Henry Goldman, who reported extensively on Smith's current
views on various matters and people, and described how he
spent much of his time writing to his wife and was looking
forward to a conjugal visit with her as permitted by California
law. "I wanted you to know," Mrs. Smith continued in her
letter to me, "that I am *not* going to see him at all and he *does
not* spend his time writing to me. He spends his time fantasiz-
ing and working up stories. I don't know what to do about him
any more!"

The exact quotation from Smith, featured in the *Record*

story, was: "But, you know, twenty years between crimes ain't bad, when you compare it with the guys who come in here every few months after shooting this one, or stabbing that one." Smith of course has a very good point, which is that people who shoot and stab other people shouldn't go in and out of jails at the currently fashionable velocity, though that was not the point he was trying to make. He was altogether disposed to analyze his weakness for the benefit of the Bergen *Record:* "I may be uncontrollable at certain moments. If I could handle that one minute, I'd be all right. But until the time comes that I have to deal with it, I don't want to think about it." But of course others will think about it, most specifically the parole board, in October 1983.

Or maybe sooner? To a friend, he wrote in July 1977: "Yes, I have an appeal in progress, and yes, I will litigate them to death. And no, I do not expect to do as much time as some people suppose."

So he will litigate them to death. He knows how to do this, but this time it will be more difficult because there is no electric chair or gas chamber waiting for him at the other end, vesting his appeals with a special urgency. Moreover, the arraignment and the trial were conducted with the care and precision of an Apollo moon launch, and it is questionable whether even Edgar Smith will succeed in seining out of the experience reversible error. How then—apart from litigating —will he comport himself? In the *Record* interview he said: "I'm going to be a good boy. Good is out. And I do want to get out. I want that very badly. I'm getting old, but I'm a survivor, I have a few dragons to slay yet. I'm not sure who they are, or what they are, but they're out there, out in the world." When Edgar Smith uses the word *slay,* the dragons of this world are entitled to feel a slight sense of insecurity. Besides, at the rate of one victim every twenty years, as he puts it, there would be time for a third; indeed, given a geriatric breakthrough, conceivably even a fourth, who knows?

"I really wish you would write [another] story [about Edgar]," Paige wrote me after the trial. "I can understand why you would be hesitant, but I feel that you owe it to yourself, to everyone else and even me. I think the story has got to be told for everyone's sake." I replied by asking her what, in such a story, did she think should be stressed?

"Did you know," she answered, "that Edgar basically has no conscience? I still don't know the reason Edgar did what he did. I wonder if we will ever know? I know it wasn't rape and I know it wasn't robbery. I have searched and searched and the only answer I came up with is the one that the psychiatrist did: Edgar can't handle frustrations. You know, after rereading his books, I can see where he is the same person he was when he was twenty-three, only much brighter. That is really sad! What I don't understand is our judicial system. O.K., so Edgar is back in jail and will be there a long, long time. But he'll get out and be the same person he was when he went in. So, what good has putting him in prison done? [Ask Mrs. Ozbun.] Another thing is that Edgar loves attention. Did you know that Mrs. Ozbun is suing him? Well, I got a letter from him saying he would fight her in court!"

Did I know that Edgar loved attention? I have always supposed that anyone in prison loves attention. The warden, back in 1965 when I first visited Edgar, told me that, after a while, the prisoners get fewer and fewer letters, and then, in some cases, none at all. Yes, I devoted a lot of attention to Edgar, am doing so at this moment. When my name was raised with Smith last year, Smith said, "He's a little upset with me and I'm a little upset with him. He was the great, infallible, always right Mr. Conservative who suddenly thought he had been had. But I don't have much sympathy for Bill Buckley. He got his two-hour TV show. He got what he wanted to use me for."

I used Smith like Mrs. Ozbun used Smith, and it will be instructive to read his counterclaim after she has filed hers against him. But what would you expect? "I got out [of Trenton] because Fitzpatrick bargained me out," Smith has said. "He says he's angry because I lied. Actually, most people are angry because they believed me. I don't know what they expected me to do. Did they expect me to go to the chair?"

Or say he was sorry? Cry, à la Julie London? Now that he tried it on the judge—and it didn't work?

Edgar Smith is a most extraordinary man, highly gifted—his many paintings executed from imagination in that death cell have a special faculty and flair—with much social savvy and wit, qualities that won him friends and partisans among persons who had never dreamed of meeting, let alone befriending, a convicted murderer. The lesson of Edgar Smith must be stated carefully, must not be formulated in such a way as to be disfigured readily into generality. I don't know about other people. But it would seem plain that Edgar Smith must never be released from custody. This is truly tragic, using that solemn word most solemnly. But it's like what his manager once said about Sonny Liston. "You know, Liston has a lot of good qualities. It's his bad qualities that aren't so good."

2

Why No Eloquence?

June 1, 1978

JAMES RESTON, who is a very eloquent man, wonders what has happened to eloquence these days. His reference is to the performance thus far at the United Nations, where the mighty of the world have met to deplore the huge planetary budget for arms. It isn't that Reston expected that anything would come of it; nothing, really, ever does under UN sponsorship. But Reston bemoans the absent voices. Men like Roosevelt, and Churchill, and de Gaulle, he said, could by their eloquence affect events. Their successors—Carter, Giscard, Callaghan—speak, and all the birdies stay perched on the trees. Meanwhile the objective situation, as described, is quite awful. He recites the figures.

We are spending four hundred billion dollars per year on arms in the world, which is more than we are spending on education.

The figures rise notwithstanding the nuclear factor. One would think that with the invention of nuclear power, there would be less of a need for the conventional weapons. But of course it doesn't work that way because the success of nuclear technology has precisely the other effect: the weapon is so apocalyptic, it is necessary to rely on lesser weapons, so that the production of airplanes and tanks and machine guns and rifles continues unabated. And the poor nations are buying weapons valued at eight billion dollars per year. Symbolic of the emptiness of the big ritual in New York is that in the opening days as much time was given over to discussing a border fracas in Zaire as to the problem of armaments.

One hesitates to instruct Mr. Reston, but one does so anyway.

True eloquence is based on reality, even mythic reality. Prince Hal, delivering the most famous charge in the history of literature, exceeded even Knute Rockne's to the Notre Dame football team.

What would Shakespeare say about disarmament? He could make almost any cause beguiling, witty, ingenious; he could harness the language wonderfully to the uses of seduction, or ambition, or even treachery, these being great human passions. Indeed, viewed through contemporary prisms, King Harry was up to no good at Agincourt, coveting French territory on flimsy genealogical authority. Still, he stirred what then were accepted as honorable passions: to fight for king and country.

But the problem with attempting eloquence at the United Nations is that that which is affirmed by all the surrounding moral maxims is regularly and systematically flouted. The United Nations is about things like a covenant on human rights; about things like genocide; about self-rule; about the dignity of man. But the countries that dominate the United Nations have no use for these goals. This does not prevent them from praising them, which they do copiously. A speech by the ambassador from East Germany praising human liberty and democracy is as routine at the UN as a water fountain in Central Park.

But how then does a statesman go about appealing to such an assembly for world disarmament? Nations take up arms for reasons good and bad: to defend their liberties—and to wrest from others their liberties. We have not fought an imperialist war in the lifetime of all but American octogenarians. But it was only ten years ago that the Russians used their vast army to douse a flicker of liberalism in Czechoslovakia. The size of our hundred-billion-dollar-per-year budget is a function of the budget of the Soviet Union. If the communists disarmed, we could disarm; if the communists armed purely for the sake of self-protection, even then we could disarm. But the reality is that two great superpowers, the Chinese and the Russians, are bent on world revolution, and every state that opposes them, however tatterdemalion—Shaba Province is their most recent objective—is a nubile target. But how do we address them?

The trouble with the search for eloquence is that eloquence cannot issue except from telling the truth. And in the United Nations one is not permitted to tell the truth, because protocol is higher than the truth. The problem, then, is not so much the deterioration of the gift of eloquence as it is that constipation that must come when we are told to speak untruths, or to build our speeches on untruths. That is why the only great eloquence in the world today is that of Solzhenitsyn and his fellows—and they are not permitted to speak at the United Nations.

3

Final Rebuke

November 30, 1978

ON OCCASION I have recalled with merriment the story of the man who walked dejectedly from church one Sunday having been subjected to a thunderous reiteration of the Ten Commandments. As he reaches his car, his face suddenly brightens and he looks up at his wife triumphantly: "I've never made any graven images!"

The story loses its flavor, but not its bite, one week after Jonestown. "You shall not have other gods besides me. You shall not carve idols for yourselves in the shape of anything in the sky above or on the earth below or in the waters beneath the earth"—how natural it now seems that this should have been the very first commandment. And how regularly over the centuries we have been reminded of its awful relevance. There was "the mad attempt of Caligula to place his own statue in the temple of Jerusalem [which] was defeated by the unanimous resolution of a people who dreaded death much less than such an idolatrous profanation," recorded by Gibbon, who in a later volume went on to write of the Fatimite caliphs, among them "the famous Hakem, a frantic youth, who was delivered by his impiety and despotism from the fear either of God or man, and whose reign was a wild mixture of vice and folly."

And yet—and yet: Did they really die in vain? Certainly the answer is, yes, they died in vain if nothing is to be learned from their dying. But to say that Jim Jones was a monster, which indisputably he was, is not to say that he presided over monsters. No more can it be said that everyone who died for Hitler or for Stalin was monstrous. The men and women who lined up as meekly as the Aztecs (I can hear Phil Harris already: "What I admire about the Aztecs is they did it without Kool-Aid") understood themselves to be dying to uphold a principle. What principle? The grisly remains, far gone in putrefaction but still fleshly, seem suddenly to have been lost to us as irredeemably as ancient civilizations. There are living potsherds, and they mumble something about how they believed that Dad would look after them, how they would build a socialist society free of strife. They were undiscriminating men and women, but they were capable of giving their own lives in return for an ideal reified in the jungle of Guyana, and it is wrong to despise them, wrong even to despise those of them who administered the poison to their children.

The energumen was the leader. But he preyed not on the worst of man, but the best. He did not exhort his flock to pillage, plunder, and conquest. Jimmy Jones had his fasces, and from all accounts they were liberally used to keep in line those whose restive intelligence or natural hedonism questioned the ideals or resisted the spartan regimen. But there is no accounting for what finally happened except that it was a collective act of hara-kiri. There are the surrounding mysteries: among them the strange, lockstep arrangement of the corpses. But perhaps that too was rehearsed, and the exalting idea of form was also disfigured by the macabre symmetry.

No doubt they will raze Jonestown, as they did Berchtesgaden, and properly so. But there is no expunging the massacre from the memory. It is the supreme rebuke of our civilization. We, heirs of Chartres and the Beatitudes, who count among our progenitors St. John of the Cross and Aquinas, breed a race of men and women who, looking about them, go to Jimmy Jones for solace, for protection, for fulfillment. Will Mr. Califano find the need for a fresh division?

No, there is no role here for the state. "In things that prejudice the tranquillity or security of the state, secret actions are subject to human jurisdiction. But in those which offend the

Deity, where there is no public act, there can be no criminal matter; the whole passes between man and God, who knows the measure and time of His Vengeance." Thus Montesquieu. There was of course a public act—the killing of the children. But mostly, the act was public in its mute rejection, under the baton of a madman, of the alternatives our civilization proffered those wretched people.

4

Who Speaks for the Gays?

April 7, 1979

IT IS CLEAR that the heavy vote against liberalizing the homosexuality laws, the most conspicuous of which was in Florida after the campaign that made Anita Bryant famous, has intended to signify something more than mere hostility to sexual aberrants. In California, when the Briggs Amendment was proposed, the voters defeated it—because in their judgment (correct) it went too far in the direction of harassing intellectuals. Even so there are those who voted against the Briggs Amendment reluctantly, because it is increasingly clear that many aggressive gays, if you will pardon the oxymoron, are out for something much more than a mere respect for adult homosexual privacy. This is made clear in a publication called *Gala,* excerpts from which have been distributed by Anita Bryant's organization. What you have in that magazine is, so to speak, a reprimand by the militants of what one might call Straight Gays.

The author, who styles himself "Spokesperson, Coalition for Lesbian and Gay Rights, New York City," insists that the gay liberation movement is not making explicit demands for genuine liberation. "It is essential," the author writes, "that the gay liberation movement as a whole recognize and fight for the rights of children to control their own bodies, free from the antisexual restraints now imposed upon them by adults and by the institutions adults control—religion, the state, the legal profession, the schools, and the family."

The author, speaking for his association, gives the "ultimate goal of the gay liberation movement." It is "freedom of sexual expression for young people and children." Nothing less than that is genuine liberation. "We gain nothing by limiting our defense of homosexual love to consensual sex between adults. It is," he writes, "absurd to charge gay men who share their sexuality with boys as 'child molesters.' . . . Those of us who are struggling for gay rights are, moreover, hypocritical if we limit our demands to the protection of consenting adults." The issue of *Gala* carrying the article in question advertises buttons reflecting its opposition to morals based on the "primitive 'revelations' of the Bible" and calling for relief for "brothers and sisters who are victims of organized religion."

Now, this is a pretty unpleasant situation. Unpleasant because on the one hand it tends to confirm the suspicions of many voters: that the homosexuals are indeed after more than their demure demands for civil rights and privacy suggest. Unpleasant also because it is correct that many homosexuals in fact want merely this, but are inevitably linked with others whose iconoclasm is total and who insist that only when pedophilia is legally sanctioned and conventional is there effective liberation.

Now, every movement has its extremists. But most movements have the advantage of acknowledged leaders who dissociate themselves from the extremists. The American liberals' renunciation of communism in the thirties was an event of historical importance. The conservative rejection of the John Birch Society, of the anarchists and other fanatics, was an act of excretion essential to political and intellectual hygiene. A cause for justified criticism of black African leaders was their prolonged failure, only recently set right, to renounce Idi Amin.

But who are the acknowledged leaders of the homosexual rights movement? Although marches by gay rights people are no longer unusual, and in that sense it can be said that gays have come out of the closet, no name or names come readily to mind, in the way that the feminist movement suggests a half-dozen names of established leaders. *Their* problem has been the failure to dissociate their movement from the lesbian movement, notwithstanding an attempt, later recanted, by Betty Friedan. But the homosexuals have no spokesman of national prominence.

The crowning question is: If such a person emerged, or a council of acknowledged homosexual leaders, would they speak convincingly for the entire movement in rejecting the enormities of those gays who write of the necessity to legalize child molestation, indeed to encourage pederasty? To assault Judeo-Christian standards, morals, and ideals? Unless something of the sort is done, voters faced with Yes or No options on homosexual rights are for understandable reasons going to be tempted to say No. If the voter cannot be given the opportunity to discriminate, what is he expected to do?

5

The Prophet

June 14, 1979

THE POPE has come and gone, and what will the Polish people do now? And the Polish state? What, as Western instrumen-
talists like to put it, has been "accomplished"?

One strains for prophetic help. It is a coincidence so bizarre
as to defy credence. But halfway through John Paul's pilgrim-
age to his own country I had reason to forage in old files. I came
upon a letter from Whittaker Chambers which, because it had
been misplaced, was not published in the volume *Odyssey of a
Friend* (1970) and therefore has never been seen other than by
the addressee, twenty-two years ago.

Chambers wrote in April 1957, six months after the Russians
had quieted the Poles by appointing the tough-minded communist Gomulka as Polish satrap. Cardinal Wyszynski—then as
now—was primate of Polish Catholics. And Cardinal Wyszynski, who shaped the present Pope's political development,
launched Poland on a controversial course, dramatically at
odds with his counterpart in Hungary, the tortured, heroic,
ascetic Cardinal Mindszenty who, having lingered in communist dungeons, was freed for a few glorious days by the freedom fighters, only to take refuge in the American Embassy in
Budapest where he would live twenty years until he became
an embarrassment to détente. The two cardinals, one of them
breathing a kind of coffined defiance, the other going about the

streets of Polish towns attending shrewdly to his workaday chores as minister to the spiritual needs of his countrymen.

"Those Poles and Hungarians," Chambers wrote, "stand looking at us from the fastness of that difference which is rooted in a simpler experience of sweat, blood, filth, death.

". . . I have been a Wyszynski man *ab initio*. I have argued that his course was right because no other course was possible. I am afraid that I have deeply disappointed (perhaps even estranged) certain Catholic friends by my unbudgeability on this point. I point [to] . . . the contrasting attitudes of their Cardinals. No one who has not suffered so much may judge Cardinal Mindszenty, even if he were stupid enough to incline to. But contrasting policy results can be appreciated; I hold that the contrast favors the results in Poland. Early in the crisis, I took part in a private group discussion on these contrasting policies; a discussion that under its formal courtesy constantly threatened to flare, in part, I believe, because one faction was astonished to find me pro-Wyszynski, and took it as a defection. It is nothing of the kind. With the knife at your throat (the situation of the Poles and of their Cardinal), there are only two choices: to maneuver, *knowing fully the chances of failure*, but remembering that Hope is one of the Virtues; or to hold your neck still to the knife in the name of martyrdom.

"But just here is the crux. We are not talking about the Church Triumphant. We are talking about the Church in this world, the world of Warsaw and of Budapest, whose streets are of a drabness that squeezes the blood from the heart. In that sad light, the figure of the Polish Cardinal is a figure of hope. I say: we know nothing about these things. I say that what makes us all sick with a sickness we cannot diagnose is that, in the current crisis, the West has gained the world (or thinks it has), but has lost its own soul. I say: the Poles and the Hungarians have lost the world (or whatever makes it bearable—they live in Hell), but they have gained their own souls. What price, Power without purpose? Dulles mouthing moralities while on the streets of Budapest children patrolled the shattered house-fronts, with slung rifles and tormented faces. I say those children, whatever their politics, will have grown to men while Dulles and his tribe lie howling. . . .

"That is why I keep beside Wyszynski. That is why Gomulka

keeps beside him and he beside Gomulka. In each other they recognize men; they are scarce enough. How lonely these two men must be. Was ever such loneliness endured, and not made less by the knowledge, clear to both, that, under necessity, Gomulka may destroy the Cardinal before he is destroyed himself. But these men at least acted: I think we must see this clearly."

It is difficult to see clearly through to the meaning of Wyszynski's successor, now the bishop of Rome, in Poland, dealing with the successor to Gomulka. But who can deny that those of us who thought Mindszenty right, Wyszynski wrong, lacked the prophetic insight of Whittaker Chambers?

6

One More Time

CHÂTEAU-THIERRY, FRANCE.—On May 27, 1918, the German army of Kaiser Wilhelm mounted an offensive fifty miles northeast of Paris designed to overwhelm the Allied forces, conquer Paris, and win the war. They were stopped, but a deep salient was held, the spearpoint of which was Belleau Wood. Freshly arrived American troops were hurled against this salient, the wood was reconquered, the Germans driven back, regrouping for the July 15 offensive that failed, giving the Allies the armistice of November 11. By the side of Belleau Wood is a cemetery comprising 2,800 graves of U.S. marines and infantrymen, less than half those killed in that single engagement. On the momument is written, "TIME WILL NOT DIM THE GLORY OF THEIR DEEDS," which is something we might put down as "battlefield prose." Valedictorians at U.S. high schools have never even heard of Belleau Wood. We lost 53,000 men in World War I, to protect Europe from a hegemony dominated by a grandson of Queen Victoria. Fifty-three thousand dead is a lot of dead Americans, but in fact we were only warming up for the Second World War To Rescue European Diplomacy From Itself. In that war, U.S. casualties came to 292,000. For reasons not instantly persuasive, we suddenly find that the strongest argument coming from the Administration in favor of SALT II is that if we don't ratify it, Europe will refuse to deploy U.S. weapons designed to protect Europe.

It does sound preposterous put that way, so let us attempt to compress their arguments in the most favorable light. They go as follows: if we do not sign SALT II, the Russians will MIRV up their European-aimed SS-20 missiles from their present strength (about two thousand) to a projected 3,500 by mid-1985.

Now (the Europeans are saying) we want to get on with the business of denuclearizing the European theater. But that can only come after we achieve some kind of limitation on strategic weapons, and that means SALT II. If you Americans don't get on with SALT II, how can we get on with SALT III?—so sour will East-West relations be.

What the Europeans threaten is to decline to deploy the cruise missiles and ballistic nuclear missiles (about six hundred) which are otherwise scheduled to be put in place over the next few years. The reasoning is that to proceed with such missiles might strike the Soviets as provocative, and to provoke the Soviets is a much more dangerous thing than to enfeeble Europe. Senator Nunn, contemplating the arguments of the Administration, put it very well: "Over the long term, I don't think the American people will continue to support an alliance that has to be convinced on most occasions to take steps to defend itself."

It is difficult to see how one can express the dilemma (if we agree to SALT, we perpetuate a critical Soviet advantage; if we don't, we threaten the Western alliance) other than by acknowledging that if it is correct—i.e., if those are the only alternatives—then, in fact, the Soviet Union has begun to assert control over European politics. And will continue to do so, giving an extradimensional meaning to Lenin's fabled arrival at the Finland Station in 1917. The Finlandization of Europe is a development that has been warned against, and predicted, for twenty-five years. It is on the verge of happening.

Now, it might have been otherwise, and even now it could change. If Mr. Carter, a year ago, had deployed the neutron bomb, and, the year before that, authorized the Defense Department to proceed with the B-1 bomber, European leaders would arrive at the next NATO conference in December with knees less wobbly. Even so, if Hitler had been stopped at the Rhineland, he would never have strutted into Paris. No doubt much of Europe was demoralized by Henry Kissinger's recent speech in which he confessed the truth of the matter, namely that the United States would not likely hostage one hundred million Americans in return for the safety of Europe: other trade-offs must be sought out, the only obvious one being preparation to successfully resist land war in Europe. In which the critical battle, one would hope, would take place somewhere east of Château-Thierry.

Europeans should be advised that American senators planning to vote against SALT are not to be likened to those isolationists who voted against the League of Nations. Senators of this breed—Baker, Nunn, Garn, Hollings, Tower, to name a few—are sophisticated men; men who have done their homework; men committed to taking every reasonable step to defend Europe; men who genuinely believe that the Soviet Union, if this treaty is rejected, will in fact acquiesce in a new treaty that makes sense. Sense here defined as sense for the West, as well as for the communists.

7

Marx Is Dead

January 24, 1980

ALTHOUGH it is likely that more academic and philosophical attention has been devoted in the last fifty years to the flowering of Marxist thought and to life under Marxism, it is astonishing how little thought is given to the great residual paradox. It is expressed in the antipodal manifestos of our time. The first is the voice of Solzhenitsyn—a single voice to be sure, but it is the voice of baptized humanity. What he said is that there is probably not one believing Marxist in Moscow. The contrary voice is the voice of—the Politburo: a great assembly of lords secular, disposing of three thousand silos armed with hydrogen bombs, the world's greatest army, navy, and submarine force commanding the greatest satellite empire since Rome's. They are fighting for the most penetrable idiocies in the history of superstition; and yet on and on they go.

What would the Soviet Union be, if you stripped it of its ideological pretensions? The answer to that question is most easily given, one supposes, if it were asked of, say, Machel in Mozambique, or Castro, or the Ethiopian sadist; or those grisly impostors in France and Italy and East Germany. There are three typhonic vectors in the postwar world. One of them is nationalism. The second—related—is anti-imperialism. The

third is Marxist imperialism. Although every nation represented in the United Nations, ourselves included, will vote
against imperialism, very nearly as many (subtract a dozen)
regularly vote to ratify the Soviet Union's de facto imperialism.
Although every nation will swear out a blood oath against
tyranny, the majority will back tyranny—as long as it is done in
the holy name of Marx. Find yourself any old country, impov-
erished, agricultural, illiterate: by rigorous definition laid down
by Marx himself, lacking the constituent parts to pass over into
communism. But you need only require that the prevailing
tyrant declare himself to be a Marxist, and the propaganda war
is half won. If Machel of Mozambique had said everything he
had said, done everything he had done, but announced that he
was just a good old-fashioned bourgeois despot, he'd have been
the target of universal obloquy from the beginning, in 1974.
He has only to say that he is a Marxist, and he is accounted
blessed among the ignorant, and the cynical, of this world.

The question arises: Why doesn't the West take better advantage of the palpable superstitions? The obvious differences
apart, Karl Marx was no more reliable a prophet than was the
Reverend Jim Jones. Karl Marx was a genius, an uncannily
resourceful manipulator of world history who shoved everything he knew, thought, and devised into a Ouija board from
whose movements he decocted universal laws. He had his
following, during the late phases of the Industrial Revolution.
But he was discredited by historical experience longer ago
than the Wizard of Oz: and still, great grown people sit around,
declare themselves to be Marxists, and make excuses for Gulag
and Afghanistan.

The Republican candidate for President of the United States
should declare himself devoted absolutely to the total atomiza-
tion of the Marxist myth. He doesn't need to conscript think-
ers-for-hire. The thinking has been done. The research has
been done. History is there begging to be used as witness
before the court of the people. The demonstration, at a private
level, has been done by the poets, historians, and martyrs of
our time. It requires only that it become an official crusade, one
to which we will attach ourselves as vigorously as if we were
spreading the word of how to extirpate smallpox from the fetid
corners of the world.

This then is the miracle that can exploit the technology of communications. The Voice of America? Hell, the voice of humanity. If we undertake a systematic, devoted, evangelical effort to instruct the people of the world that the Soviet Union is animated not by a salvific ideology, but by a reactionary desire to kill and torture, intimidate and exploit others, for the benefit of its own recidivist national appetites for imperialism —we will have done, by peaceful means, what is so long overdue. We will have buried Marx, and Marxism, in that common grave in which he belongs, together with such recent historical figures as Jim Jones, or such ancient historical impostors as Lucifer.

8

Do You Favor the Draft?

April 24, 1980

ACTIVISM at the college level, one learns, is all but dormant, with one or two exceptions. The enthusiasm for John Anderson is considerable, and that's a good sign, suggesting that Anderson wouldn't stand a chance nationally. The only other cause militant is the question of the draft. And that of course is understandable. The draft is democracy's contribution to total servitude. Not only do you have to get up in the morning at six in order to perform calisthenics, you have to dig trenches, sleep in them on occasion, face bullets of the same caliber used by execution squads and—worst of all—address your tormentors as "sir."

Still, the draft-protest statements are being circulated in the colleges; if the single example of them that I have seen is typical ("I [do] [do not] approve of a national registration designed to facilitate a draft" . . .), then the questionnaire is not as searching as it ought to be. I submit the following as a suggested questionnaire to replace the versions being circulated.

STUDENT POLL:

1) I believe there should be a national registration of Americans between the ages of 18 and 26 in order to facilitate, if and

when Congress deems it necessary, the induction of men (and possibly women) into the armed services.

1a) I do not believe there should be a national registration (check one):

1a(i): at this time; 1a(ii): at any time.

If you have checked 1a (ii) above, please proceed with the following:

2) I believe that national registration should be for Americans older than 26, but younger than 36.

2a) I believe that national registration should be for Americans older than 36.

2b) I believe that there shouldn't be a national registration under any circumstances.

If you have checked 2b above, please proceed with the following:

3) I believe that the manpower required to underwrite our foreign policy should be drawn from volunteers. If there are, at the present level of induction, insufficient volunteers, I would favor offering a draftee (check one):

3a) $5,000 per year

3b) $10,000 per year

3c) $15,000 per year

3d) $20,000 per year

3e) $25,000 per year

3f) (supply maximum figure)

If you have checked 3c above, or any figure in excess of 3c, please proceed with the following:

4) I believe that the money necessary to finance the volunteer army should be drawn from:

4a) Windfall profits taxes.

If 4a should prove insufficient, please proceed with the following:

4b) Send the bill to Mom and Dad.

4c) Increase my tuition at college, as required.

4d) None of the above: I don't believe in increasing our defense budget above the present level.

If your answer to the above is 4d, please proceed with the following:

5) The United States should withdraw from its outstanding alliances.

5a) The United States should withdraw from its outstanding alliances with the exception of:

5b) Israel.

5c) Other (please state).

5d) No exceptions.

If your answer to the above is 5d, please proceed with the following:

6) U.S. policy should be confined to the defense of the fifty states of the Union.

6a) Provided those states can be defended by the existing defense budget.

6b) Alternatively, we should rely exclusively on our nuclear deterrent.

If your answer to the above is 6b, please proceed with the following:

7) I am in favor of the use of nuclear power to deter attacks on U.S. sovereignty.

7a) I am not in favor of the use of nuclear power to deter attacks on U.S. sovereignty.

If your answer is 7a, please proceed with the following:

8) I am in favor of surrendering to the Soviet Union now.

8a) I am in favor of surrendering to the Soviet Union (check one):

8b) Tomorrow.

8c) A year from tomorrow.

8d) (supply date)

8e) Never.

If your answer is 8e, please begin again with question No. 1.

9

Cardinal Arns, Socialist

November 15, 1980

SÃO PAULO, Nov. 11—If you think it is easy to probe the thought of Catholic socialists, try spending one hour with the senior figure in the Brazilian hierarchy, the Archbishop of São Paulo, Paulo Evarista Cardinal Arns.

He walks into the studio radiating benevolence. Here is a man who studied literature at the Sorbonne in Paris, where he achieved his doctorate; who taught patrology and didactics at highly respected universities; who has written twenty-five books, including abstruse treaties on medieval literature. At the end of an hour, one seriously doubts that he knows what a supply-demand curve is; or cares. But, when you come down to it, if you had an hour to spend with St. Francis of Assisi (who founded the order of which Cardinal Arns is a member) you probably wouldn't talk to him about supply and demand; I'd have felt better just sitting and cooing with Cardinal Arns. Come to think of it, he did treat me about as St. Francis did the wild animals.

Last July, when the Pope was in town, everyone's eyes were trained on him to see how he would handle the problem of Cardinal Arns. The problem of Cardinal Arns is roughly defined by his gentle and plainspoken contumacy. Two years ago he egged on the metal workers in São Paulo, who were striking illegally. Brazil is a dictatorship of sorts (Goulart, who was

Brazil's Allende, was overthrown in 1964), and only in the past year or two has there been a genuine liberalization. Torture is, by everyone's admission, a perversion of the past; and in 1982 elections are expected, right up and down the line. But there are many who doubt they will eventuate. There are signs of deterioration, including in the morale of a normally indomitably happy race of people. And there is the turmoil in the most stable of Brazil's institutions—the Church.

So that when Pope John Paul stood up in the huge soccer stadium, it was everywhere noticed that he hugged with special tenacity Cardinal Arns. To be sure the cardinal was the senior hierarchical figure in São Paulo, but the Pope, it is generally conceded, intended more. What did he intend?

Again, try to get it from Cardinal Arns. He will smile. His English, though thoroughly functional, is imperfect. He would rather, he smiled—a smile so warm and ingenuous there is no doubting the sincerity that animates it—he would rather, he says, speak to you in Brazilian, Italian, French, German, or Latin. But the exchange is being televised; and, although the swanks at PBS are pretty proud of their audiences, an exchange in Latin would probably be thought *de trop*. What, concretely, you ask the cardinal, is his economic program for the poor in Brazil? He will answer that neither capitalism nor communism has helped the poor. You reply that in America capitalism has greatly helped the poor. He will answer that the people must know each other, in small communities, must love each other, and work together, and pool their talents. You agree, and you say that the income per capita in Brazil is on the order of $600 per person, and taking the money from the rich and giving it to the poor wouldn't help the poor to the point where they would even notice it. The cardinal smiles, and says gently that he was invited to talk about religion, and suddenly he is asked questions about economics, which is not his field.

Manifestly. A number of years ago Roberto de Oliveira Campos, Minister of Planning in the government of Castelo Branco (who overthrew Goulart), wrote about the *"profundo desinformacao clerical"* in respect of economics. Archbishop Pirés of Paraiba distributes visual-aid cards, on one of which is a huge bloated steer. The caption: "The name of the steer is capitalism, and capitalism is the gimmick of the wealthy minority to

mislead society into thinking that the most important thing is
money and profits. There are actually very few who profit, and
they do so by making the poor much poorer. Capitalism puts
money in the hands of the few, money that was obtained
through the sweat of many poor workers." I read that passage
to Cardinal Arns and asked if he agreed with it.

He smiled. Archbishop Pirés, he said, is a wonderful man, a
holy man. You give up.

10

On Right and Wrong

March 7, 1981

A CASUAL LINE, thoughtlessly dropped in *Newsweek* in a report on stalled SALT negotiations, gives us a clue to the principal moral responsibility of the Reagan administration, which is persuasively to reassert certain truths that distinguish us from those we seek to protect ourselves against. In citing the dangers of a nuclear buildup, *Newsweek* correspondents conclude: "At best, the extra billions of dollars for defense would severely drain both countries' economies. At worst, the pell-mell, action-reaction cycle would produce a temporary advantage for one side that it might be tempted to exploit."

Both sides. Who began that stuff? Probably the worst expression of it was in a speech given at Yale by Senator William Fulbright in the sixties. George Kennan, when he gets clinical, oversterilizes his vocabulary, and before long you see the Soviet Union as the A team and the U.S. as the B team, all very simple. Probably the worst of the lot, both because he spoke always from an august pedestal, and because he spoke augustly, was Charles de Gaulle. Above all because his statements were taken to be informed by a distinctive historical sweep and guided by right reason. He referred, on several occasions, to *"les deux hégémonies."* "The two hegemonies." He would have been altogether dumbfounded if Winston Churchill had referred to the Vichy government, dominated by the Nazis, and the exile government, dominated by de Gaulle, as "France's two contending governments."

The nadir in our period of self-abuse came during the Vietnam war, when such as Noam Chomsky of MIT, and others mostly forgotten but whose moral reasoning continues its extraordinary resonance in the academies and in the press, denounced America. It became altogether routine to make comparisons between Americans and North Vietnamese, to the disadvantage of Americans. For Soviet propagandists to construe the United States as the aggressor nation is routine stuff. It ought not to be routine stuff for Americans to accept lackadaisically the most significant triumph of the communist-aggressor movement, which is to persuade so many that there are, as between the Soviet Union and the United States, merely historical-cultural differences. The difference between us isn't that we are saints and they sinners. It is that we seek to be saints and they seek to be sinners: sainthood here defined as the acceptance of the individual human being as a man born to be free; sin here defined as the de-divinization of man in pursuit of secular ideology.

What's the matter with *Newsweek*? For twenty years the United States had conclusive military and nuclear superiority. I don't know a single public figure who proposed that we should use it to dispose preemptively of the creeping Soviet menace. At the end of 1945 we occupied Germany, Japan, Italy, and a dozen peripheral countries. We could, had we been so disposed, have colonized Great Britain and France. Instead we got out of all those countries, gave the Philippines their independence, and, after a generation's entreaty, agreed to annex Hawaii and Alaska as sovereign states.

Newsweek secured an interview with Rubin Zamora, who is emerging as the principal spokesman for the revolutionaries in El Salvador. *Question:* "Why did the American government release its so-called white paper claiming [note: 'claiming,' not 'demonstrating'] outside meddling in El Salvador?"

Answer: "The United States is up to its neck in support for a genocidal government . . . It's so similar to what the United States was saying just before its 1965 intervention in the Dominican Republic. My personal feeling is great sorrow."

My personal feeling is that talking with Mr. Zamora other than behind bars is a waste of time. Find me a member of the Reagan administration interested in genocide. Why did the overwhelming majority of the Organization of American States support President Johnson's intervention in the Dominican Republic? How long did U.S. troops stay there? Who backed democratic practices there during the last election?

The government of El Salvador is a mess. It has gone through thirty upheavals since 1932. The notion that the clouds would part and posies spring up in the pavements of San Salvador if only the junta redistributed the land is as naïve as that we are intervening in El Salvador because we like to support people engaged in killing other people. Reagan is right: the distinction between the Duartes of this world and the Zamoras of this world is a distinction within which we need to maneuver. But let us be morally assertive. It is not chauvinistic to announce that the United States will not tolerate another Soviet-dominated abscess in the Western Hemisphere, and if people don't understand why, then they are moral idiots.

11

Say Again?

March 17, 1981

ALFRED NORTH WHITEHEAD is often quoted as having observed that historians learn the most about any culture by studying what it is that that culture never got around to saying about itself. Because that is what a culture takes for granted: the inbuilt premises, the planted axioms. The headline in the *International Herald Tribune* splashed across five columns is "U.S. Budget Seen as Hurting the Poor, Aiding the Rich." The story is from the Washington *Post* service and written by Robert Kaiser, a superb journalist who ought, really, to know better, though it is the point of this cautionary tale precisely that, with luminous exceptions, people *don't* know better. They look at Reagan's budget and say, as Kaiser does, "its most obvious effect would be to redistribute income in the United States. The money would go from poor to rich."

The superstition is that to restore to somebody something that is his is to take something from somebody else. Perhaps Mr. Kaiser would have greeted Lincoln's Emancipation Proclamation with the headline: "President Lincoln Endorses Massive Tax Break for Black Poor." It appears to be impossible to get anyone to acknowledge that if someone is paying 70 percent of his, repeat his, income to the government, and you propose to reduce taxation from 70 percent to 63 percent, you are not "giving" that man something. What you are doing, of course, is taking less than what you were taking. If you stop blowing cigarette smoke into the face of the man seated next to you, you are not "giving" him clean air, you are desisting in your pollution of the air he breathes. It is thirty years since two scholars in Chicago published their book, so felicitously titled *The Uneasy Case for Progressive Income Taxation.* Well, it is to say the least uneasy: it violates the most fundamental rules of equality under the law. The same people who in behalf of women's rights or minority rights will go anywhere except Vietnam to fight for equal pay for equal work are quite prepared to make a woman or a black pay twice as much as a white male if that woman or that black goes out and earns twice as much money by working longer hours or by cultivating special skills.

So that at a philosophical level, the story is illiterate. It is equally offensive, however, as a piece of "news analysis"—which is how the editors presented it, at least in Europe—in its failure to make the dominant economic point, which is that under existing economic arrangements—i.e., the existing configuration of taxes, spending, and deficits—we are running an inflation rate of 13 percent and achieving a zero growth rate. Inflation doesn't, noblesse oblige, decline to afflict poor people. It is entirely undiscriminating. But it is poor people who suffer the most because net decreases in their purchasing power deny them items necessary to physical, not merely psychic, comfort. It requires a very hard commitment to the vocabulary of class antagonism to suggest that a budget primarily designed a) to fight inflation, and b) to increase productivity, is a budget aptly described as "Hurting the Poor, Aiding the Rich."

Mr. Reagan has high hopes that his program will slowly arrest and finally reduce inflation to 3 or 4 percent. If he can contrive to do this, and also resume economic growth, he will have done more to help poor people than two-thirds of the social legislation on the books.

The writer Tom Bethell, for the exercise of it, counted the cross-references over a period of one month, while watching the nationally televised news, to causes of inflation when the subject was inflation. Time after time the best-informed men in America, commanding the greatest research facilities, would mention, oh, OPEC oil, and corporate profits, as the putative causes of inflation; and hardly ever a) deficit financing, b) lower productivity, c) increased public spending, d) high marginal tax rates.

It is extremely difficult to get used to pristine conceptualization. I suppose that if every day during the past twenty years the editor of the Washington *Post* had begun his morning by giving Mr. Kaiser a hotfoot, and suddenly he stopped doing so, Mr. Kaiser would instinctively write a story crediting the editor with stabilizing his body temperature. Mr. Reagan really ought to devote one entire speech to teaching American journalists how to climb out of the superstitions in which they were inculcated at places like Yale.

12

A Reasonable Compromise

April 14, 1981

Friends whose reasoning and emotions are highly esteemed
have asked that I reconsider my position on gun control, and
these words are written to honor that request.

Let us, instead of rehearsing the usual arguments, inquire
into what actually would happen if gun control were to go into
effect: specifically, a law that required owners of handguns to
turn these in. Let us assume a law as sensible as we can conceive it. Call it the Small Arms Control Act of 1981 . . .

1) SACA begins by making exceptions. Licenses to own and
carry pistols will be granted to persons whose professions logically suppose that they be armed. The Secret Service, the FBI,
policemen, Brinks guards—that, substantially, would be it.

2) Non-license holders would be required to turn in their
handguns by, let us say, October 1, 1981. Federal buildings
would be designated to receive these weapons during the
month of September. A schedule of values would be posted so
that everyone turning in a gun would be reimbursed such
sums as are listed on the same kind of schedule one consults to
ascertain the value of a used car.

3) Anyone caught in the possession of a pistol after October
1, 1981, would be sentenced to spend one year in jail. SACA
would provide for no exceptions to this rule.

What would happen?

To begin with, something on the order of a national debate on the issue of compliance. It is generally accepted that if noncompliance is endemic, prosecutions are at best erratic. There are laws in most states against the possession of marijuana, and in all states against the purveying of marijuana. As much is true for heroin and other drugs. Marijuana is not much more difficult to obtain than beer. In fact it is said to be easier to purchase in areas thickly populated by young people. The reason for this is that a liquor store selling beer to a minor stands to lose something of substantial value, namely its liquor license. Marijuana salesmen don't have expensive overheads, and so are not easily punished. If by the end of September something on the order of explicit, massive resistance to SACA were to consolidate, the act would be dead.

Let us, however, assume that the American people decided that, after all, the law is the law; decided, in overwhelming numbers, to comply. Let us go so far as to say that 90 percent of all handguns were turned in.

That would leave five million illegal handguns.

During the ensuing year, let us suppose that 1,000 prosecutions of persons caught possessing a handgun were initiated and let us suppose, just to suppose, that all of them proved successful. So, 1,000 people go to jail, generating enormous publicity, and we have arrived at October 2, 1982. The President goes on television and announces that he will grant a general amnesty to all Americans who did not turn in their handguns as required under SACA, an amnesty that will extend through the month of October, expiring on November 1. A sulky line of men and women forms the next day outside the federal office, and during the next three weeks three million guns are turned in.

That leaves two million still in illegal hands.

I should think that the figures, given the scenario, would be instantly reassuring at the level of handgun crime of the domestic variety. Fewer husbands would be shot by irate wives, and fewer wives by irate husbands.

Would fewer nondomestic crimes aided by handguns occur?

It isn't easy to say. Probably not at the level of assassinations. Governor George Wallace, asked for his views, said last week in his best anti-pointy-head prose that a man willing to suffer the consequences of an attempted assassination is willing to suffer the consequences of being caught carrying an illegal handgun. Conceivably—let us permit ourselves to think it—we would have given birth to a slowly gestating ethos. An example would be the strides made during the past forty years in arresting anti-Semitism. There came a point where it wasn't accepted. A very prominent New Yorker told me a while ago that he would leave the room if such a remark as was routinely made at the dinner table of his parents were made in his presence today. Would such an attitude toward handguns materialize?

At this point one asks, really, the ultimate question: Would *you* obey that law? I guess I own four or five of those things, always have, used to shoot snakes and things as a boy, and woodchucks. I even have a permit to carry one in my pocket in New York City, dispensed after a rather imaginative threat on my life when I ran for mayor of New York. Would I hang on to one of these, in my home, against the contingency of the man with the knife—or with the gun—coming at me or my wife?

If I could answer that question with assurance, I'd have a better idea of whether SACA would work.

13

Growing Up Absurd

April 21, 1981

I HAVE BEEN traveling about colleges, and remit information and impressions of general interest.

College A. The university in question has a considerable enrollment, and it transpires that it is an Open Admissions institution. That means that in order to gain admission it is required only that you produce a high school diploma.

"I was disappointed," I said to a professor later in the evening, in isolated circumstances, "that there weren't any black students at the lecture."

"They won't come out in any numbers other than for Jesse Jackson or Coretta King. They constitute 20 percent of the college population. At least the same percentage of white students are as listless. I would guess that half the blacks and half the lower quintile whites can't a) add fractions, or b) read a newspaper."

"You're kidding."

"I am not kidding."

"How do they pass their exams?"

"They don't. But the administration doesn't expel them, because to do so means one less body against which to claim the annual subsidy from the state capitol."

"So what happens to them?"

"They are put on probation. It isn't easy for a student here to

know what the difference is between being on probation and
not being on probation. Life goes on exactly as before. After
about two and a half years they have to weed out. The student
leaves, and he's mad at the college, mad at his teachers, mad at
the state, and probably mad at the truck-driving firm that gives
him a job."

College B. An informal situation, before the main event.
Question period. A student asks whether the state isn't
"wrong" in exercising such powers as were exercised e.g. by
Franco and Allende to maintain power.

I answer: States are amoral institutions. In a "state" inheres
the authority to preserve itself. My sympathies, obviously, are
with George Washington, but if the British had captured
George Washington, tried him for treason, and hanged him, no
one would with any historical or philosophical justification
have had a case against the behavior of the Brits who hanged
the Father of Our Country. "A state exercises power with the
same authority whether the state is governed by Pericles or
Caligula."

Big Scene, following the episode above recounted. Woman
reporter approaches speaker:

"Just where do you get off mentioning 'Caligula' and 'Pericles' when talking to college students?"

"Excuse me, ma'am?"

Repeats question.

"I was talking to fifty seniors in a college that ranks among
the top twenty in the United States. Just what is your point?"

"My point is that there is no reason whatever for you to
suppose that these students have ever heard of Caligula or
Pericles."

—For want of another formulation: "You must be kidding."

"I am not kidding."

"I don't believe you."

"Would you like me to go out and ask?"

"Yes. But before you do that, wait one minute. Let's assume
that these college seniors did once know that Pericles was a
famous Athenian general, that he became the ruler of Athens,
was widely regarded for the grandness of his rule, indeed giving rise to the designation, 'The Age of Pericles.' And can we
grant, that even before the *Penthouse* people made a grisly

movie about the Emperor Caligula, he was known as a sadistic maniac, as well known as Nero—who is surely well known if only because we can't think who else fiddled while Rome burned? And anyway, in a rhetorical formulation in which the speaker is clearly reaching for antipodes, he needn't depend absolutely on a student's precise knowledge of history to be satisfied that if he speaks such a sentence as, 'irrespective of whether you're talking about Adolf Hitler or Florence Nightingale,' the student will know that one of the above characters was a bad guy, one a good guy, and will probably guess by the rhetorical accents of the speaker which was which."

The lady went out with paper and pencil to establish how many students knew the difference between Pericles and Caligula. A few minutes later she sent word that her score was, so far, four out of four—who didn't know the difference.

I don't believe it. But if it's true, shall we all just agree—fatalistically—to give it all up?

14

The Reign of Spain

April 23, 1981

SEVILLE.—At a little kiosk near the park is a child's mechanical rocking horse. You insert 25 pesetas, and for ten minutes your little boy or girl rocks around the clock, gasping with pleasure while holding on hard to the little wood extuberances that serve as bridles, while the child's feet rest on stirrups adjustable to the length of his legs. As the horse bounces about, your eyes focus behind the child at the windowpane of the kiosk. A magazine is held open by clothespins. It depicts, six inches from the child's head, in photographic detail, acts of male homosexuals.

A few minutes earlier, the cardinal of Seville, officiating at mass on Holy Thursday at the great cathedral, addressed a reverential mass of people. Seated directly in front of the cardinal, a few yards removed from the steps to the altar, is the mayor of Seville. And directly behind him is Calvo-Sotelo, the prime minister of Spain. They are listening to the cardinal's words, but the mind almost necessarily wanders. The kiosk outside is in the same town whose antecedent primate, the famed and feared Segura, died twenty-five years ago shortly after pronouncing excommunication on anyone—man, woman, married, unmarried—who danced. A pious people, the Andalusians; but a few weeks after the death of His Eminence, a tourist guide, answering a question from an American about what was it like in Seville with the cardinal dead, answered: "When Cardinal Segura died, he, and we, passed on into a better world."

The differences between then and now flash through the minds of the worshippers, who that night would not, most of them, go to their beds until after seven in the morning, since the long evening would be given over to marching in one or more of the many processions, along with huge elaborate gilded, silvered floats, bearing thousands of candles weighing up to four thousand pounds, carrying statues of the Virgin, images of Christ and his tormentors, released from their sanctuaries in neighborhood churches to wander through the crowded streets of the city during the holy days. They would stop every hundred yards—the men who bore the weight could not go farther without pausing—and from time to time they would be greeted by a lone voice, male or female, rising up from the crowd, singing out devotional chants in the strangled, erotic, minor mode of the flamenco singers. Three, four, five minutes of silence from the crowd while the singer, deserting his profane art, turned his talent to the service of God.

And when they would sit down, finally, to eat, at two or three or four in the morning, the conversation would turn to politics. Turn, specifically, to the great trauma of February 23. No historical event in Spanish history since the civil war has had a greater impact upon the Spanish people. Suddenly, viewing on television one army officer, machine gun in hand, holding the parliament at bay, they recognized that the changes are perhaps disordered: something on the order of hysteresis, a lag that follows an effective cause. From zero political freedom to freedom for communists, and something less than effective repression of terrorism. From unquestioned national unity to separatism in the north. From suspicion of normal heterosexual dancing in Seville to open displays of perversion, literally in the line of sight of children.

Everyone has his theory of things. One (highly popular) is that the king himself, recognizing that the social and political trajectory could not go on without creating disorder, obliquely and contingently colluded with the generals. A second has it that precisely because the king was the clear and present abortifacient of the revolution, the king (next time) would be the first to go: either by assassination (less likely), or exile or confinement (more likely). Others say that Calvo-Sotelo has, maximum, three months during which to *"imponerse"* (hard to translate: so to speak, to become the dominant figure); otherwise, incipient chaos, and back to the generals. The position on the generals is ambivalent. Say what you like about Franco, the Spanish people—those of them who were willing to let their political appetites hibernate—did well. They prospered economically—all classes of Spaniards. And the peace was longer under Franco than at any other time in Spanish history. Forty years of relative prosperity, peace and independence are, for many Spaniards, a wistfully attractive substitute for political, social and moral anarchy.

15

Cut This Out and
Put It in Your Wallet

October 10, 1981

THIS ESSAY is going to be full of figures, but I venture that you will not wish to be without them. I tried to arrange with the editors to publish this piece with perforated edges, but I found this impractical. Under the circumstances, get out the scissors or the razor blade.

A soundly run country will, as surely as the soldier keeps his rifle lubricated, labor to maintain its essential plant, correct? Another way to put this is that if our per capita income were as low as, say, India's or Brazil's, there would not be much left over to a) guard the common defense, or b) look after the unfortunate. In order to do either of these there has to be a certain residue. That residue can be mulcted from the masses as in the Soviet Union, leaving them without the essential freedoms to engage in commerce or to blunt the sharp edges of life, or it can come out of what might reasonably be called a "surplus."

So that in deciding what percentage of the gross national product should be handed over to the government to be spent as the legislatures dictate, one should from time to time take the temperature of the economic plant. These figures, culled from the Tax Foundation and the Grace Company's economists, to whom we should all be grateful, are straightforward.

Between 1962 and 1980, we wish to know: 1) What was

government spending, as a percentage of GNP? 2) What was the average investment, as a percentage of GNP? 3) What was the annual increase in GNP (in every case, we are talking about the average between 1962 and 1980)? 4) What was the percentage increase in productivity?

Here are the answers, in percentages, to the above for six countries:

Japan:	1)	8.7	2)	32.5	3)	7.9	4)	7.8
Italy:	1)	15.4	2)	20.6	3)	4.1	4)	5.6
France:	1)	13.8	2)	22.9	3)	4.4	4)	5.4
Germany:	1)	17.5	2)	20.6	3)	3.6	4)	5.2
United Kingdom:	1)	18.7	2)	18.4	3)	2.3	4)	2.7
United States:	1)	20.6	2)	17.8	3)	3.5	4)	2.2

These figures speak volumes. The United States spends over twice as much of its gross national product through the public sector as Japan, and more than any other nation listed. The United States invests about one-half as much as Japan, as a percentage of its gross national product, and less than any other country listed. The United States' real average growth in GNP is less, as a percentage, than one-half Japan's, and less than that of any other country listed, with the exception of the United Kingdom. The United States' percentage of productivity increase has been only 35 percent that of Japan, and less even than that of Great Britain. Something, then, would appear to be wrong in the care and feeding of our capital plant.

What about corollary figures? In 1966 federal spending amounted to 18.6 percent of the GNP. By 1980, that had grown to 22.4 percent.

During that period, unemployment increased by 28 percent. Real GNP, measured as the average annual percentage change, went down by 46.7 percent. Real business investment, measured annually, went down by 74.7 percent. Productivity —again annual average—down 85.3 percent. Inflation—average annual percentage change—increased by 513 percent. The federal deficit, on an annual average, increased by 3,115 percent (i.e., it went from $1.3 billion to $41.8 billion).

And, finally, and here is a show-stopper: After *all* Reagan's tax decreases have been enacted—i.e., in 1985, if we assume an inflation between now and then of a mere 7 percent—the man in the $10,000 bracket will be paying 27 percent more tax on the marginal dollar than he was in 1972. The man earning $25,000 will be paying 17 percent more on the marginal dollar. The man earning $40,000 will be paying 9 percent more. In other words, after the great tax reform of Ronald Reagan, in 1985 every category of taxpayer will be worse off than in 1972. Question: Is this sufficient reform?

16

Next in Central America?

March 20, 1982

Concerning the deteriorating situation in Central America, a few observations:

1) There is no practical means by which the United States can arrest the violence sweeping the area. The "Roosevelt [Teddy] Corollary" to the Monroe Doctrine asserted a general right to intervene in Latin America in the case of (get this!): "chronic wrongdoing or an impotence which results in a general loosening of the ties of civilized societies." Such language can keep the Marines busy—and did, a couple of dozen times during the ensuing twenty years.

It is not intended as ethnically invidious to remark that history shows a propensity for violence in Latin America. We have our crime in the streets, the Germans had Hitler, the Russians had Stalin and his successors, the Asians Mao Tse-tung and Pol Pot; the Latin Americans incline to massive political violence. During the civil war in Colombia that began in 1948, whose motivations are almost as difficult to recall as those of the great powers that gave us the First World War, violence reached heights that, by contrast, make El Salvador sound like Waikiki Beach.

Historian Alistair Horne, in his book *Small Earthquake in Chile*, merely suggests what it was like. "Accounts of the atrocities committed during *La Violencia* (the period of violence) turned the stomach. Luckier victims escaped with nose, lips, or ears cut off. Crucifixions were commonplace where the most refined tortures had their own special names (I eschew the description of some of these). The forces of law and order were themselves often involved. There were no battle fronts in the civil war. By its end, 300,000 Colombians were estimated to have been killed. In one small community alone, 503 out of 509 families were found to have lost some close relatives." That, in American terms, would amount to four to five million deaths by violence, far more than have died at war throughout the history of the United States: about 100 times our losses during the excruciating war in Vietnam.

2) This does not mean that the United States should be indifferent to the scale of political violence in Central America, but does mean that we must jealously guard the relevant distinction. And it is this: Where is violence being cultivated, with a view to exporting it? One should not tire of repeating the fatalistic but wise maxim of Senator Fulbright, that the United States government has no proper quarrel with any nation no matter how obnoxious its domestic policies, so long as it does not seek to export them. As much was said by President John Quincy Adams when he stressed that Americans were friends of liberty everywhere, but custodians only of their own.

3) However grotesque, then, the leaders of Guatemala, or the death squads associated with the government of El Salvador, our concern is with Nicaragua. Why? Because it is becoming a staging base for exported political violence. Why does Nicaragua need an army of 70,000? You will say: to guard against being overthrown by the CIA. But the mobilization was under way well before the United States turned hostile toward the Sandinistas.

And, of course, Nicaragua becomes an arsenal as a result of another staging base, namely Cuba. And Cuba? We all know the answer. Cuba would be prostrate economically if it were not for the Soviet Union, which incidentally would not be able to finance revolutions throughout the world were it required to meet conventional credit standards which, in their wisdom, the capitalist nations of the world proudly waive when dealing with the Soviet Union.

Our direct quarrel, then, is with Cuba. It is perhaps too late to arrest the decline of El Salvador. The reach of terrorism is underestimated in a country that has never experienced it. But the notion that the elections of late March will establish anything, when the guerrillas have publicly promised death to anyone who votes, is ludicrous. And so the demoralization of an army largely untrained proceeds. Answer?

We have got to get at Cuba. A declaration of war, given the record of its hostility to the United States, could plausibly be framed. But meanwhile it behooves us to blockade Central America, by air and sea, arresting all movement of arms to the area. Our diplomacy should focus directly on harnessing sponsoring resolutions by Latin American nations. And here, Mexico is critical.

17

The Missing Perspective

March 23, 1982

PROFESSOR GALBRAITH has a nice wisecrack—as one would expect, self-serving—about how the Republicans' insistence that they are not wholly responsible for the economic mess won't work, because if you play that game you can complain that all our economic woes trace to Alexander Hamilton. A nice try (one has only to look at the economic indices since Gerald Ford: inflation doubled, the growth rate halved, the deficit doubled, unemployment up, etc.). We are reminded, however, how easily public attention is distracted from the greater issues, the greater responsibilities.

We have the governors of Mainland China calling in diplomatic representatives from all over to announce that relations with Taiwan, however informal or surreptitious, will not be tolerated. And it is predictable that the republic will be engrossed in discussing this subject rather than others that come to mind—for instance, the responsibility of the governors of China for the continuing misery of those Chinese not enterprising enough to flee to Taiwan in 1949. We hear talk about how we should behave diplomatically from the same people who give testimonial dinners to Pol Pot, whose only claim to Chinese hospitality presumably is that his depravities exceeded even those of Hitler and Stalin.

Every newspaper is crowded with tales of El Salvador—lurid

descriptive details of the horrors there, most of them the work
of government death squads. In the ghetto pages of the newspapers one may come upon an occasional reference to Afghanistan, where a mountain people are fighting tanks, machine
guns and in all probability chemical weapons, in a continuing
struggle that engages the energies of 100,000 Soviet soldiers.
Student or church protests against the campaign in Afghanistan, if they take place, do not attract public attention.

Poland is in the news sporadically. But watch: it is easing out
of the most energetic headlines, the galvanizing headlines. We
are, in the West, a psychologically hopped-up race of people,
and we have little patience with that which goes on and on. It
will not be more than a few months down the line before
barbarities in Poland become about as interesting as barbarities in Cuba: So what did you expect, chimes?

Brezhnev steps forward to claim public credit for not install-
ing more, and highly redundant, nuclear weapons along his
western frontier. And, sure enough, there ensues talk about
the contrasting flexibility of the Soviet Union over against Reagan's intransigent zero-option position. When Ed Meese suggests that Brezhnev's proposals can be compared with the
team leading the football game at the third quarter by a score
of 50–0 coming out for freezing the status quo, James Reston
becomes impatient, in a general broadside against the hard
language of the Reagan administration, and sure enough before we know it we are nodding along, considering the question of Reagan's excesses. Not Brezhnev's. Reagan's.

The Vice President of the United States is criticized for
making a specific reference to President Marcos of the Philippines, notwithstanding the general countenance of diplomatic
cant, while the chancellor of Austria provides official state hospitality to Madman Qaddafi, only weeks after Qaddafi commissioned a death squad to effect the assassination of the president
of the country without whose presence on the scene the chancellor of Austria would today be whoever the Kremlin decided;
and a generation after the United States prevented Austria
from being run by a designee of Adolf Hitler.

Where is the perspective, with which for instance we can
evaluate the complaints of college students? Why are they
paying $13,000 per year to go to Yale? Because of economic

excesses of Ronald Reagan and Gerald Ford? Why are college-educated people the last to understand that it is literally true there is no such thing as a free lunch, that they are paying, and their parents are paying, for policies which they now wish to continue to be enforced, lest they should themselves suffer?

It is true that current contentions are not readily illuminated by pointing out that man was born with Original Sin. But neither are they readily illuminated if we assume that today there is no burden to be borne in virtue of yesterday's excesses. And little to be gained from permitting the great social internationalist disrupters of peace, and hope, to direct our attention to what they desire us to consider and condemn, while they continue to pass the ammunition, and smile a smile of guile, and death.

18

The Hinckley Mess

June 29, 1982

THE MATTER of Hinckley's "vindication"—a strange sound that word has, used in the circumstances—provokes several observations:

1) The notion that a law that is clearly seen now as having purely abstract architecture will quickly be reformed, lessening the likelihood of Hinckley II and Hinckley III, is—well, remote. Mr. Morris Abram, the distinguished educator, lawyer and civil rights champion who has just issued his memoirs (*The Day Is Short*) said, on the day after the acquittal was announced, that it would surely catalyze legal reform, to which the answer is that no such thing is by any means predictable.

Twenty-year olds who have mugged and tortured grandmothers on Monday are regularly arraigned on Tuesday, spend Wednesday yawning through the procedures to which they are submitted, and are out on Friday looking around the neighborhood for fresher meat. They would smile. We have had a crime wave that mounts, about which we have done practically nothing; a creeping illiteracy that mounts, about which we have done practically nothing. We may have got our reputation back there as a can-do society. We don't deserve it.

2) Mr. Abram also said that the adversary system in America is our way of ascertaining the truth. But as soon as he said it he was, really, sorry. The adversary system, before a tribunal, is

America's way of deciding public questions, for instance whether Hinckley will be punished as a murderer or merely detained as a psychiatric patient. A judicial trial resolves public policy on how to deal with someone. Nothing else. Those who desire to believe that Hinckley is "guilty" in the communicable sense of that word are free to do so without fearing that they are obscurantists who stand in the way of scientific epistemology. Dr. Johnson said that it does not defame speculation to say about it that it errs when it announces that two plus two are equal to some figure other than four.

3) The spectacle, at the Hinckley trial, of experts, so-called, arguing with other experts, so-called, for the benefit of a jury on such tangled questions as whether Hinckley knew what he was doing, and knew that what he was doing was wrong, gives us a textbook example of the presumptions of scientists moving in on public policy. The word "expertise" means "a body of operative knowledge." If no such knowledge exists—for instance, on the question of whether Hinckley knew what he was doing and that it was wrong—then no one is by definition an "expert" except in the sense that he is devoted to trying to answer a question about which there is no expertise. If you attempt to play Rachmaninoff's Second Concerto, devoting your lifetime to the effort, but what comes out is disharmonious sounds, unrelated to what Rachmaninoff wrote, you simply have not mastered the Second Concerto. At least, however, we know that the concerto exists. What we do not know is whether there is any way in which Hinckley can be proved to have known that what he was doing was evil and unlawful.

Now the notion that a body of inoperative knowledge can be presented to a jury, an "expert" advocate on one side and an "expert" advocate on the contrary side, in the expectation that that jury can adjudicate as between the antagonistic positions is quite simply, well, voodoo law. If, say, Einstein and Fermi could not agree on, oh, the way in which to weigh matter in space, that a jury could, listening to both men, come up with the "right" answer is—well, a superstition. So that we went to elaborate lengths to underwrite a superstition, the purpose of which was to let Hinckley go unpunished. Because he didn't know he was trying to kill the President? Hardly. Because he didn't know it was unlawful? Hardly. Because . . . because we are a Freud-obsessed society, riveted to the angel-explanation of human behavior, and if somebody does something bad, it's got to be because he didn't get enough food stamps when he was a kid.

4) So where do we go from here? Probably nowhere. But if there is comfort to be taken, it is in the solid judgment of the American people that their institutions are running the danger of being, simply, useless. The law as regards curbing crime is about as useful as the United Nations in curbing aggression. Cynicism isn't the answer. Realism, however, helps. And realism begins by sticking out our tongues at the judge and the jurors who went along with the expensive charade.

19

The Averted Gaze

December 2, 1982

A COLLEAGUE tells the story of the lieutenant and captain waiting in the hotel lobby for their companions to come down.

Two women are spotted descending the staircase. The lieutenant leans over and whispers, "That's got to be the ugliest woman I've ever seen."

"That's my wife," the captain hisses.

"Oh. Well, I didn't mean her. I meant the woman next to her."

"That's my mother."

The lieutenant pauses, and then: "I didn't say it."

One is reminded of the Thanksgiving flurry involving the Reagan administration and the proposal that at some point, at some level, unemployment benefits be taxed. It is rumored that the President first heard that this had been listed among the hypothetical options to diminish disincentives to working, whereupon he pushed every executive button simultaneously, causing fifty-five Administration spokesmen to pronounce that the proposal in question a) would not be adopted, b) was not being considered, c) was invisible the whole time, and d) probably never existed in the first place. In politics you simply don't say certain things.

It doesn't matter if they're true—still, you're not supposed to say them. Martin Feldstein, the Administration's principal economist, noted a few years ago that at a certain salary level a Massachusetts taxpayer who lost his job would, during the first year, bring in 93 percent of his post-tax income made while working. This by adding federal, state and city benefits, tax free. There are people, rich and poor, who would consider trading 7 percent of their net income for forty free hours per week. You can catch up on your reading, for one thing.

Among the unemployed in America there is a division. There are those who cannot find work. And there are those who cannot find work they are willing to do. Nobody disputes that there are eight million (or more) illegals in America. And nobody disputes that they are working. Where did they find the jobs? Still, one does not say "it." And, of course, in some cases "it" does not apply.

Here is an interesting figure. Suppose you were to tax everyone in America 44 percent of his salary—this in addition to the taxes he is already paying. What do you say to that proposal? I agree. I mean, talk about disincentives.

But that is exactly how much tax Americans would need to pay by the year 2035 if current arrangements concerning Social Security prevail. The Kennedys and Moynihans and Peppers and O'Neills treat any suggestion about modifying Social Security benefits as if President Reagan, paintbrush in hand, was setting out to touch up the Mona Lisa. Well, just what is it that they propose to do about it? Once again, speaking of Social Security, a division is in order, i.e., to distinguish between those who need every penny of their Social Security check and those who do not. It transpires that 30 percent of Social Security benefits go to the wealthiest 20 percent of the elderly, here defined as families with an income in excess of $30,000 per year.

Robert Lekachman is a witty socialist and economist in New York. His idea of a truly perfect society is one in which 100 percent of all the money above whatever his salary is at City University would go to the government. Professor Lekachman writes, "Even today Social Security and Medicare owe their relative invulnerability from David Stockman's budget bleeders not to the non-voting poor but to politically alert, middle-class Gray Panthers and members of the American Association of Retired Persons."

Abraham Lincoln once asked a question which, in our smugness, we have always taken to be rhetorical. We are here, he said at Gettysburg, to test the proposition whether a government of the people, by the people and for the people can long endure. But the question is very serious. And the Averted Political Gaze, when unpleasant questions are asked, is a hideously eloquent means of answering Mr. Lincoln: No.

20

Who Is Responsible for Unemployment?

December 9, 1982

THE RISE in the unemployment rate to 10.8 percent was bad news. Public ire was directed at Ronald Reagan.

Why?

In Canada, unemployment is at 13 percent. Everyone is mad at Trudeau more or less as a matter of principle, and that is understandable. On the other hand, Trudeau is a socialist of sorts, so why doesn't he do something about Canadian unemployment, which is two points higher than ours? Or, while we are at it, we have some superheated socialists in Mexico, where unemployment is at 50 percent. Is that the way to go?

So what is Reagan supposed to do? Mitterrand, running for president, announced that he would hire an extra 150,000 bureaucrats. He proceeded to do so. But by the time he was inaugurated, unemployment had dipped far beyond the number of bureaucrats he hired. So what is Reagan supposed to do, hire a couple of million extra bureaucrats? What are they going to do, and who will step forward to pay for them?

Should Reagan place a government order for a couple of million cars? For 50 million tons of steel?

Should he lower the interest rate? How does a President lower interest rates? By asking Congress for legislation to take from the Federal Reserve Board the right to buy and sell government securities? The establishment of the Fed, dating back to the administration of Woodrow Wilson, has for years been hailed as a progressive step, removing from government capricious authority over the money supply. The gold standard and gold convertibility having since then been abolished, this would appear all the more desirable.

But what if Reagan managed, through legislation, to acquire de facto authority over the money supply? Should he then flood the country with paper money to drive down the interest rates, so that more people could borrow to buy cars? And, by so doing, drive down the value of the dollar? Should he, in short, attack the earnings and the savings of the 99-plus million Americans who are working, in order to stimulate jobs for the 11 million? And how long would they then have work if he were to do so, pursuing an inflation that everyone was complaining about when Reagan took office, and which since then has been halved?

Lane Kirkland, head of the AFL-CIO, was on television when the figures came out. What did he say? He said that if "they"—meaning Reagan's White House—would not "do anything" until there is "turmoil in the streets," then "we'll give them some turmoil in the streets." Kirkland managed to sound like Stokely Carmichael. Is the head of the largest free trade union organization in the world proposing street anarchy?

Which reminds us: Now that we have examined what Reagan can and can't do about unemployment, has anyone asked Lane Kirkland what he might do about unemployment? Why do foreign cars amount to so great a share of the market? If the American worker's wage is pegged to a scale that keeps him earning about twice as much as the Japanese worker, is this a possible reason why so many Americans are buying Japanese cars? If the steelworkers are earning half again as much as German steelworkers, could this be why steel is being produced at 30 percent of capacity? We all know that workers can earn more money if their tools are so refined as to give them an advantage over the competition. Thus one worker with an electrical loom can be as productive as ten without such a loom.

Well, what has Lane Kirkland done to encourage savings and investment and recapitalization? He has been around longer than Reagan. Why not ask Mr. Kirkland to take a little time off from breaking windows in the streets to answer the question: Where is the statesmanship for which he has called? The Detroit Chrysler workers have been courageous and intelligent. But what about their counterparts?

It is time someone pointed out that Lane Kirkland is far more responsible for unemployment than Ronald Reagan. Come to think of it, someone *has* now pointed this out.

And by the way: During the same month the joblessness rose, 4.1 million Americans who had been unemployed got jobs.

21

A Matter of Style

January 1983

I FEEL the need to admit that I have not given much explicit thought to the definition of style, notwithstanding that I am said to possess it, by which a compliment is sometimes but not always intended ("style" is widely misread as affectation). But finding myself in the pressure cooker, it came to me after very little ratiocination that style is, really, timing. Let me tell you, by giving you a story, what I mean by this.

It is a story by one of the nineteenth-century Russians, and timing here is one factor for not going to the trouble of finding out which one it was, since it doesn't matter. Tolstoy, I think; in any event, the story I read sometime during my teens was about a very rich young prince who one evening engaged in a drinking bout of Brobdingnagian dimensions with his fellow bloods, which eventually peaked, as such affairs frequently did in that curious epoch of genius and debauchery, in a philosophical argument over the limits of human self-control. The question was specifically posed: Could someone succeed in voluntarily sequestering himself in a small suite of rooms for a period of twenty years, notwithstanding that he would always be free to open the door, letting himself out, or others in? In a spirit of high and exhibitionistic dogmatism, the prince pronounced such hypothetical discipline preposterous, and announced that he would give one million rubles to anyone who succeeded in proving him wrong.

You will have guessed that a young companion, noble but poor, and himself far gone in wine's litigious imperatives, accepted the challenge. And so with much fanfare, a few days later, the rules having been carefully set (he could ask for, and receive, anything except human company), Peter (we'll call him) was ushered into the little subterranean suite of rooms in the basement of the prince's house.

During the first years, he drank. During the next years, he stared at the ceiling. During the succeeding period, he read—ordering books, more books, and more books. Meanwhile the fortunes of the prince had taken a disastrous turn, and so he schemed actively to seduce Peter to leave his self-imposed confinement, dispatching letters below, describing evocatively the sensual delights Peter would experience by merely opening the door. In desperation, as the deadline neared, he even offered one half the premium.

The night before the twentieth year would finish at midnight, half the town and thousands from all over Russia were outside to celebrate and marvel over the endurance of Peter upon his emergence. One hour before midnight, the startled crowd saw the celebrated door below street level open prematurely. And Peter emerge. He had, you see, become a philosopher; and in all literature I know of no more eloquent gesture of disdain for money. One hour more, and he'd have earned a million rubles. What *style*, you say; and I concur.

But what is it about that one hour that speaks so stylishly, in a sense that Peter's emergence one year before the deadline would not, lacking as one year would be in drama; or, at the other end, one minute before midnight, one minute being overfreighted in melodrama?

It is style, surely.

Even so the speed of human responses which, indicating spontaneity, communicate integrity. "Is it all right if I bring Flo's sister and her husband along for the weekend?" demands *instant* assent; the *least* pause is, to the quick ear, lethal. When such a proposition is posed, the man of style will make one of two decisions, and he must here think with great speed. He will either veto the extra guests, going on to give whatever reason he finds most ingenious, or he will accept them *on the spot*. Absolutely nothing in between. In between is many other things defined as lacking in style.

It is so, I think, with language, and with that aspect of language on which its effectiveness so heavily relies, namely rhythm. It matters less what exactly you say at a moment of tension than that you say it at just the right moment. Great speed might be necessary, as above, or such delay as suggests painful meditation as required to ease, console, or inspirit the other person. Style is not a synonym for diplomacy. Style can be infinitely undiplomatic, as in the stylish means selected by John L. Lewis to separate his union from the CIO. "We disaffiliate," he wrote on an envelope, dispatching it to headquarters. It is sometimes stylish to draw attention to oneself, as Lewis was doing. Sometimes the man of style will be all but anonymous. Some men are congenitally incapable of exhibiting a stylish anonymity. Of Theodore Roosevelt it was said that whenever he attended a wedding, he confused himself with the bride. The Queen of England could not feign anonymity, neither could LBJ, or Mr. Micawber. But whichever is sought —being conspicuous or inconspicuous—timing is the principal element. Arrive very early at the funeral and you will be noticed, even as you will be noticed arriving at the very last minute. In between, you glide in, on cat-feet.

In language, rhythm is an act of timing. "Why did you use the word 'irenic' when you say it merely means 'peaceful'?" a talk show host once asked indignantly. To which the answer given was: "I desired the extra syllable." In all circumstances? *No, for God's sake.*

In the peculiar circumstances of the sentence uttered, and these circumstances were set by what had gone just before, what would probably come just after. A matter of style. A matter of timing.

22

China Over Lightly

February 4, 1983

No STATE has absolutely impermeable frontiers, but some come pretty close and China was one such for years. Now anyone can go to China, but on *their* terms. There are the fascinating exceptions: in Peking the U.S. ambassador told me that every now and then he runs into, or perhaps more properly is run over by, an American hippie-type who actually arrives in China—somehow; then sets out with his backpack; knows no Chinese; has some, but usually not much, money. "Damned if some of them don't get all the way to Lhasa and back." Lhasa used to be where the Dalai Lama governed by the will of God, until God lost interest, in 1959; and now it is the capital of Tibet, the westernmost province of China.

The fancy way to go to China is what one might call Kissinger Class: which is all jets, most of them private, and Red Flag limos. They manufacture two hundred of those per year in China. And get this: if your driver runs over and kills a pedestrian, why that's too bad—for the pedestrian. You see, the driver of a Red Flag is not supposed to take drastic braking action because if he did, the man sitting in the back seat might get hurt, and that man's presumptive value to the state, given that he is entitled to a Red Flag, is legally higher than that of a random pedestrian. (People's stations in China are as polarized politically as they are economically. The peasants earn about

one-fifth what the city folk do.) Kissinger Class gets you ban-
quets, and conferences with Deng Xiaoping (the sovereign),
and Hu Yaobang (the Prince of Wales); plus the usual ration.
Of? Ping-Pong, acrobatics, children's concerts, ballet, tombs,
temples, the Great Wall, the Forbidden City, cultivated gardens, and meals meals meals, figure roughly about as many
courses as you spend hours in China. To qualify for Kissinger
Class isn't easy. Nixon is the most conspicuous consumer in this
category, and once, soon after he was driven from office, Mao
Tse-tung sent a 707 jet to bring him all the way from California
for a visit, a gesture absolutely emperor-like, never mind that
the Chinese emperors these days wear their equivalent of blue
jeans.

There is the other way, now standard. You ask your travel
agent to link you up with a group, it doesn't greatly matter
what group. Choose one with reference to how long you want
to spend in China. One week, two; the usual maximum for
China, and certainly for you, being three weeks. All twenty, or
thirty, or sixty of you will land together, and twenty-one days
later you'll depart together. Meanwhile you will have seen
China, meaning of course that China China wishes Americans
to see. Last year there were eighty thousand visitors, an exorbitant number, really, given the exiguous network of hotels,
trains, guides, and buses—which simply isn't developed to care
for so many transients in a mere twelve months. Contrast
Spain, where last year forty million tourists visited.

But now there is another way, and that is by cruise ship. It
has the disadvantage that you don't get total immersion, if that
is what you are looking for. I remember my astonishment on
learning, as a boy, that the athlete who set out to swim across
the Atlantic was permitted to pause, at the end of eight hours
or so, to board his escort vessel: wherein he would eat, and
sleep, before resuming his struggle.

It is so with the cruise ships. Mine (the *Pearl of Scandinavia*)
contrives its fourteen-day sail from Kobe, Japan, to Hong Kong
(and vice versa) so as to leave you only two nights having to
sleep on Chinese soil (in Peking). That way you miss something
of the exotic impact: the fighter pilot returning to his aircraft,
compared to the infantryman in the field. But you miss, also, a
lot of the irritation. If you stay in China you begin to feel an

alienation from circumstances which you are accustomed to controlling, but now they are controlled by your tour guide, or by the hotel clerk, or by the taxi driver, and communication is always vexing.

This point is worth stressing. Because life in China is substantially a reflection of the tension: you versus circumstances outside your control. Whether it's the emperor whose identity you cannot pinpoint or the chicken you cannot find in the market (where the average Chinese spends two hours per day foraging for that day's food). You may, if inclined to the juridical, call this an extension of habeas corpus. Do you have control over your body—or do *they* have it? When you tour China over an extended period, it is easy to surmise, you discover that the tendency is for your body, well, to incline—it is much easier that way—to what the Chinese call the *li*, a Confucian term suggesting, at its most exalted, divine order. And it is generally supposed that where the body goes, the mind tends also to drift.

That this does not necessarily happen is, of course, one of the things that got in the way of the evolution of Mao man, a species prematurely taxonomized by many Western intellectuals and journalists, most notably (in my own memory—perhaps because the words he used were so . . . chiliastic) James Reston. After his appendix was taken out in Peking, in 1971—the year before the great Nixon-Mao rapprochement—he told reporters in Tokyo, "I'm a Scotch Calvinist. I believe in redemption of the human spirit and the improvement of man. Maybe it's because I believe that or I want to believe it that I was struck by the tremendous effort to bring out what is best in man, what makes them good, what makes them cooperate with one another and be considerate and not beastly to one another. They [the Chinese] are trying that." They certainly did try something transmutative. Professor Edward Luttwak came up several years ago with a hauntingly bright aperçu calculated to distinguish between Mao man and Soviet man. In Russia, he said, the people were given an almost infinitely long list of what it was they could not do. Anything not on that list was okay. And so Russians spend their very long days slithering in and out of the interstices, and this creates a perpetual sullenness, and an apprehension, lest a frontier between what might be done, and what might not be done, was traversed.

Mao man, on the other hand, was told that Nothing could be done—except as a directive came in to do it. These directives were refractions of the Chairman's thoughts, and these came in bewildering profusion, often contradictory. The superficial effect was that of the compleat sycophant. Have you read *The Story of O?* The story of Mao man; only, of course, he never really materialized. James Reston would have had the greatest anthropological beat in history.

For heaven's sake I am not suggesting that the spiritual inertia of the regular guided tour through China ends you up thinking Mao thought, though this did happen to otherwise skeptical people. No more would I suggest the opposite, that brief encounters immunize you. Merely that if you want only to *experience* China, a physically and emotionally comfortable way to do this is off a cruising boat.

What, concretely, happens? I speak of the *Pearl of Scandinavia,* having sailed aboard that thoroughly pleasant boat with its thoroughly pleasant people (the cruise director is so well organized that his note congratulating me on my lectures arrived in my cabin before I had delivered them). The *Pearl* is, at this writing, unique. But its pioneering is bringing in the competition, and in a few months one of the *Vikings* will be doing the coastal tour as well. Let's face the probability that within five years, if Reaganomics comes through for us, a Chinese coastal cruise will become almost as routine as a Caribbean cruise. But in the meantime, Reaganomics has a long way to go. Roundtrip airfare to the Orient is a couple of thousand. Triple that if you count in the ship, a souvenir jade tree, and fifty air-mail postcards.

But China has much further to go than Reagan, if the annual tourist figure is to rise from the existing level of eighty thousand to, say, one million. Because even now you have the feeling that your tour group is the incremental strain on the Middle Kingdom: that China is so close to not-quite-making-it, having to feed and house one billion Chinese, that that marginal imposition of four hundred people from your cruise trip threatens the whole national enterprise. For instance, only two of the six elevators in the huge new Hua Do Hotel in Peking work: so that you are likely to find yourself running down the stairs carrying your suitcase, for fear of missing the bus, and oh God, what happens if you miss the bus? Make your own arrangements to get from Shanghai to Tianjin, there to catch the boat? As well make your own arrangements to launch from Cape Canaveral.

In Shanghai, they have put together a special train to take you to the fabled Suzhou (Soochow—Question: Why did the Western press go along on the Pinyin bit, which has caused a quite unnecessary orthographic revolution of no imaginable usefulness to us? Why should we now call it Beijing? We don't call Cologne Köln), where you see one of those breathtaking sights, in this case the leisurely, terraced, endless garden, and the bonsai trees, maybe four hundred different species. Anyway, you need to have breakfast at 5:30, and breakfasting at 5:30, if you're not used to it, so to speak affects your movements the night before. Why 5:30? Because there is track available for the special train only at 6:45; so that the straitened facilities of Chinese travel affect you very directly. And then, after the long day seeing the gardens, the silk factory, the endless lunch, together with toasts back and forth, you are really out of steam.

Ah, but you must go out a few miles to see a bridge built during the days of the T'ang Dynasty. You get there and look at the remains of a stone bridge running low over the sleepy river, and you say to yourself, So what? You photographed the Colosseum in Rome way back when you were a little boy, and they built that seven hundred years before T'ang got around to building his bridge, so what are we doing here? Later on the guide confides in you. What we are doing there is killing time. Because, you see, there is no railroad track available until 6 P.M. The first four thousand years of China produced four hundred million people. Under early-Mao, birth control was held to be bourgeois. So that in a decade, that four-hundred-million figure doubled. Not so the railroads, let alone hotels, quite the contrary. There were ten thousand restaurants in Shanghai when Mao took over, fewer than one thousand today.

But then there is a conspicuous difference over ten years ago. Granted my visit at that time was as a member of the press following Nixon around, and all the sights were presumably reserved for the visiting foreigners (we were, in total, about two hundred). But now the public sights are open to the public, and even though the Chinese get different days of the week off, the public sights are very crowded. The Forbidden City in Peking, when last I saw it—that magnificent 250-acre compound of palaces and temples and stately, discrete houses, in one of which the Great Helmsman lived—was as empty of unofficial Chinese as a Chinese Friendship Store. (No dollee, no entree.) The great, standard Chinese sights aren't yet crowded like a Rolling Stones concert, but I warn you, that is the way they are headed. And why not? It is splendid that the most oppressed, most regimented people in the world have something to look at other than the *People's Daily,* the face of Mao Tse-tung, and the Chairman's book of quotations. This is a startling change. And there is television now although the price of a set is ten months' salary. Never mind. Escapism of any kind in a deadly dull society (that is what its most reluctant critics concede about the People's Republic of China, though better today's dullness than the sadistic convulsions of yesterday) is to be expected. But along the way, the foreign tourist should be warned that the photograph he intended to take of the Palace of Accumulated Elegance is going to have the palace *and* seven hundred Chinese in it, unless he can manage to get there before opening time, or after closing time.

So. The night before, you cruised into the Yellow Sea, having stopped in South Korea's Pusan for a few hours. There is nothing that strikes you, in mid-October, as distinctive. Seas sometimes have a way of looking like any other sea. As you come closer to the mainland, you see more boats. The most bedraggled fleet in the world. The tempo of commercial traffic in and out of China is increasing heavily. That night, on board, you could see a movie *(Chariots of Fire),* or a musical revue. First sitting at 6:30, second at 8:15, dress formal. The blackjack tables open after dinner, and two girls from London operate them until they run out of customers, usually about one in the morning, a half-hour before the buffet closes, though the Poseidon Lounge is open 24 hours a day if you want fruit juice, tea, or coffee; indeed you can ring from your room, and a Filipino is supposed to come, even if it is three in the morning, and bring you something. To experience all of this as you approach a country whose per capita income is under $500 per year adds to the piquancy, if you use that word properly: i.e., with reverence.

You have disembarked and are in China. You are led to your bus, one of twelve. Your guide talks to you as you drive north to Ji Xian, where you see a temple and have lunch before the train. The guide chats with you ("The population is the major concern of the government"); reassures you about the civil quality of Chinese society ("The teachers are very kind and are very sweet with everyone"); leads community singing ("Jingle Bells," "Old Black Joe," "I've Been Working on the Railroad"). You have lunched (eight courses), and now are taken to the railroad car, so primitive as to be almost exciting, for the first ten minutes. Its backrests would do as plumb bobs. The scenery is unremarkable, save for the absence of mechanical contrivances—only every now and then is there a truck facilitating the farmwork. Mostly it is oxen. Actually, mostly it is human beings. In two and one-half hours, you are in Peking. The railroad station there, by the way, is as dirty as any you have seen anywhere in the world, and you reflect on all those rhapsodies you used to hear about Mao-hygiene. It is true that Moscow's subways are beautiful and clean. It is not true that in China socialism has brought cleanliness, let alone defeated pollution.

What is there to say about Tien An Men Square, or about the temples, the Great Wall, the Summer Palace, except that they are overwhelming examples of power, beauty, and obstinacy of design, and breadth of conceptual imagination? It is so terribly important, however, to read Simon Leys's *Chinese Shadows,* because without the help of this learned and passionate Belgian art historian you will not know what have been some of the ideological desecrations of what once was there, like the great walls of Peking, and the gravestones. But somewhere along the line the passion to destroy stopped, in China even as in Russia, and the tourists, mostly, are taken to where the beauty is, and it is very old.

The Hua Do Hotel ranks after the Hotel Peking, which is very difficult to penetrate, even with its new wing. There the diplomats and journalists and businessmen get the rooms. Hua

Do is considered luxurious in Peking, and would not last a week in Atlantic City. The two dining rooms, one serving Western food and the other Chinese food, are lit like solariums, and the tables set up as though to feed passing divisions of soldiers. There is a touch of coziness in one bar, and the staff is as helpful as it can be, considering that they do not, really, know how to speak in English. Forty-eight hours later you are back on the train, and just as she reached for the overhead compartment, one of our passengers fell. Dead, as it turned out. The word was whispered about that her traveling companion had revealed, through tears, that she was eighty-five years old. She was taken out on a park bench, brought in from somewhere. Here and there passengers reached into their overnight bags (no porters: everyone had to carry everything he brought along or bought while there) for those emergency little bottles, and the vodka and other spirits helped; and the consensus gradually crystallized that the lady, at that age, had had a most dignified and utterly painless end; and before long, in anticipation of the pleasant cruise ship three train-bus hours away, and the hot showers and hot food, the mood picked up; and in due course someone even mentioned that, all things considered, the mortality rate of a visit to Peking was proving tolerable.

The following day Qingdao, dominated for the greater part of this century by Germans; its substantial architecture remains distinctively European, and its beaches accentuate its attraction as a resort. The guide, clearly happy to practice his English, is chatty, and advises us that in China, "more work, more pay." There are eight economic levels of work in China, he says, and compensation rises from 40 to 108 yen per month. The yen goes at two for one dollar. "Our pay is enough for an apartment or a house, and we use the rest for clothes and TV, etc." In Chinese urban areas, the per capita allocation of space comes to 3.6 square yards. At the embassy yesterday I saw Robert Myers, an old friend and business partner in the odd enterprise of attempting to sell joint advertising space, he as publisher of *The New Republic*, I as editor of *National Review*. "I've tried for years," he said, "to persuade Bill Rusher [the publisher of *National Review*] to come to visit China." We

discussed then the interesting question of exactly what ideological point is made by persuading people to visit countries
that they will find operate pretty much as they had supposed
them to operate. Invite someone disbelieving the figures about
American agricultural productivity, say (110,000 pounds of
grain per year per farmer, fifty times that of the Chinese), and
an empirical purpose is served. It is hard to imagine exactly
what political purpose is served by inviting people to visit
Cuba, or China, or the Soviet Union; i.e., assuming them to be
cosmopolitan in the first place, what is it that is supposed to
surprise them? Gulag is not in downtown Moscow, nor the
"retraining camps" in Qingdao Square. One would not want to
advance the line of reasoning that because one did not see the
Lubyanka it does not exist: like the Irishman at the trial who
volunteered to produce thirty persons who had not seen him
murder the girl . . . But with guides one is passive, and
should be. I wrote once that one doesn't argue transubstantia-
tion with an altar boy. Nor the delights of life under Mao with a
guide. Not in public.

You pause in Dalian (Dairen), an unexceptionable and not
particularly interesting port where, however, your taxi driver
asks whether you would like to see the Christian church. The
minister in the courtyard makes the sign of the cross, not
attempting piety but as a means of communication: Were we
Christians? Inside is a substantial building, in which at one
time five hundred people might have sat, staring at turn-of-
the-century stained-glass windows depicting WASP-featured,
WASP-complexioned heavenly characters. One wishes one
might have learned something about the church and its recent
tribulations. The guide in Peking advised us with obvious pride
that only 3 percent of Chinese "believe in religion," much as
he might have advised us that only 3 percent of Chinese were
illiterate (the figure is 14 percent). Still, the church, although
empty, is open; ten years ago, in Peking, Tom Ross, then with
the Chicago Sun-Times, and I attempted to visit a church in
the central part of the city but it was locked—very tightly, we
ascertained when we finally succeeded in rousing its resident
gargoyle, who stared dumbly at us and pointed us away. Any
direction would do.

Two days later we woke in Shanghai harbor. We were twice

told by the ship's captain the night before just how lucky we were. Because space is so highly coveted in the central city. The *Pearl* was advised only late the day before our arrival that the harbormaster would give us a berth by Zhongshan Road, the old Bund, where the palatial buildings of the colonial period still stand. Alternative berthing is a full ten and a half miles away, and the difference is the loss of personal mobility. As it stands, one can call a taxi and—this one learns quickly in China—set out with one's own glossary. You make a list of places you wish to see—museums, temples, shops, restaurants. Alongside the English, a Chinese-speaking tour guide aboard the vessel writes the Chinese equivalent. And with this, you negotiate with the taxi, using also the phrases listed in the appendix of the *Fodor Guide* or in the State Department's briefing manual.

The throb of Shanghai has always been remarkable, and there are those who say it is now the largest city in the world. Difficult to establish, because as many as two million Chinese may be living in Shanghai without permits, and they do not cooperate with census takers. The city is unimaginably dirty; its river might have posed for one of Bosch's detailed nightmares. Here is the commercial mecca of China, where everybody unwedded to tranquillity would wish to be. Because here there is everything—even, they whisper, a little free-enterprise vice, cautiously celebrating the passing of prim Mao, whose own concubining was done discreetly, although he did list four wives, the last one of whom makes up one-quarter of the Gang of Four. It was she who in 1965, after seeing an operetta she thought insufficiently obsequious to the ideas of Mao, depressed the little trigger that brought on the Cultural Revolution and, it is widely felt, the end of Maoist illusions—among Chinese. Because the Cultural Revolution was to Mao what Jonestown was to whatever-it-was that other madman was promoting.

And so, before midnight on the second day, you set sail. Destination, Hong Kong, two and one-half days down the line. You began at Kobe. During your 336-hour fortnight you have spent 112 hours in China, eating thirteen meals ashore. And how much do you know about modern China?

At least for the next few years, I'd venture to say that that

depends on whether you have taken along to read Fox Butterfield's book *China: Alive in the Bitter Sea.* It is unlikely that
if you spent six months in China you would know one half as
much as you do from reading this startlingly important book,
by a reporter for the New York *Times,* a Sinologist fluent in the
language who spent twenty months in China and wrote a book
hailed by the dean of American Sinologists, John K. Fairbank,
who back in 1972 pronounced Mao the "best thing" that had
happened to China in millennia, and is cautiously, and belat-
edly, retreating from that position. It is all there in that volume, the whole incredible story, with details richer than you
yourself would ever succeed in unearthing, because you are
less talented and less industrious than Mr. Butterfield, and
because you do not speak Chinese. Learn Butterfield, and
know China. Travel to China, and experience China: in that
limited sense in which a tourist experiences a country, by fleeting contact with its people and a brief, voluptuarian gaze at its
treasures; in China's case, all of them antedating Mao's reign,
and most of them, his birth.

23

Who's Squealing Now?

March 5, 1983

THE FUROR over the squeal law appears endless. In part, of course, the controversy has been prolonged by the curious decision of a federal court to the effect that the same Congress that desires to diminish teenage pregnancy cannot logically endorse a protocol (advising the girl's parents that she has put in for birth control information) the effect of which might be to frustrate Congress's objective. The reasoning here is that the more information you distribute to teenage girls about how to conceive a baby, the fewer babies there will be.

Unhappily, not much attention, in disputes which are fundamentally ideological, is ever given to available data. The country in the world in which access is easiest to birth control information is Sweden, where the number of bastard births is highest. The profusion of information about cigarette smoking and cancer is not seriously affecting the rate of addiction. As for alcohol, which is probably the single greatest threat to individual health and productivity, the same country that gave us Gulag as a means of controlling its people can't seem to figure out how to keep those people away from booze. The good news, recently got out by a gentleman whose hammerlock on Soviet data never ceases to amaze, is that the tax on vodka in the Soviet Union is proving sufficient to generate revenues to finance the entire military establishment. Our lawmakers should perhaps cope with the budget deficit by inducing more drunkenness. They could be encouraged to give the public an example by their own conduct, except that one would not know the difference.

Beyond the failure of the birth controllers to establish a causal relation, a few other points ought to be stressed.

The first of these is that teenage sex is most usefully thought of as a drug. That is to say, sex gives pleasure, as drugs give pleasure; and sex is somewhere between a habituate and an addiction, which is true of many drugs. Alcohol, which is a drug of sorts, is innocently consumed in moderation, and the point is therefore to instruct potential victims on where the point of moderation lies. The analogous question in sex is to instruct those who are unaware or uncaring of the implication of wanton sex of its limitations. Just as the drug taker who overdoes it can damage himself physically, so the human animal who looks on sex merely as one of the smorgasbord of pleasures available to the pleasure-seeker needs to be instructed in the discipline of sensible self-limitation. The fifteen-year-old girl who has had no instruction at all in the subject is really quite helpless, particularly inasmuch as the routine inducements are to libertinism rather than to self-restraint, even as you will find more advertisements to buy this or that alcoholic drink than you will find warnings against buying it. What happens, then, is that the fifteen year old girl runs a number of risks. One is that of finding herself, though unprepared, pregnant. Other risks include diseases and emotional derangements. Insufficient attention, it seems to me, is paid to the question of whether the male (or female) animal whose sex life is undisciplined is happier than his/her complement. I see no evidence that this is so.

Accordingly, since most of the instruction in sex discipline issues from parents—and issues from them more often indirectly than directly—it would seem sensible to pass along to the parents information about a child's misgovernance. This would appear to be a point especially relevant given that the question of sexual activity is significantly informed by matters that deal with right and wrong, which is the dominion of religion. One is constantly surprised that those who oppose any religion in the schools, usually giving as a reason that religion is a matter for the home, are almost uniformly opposed to parental authority being exercised at home in matters that pertain to religion.

The Voice of America is in a tizzy over what kind of rock lyrics should be countenanced, and poor Mr. Scott, the director of programming, is discovering that if you rule out rock songs that are an invitation to round-the-clock sex, you pretty well rule out rock music. The measure of civilized activity, then, is equilibrium. And equilibrium in sex (as in most other matters) is informed by empirical studies (too much booze equals alcoholism), and by codes of behavior (thou shalt not covet thy neighbor's wife), which are informed primarily by religion. So that the lesson of the day is that parents ought to know when their children are falling into habits that could wreck their lives and those of others.

24

When Change Is Necessary

May 14, 1983

THE LEAD EDITORIAL in the New York *Times* for May 11 begins, "Whatever happened to the balanced budget amendment? It's obviously gone, to the burial ground for bad ideas. But whatever happened to the idea of reducing the budget deficit?"

It is correct that nothing appears to be happening to advance a balanced budget amendment, and clear that the second half of the rhetorical questions asked by the New York *Times* answers the first half. There being no budget amendment, less thought is being given to balancing the budget. So?

When it is not necessary to change, it is necessary not to change. That adage—was it by Lord Falkland?—is held as revealed conservative doctrine, and very much so in the matter of changing the Constitution. James Jackson Kilpatrick, who as a dispenser of wisdom in most matters sits at the right hand of Solomon, sometimes gives the impression that he would rather paint over the Sistine Chapel than approve a constitutional amendment. And, of course, the presumption is against changing the basic law of a society. But there are twenty-six amendments to the Constitution, and although by no means all of them are, in retrospect, sound, they indicate that from time to time a change is thought to be in order.

Any constitution that seeks to bind the political conduct of a people needs to take into consideration two things—one of them human nature, the second the cultural distinctiveness of the members of a particular society. A modern political miracle was the fashioning of an instrument in Philadelphia almost two hundred years ago that accommodated both human nature and American habits of mind and behavior. But in two hundred years we look back on when the Constitution was founded much as the Founding Fathers, looking back, could see the foundation of the colony at Plymouth. Postconstitutional America, in other words, is now older than preconstitutional America. So that we can with some gravity weigh what has become a national habit, and that is the unbalanced budget.

Sometime after the automobile was invented, it generally transpired that automobiles could not be permitted to drive as fast as engineers could make them drive. Because something other than the chauffeur's life was at stake—the lives of other people. So there came: the speed laws.

Sometime after the development of a parliament whose authority over money was unchecked, there transpired the need to provide such a check. This need for a check is an aspect of the human condition. A phrase incorporated into the most commonly recited prayer in Christendom is: "Lead us not into temptation." It isn't undignified to keep stray cigarettes out of sight of the man who is trying the kick the habit, or booze away from the alcoholic struggling to reform. Why do we suppose that politicians are not subject to temptation in that, as members of the human race, we are all of us sinners?

Representative Phil Gramm of Texas, who before going to Congress taught economics, a few years ago did a study. For convenience I have rounded off the figures, but inconsequentially. What he said was that the typical money bill that comes before Congress is for $50 million. The typical beneficiary of that money bill stands to get $500 if the bill is passed. The taxpayer stands to pay out fifty cents extra in tax if the bill is passed. Now: On which shoulder is the congressman likely to feel the greatest pressure on the day the bill comes up for a vote? The shoulder on which the people are leaning who will gain $500? Or the shoulder on which they lean who stand to lose fifty cents? You guessed it.

Mr. Gramm then gave a concrete example. A few years ago it was suggested in the House of Representatives that at a time when there was zero economic growth among American workers, the biannual indexation of Social Security was both unwise and unfair, and that, instead, indexation should take place only once a year. The motion was carried by voice vote. Then—one congressman asked for a roll call. You guessed it again: The economy was voted down, 2 to 1. Temptation is precisely, as Oscar Wilde said, the only thing most people cannot resist.

The time has come to mitigate the lure of temptation. If we had a balanced budget amendment—one carefully drawn up to take contingency into consideration—we would have the constitutional equivalent of speeding laws. How good it would be if bipartisan support could be got for such an amendment. Why not begin with a joint statement by Common Cause and the Heritage Foundation?

25

More Calisthenics
than Passion

March 25, 1983

I MUST ADMIT that, in contemporary seasons, Lent has a way of coming and going. Not so, obviously, for those more disciplined than the average. But the phenomenon reminds me of yet another of the habits of the past that are still fresh in the memory, and that serve pointedly as reminders that there is a little nexus between flesh and spirit that needs rather to be stimulated than ignored.

At the risk of sounding yet another atavistic tocsin, I say it flatly that it was a serious psychological mistake for Vatican II to dispense with the habit, all but international among Catholics, to refrain from eating meat on Fridays. I shall not step into the obvious trap of suggesting that Friday fish-eaters find themselves on the golden road to the everlasting. At the same time, I doubt that any purpose is served in recalling the frequency with which Our Lord submitted to fasting.

Lent used to be a season that almost demanded some conspicuous mortification of the flesh. For me as a schoolboy it was as simple as not eating candy, save on Sunday. This was difficult to do. By the standards of a thirteen-year-old, extremely difficult. That little sacrifice graduated, in college years, to abstinence from tobacco. Not quite all day. My rule became: No cigarettes until dinnertime. This was so agonizing that notwithstanding a most awfully exigent academic and extracurricular schedule, I took to going to matinees in midafternoon, because I had become inured, that being the rule in Connecticut movie houses, to not smoking for two hours. The idea was to make the time pass. By custom a late eater, I would find myself in the college dining hall not at seven-thirty (closing time) but at six (opening time): that way, I could smoke earlier.

Were these exercises spiritually orienting? In a way I think that they were. So was it remarkable, I thought, that at a certain point in Lent one no longer was able to look into the face of the cross, because it was shrouded in purple. Grief time. The conjoining of the petty griefs of minor abstinences, on over to a consideration of the overwhelming grief brought on by the suffering of the son of God had, in its quiet way, an electrifying sense of participation in the mysteries of divine providence.

Last year I attended what I suppose is the world's leading spectacle commemorating Holy Week. I mean, of course, the holy week as "celebrated"—always a word uncomfortably used in the circumstances—at Seville. It all begins on Wednesday night, and Thursday night stretches into six in the morning, with spectacle after spectacle, a magnificent ongoing pageantry with hundreds of thousands of—are they penitents, or are they celebrants? An interesting question. There are people who go to Seville in the same sense in which Dwight Macdonald once told me he read the Bible—as the greatest book in the world "which, however, does absolutely nothing at all for me on the business of believing in God." No doubt the spectacle of Seville would survive the disappearance of Christianity as, after all, Marxist ideology survives the historical anachronization of Marxism. I make only the point that we can still be reminded of the joys and the passion and the entirety of one's sometime devotion to the Lenten season.

I do not doubt that the passion will reawaken one of these days, and I pray that it will. The passion, primarily, to reflect on what genuine sacrifice can be, that which Our Lord underwent for reasons so monstrously silly as that you and I are worth His suffering. But that thought, so unspeakably frivolous, is the great catalyst of human equality: the means by which we are reminded of the nature of human fraternity. That God should love us equally says everything about Him, and almost everything about us. Certainly it reminds us that Lent is here to put us in our place, humble and sublime.

26

Gentlemen, Please

May 26, 1983

GENTLEMEN, gentlemen—please. Quiet—just a minute—let me speak now, OK? Thank you, thank you. Thank you very much.

Now I was born with a balanced-budget spoon in my life. I was for a balanced budget when I was sixteen, and if I had been precocious, I'd have been for a balanced budget when I was six. But it was in my blood is my point, and in due course it trickled to the brain, notwithstanding that I majored in Keynesianism at Yale. So please don't proceed as though I were indifferent to the ramifications of an unbalanced budget. In fact, I'm in favor of a balanced budget constitutional amendment, so my orthodoxy is absolutely straight.

And yes, I know that Ronald Reagan criticized the hell out of Jimmy Carter for having run a budget deficit of $160 billion in the course of his four years in office, and yes, I know our deficit this year is going to be in excess of that figure.

What was that, Mr. Mitterrand? Our deficit is endangering the French economy? But when you ran for office, you complained that the principal danger to the European economy was the U.S. inflation rate. It was 13 percent then and is down now to 4 percent.—What's that? Interest rates?

Well, our interest rates were running at over 20 percent

when Reagan took office, and they are half of that now. What's that? They're going to head back up because of our deficit?

Yes, I think that's true. Only not as much as is widely held. It is true that credit is finite, and that to the extent the unbalanced budget eats up that credit, there is less of it left for other needs, and it's true that scarcity breeds price increases. It's also true that the feds, if they step in to mitigate the credit shortage by creating a lot of money, will bring inflation back. So it would appear that we are headed for either a) higher interest, or b) higher inflation. I think that is correct. But you people—yes, Fritz, I'm looking at you, and Gary and John (how does political campaigning compare with weightlessness, John?) and also the neo-Rockefellerites, if that's what you want to call Bob Dole, John Chafee, Mac Mathias—are suggesting two things. They are: a) cut down on defense expenditures, and b) raise taxes.

Now the Constitution vests the President with the responsibilities of commander in chief. That doesn't mean it vests him with infallibility. It does mean that his evaluation of the defense needs of the country becomes a grave statistic. And remember that if we were to go the freeze route and the no-nuclear route we'd have to double, maybe triple our defense spending.

On the matter of taxation, what's the quickest way of saying it? How about this: During the Second World War, when nothing counted except victory, when 15 million Americans were drafted, we were taxing the American people 29 percent of the gross national product. Right now we're taxing 39 percent of the GNP. Colin Clark, the Oxford economist, cautioned a generation ago against taxing more than 25 percent of the GNP.

Does that mean I'm resigned to a big deficit and what it portends, you ask?

You're asking a political question, and I'll give you a political answer. We have an election coming up, as God knows this group knows. Military spending accounts for 23 percent of total federal spending. What spending program has Reagan initiated, other than in defense? When last, before 1980, was either house of Congress controlled by Republicans? That's right, 1954. So that every dollar being spent, creating the huge deficit, is a dollar voted to be spent by Democratic Congresses, and authorized in most cases by Democratic Presidents. Reagan has no authority to repeal entitlement programs.

So Congress needs to take the blame for the deficit. That part of the deficit that represents increased defense spending Reagan can take the blame for, if that's the right word for the culpability of mounting our defense. Take what Carter wanted to spend in defense—$138 billion—and what Reagan proposes to spend—$170 billion. A difference of $32 billion. Assign Reagan the blame for that much of the deficit. The rest is a Democratic responsibility.

OK, go ahead and boo me. But I got under your skin, didn't I? OK, OK, I'm leaving. Just wanted one word. Pluralistic society, remember? Ask the ACLU. They'll be here any minute now. They're all home praying.

27

Down Mexico Way

July 5, 1983

THE BIG NEWS out of Mexico is that the government has actually indicted (for fraud) somebody who counts. Mind you, not a former president, but the target, Jorge Diaz Serrano, was the head of the Mexican state oil monopoly (Pemex) and it is charged that he was involved in buying a couple of freighters at $34 million more than they were worth.

Now that sum—$34 million—may strike us Americans as enormous, but that really is an index of how naïve Americans tend to be in the world of graft. The Mexican Workers' Party has filed charges, apparently documented, to the effect that 317 million more barrels of oil have been brought out of the ground in Mexico during recent years than Pemex records having received. Depending on the price of oil, the resulting loot comes in at not less than $10 billion nor more than $15 billion. U.S. journalist George Lake comments that "if true," this would "compare with Teapot Dome, the notorious U.S. oil scandal of the 1920s, as a whale compares with a sick minnow."

What everyone is speculating about in Mexico is the former president.

Mr. José López Portillo, the people's friend who left Mexico with a foreign debt of $90 billion and as a final gesture of contempt for the private sector nationalized all the private banks, has been having a tough time lately. The people have

got to referring to him as JoLoPo, which is not the most re-
spectful compression one can think of for someone who as
recently as a year ago was the undisputed boss of Mexico. But
going around being called JoLoPo is nothing compared to
other problems the former president has.

You see, before he became president, JoLoPo was a university professor, and we all know that university professors are
not millionaires. Now, having left office, JoLoPo's principal
residence is a 32-acre hilltop estate in a suburb of Mexico City.
JoLoPo is a family man, and accordingly he built not merely a
house for himself and his wife, but also one for each of their
three children. Very nice houses, in that each has its own en-
closed swimming pool heated by a central facility, and of
course there are tennis courts and gardens and lawns. Also an
astronomical observatory, useful for tracking friendly astrolog-
ical concatenations, if indeed JoLoPo acquired all that money
by speculation. We say "all that money" because a building
expert in Mexico has calculated that the Mexico City compound would have cost 100 percent of the salary of the president of Mexico if he had served for 107 years.

JoLoPo is vividly remembered for the speech he gave sometime before leaving office in which he said he would "fight like
a dog" to prevent the devaluation of the peso. This speech was
quickly followed by the second devaluation of the peso in four
months. The result is that not only have the Mexican people
given JoLoPo a bad nickname, they have also given a name to
his compound. They call it *Colina del Perro*, which is to say,
Dog Hill.

You may think that was bad enough, but you would be
wrong. The other day, JoLoPo was at a fancy restaurant with a
good friend, Rosa Luz Alegría, former secretary of tourism,
when suddenly from the rear of the dining room a human bark
was heard. Before long the entire place was barking, and poor
JoLoPo had to flee the restaurant and leave for an extended
stay in Europe. In his private airplane.

President de la Madrid coasted into office promising to clean
up corruption. JoLoPo had meanwhile promised that a list
would be published of those Mexicans who had secreted their
money and sent it abroad. They are said to have got out $24
billion. The trouble was that when time came to publish that

roster, it was the political equivalent of publishing a list of JoLoPo's brothers, sisters, aunts, uncles, cousins and mistresses. The list continues unpublished.

There is a very dark side to all this. The Mexican people are suffering very acutely. President de la Madrid has a tough time. On the one hand, bringing JoLoPo to justice may be to pull the linchpin on the reigning political party. On the other hand, the failure to do so may convince the people that nothing, really, is changing. That's OK for people who have a job, food to eat, and shelter over their heads, but the number without these amenities is growing at a perilous and tragic rate.

28

How to Make a Crisis
Go Away

August 2, 1983

Every now and again despondent observers of the world
scene mutter thoughts to the effect that democracies simply
cannot contend against totalitarian powers because of the inherent advantages of decisive rule uninhibited by the need for
public sanction. The consolidation of the Polish question, con-
trasted with the continuing turmoil in Central America, illus-
trates both the advantages of communist practice and the col-
lusion of the West in bringing on their successes.

Would any stray diplomat, if collared on the street, say that
there is at this moment a "Polish crisis"? The answer is, very
clearly, no. Why is this so? It is so because there is no Polish
crisis. But then why was there ever a Polish crisis? There was a
Polish crisis because a labor movement called Solidarity cap
tured the public and national imagination and served demands
on the communist overlords to acknowledge such basic human
freedoms as were enunciated in the Helsinki Accords.

But, then, why is there no longer a Polish crisis, given that
the Poles do not enjoy the freedoms they set out after?

Answer: There is no Polish crisis because the West has
agreed that nothing is going to be done to challenge the hegemony of the Soviet Union over Polish affairs.

Question: Then why was there ever a Polish crisis?

Answer: Because Western leaders take public positions that

side with those who call out for freedom, and the hypothetical possibility arises that the West will do something concrete to help the oppressed. For that reason, for brief moments in history the world stirs: it did over Poland in 1952, over East Germany in 1953, over Hungary in 1956, over Czechoslovakia in 1968, and over Poland in 1981. The crisis then goes away by the simultaneous workings of Soviet resolution and Western irresolution.

Lech Walesa pronounced the final judgment on the end of martial law in Poland under present circumstances. It would be preferable, he said, to live in Poland under martial law than to live in Poland under the circumstances imposed by the new constitution.

So normal are things now that you can expect that the Polish government will put in for Western rescheduling of its loan, which stands at $25 million. What will the West do? It will accede. And, if you can stand it, it will do so "in order to avert a crisis." The crisis is here defined as anything that might cause serious discomfort to the Soviet Union.

Now the peculiar working of the Western mind is that not only do crises go away when the Soviet Union resolutely steps in to stop the threat of disorder. Crises also go away when the West contrives to make a bad situation worse. Anyone not blinded by race prejudice would probably admit that life in Rhodesia is worse for white and black under Mugabe, whose government we not only recognize but sustain economically, than it was under the predecessor government, which we boycotted. If we have not, by the end of this decade, succeeded in overturning the government of South Africa in order to visit on the people a black-dominated dictatorship, no American liberal will sleep peacefully. Having twenty years ago collaborated in the ouster of a penny-ante dictator in Cuba and replaced him with a finished totalitarian proconsul, we considered the Cuban crisis ended—after an ineffective attempt to overthrow Castro, followed not much later by a public promise not to try to unseat him.

The Vietnam crisis ended when we surrendered Vietnam to communist aggression. We conspired to overthrow Somoza in Nicaragua, and all the commotion today that adds up to a Nicaraguan crisis has to do not with Nicaraguan efforts to subvert adjacent countries, but with American efforts to prevent the Sandinistas from doing so. The Salvadoran crisis—I do not exaggerate—will end a month or two after the insurgents take power. If we succeed in giving marginal aid to the government sufficient to quell the rebellion, the Salvadoran crisis will endure for years. A corollary to the above definition of crisis is that a crisis endures for as long as the Soviet Union's position does not prevail.

When we reflect that Ronald Reagan is the President of the United States, and that even so we accept such defeats as have been handed to us in Poland, a great and bitter despair threatens to take us over, and in such moments as these one concludes that if the West is going to win, it will do so because of the failure of communism, not because of the resources of freedom.

29

The Sweet Sound
of Saber Rattling

October 27, 1983

IT PAYS to remind ourselves every now and then that many clichés once were aphorisms. "The fault, dear Brutus, is not in our stars, but in ourselves, that we are underlings" is a yawn-maker today, but was a hot thought, poetically expressed, five hundred years ago. "The trouble with Hamlet," the lady is said to have complained, "is it's so full of clichés." One of the clichés to which we have plighted our troth since the end of the Vietnam war is that we must not go about saber rattling. My own opinion is that we are overdue for a little saber rattling.

Begin by asking the question: Why do nations have sabers? Answer: to threaten to use them if necessary.

What then is it to rattle one's saber? Answer: to remind those who need to be reminded that the saber is there, and that indeed there are circumstances in which it will be used.

Now Ronald Reagan, without saying so in so many words, is totally committed to using our ultimate saber against the Soviet Union if the Soviet Union uses it against us. It is below the level of atomic exchanges that the United States approaches something on the order of impotence. In Central America we have managed to insinuate something on the order of sixty military advisers into El Salvador. One sometimes has the feeling that if the commander in chief dispatched five more, Congress would impeach him.

Nor has the commander in chief helped things very much by saying on more than one occasion that we will not have a Vietnam in Central America. If he had been clearer, the statement would have been all right. In order to be clearer he should have said, "If we find it necessary to become militarily involved in Central America, it will not be another Vietnam, believe me." Castro and his epigone would have understood that one. As things stand, positively the safest political thing to do in most of Central America is to defy the United States. The next easiest thing to do is to emigrate to the United States.

A scholar who recently visited in the area reports that his contacts with knowledgeable Latin Americans lead him to the conclusion that they have concluded that the Congress of the United States will not back tough, decisive resistance to Marxist aggression in the area. The likely result of our anemic response to Castroism is the collapse of effective opposition. Such a move, the thoughtful gentleman reports, would in the opinion of many forecasters bring on the collapse of political authority in Mexico. This could lead to—one reaches for just the descriptive word—an avalanche of Mexicans, fleeing chaos and poverty in their native land, coming into the United States. Imagine—and we must force ourselves to do this—what would be the social and political and cultural consequences within the United States of, let us say, 15 million Mexicans pouring in illegally, in a period of a year or two.

"It is impossible," my friend writes, "to persuade academic specialists on Mexico and Central America to give serious attention to such a development. I know of no weighty study of the implications for our domestic tranquillity on such a tide of immigrants."

What are our contingency plans for containing such a flood? How do we fuse humanitarian and realistic elements in considering the problem? How widely is it known that since the collapse of the Mexican peso eighteen months ago, illegal immigration has risen by a factor of 400 percent and that frontier officials privately concede that anybody in Mexico who has two cents' worth of wit can cross the border?

But the existing problem is as nothing compared with the projected problem in the event that El Salvador, then Guatemala, Honduras and Costa Rica, went the way of Nicaragua. And why should they?

Not because the people desire it. Not even because a non-Marxist government is often weak and ineffectual. It is because more and more people feel it in their bones that the future belongs to the kind of governors who say no to the liberalization of Poland and mean it, who march armies into Afghanistan and stay there, and who shoot down uninvited airliners as they would swat down a mosquito. While the other superpower agonizes at peace rallies over disarmament treaties which, when effected, mean nothing to the Soviet Union and self-castration to the United States.

Indeed, it is time for saber rattling over here.

30

The Problem
Is Something Else

January 6, 1984

IN DISCUSSING the business of terrorists and death squads and U.S. policy in general recently, *Time* magazine emphasized a solidifying U.S. consensus. It said that Vice President "Bush was in El Salvador for just seven hours, but his warnings about 'these right-wing fanatics' were stark and powerful. 'Your cause is being undermined by the murderous violence of reactionary minorities,' he said to an assembly of the country's politicians and military men, '[which] poisons the well of friendship between our countries. [Do not] make the mistake of thinking that there is any division in my country on this question.'"

Now, let us concede that the death squads are composed primarily of sadistic opportunists who, taking cover in the civil war, pursue their acquisitive and sanguinary interests relatively unmolested because of the preoccupation of civil authority with that civil war. Is it a strategically decisive problem that they are unregulated? One on which plausibly hangs the question whether we should aid the government of El Salvador?

One's instinctive feeling in the matter (perhaps I should not go so far as Mr. Bush and suggest that there is no "division in my country on this question") is that the world would be better off if a dozen Salvadoran government sharpshooters, in the middle of the night, were to visit the homes of the leaders of the death squads and, in the brisk style of Charles Bronson in the movie *Death Wish*, simply do away with them. To be sure, there would then be those who accused El Salvador of commissioning a Super Death Squad; but we could leave that discussion to the American Civil Liberties Union to fret over, and go to sleep a little bit more peacefully in the knowledge that the country we were sending military and economic aid to was not co-existing peacefully with squads of men who go out at night and murder missionary nuns.

But what one must guard against is the notion that our alliance with the government of El Salvador is a function of its civilized deportment.

A generation ago we joined hands with Josef Stalin, whose entire government one might charitably refer to as a death squad. He would not have welcomed any advice on how to reform Gulag; which advice, for the record, nobody in the government of Franklin Delano Roosevelt felt any compulsion to tender.

Twenty years later, we began telling President Diem in Vietnam to mend his ways sufficiently to keep Buddhist monks from immolating themselves in protest against his policies. What we ended up with, in due course, was the boat people.

A half-dozen years ago we decided we had better begin running Iranian internal affairs, and began inveighing against the (demonstrated) cruelties of the representatives of the Shah of Iran. In due course we got the Ayatollah.

Last month, the newly elected president of Argentina indicted a handful of military figures whom he will hold responsible for the six thousand *desaparecidos* wasted during Argentina's civil war. This grand gesture toward a historical reconciliation between Argentina and justice does not belie the chronological point, namely that at the time the Argentinian death squads were operating, either the government could not, or, if it could, it did not impede their activity. And now Argentina is being run by a democratic government. It would be glib to suppose that that would necessarily have come about if the counterrevolutionary activities against the Montoneros, the Argentinian version of the Sandinistas, had been conducted according to rules of warfare that nowadays satisfy the refined consciences of American congressmen. Argentina is in the hands of democrats, not totalitarians. How that came to be is a subtle question, deserving of subtle analysis.

We are in El Salvador because its government, for all its impurities, is geopolitically allied with us in the great cosmic effort, however disheveled, to give freedom and democracy and decency a chance against the communist monolith. To suggest that United States support should be contingent on El Salvador's regulation of its grisly death squads is, simply, to miss the point; and to raise to primacy, in the formulation of foreign policy, considerations that are, simply, extrinsic to strategic U.S. concerns.

31

For Moderation
in Osculation

February 16, 1984

I WANT TO KNOW one very simple thing: Why do nontotalitarian leaders embrace totalitarian leaders? By "embrace" I do not intend a metaphor, as in "During the Second World War, President Roosevelt embraced Josef Stalin." I mean the real thing. I am staring at a picture of two men smiling at each other, their arms about each other, their noses not two inches separated. Any closer, and they'd have skirted sodomy. The caption reads: "A friendly meeting—President Fidel Castro of Cuba, right, is greeted by Prime Minister Felipe González of Spain at Madrid's airport."

We all recognize that the business of diplomacy requires interpersonal contacts, as for instance between Neville Chamberlain and Adolf Hitler in the fall of 1938. But why is it that such meetings need to communicate a personal relationship that transcends politics? Felipe González and Fidel Castro managed to look like the Smith Brothers greeting each other after receiving Nobel Prizes for their cough drops.

Now the news story reveals two interesting data. One of them is that Felipe González is something of an old friend of Castro. Most of Castro's old friends Castro has shot or imprisoned, so that one possible motive of Felipe's delight was to celebrate the fact that he is an exception. The other datum of interest is that King Juan Carlos telephoned his greetings to

Castro, whose stay in Spain was for a mere four hours (he was flying back from Andropov's funeral). King Juan Carlos evidently hopes to make a state visit to Havana, one knows not why, and was evidently anxious not to be left out of the celebration of Fidel Castro's very first visit to any country in Western Europe. Always before, he has overflown Europe en route to Moscow and the satellites. The Reuters dispatch records, "The gesture"—the royal phone call—"was a reflection of the enthusiasm in Madrid for Mr. González's action."

Why this enthusiasm? I mean, is there any reason anyone can think of why in a country in which Francisco Franco has become a dirty word because he imprisoned a dozen people every year and exercised a light political censorship of the press, Fidel Castro should be lionized? Fidel Castro, who exercises totalitarian power, imprisons priests, is an excommunicated Catholic, tortures poets, incites revolutions, protects terrorists, husbanded Soviet thermonuclear missiles: Why does a socialist democrat wish to embrace Castro?

You will say: Ah, but don't you see, it is a part of the Mediterranean style. You cannot, if Spanish blood runs through your veins, greet another leader without embracing him. To do otherwise would be to offend him.

And it is true that President Carter bussed President Brezhnev when they signed SALT II. And true that although Richard Nixon was a little more platonic in Peking that first night, he did approach individual survivors of the Cultural Revolution with sheer ardor in his eyes, a toasting glass in hand. Is this necessary to effective diplomacy?

So far as one can remember, if this is so, it is something new. There are no pictures easily recalled of President Roosevelt smooching with Josef Stalin. FDR did give Stalin a few countries, as souvenirs of their meetings, but he drew the line at a public embrace. Neville Chamberlain did not embrace Hitler (ugh!). Why did Austria's Kreisky feel the need to embrace Arafat? And anyway, in our heart of hearts, don't we know perfectly well that there isn't a leader in the world who would kiss the prime minister of South Africa—unless he were black? We know this intuitively, and our knowing it intuitively makes all the more mischievous the promiscuous bussing against which I rail. Because you see, if we acknowledge that there are some people one simply will not embrace publicly, then one acknowledges that there are moral criteria that govern these matters. And then one asks, What moral criteria are drawn so loosely that Fidel Castro should not fall within their proscriptive range? What is the use of having any criteria, if Brezhnev is not excluded by them? If the Boston strangler is a member of the club, what is the use in having an admissions committee?

Accordingly, herewith a proposal to be incorporated into the Republican Platform. "No American President should embrace any world leader responsible for the death and/or torture and/or imprisonment of more than 0.01 per cent of his people." For short, it can be called the Osculation Clause.

32

On Preempting
the Categories

July 6, 1984

M ANY YEARS AGO when he was running the summer school
at Harvard, Henry Kissinger spoke ruminatively about how
the liberals in America have "preempted the categories." So,
in international affairs, have the communists preempted the
categories.

It is quite dazzling to think that the Reagan administration is
actually on the defensive where intellectuals meet, with such
policies as have resulted in the interest rate being cut in half
and inflation cut by 75 percent. By the same token, in the
academic corridors in Europe and Latin America and the
Third World, the United States is thought to be dragging its
feet on the matter of world peace. We are held responsible for
the Soviet Union's pouting.

Take, as an example of what the Soviet Union nonchalantly
gets away with, the matter of Cuba. John Silber, the sharp-eyed
and acid-tongued philosopher who is president of Boston University, spoke a while back to the American Legion and reminded that body that the agreement reached between President Kennedy and Premier Khrushchev in 1962 has been,
quite simply, broken.

If your reaction is: How can that be? The Soviet Union has no
missiles in Cuba—then you are proof, redundant proof, of how
successfully the Soviet Union has preempted the categories.

Because the agreement reached in October 1962 was only in part about missiles.

When President Kennedy issued his proclamation of June 23, he used the following language: "The United States is determined to prevent by whatever means may be necessary, including the use of arms, the Marxist-Leninist regime in Cuba from extending, by force or by the threat of force, its aggressive or subversive activities to any part of this hemisphere, and to prevent in Cuba the creation or use of any externally supported military capability endangering the security of the United States."

When Khrushchev capitulated, he didn't merely withdraw the nuclear weapons. He withdrew 10,000 to 15,000 Soviet combat and support troops, and all his bombers. By his deeds, he confirmed his acquiescence to Kennedy's terms.

What then happened, over a period of twenty years, was a gradual erosion of the Cuban commitment except insofar as nuclear missiles were concerned. As it happens, during those twenty years the need for nuclear missiles on Cuban territory has greatly diminished for the simple reason that Soviet submarines prowling our waters dispose of far greater nuclear power than was projected for Cuba in 1962. But the other half of the agreement, to demilitarize Cuba, is spectacularly violated.

Cuba has now a standing army of 230,000 men (second in size only to Brazil's, which has thirteen times the population of Cuba), the best equipped in Latin America, and rated by the experts the second most potent military power in the hemisphere. Why, if not to threaten its neighbors and export its revolution?

Cuba has a submarine base at Cienfuegos that threatens our water passages to the south. It houses a Soviet combat brigade. It has Soviet Bear (TU-95C) reconnaissance planes, which give way now to TU-95F, capable of antisubmarine warfare. Cuba's airfields, deserted by the Soviet military pursuant to the Kennedy-Khrushchev agreement, accommodate Soviet Backfires. These are the nifty Soviet supersonic bombers that can fly nonstop from the U.S.S.R. across the United States to Cuba. The Soviets sent some MiG-23s and MiG-27s, the latter capable of supersonic speeds and the delivery of nuclear weapons.

Why aren't we out there in the chancelleries of the world, in the United Nations, in the corridors of academe, demanding that the 1962 agreement be honored by the demilitarization of Cuba? Why isn't what's happening in Cuba, as distinguished from what's happening in Nicaragua and El Salvador, being discussed? Nicaragua and El Salvador would, but for Cuba, be fighting merely routine banana-republic Colonel-Gonzales-*v.*-General-Gómez-type wars—but for the violation of the 1962 agreement and all that this has meant in planned-in-Moscow chaos.

In Europe, it goes as follows: The Soviets deploy SS-20s. We back up NATO with Pershing IIs. The Soviets scream and yell and go home to mother. And we are blamed for intransigence. In the Caribbean, we make an agreement, the Soviet-Cuban axis violates it, which brings on a crisis in Central America. And we are blamed for it.

Sometimes it causes one to wonder, wonder, wonder. A Negro spiritual is relevant: Were we actually there when all this happened to us?

33

Keep Your Eyes on Mario

August 1, 1984

M R. CUOMO has accused President Reagan of "pandering" to the Catholic vote, and the occasion is ripe to touch on the meaning of the word.

Webster's Third gives three definitions, the first two having to do with prostitutes and the role of the panderer. These are irrelevant to a political discussion save when the intention is to suggest that a candidate is offering his services (the endorsement of a political plank, let us say) in pursuit of an unprincipled purpose (for instance, subsidies) in exchange for money (votes). The operative word here is "unprincipled." A moral whore is not only an oxymoron, it is a contradiction.

The third definition of a panderer is one who "caters to, and often exploits the weaknesses of, others." This last definition isn't one that a politician like Mario Cuomo would rush to emphasize, inasmuch as it would find him required to elaborate on just what are these weaknesses of American Catholics to which Ronald Reagan is pandering. Mario Cuomo would change the subject.

Concerning the first two definitions, a reminiscence.

Sometime after he (in effect) announced his candidacy for President in 1952, Adlai Stevenson telephoned his former wife and told her to prepare "the boys" to be picked up on Sunday at 10:45. "Why?" Mrs. Stevenson asked. "I am taking them to church," said Adlai. "That was when I knew he was going to run," Mrs. Stevenson told a friend later. And sure enough, the photographers were there to record the hebdomadal piety of Adlai Stevenson.

Could we then say that Adlai Stevenson was "pandering" to the churchgoing community? No, not really. One might accuse him of hypocrisy—but even then, we would need to do this with caution. Men of standing are expected to do certain things whatever their internal inclination. For all we know, Ronald Reagan might, a polygraph strapped to his arm, admit that he loathed baseball and choked at the very thought of spaghetti. The old saw of La Rochefoucauld was that hypocrisy is the tribute that vice pays to virtue. To like baseball is considered, in America, not merely a workaday preference, like for instance an innocent preference for chocolate sundaes or catamites, but a virtue, very possibly ennobling. It is not a part of any political candidate's moral mandate to shake that confidence. And if indeed Adlai Stevenson was an agnostic or an atheist, he did not feel that it was his mission to go out and preach iconoclasm to the American people.

So what, then, is Mario Cuomo talking about?

The event to which he referred was a spaghetti dinner given under Catholic auspices in New Jersey and a speech in which Mr. Reagan reiterated his conviction that family life and religion are fundamental American institutions.

The question before the house is: How is this to pander? We have disposed of the problem of eating spaghetti—it is simply good manners to pretend to enjoy what you are served, though an exception might here be made of gefilte fish, the consumption of which, reasonable epicureans might conclude, is not worth going through to gain admission to the White House. What was it that Mr. Reagan did that "pandered" to Catholics? President Reagan opposes abortion, as do many non-Catholics; as do 49 percent of registered Democrats. Is it to pander to Catholics to express beliefs that harmonize with their own? Is it to pander to Jews to profess one's belief in the right of Israel to exist? Was Mario Cuomo anywhere around in his own state during the Democratic presidential primary campaign? Murray Kempton, the brilliantly amusing columnist, remarked on television that the Democratic presidential candidates had jumped on Jesse Jackson for saying that New York was Hymietown, and then proceeded during the campaign to prove, by their explicit solicitation of Jewish support, that they thought Jackson was right. An amusing formulation, and indeed Gary Hart went further in his public pledges to the territorial integrity of Israel during the campaign than he'd have been willing to go on behalf of Iowa.

But there was nothing heard from Mario Cuomo in protest.

Governor Cuomo is beginning to grate. This happens when men affect to speak from high moral ground (George McGovern comes to mind) and are regularly subversive of principles by which they profess to abide. Keep your eyes on Mario. Or am I pandering to the patriotic vote?

34

The Bankers Take Us
for a Ride

August 6, 1984

In New York, as presumably elsewhere, the Continental
Illinois National Bank took out a full-page ad on Friday, Deliv-
erance Day. If Leon Trotsky had written it, it could not more
effectively have undermined respect for American capitalism.

Starting with the headline "At last, a rumor we can confirm,"
it stayed right in that jaunty mood. Its lead sentence read:
"These past few months you've probably heard more about
Continental than you'd care to know."

That is what I call leading with your chin. The average
American is as interested in Continental Illinois as he is in the
annual rainfall in Tierra del Fuego, which for all we know is
one of the principal investments of Continental.

Next: "Now, we're happy to report, we have a plan designed
to solve our problems in the best interest of everyone concerned." There are several problems with that sentence. The
first is that it wasn't Continental's plan, it was a plan of the
comptroller of the currency, the Federal Deposit Insurance
Corporation, and the Federal Reserve Board. A plan certainly
designed to make the shareholders and bondholders of Continental "happy." Making them happy was not a plan incorporated in the Declaration of Independence or in the Constitution. Most banks can be made "happy" if you underwrite $4.5
billion of their bad debt. The "plan" was the government's,

and it was designed to avoid the chaos that would have resulted from requiring Continental to face the market discipline of its foolish practices.

"The key provision of the plan is that Continental will continue to operate as a vital financial institution, free of the bulk
of the problem loans which had become a burden on our financial and human resources." A burden on their human resources. Sure. Any burden on one's financial resources can
become a burden on one's human resources. It is also a burden
on one's human resources when one goes to jail. The moral
question that some Americans are considering is: Why did
Continental's burden become our burden?

Now, there are a lot of plausible answers to this, primarily
that the entire banking system would suffer a grievous shock if
Continental went down. That, most Americans can understand. If emergency action is needed to prevent a lot of banks
from sliding over Niagara Falls, then take that action. But
there is no moral reason to shield the $800-million equity of
Continental shareholders by using public money. Public
money is here defined as money printed by the Federal Reserve Board.

On May 18, the Fed made an error of grave psychological
consequence. It was then that the regulators announced that
all depositors of Continental would be protected, never mind
the $100,000 ceiling set by the Federal Deposit Insurance Cor-
poration. Protection for individual depositors by the FDIC is
an accepted convention of the New Deal, designed to protect
depositors against collapsing banks. To enlarge that guarantee
in order to protect general creditors is primarily a political act,
i.e., an act designed to weigh alternatives and to select the one
that gives least pain to most people.

The trouble with political solutions, however, is that the
individual American taxpayer becomes, increasingly, a general
creditor—left with highly illiquid returns. The federal pool
that salvaged Continental via the FDIC is out $1 billion. It has
access to equity that may or may not, in the years to come,
return some of its investment.

But whether it does (as in the case of Chrysler, where the
government ended by profiting from its bailout) or it doesn't,
the psychological precedent is set according to which any sub-

stantial group of investors in any enterprise can cite Continental—as, before it, Chrysler; as, before it, Lockheed—to make a social point. "Bail us out, because the alternatives are too painful." As Continental puts it, you need only proclaim that your business has "become a burden on our financial and human resources" and the Feds will come running to help.

Congress had better grope its way out of the crystallizing paradox. On the one hand we favor deregulation of the banking industry as economically healthy for America. On the other hand, we appear to be weaving a security blanket that argues that competition is ultimately meaningless because, when all is said and done, government is there to protect against risk.

You will hear the name of Continental on the lips of every special-interest advocate of cradle-to-grave protection for American businesses; except that graves, by the dictates of the New New Deal, will be abolished.

35

Can't Stigmas Be Useful?

August 20, 1984

THE PERMISSIVENESS of which modern liberals are so proud turns out, in situation after situation, to usher in circumstances liberals—and others—deplore; and so it is time now to check on our hierarchies and integrate our thinking.

During the past twenty years, erotic and pornographic books and magazines have become universal. It is as easy to buy *Penthouse* as *The Wall Street Journal.*

During the past twenty years, information about birth control has become quite generally available. Moreover, technological achievements, most notably The Pill, have made the control of pregnancies easier. Indeed, the word went out that The Pill in and of itself was the great emancipator of women.

During the past twenty years we have had an organized national war against poverty, to use the martial metaphor so often used. Whereas the military budget, twenty years ago, was twice the size of the welfare budget, now it is the other way around.

Now, what has happened, as a result of all these blessings?

At one level of permissiveness we have rampant homosexuality. This would appear to mean that whereas twenty years ago homosexuals were encouraged in continent behavior, no such self-discipline is any longer a part of the governing ethos. One result of this is a new and fatal disease, AIDS—which torments homosexuals primarily—plus other venereal diseases.

At the level of heterosexual experience, the result has been an extraordinary rise in illegitimate births. Surely, given the abundance, variety, and ubiquitousness of birth-control information, there should flow a sharp diminution in accidental pregnancies. But this didn't happen. In New York City out-of-wedlock births are one-third of the total. In Harlem, 80 percent. In Newark, 60 percent. In Baltimore, 58 percent.

Well, what about poverty?

In 1965, 17 percent of Americans were "poor." By equivalent standards, today 15.2 percent are poor. So the figures would appear to tell us that after the expenditure of perhaps a trillion dollars, the poverty level was reduced by only two percentage points. But then we note that in 1974—ten years ago—the poverty level had sunk to 11 percent. And the figures are not entirely reliable, given that the poverty census takers don't count nonmonetary forms of income. If these were counted—such things as food stamps and subsidized housing and medical care—poverty would be cut almost in half, to 8.8 percent. Still, there are a lot of poor people, when you consider how much money we are spending toward the eradication of poverty.

Comes now the integration of these phenomena. Is there a correlation between illegitimate births and poverty? Answer: Yes, there is. If you are illegitimate, you probably will be reared in poverty.

What is it that brought about the twin conditions?

Dr. Sol Blumenthal, the New York City Health Department's director of biostatistics, informs the New York *Times* that the growth in illegitimacy is owing to a shift in society's attitudes toward the idea of having children out of marriage and to the lessened stigma attached to out-of-wedlock children, to quote a story by Joseph Berger. "People who were in that class were once held to ridicule and abuse," Dr. Blumenthal said. But now, "if there is no father around, there's nothing to berate anybody about," because in some neighborhoods a majority of the births are out of wedlock.

And the second reason? Dr. Blumenthal says that—to quote the story—"society has cushioned the blows of having children outside marriage by providing welfare payments and day-care programs."

So let us look the facts in the face, as Walter Mondale and Mrs. Ferraro are not doing, preferring instead to attribute high rates of poverty to Ronald Reagan, whom they may as well get mad at for not having any illegitimate children, proving that he does not have the common touch.

1. Sexual permissiveness has caused a rise in disease and death.

2. Sexual permissiveness has caused a rise in illegitimacy.

3. Illegitimacy has caused a rise in poverty.

4. The general availability of birth-control information has caused a rise in illegitimacy.

5. Liberal approaches to social life have really hit the jackpot: reduced morals, betrayed children, disease, and poverty. Nice going, gang. What's the next welfare trillion going to do for us?

36

They Used to Call It
the Resistance

October 28, 1984

THE BUSINESS about the CIA and the little booklet in Nicaragua brings to mind, yet again, as so much so often brings to mind, Henry Kissinger's wistful statement twenty years ago that "the liberals have preempted the categories." Applied to the current situation it adds up to: No serious attempt to liberate Nicaragua is tolerable, because the liberation of Nicaragua from the Sandinistas, as distinguished from the liberation of Nicaragua from Somoza, is not on the liberal agenda.

A generation ago it was accepted that patriotic and courageous Frenchmen would do what they could to liberate their country. There were a lot of Nazis in France, but most of France was governed by Frenchmen—Vichy French they were called—who had completed a treaty with Hitler under which, in effect, France became a Nazi German satellite. The order of the day for Frenchmen who did not want the permanent nazification of their country was to do something about it. Aided by the British and the Americans, they relayed military information to the Allies, they blew up bridges and trains and power stations, they killed both German and French officials, they kidnapped, interrogated, and executed. They were called the Resistance.

Now it is the central contention of the architects of our policy in Central America that Nicaragua is not an independent country. For the sake of convenience, multiply any figure involving Nicaragua by a factor of one hundred in order to feel out what the figure would be, cast in an American perspective —there are 2.5 million Nicaraguans and about 250 million Americans.

Nicaragua proposes a 250,000-man military (read, 25 million).

There are thirty-six new military bases in Sandinista Nicaragua. Forty-five tanks, and equivalent armored personnel carriers, mobile rocket launchers, and helicopters. There are three thousand Cuban military and security advisers and five thousand Cuban civilian technicians. There are fifty Soviet military advisers, several thousand Eastern-bloc technicians. Adding up to?

"There is something you have to understand," said Alfonso Robelo, a former member of the original five-man junta in Nicaragua. "Nicaragua is an occupied country . . . The national decisions, the crucial ones, are not in the hands of the Nicaraguans, but in the hands of Cubans. And really, in the end, it is not the Cubans, but the Soviets." That is why Alfonso Robelo is now a leader of the dissident Revolutionary Democratic Alliance.

The Nicaraguan people are oppressed at every level. Real wages are down 71 percent since Somoza was ousted. There are 4,100 political prisoners (remember the times-100 factor). "There is," in the summary of Roger Reed, formerly with the Council for Inter-American Security, "no right to strike, no right of habeas corpus, no right of assembly, no right of political parties to hold public meetings." There is persecution of religion. And there is brutality. James Whelan, former managing editor of the Washington *Times,* and Patricia Bozell, former managing editor of *Triumph* magazine, in a wonderfully useful new book *(Catastrophe in the Caribbean)* discuss the methods of Nicaraguan interrogators trained by Cubans: "It must take training to devise the 'vest cut,' whereby captured counterrevolutionaries are taken to the nearest village, their arms and legs lopped off, and their torsos left to die by inches, a grisly inspiration of behavioral science for the inhabitants—men, women, and children alike."

Now the CIA was once routinely expected to help those who

wished liberation from communist tyranny and could hope to effect this (e.g., help the Greeks, the Guatemalans, the Afghans, the Nicaraguans; don't try—it is too late—to help Bulgarian dissidents, or Czechoslovakians). Why not help from the CIA for all dissidents against oppressive governments? Answer: Because we can't hack it. Fulbright reminded us that the government of the United States has no proper quarrel against any government, no matter how odious its policies, if it does not seek to export those policies. That is what distinguishes the tyranny of Castro from the tyranny of Papa Doc.

So a manual is worked up that outlines the techniques of resistance. Somebody in the CIA evidently had a hand in preparing it, though it was published, edited, and distributed by the Nicaraguan Resistance. And that causes Tip O'Neill to go into one of his high fustian outbursts against CIA director William Casey, who may not even have known about the CIA's role in the preparation of the manual but can hardly believe that the Contras are going to limit themselves to using poison ivy against the Sandinistas. "I say it's time Mr. Casey should leave his job. I want him to get out of there."

There are others who say it is time for Tip O'Neill to grow up. There is a real world out there, and *sic semper tyrannis* is still the guide of American emotions; either it is, or we should repeal "The Star-Spangled Banner," lower the flag, and be done with it.

37

Please Just Go Away

November 7, 1984

IT SEEMED never to occur to candidate Mondale that, in America, the idea of progress presupposes a state of mind Mondale never acknowledged, in all that caterwauling he did for all those weeks and months. That idea is that progress should entitle an American to a certain limited security; that having worked, earned, and saved, that American doesn't think it correct that his life's work should be subject to political vicissitudes: here today, gone tomorrow in inflation and in taxes. Moreover, that American doesn't feel that he made headway at the expense of other Americans. When the voter began listening to Mondale, he found himself invited to think of himself and others he knew and worked with as base creatures, dominated primarily by greed. He knew this wasn't so, and he came, I think, to resent this being said about him. He turned against Mondale, a rejection that didn't necessarily comprehend local Democrats not associated with Mondalean censoriousness.

The final speech of Walter Mondale in Corpus Christi said it all in direct language. "There are a lot of things we can't afford in this country, but one thing we can't afford to be is just cruel, uncaring, brutal, unkind, and vicious to the helpless in America."

Now the clear assumption, here invited, was that those

Americans who favor the policies of Ronald Reagan are cruel, uncaring, brutal, unkind, and vicious. ("Darling, am I cruel, uncaring, brutal, unkind, and vicious?" "No, dear, you are gentle, thoughtful, tender, kind, and civilized.") This is not to deny that we are a race of sinners. But it is to deny that on the day of the Great Accounting one will need to include in the list of one's sins that one had worked for Ronald Reagan.

The conviction runs deep in America that the Marxist notion that any success is exploitative is quite simply mistaken. Walter Mondale—and his counterparts in the academy; one thinks of Professor John Kenneth Galbraith—was in fact tendering this assumption to the people. That what they got was ill-gotten, and that what they had, they owed, in fact, to those who did not have so much. It is no slur on the deep philanthropic reserves of America that this proposition was emphatically rejected. Rejected not only by the comfortable, but by the many not now comfortable who see in the Reagan program the means by which they can rise, in the American tradition, from discomfort toward modern affluence. The figures indicate that 30 percent of the Americans who voted and whose incomes are less than $5,000 per year voted for Reagan. And that 50 percent of those whose income is between $5,000 and $10,000 voted for Reagan. They were registering an affinity for policies that suggest that hope is a realizable ideal. They were rejecting the proposition that Mr. Mondale's "helpless" are a class of the congenitally deprived.

The week before the election, Professor Galbraith, lecturing about the country, was insisting that Ronald Reagan had brought to America the first true political polarization in modern times. It is hard to take this position seriously after Tuesday's election.

No, the nation is not polarized. There are, as there will always be, differences. But there is a flat popular rejection of the proposition that policies that favor lower taxation and greater opportunity are misanthropic in nature. Wise Democrats ought, really, to catch on by now. The American people have spoken three times on the subject, emphatically rejecting McGovern, then Carter, then Mondale. They don't want McGovernism, and they are saying that not wanting

McGovernism is not the same thing as hating the poor and the needy. That to say no to Fritz Mondale is not the same as being cruel, uncaring, brutal, unkind, and vicious. They just want him please to go away.

V
CORRESPONDING

Notes & Asides
from *National Review*

- To the Editor
The Washington *Post*

Dear Sir:

In your story of Sunday January 15 ("NOBODY BUDGES IN BUCKLEY–REAGAN CANAL TREATY DEBATE") your reporter Mr. Ward Sinclair wrote: "Cameras are running. Buckley gives his side. Witty, rapier-like, observing the anomaly of disagreeing with his favorite politician. Supersure of himself, he says, 'I fully expect that someday I'll be wrong about something.' Moments later, he is. He is wrong about something basic, but the opposition misses it. He says Cortez crossed Panama and was the first to espy the Pacific Ocean. It was Vasco Nuñez de Balboa."

What I said in my speech was, "If there is a full-scale atomic war, the Panama Canal will revert to a land mass, and the first survivor who makes his way across the Isthmus will relive a historical experience—like stout Cortez when with eagle eyes he stared at the Pacific, and all his men looked at each other with a wild surmise—silent, upon a peak in Darien."

The lines are from John Keats. His sonnet, "On First Looking into Chapman's Homer." I felt presumptuous enough correcting Ronald Reagan's foreign policy without straightening out Keats's historical solecism. But tell Mr. Sinclair not to worry: it happens all the time, people's inability to tell where I leave off and Keats begins. Yours cordially,   WFB

• Dear Mr. Buckley, Jr.:

Preceding WW2 I went thru the Panama Canal—with my mother.

A Jap was on the ship. He was taking pictures of the locks on the Canal.

Respectfully yours,
Mrs. James A. Sullivan
Denver, Colorado

Well, obviously that was *one* fat Jap who was a lousy photographer, because when they tried to bomb the locks at the outbreak of the war, the nearest they got to them was Pearl Harbor. Right?   WFB

• Dear Mr. Buckley:

Can you allow the sanctioning of a complete and total waste of a human life?

There is no justifiable reason why the medically ill and impaired should not be allowed to be the recipient of a healthier and extended life. This can be done by using the organs of a person that is facing an unavoidable death by execution.

The popular method of execution by electrocution is barbaric in that it deprives thousands of people of the above type of life. There is a better method of execution, one that is far more humane, because of the immense benefit to mankind.

I am on death row in Alabama and my death is very imminent. Therefore, it is my profound wish to be put to death in such a manner that will benefit others. My proposal is that my execution be done on an operating table so that my vital organs can be removed for donation to the vast number of people that are so urgently in need. I am writing to plead for your help and support in getting the legislature to quickly enact a law that will give a condemned man the choice of the aforementioned mode of execution.

I sincerely thank you for your patience in listening to me, and I would greatly appreciate your ideas or suggestions.

Sincerely,
John Evans
P.O. Box 37
Holmon Station, Ala.

Dear Mr. Evans:

Inasmuch as you are scheduled to be electrocuted on August 4 and have declined to appeal your death sentence there would appear to be little time for maneuvering to change the law so as to introduce alternative means of execution. Your sentence (for first-degree murder) mandates that means of execution (electrocution) specified by the law. Let us pray that your death, if indeed it is to be, will mean that something less than "thousands" of people will be deprived of the use of vital organs recapturable from men and women sentenced to death. Win or lose, may God have mercy on your soul. WFB

• United States Senate
Daniel Patrick Moynihan

Pindars Corners, New York
September 4, 1978

Dear Bill:

This is a letter that will do me more good than you.

I've had a week here, reading and fussing with a great mound of research reports on the guaranteed income experiments which we started in the late 1960s in the expectation that no government would propose one until the case was proven. (Well, of course, as you know, one did. Since then, another.) My sense in 1969, when I found to my amazement that Finch et al. would go along, was to do so (i.e., propose it) as an earnest that social progress was not an end, etc. I don't entirely think I was wrong about that.

But were we wrong about a guaranteed income! Seemingly it is calamitous. It increases family dissolution by some 70 percent, decreases work, etc. Such is now the state of the science, and it seems to me we are honor bound to abide by it for the moment. True, as chairman of the Subcommittee on Public Assistance of the Committee on Finance, I propose to hold hearings after the election, confronting one and all with the evidence.

And so you turn out to be right, in addition to which your recipe for apple soup works.

Your piece on the Pope was fine. Did we get the man you hoped for? I hope so. He likes Chesterton.   Best,
                                                                        Pat

Dear Patrick: Thank you for your graceful note, to which I shall give discreet attention. I am fascinated by your findings and will follow closely your disclosures, on which you are welcome to elaborate in *NR*, should you choose to do so. I wonder if Milton Friedman will also change his mind? On the other hand, his social arithmetic tends to be more atomistic than yours.   Cordially,
                                                                        Bill

• Dear Bill:

Having been a subscriber to *National Review* for many years, I am still amazed at two things: 1) your amazing ability to use precise language to communicate your exact meaning, and yet 2) your equally amazing lack of understanding of precise language, taught throughout the Bible, concerning salvation or eternal life.

For example on Page 1102 of *National Review*.

No man ever tried harder than Pope Paul, nor ever *earned* more convincingly his safe passage from this vale of tears.

Can you explain your use of the word "earned" in the light of such Biblical passages as:

. . . but the *gift* of God is eternal life through Jesus Christ, Our Lord. *Romans 6: 23*

For by Grace are you saved, through Faith, and that not of yourselves, it is the *gift* of God: not of works lest any man should boast. *Ephesians 2: 8–9*

And I *give* unto them eternal life, and they shall never perish. *John 10: 28*

Can you not see that your words as quoted above express a meaning which is completely unscriptural?

In view of your demonstrated ability always to use the word or words which will convey just the shade of meaning which you have in mind, I trust that you will take time to study from the Bible—how man can obtain a *safe passage* from this vale of tears.

Yours,
Edward D. Cross
West Bridgewater, Mass.

Dear Mr. Cross: Behold Matthew 16: 27: "For the Son of Man shall come in the glory of His Father with His Angels: and then He shall reward every man according to his works." But a note to all Pelagians: This is not an invitation to reopen The Controversy. Cordially,   WFB

• Dear Mr. Buckley,

Gene Genovese, Editor of *Marxist Perspectives*, sings the praises of *National Review* as a model of popular political journalism. The efforts of those of us who work in the office of *MP* to keep track of the enemy would be aided by a comradely (whoops . . . collegial) exchange of subscriptions. I hope you will look favorably upon my modest proposal.

Cordially,
Jacques Marchand, Publisher
Marxist Perspectives
New York, N.Y.

P.S. Our list of subscribers includes several *NR* staff members. While I welcome such august converts, I assure you we have not yet placed moles in your organization.

Dear Mr. Marchand: If you have, you can fire them for incompetence. Cordially,   WFB

• Dear Bill:
   I write to tell you of a conversation I had yesterday morning on the ferry from Vineyard Haven to some place on the mainland in the general vicinity of Falmouth. It was as follows:
   A man in plaid pants: "Did you know, Professor, that your friend William Buckley got stuck last night in Menemsha Channel? He was too far over to the side."
   JKG: "It doesn't surprise me."
   Plaid Pants: "What do you mean? I don't understand."
   JKG: "William Buckley rarely gets anything right."
   Plaid Pants: "I think that comment is unnecessary—and unkind."

My regards,
Ken
[John Kenneth Galbraith]
Harvard University

Dear Ken: Channel markers are not maintained by the private sector. Cordially,

Bill

• Dear Mr. Buckley:
   I answered my doorbell last Halloween evening and found two grade-school boys dressed in three-piece suits, carrying briefcases and toy pistols. They told me they were IRS agents. They said that if I didn't fork over a share of the candy, they would take it from me.

Either trick-or-treaters are getting more sophisticated, or the IRS is implementing some new tax legislation that I haven't heard about.

Best wishes,
Scott Ferguson
St. Paul, Minn.

Dear Mr. Ferguson: Right, you hadn't heard of it. It's a division of Operation Head Start. Cordially, WFB

• Miss Virginia B. Smith
President
Vassar College
Poughkeepsie, New York

Dear Miss Smith:

On March 20 you sent me a telegram the first sentence of which read, "The Class of 1980 at Vassar College invites you to speak at their graduation on the morning of Sunday, May 25, 1980."

On March 24, acknowledging my acceptance, you began your letter, "I am delighted that you have agreed to be our Commencement speaker. I shall inform the president of the senior class when the students return from spring vacation today, and I know that the class will be pleased and excited."

On April 24, someone from your office called my secretary to ask if I might make a special pre-Commencement appearance at Vassar—to "answer a few questions some of the students have raised." I asked to be informed about the character of those questions. On April 30 I received your letter, beginning with the sentence, "Spring at Vassar is traditionally lively," and enclosing four issues of the Vassar student newspaper, revealing among other things that 53 percent of the class now opposed the invitation. Having read those issues, on May 2 I telephoned you with a proposal I deemed appropriate. You replied that you thought my idea useful, would consult with your colleagues, and would get back to me on May 6.

However, I did not hear from you again until May 14, when you left word with my office (I was traveling) where I could reach you on May 15. You discussed my proposal, the reasons you now thought it inadvisable, and once again reconfirmed the invitation. I advised you that I would reflect, over the weekend, on the whole matter, and communicate with you on Monday. This I am now doing.

I decline the invitation to participate in Vassar's Commencement exercises.

You stressed the point, in your open letter to the student body of April 21, that you had invited me pursuant to established procedures for selecting a Commencement speaker. I do not doubt that you did, but there is no gainsaying, notwithstanding that your invitation was issued in the name of the senior class, that a numerical majority of that same class have recorded their opposition to my speaking at Commencement.

Moreover, I tend to agree that Commencement speakers are an integral part of a ceremony, broadly viewed; and although Commencement speakers cannot reasonably be expected to incarnate the institution at which they speak (unless they are Douglas MacArthur, addressing West Point), their physical presence should not ordinarily be offensive to the majority of the graduating class: indeed, it is for this reason that most colleges consult the senior class on the matter of a Commencement speaker.

The majority of the senior class of Vassar does not desire my company, and I must confess, having read specimens of their thought and sentiments, that I do not desire the company of the majority of the senior class of Vassar. Really, they appear to be a fearfully ill-instructed body, to judge from the dismayingly uninformed opinions expressed in their newspaper, which opinions reflect an academic and cultural training very nearly unique—at least, in my experience. I have spoken, I suppose, at five hundred colleges and universities in the past thirty years, and nowhere have I encountered that blend of ferocious illiteracy achieved by the young men and women of Vassar who say they speak for the majority of the graduating class and, to some extent, say so plausibly by adducing the signatures of the majority of that class in their recall petition. One professor of English writes to the newspaper, "It was

Buckley who offered pridefully in those days the caste of mind and insinuating attitudes toward academic which intellectually veneered the crudities of Joe McCarthy, and in so doing, fueled 'McCarthyism' at its most virulent pitch with respect to the academic community." That the man who composed that sentence should be teaching English at Vassar rather than studying it suggests that Vassar has much, much deeper problems than coming up with a suitable Commencement speaker.

I thank you for your kindnesses, and apologize for the inconvenience for which, however, I think you will agree I am not wholly to blame.

Yours faithfully,
Wm. F. Buckley Jr.

• To the Editor
American Spectator
Bloomington, Indiana

Your reviewer, Mr. Joseph Shattan, writes about me (Who's on First, by William F. Buckley, Jr.; June 1980), "The Yale-educated Mr. Oakes is no mere fop. On the contrary, he was trained as a nuclear physicist, he gained renown as a fighter pilot during World War II, and he reads the geopolitical works of James Burnham for relaxation. Fluent in many tongues and related to—among other luminaries—the Queen of England, the young Oakes is at once effortlessly cosmopolitan and deeply patriotic." Elsewhere, Mr. Shattan advises us that he read Mr. Buckley's book about me in a single sitting. Could that have been the trouble?

You see, I took my degree at Yale in mechanical engineering, not nuclear physics. It is true that I fought in the war and knocked down two Nazi planes, but I took sick, and didn't therefore have the opportunity to gain renown, though I appreciate Mr. Shattan's assumption that, had my health stood up, I'd have shortened the war. It is true that I have read the works of James Burnham, hardly true that I read them "for relaxation." It is more nearly true that they are to be read as realistic substitutes for horror stories. And, then, unhappily, I am not a polyglot. I made a considerable effort in the spring and summer of 1952 to achieve a limited fluency in German. But my French, as Mr. Buckley pointed out, is at the level of *savez-vous-planter-les-choux*. I am mystified at the news that I am related to the Queen of England. It is correct that Mr. Buckley penetrated my penetration, but he never suggested that I am related to the Queen, though perhaps he knows something about me I don't know, not surprisingly since he is a very clever fellow.

Mr. Shattan shouldn't feel too bad, however. The reviewer for the New York *Times*, Newgate Callendar, pronounced me a "devout Catholic," which certainly qualifies him as a sleuth inasmuch as my mother is Episcopalian, my father Presbyterian, and I am somewhere in between. To be sure, I have a great admiration for Catholics, some of whom are among my closest friends; but I am mystified at how this datum was derived from anything Mr. Buckley, a careful writer though given, I think, occasionally, to euphuism, wrote. My regards to Mr. Shattan.

Blackford Oakes
Langley, Va.

• Dear Bill:

You figure most agreeably in Evelyn Waugh's letters, which I am currently reviewing. It was a major act of imagination but contrary to the basic principles of the free-enterprise system that the younger Buckley should ask the greatest prosemaster of the century to write for his magazine for, I figure, $200 a time. I believe it is called hard-headed philanthropy.

Out of friendship and a well-known ability to corrupt, I am concealing your whole relationship with Waugh.

Yours faithfully,
[Ken]
John Kenneth Galbraith
Harvard University
Cambridge, Mass.

Dear Ken:

Your mathematics are, for once, counter-inflationary. I figure it came to slightly over $400 a time, and that was three Democratic administrations back, i.e., real money.

The editor of *The Letters of Evelyn Waugh* [Mark Amory, London, Ticknor & Fields, 1980] did a curiously selective job of presenting Waugh's letters to me. Certainly (see below) the editor conveyed the impression that Waugh thought poorly of *National Review* and—can you believe it?—of my own writing. I am publishing (marked with an asterisk: *) the letters reproduced in the collection. I intersperse letters *not* reproduced in the collection. These letters, to say the least, suggest that on the subject of *National Review* and my own readability Mr. Waugh's views matured. It is, you will agree—will you not?—a pity that the later Waugh's views were kept from you.

Yours cordially,
Bill

February 29, 1960, WFB writes to Evelyn Waugh to comment on Waugh's expressed skepticism in reviewing Richard Rovere's book on McCarthy for the Spectator. WFB offers to send Waugh a copy of Buckley and Bozell's McCarthy and His Enemies *(Chicago, Regnery, 1954).* "Probably you will not want to spend the time necessary to learn the story, which is understandable. But I urge you then to heed the misgivings you clearly feel and give anti-McCarthyism a wide berth in the future." *WFB's P.S.:* "I am sending you a copy of my book *Up from Liberalism.* Please read the chapter on the great anti-McCarthy confidence man, Paul Hughes (p. 70). You will never forget that story."

FROM MR. E. WAUGH, COMBE FLOREY HOUSE, NR. TAUNTON

Many thanks for your interesting letter.

If you can spare a copy of your *McCarthy & His Enemies* I should greatly like to read it.

EW
5th March 1960

March 22, 1960, WFB replies that he is dispatching a copy of McCarthy and His Enemies. "I enclose the current issue of

National Review because you may want to see Colm Brogan's description of the British hysteria."

* [published in *The Letters of Evelyn Waugh]*
To WILLIAM F. BUCKLEY   Combe Florey House
4 April 1960
Dear Mr. Buckley:

I have to thank you for a) *Up from Liberalism* b) *McCarthy and His Enemies* and c) the *National Review* containing Colm Brogan's description of "British hysteria." I don't think you must take the last too seriously. McCarthy is certainly regarded by most Englishmen as a regrettable figure and your *McCarthy and His Enemies,* being written before his later extravagances, will not go far to clear his reputation. I have no doubt that we were sent a lot of prejudiced information six years ago. Your book makes plain that there was a need for investigation ten years ago. It does not, I am afraid, supply the information that would convince me that McCarthy was a suitable man to undertake it. Rovere makes a number of precise charges against his personal honour. Until these are rebutted those who sympathise with his cause must deplore his championship of it.

Yours sincerely,
Evelyn Waugh

May 24, WFB acknowledges Waugh's letter, and comments: "For the record, I should like to remind you that the virulence of the anti-McCarthy press was as marked at the time I wrote my book as it is now . . . Believe me, I am not saying all this because I care so much at this point for historical rectification (I have other things on my mind). But I care that you should not be victimized by the myth-makers. You have not spent your life jumping through their hoops, and you are too venerable to begin." *WFB offers Waugh a subscription to* National Review. "If you champion McCarthy's cause, while deploring his championship of it, you should look, now and then, at *National Review.* We do not make the mistakes he made and, *Deo volente,* never shall. . . ."

On May 30, 1960, WFB was sent by an old friend a clipping from the Manchester Guardian *reporting on a speech by*

Waugh in which he complained of the niggardly returns on his biography of Ronald Knox. ("At this rate, I shall end my life writing a history of the cobbler industry.") *Without alluding to the article, WFB wrote to Waugh on May 31, 1960, asking if he would be interested in writing a monthly letter.* "I am prepared, because of the admiration which I and the editors have for your writing, to offer you a guarantee of $5,000 a year for a piece every few weeks, of two thousand words. That is higher pay by far than we have given before, higher than what we have paid to Max Eastman, John Dos Passos, Whittaker Chambers, and other freelance writers who have frequently written for us . . ."

* To WILLIAM F. BUCKLEY   Combe Florey House
3 June 1960
Dear Mr. Buckley,

Thank you for your letter of 31st May.

It is most gratifying that you would like me to contribute to the *National Review* & I appreciate that in the circumstances your offer is a generous one, but until you get much richer (which I hope will be soon) or I get much poorer (which I fear may be sooner) I am unable to accept it.

Yours truly,
Evelyn Waugh

Excerpts from page 337 of McCarthy and His Enemies, *where the authors (WFB and Bozell) single out as an example of the views on McCarthy those of an addlepated European:*

Let us turn, for a short but first hand account of the European position, to a few passages of what purports to be a fairly representative statement of prevailing European sentiment on the crisis of the day. We quote from a statement that appeared in *Time* magazine, October 12, 1953, putting forward the views of Mr. Tom Driberg, MP, introduced by *Time* as "an influential Christian Socialist."

"Many Europeans and Asians," Mr. Driberg says, "mistrust the tendency to dragoon the whole world into two big-power blocs, each professing the noblest intentions and emitting, alternately, high-falutin slogans about democracy and Tarzanlike boasts of invincible might. We have seen this tendency in American and Soviet policy alike. . . .

"Many of us also feel impatient when, like kids after a street fight, each side accuses the other of having started it. Did the Russians start it in Czechoslovakia in 1948? Or the French in Indochina in 1945? Or the British in Greece in 1944? Any competent attorney could make a case either way.

". . . After all, we agree on some issues with either side: with the Russians, we reject what seems to us the jungle philosophy of big-business capitalism; we stress political liberties as strongly as the Americans do—or did before the era of McCarthy. . . .

"To equate Soviet Russia with Nazi Germany is a dangerous oversimplification. They seem to me essentially different, in several ways: 1) ideologically, Communism is a Christian heresy, but Naziism was anti-Christian paganism; 2) hence, in practice, though there has been much cruelty in Russia, there is nothing comparable with the calculated horror of the gas chambers and the extermination of the Jews; 3) geographically and economically, the Soviet Union is far more self-sufficient and therefore not intrinsically expansionist. . . ."

* To Tom Driberg   Combe Florey House
[6 June 1960]
Postcard
Dear Tom,

I read with great interest your article on the new Buchmanism in *New Statesman & Nation.* Can you tell me: did you in your researches come across the name of Wm. F. Buckley Jr., editor of a New York, neo-McCarthy magazine named *National Review?* He has been showing me great & unsought attention lately & your article made me curious. Has he been supernaturally "guided" to bore me? It would explain him.

Yours ever,
Evelyn

* To Tom Driberg   Combe Florey House
11 June 1960
Dear Tom

. . . I have thrown away all copies of *National Review.* These are the directors. Only one familiar name,† Chambers (who kept secret documents in a pumpkin). Buckley wrote *Up*

† *Paris Review,* Interview with E. Waugh, Fall 1963:
Q: Have you found any professional criticism of your work illuminating or helpful? Edmund Wilson, for example?
EW: Is he an American?

from Liberalism (unreadable); his magazine is mostly devoted to attacks on American "Liberals." I don't think he is a Papist. He would have told me, I think, if he were. Chambers certainly espoused some form of Christianity—Quaker? It would be interesting to know if this was a nest of Buchmanites. . . .

Yours ever,
Evelyn

June 16, 1960. WFB writes to express his disappointment at Waugh's letter of June 3, and to say that the complimentary subscription to National Review *will continue.*

July 10, 1961. WFB writes to Waugh requesting permission to quote from his letter on Joe McCarthy for a new introduction to a new edition of McCarthy and His Enemies. *Waugh grants permission. On March 30, 1962, WFB sends proofs of the new introduction to Waugh. He encloses the current issue of* National Review, *including a review of the latest Waugh novel* (The End of the Battle) *by Joan Didion.*

COMBE FLOREY HOUSE,
COMBE FLOREY,
NR. TAUNTON.

4th April 1962

Dear Mr. Buckley

Thank you for sending me the proof of the preface to the new edition of your book on Senator McCarthy.

The only correction I would suggest is that it is improper to call Bertrand Russell "Lord Bertrand Russell," a style only used by the younger sons of Dukes and Marquesses. He is properly called either Earl Russell or Lord Russell.

Please thank Miss Didion for her kind review. I could not understand the opening, but the rest of her article showed her to be a most agreeable young lady.

Yours sincerely,
E. Waugh

COMBE FLOREY HOUSE,
COMBE FLOREY,
NR. TAUNTON.

October 27th, 1962

Dear Mr. Buckley

I have just finished an article of about 3,500 words, which will eventually appear in the English *Spectator,* on the subject of the Vatican Council.

As you know, the Council will sit for a long time before any decisions are made, so there is no urgency about publication. *The Spectator* can delay publication until it appears in America.

The title is "The Same Again Please: An English Layman's Hopes of the Vatican Council." The theme is that the Conciliar Fathers have been imposed on by a minority, comprising an unholy alliance of modernists & archaeologists, into supposing that there is a strong demand among the laity for changes in the liturgy. Hands off the Mass.

I have not yet offered it to any American magazine. Would you care to make an offer for it before I put it into the hands of my agent?

Perhaps you would be so kind as to reply by cable.

Yours sincerely,
Evelyn Waugh

Several letters are missing, including one in which WFB requested Waugh to review Garry Wills's book on Chesterton (Chesterton: Man and Mask, *New York, Sheed and Ward, 1961), which Waugh consented to do (published April 22, 1961).* ("A second cause which Chesterton might have for complaint, is Mr. Wills's literary style. It is not uniformly bad. Indeed, again and again he shows himself capable of constructing a grammatical, even an elegant, sentence. . . . [Chesterton] was a lovable and much loved man abounding in charity and humility. Humility is not a virtue propitious to the artist. It is often pride, emulation, avarice, malice—all the odious qualities—which drive a man to complete, elaborate, refine, destroy, renew, his work until he has made something that gratifies his pride and envy and greed. And in doing so he enriches the world more than the generous and good, though he may lose his own soul in the process. That is the paradox of artistic achievement.")

COMBE FLOREY HOUSE,
COMBE FLOREY,
NR. TAUNTON.

2nd April 63

Dear Mr. Buckley

Very many thanks for *Rumbles*. [*Rumbles Left and Right*, by WFB, New York, Putnam's, 1962.]

Some of the essays were familiar to me from *National Review*. I reread them with the same zest as those which were new. You have the very rare gift of captivating the reader's attention in controversies in which he has no direct concern. I congratulate you on the collection. At your best you remind me of Belloc; at your second best of Randolph Churchill.

I hope you enjoyed your visit to London. I never go there nowadays except on my way somewhere else. They have destroyed all its character both architecturally and socially.

Please accept my greetings for Easter (which I shall be spending in Rome).

Yours sincerely,
Evelyn Waugh

• Dear Mr. Buckley:

I speculate about the reason writers for *NR* especially are fond of Latin quotations; perhaps it is difficult to find a Greek font?

Ralph de Toledano's letter (Sept. 5) defending his own general ignorance of late classical culture would be merely funny if it were not also typical of *NR*'s pretense to some general knowledge of the classics.

The decline of classical learning has been variously dated. Cardinal Newman, in his *Idea of a University*, summarized much argument in an anecdote: he asked a student (who could translate Xenophen with precision) what the title *Anabasis* meant. Newman's examination of that student demonstrated the shell a classical education had become. But at least the student could still read the language. Some writers *NR* publishes even further demonstrate this decline by an implicit nostalgia for an education they never had, but would have hated.

Ralph de Toledano, in his letter, blames his fundamental ignorance of antiquity on his source, yet he presumes to interpret a fifth century account of the Emperor Julian's last words, *Vicisti, Galilaee*, completely against all tradition, not as a cry of despair, but as a plea for Grace. Is this conservative revisionism or plain ignorance?

Jerome Downes
The Minneapolis Institute of Arts
Minneapolis, Minn.

cc: Gore Vidal, Henrik Ibsen, Ammianus Marcellinus, Gregory
    of Nazarenus

Dear Mr. Downes: I've asked around the shop here, and you've left us puzzled, sort of. Right up and down to the cc's, where you refer to "Gregory of Nazarenus," which you can't mean, 'cause Gregory was from Nazianzus, which is in Cappadocia, not Galilee. (Jesus was from Nazareth.) And then you send a copy to Gore Vidal; strange, because in his novel *Julian* he dated the "decline of classical learning" earlier than you do, to wit, "Julian, Priscus, and Libanius, the three narrators of this story, all wrote Greek. Their Latin was rather shaky, as they are quick to remind us, but they occasionally use Latin terms, much the way we do." So do our folks. Did you notice that Vidal adds, "For those readers who will search in vain for Julian's famous last words, 'Thou hast conquered, Galilean!' he never said them. Theodoret must take credit for this fine rhetoric, composed a century after Julian's death"? Now, Theodoret wrote in Greek. That means that *"Vicisti, Galilaee,"* as you give it, was an early *translation*. In the source, after that cry, Julian adds his very final words, "Yet still do I renounce thee!" Hardly a plea for Grace, but not quite despair either. Oh yes, a final, little point. You refer to the author of *Anabasis* as "Xenophen"; puzzling. Because you say that not getting that word right (in the John Henry Newman story) "demonstrated the shell a classical education had become." So, Newman's student got the book's title off, you got the author's name wrong; some say potato. *Anabasis* is a tough word to translate, which maybe is the reason the translators maintain the original. One of the guys working the typesetters upstairs said forgodsake, don't say to you: *Anégnon, égnon, katégnon*—Julian's *jeu de mots* in replying to Apollinarius' attack on his paganism. He predicted you'd come back with the retort of St. Basil. Quite right, so now I can't spare him the pain of grinding it out on the typesetter: *Anégnos all'ouk égnos. Ei gar égnos ouk an katégnos!* But boys will be boys, I told him, and it's wrong to spread the rumor that you're not allowed to tell a joke in Minneapolis! Cordially,   WFB

* Lans, Tyrol, Austria

Dear Bill:

On arriving home I found your novel *Who's on First* and read it immediately. I found it most exciting. But I clearly see the difficulty German publishers have with your novels. You should know that we do not have thrillers in German. We don't even have a word for it. (Only one or two books by Helen MacInnes have been translated—and no one ever heard of them.) Detective stories are something else, because there you have a riddle, which the reader is challenged to solve.

But when your book appears in German, you should make some corrections, or run the risk that pedantic readers will pick them up. Germans are sticklers!

pp. 2–5: Dohany Street in Budapest is in the heart of the shabby Jewish district, but Pest, unlike Buda, is a *very* recent city. No Gothic houses, no cobblestones.

p. 5: Not impossible, but most unlikely that a Hungarian girl should be called "Frieda." Call her Mária, Sarolta, Kinga, or Judit (Juci), or Etelka. Dohány is better than Dohany. People might remember Dohenny!!! Incidentally, Dohány means tobacco and you mention Tobacco Road.

p. 30: Pokrovskiy is more likely than Pekrovskii.

p. 34: Stick to one transliteration: Vitkovsky. The right ending of these Russian names is, in *German*, "ij": Witkowskij.

p. 35: Kapitsa is almost impossible since there exists a famous

Russian atomic physicist with the name of Pyotr Kapitsa—who was kidnapped by the Soviets. If he hasn't died, he is still alive in the U.S.S.R. This is like inventing an Austrian composer named Kenneth van Beethoven. Kapitsa is a *very* rare name!

p. 42: Ust' alone is too little. All Ust's in Russia are hyphenated places. And is there such an Ust' near Vorkuta? I doubt it.

p. 62: Is that French text faulty on purpose? I think that it should be correct.

p. 67: Sverdlov did not give the order to execute the Czar. He carried out the orders of Lenin and Yurkovskiy.

p. 85: Surely Jozsef Nagy? Nadi is *impossible.* Nagy is OK because it is a very frequent name, like Smith, or Fisher.

p. 86: Ernö, not Erno.

p. 86: Zlaty is a very un-Hungarian name. (It is Czech.) IMPORTANT. The Hungarian Revolution of 1956 was *totally* unprepared. It emanated from public meetings of a poetical association.

p. 93: In 1956 a Hungarian beer would not have been obtainable in Paris.

p. 94: Tóth is better than Toth.

p. 125: There is a Ferenc Boulevard or a Ferenc Square, but no Ferenc Street in Budapest.

p. 145: In 1957 a ship going from Odessa to Indonesia would necessarily pass by Bizerta, because the Suez Canal was then closed!!!

p. 149: Louis XIV never said *"L'Etat, c'est moi"*—it is apocryphal. The old czars called themselves *samodyerzhets,* or *avtokrator,* but this term was intended to suggest that they were independent of the Tartars, not that they were absolute monarchs. (There *is* also a Slavic term.)

p. 209: I would transliterate Mechta into Metshtá for the German.

p. 250: It's Punta Delgada.

p. 251: There is no "college" in Sweden—and, I suppose, hardly a single secondary school—teaching Russian.

I am not too happy about the names Spektorsky and Vlasov. The talks between Allen Dulles and Dean Acheson will hardly ring a bell in Germany. Few people realize how stupid Eisenhower was. And how can anybody translate Punky's speech? There are practically no swear words in German. "Kiss my arse" is the only indelicate expression. It is, of course, quite legitimate to introduce real persons. I feel very honored to appear in these pages. One more thing: I have never met a Hungarian with the name of Theophilus. Should be: Teofil.

All the best,
Erik [von Kuehnelt-Leddihn]

PS: Ilyitch is a patronymic, not a family name.

PPS: p. 99: The Transsiberian does not run through that area.

Somewhere in the book, a Russian refers to the "Eastern front." No Russian would have done that, because for him it was a Western front. I don't think that he would have said "the Western front" either, but just: "the Front" (there *was* an Eastern front for a few days in Eastern Siberia: Manchuria).

p. 239: No Russian soldier says to a higher officer, "sir." Such a word does not exist in the Soviet language, and I do not even know how a soldier addressed his superior in the Imperial Army. In Germany and Austria it was "Herr Lieutenant," "Herr Major," etc. "Sir" has no Continental equivalent. And "sir" in the U.S.S.R. is out of the question. In Imperial Russia, in civilian life, *barin* or *gosudar'.*

As ever,
Erik

Dear Erik: Forget it. Am resigning, going back to school. What can I pay you not to read my next book? Gratefully,   Bill

• To the Editor
Playboy
Dear Sir:

Your attack on my attack on the Anti-Defamation League's misbegotten award to Hugh Hefner amuses me, and I receive it good-naturedly. But I am left owing your readers and Mr. Hefner an explanation or two:

1. I didn't imply that Hefner is a man of "essentially criminal mentality," crime being something the commission of which usually gets you behind bars, whereas the informal legal

arrangements of our time concerning the publication of pornography leave Mr. Hefner on the safe side of the law, at least as currently interpreted.

2. I am astonished that you are astonished that a writer can at one and the same time write for a journal while disapproving the philosophy or habits of its editor. Your five million readers, of whom I am however irregularly one, should not be deprived of my perceptions (or Nabokov's, or Jimmy Carter's, or Reinhold Niebuhr's—or Cotton Mather's, for that matter). Even if the principal motive that brings these readers to the journal is lubricity. Count me in as one who is not put off by the presence of a Bible in a brothel.

3. You say that "the First Amendment protects not only Nazis but everyone else. Perhaps Buckley thinks it shouldn't, in which case he should say so directly." I don't think it should, and I *have* said so. Shall I say it again? I don't believe Nazis have the right under the Constitution to propagate or agitate in behalf of their racial doctrines. Neither did Justice Felix Frankfurter; see *Beauharnais,* which by the way is about an Illinois statute as widely disregarded as Illinois's obscenity statutes.

4. "The crux of the matter is that Buckley feels qualified to determine what God loves and what He doesn't." Not quite right. But Buckley does read in the Bible exhortations to modesty, fidelity, and abstinence which no literate person could confuse with the Playboy Philosophy. That we are all sinners is a part of the Bible-Buckley Philosophy.

5. Re "parted pudenda," you say *"Playboy* doesn't photograph women quite so graphically." Why?

Yours truly,
—WFB

• Dear Mr. Buckley:

One of my friends wrote to Senator Bill Bradley, to urge him to support the President's proposed budget cuts. Senator Bradley replied, in part:

Reducing federal expenditures and tax burdens are a necessary part of the solution to high inflation and low productivity. However, it must be done in a way that builds a consensus for increasing our competitiveness in the world economy and provides a base of innovation for long-term, stable development.

My friend asked if I could explain to him what this means; I could not.

My wife says that Senator Bradley was a Rhodes Scholar, and maybe that's why I can't understand him.

Can you help?

> Yours sincerely,
> Paul Nix
> Summit, N.J.

Dear Mr. Nix: Senator Bradley is saying that in order to have square pegs, you must have round holes, but not too round, because love conquers all. Cordially,

> —WFB

• Dear Mr. Buckley:

Your letter agonizing over the financial woes of *National Review* is the first good news I've had all summer.

If things get really desperate, please keep me informed. Good news is really hard to find under this Administration.

With best wishes to you personally, but no check for *National Review*, I remain

> Sincerely,
> Jerry Wurf
> International President
> American Federation of State, County,
> and Municipal Employees
> Washington, D.C.

Dear Mr. Wurf: Isn't it a pity we can't just direct our subscribers how much to pay into the coffers! Any advice on how you manage these, ah, matters is always welcome. Cordially, WFB

• Mr. Buckley,

Your recent column "On Argentine Colonialism" is the most inane, stupid, and unintelligent piece of writing that I have read in some time. You have outdone yourself once again.

I was not aware that Mexico made any claim to Texas. Of course, you look half asleep, sound like you are half asleep, and perhaps you became aware of this "claim" while in a dream-like state.

Anglomania is a disease of the unread, unintelligent, uninformed, and unaware. Anyone who can read and who has read even a little history can not but loathe and hate everything English. It is apparent that you are as confused as you sound.

Perhaps you should see some sort of doctor. You may be suffering from a chemical imbalance or some chemical insufficiency. I do not wish to be unkind but I really do feel sorry for you and I must say I am ashamed that you are an American. You represent everything that is un-American and anti-American.

Yours,
Patrick McVeigh
Floral Park, N.Y.

Oh, come on, McVeigh. Are we also supposed to hate the English language? On the other hand, you obviously do.
Cordially,　　　　　　　　　　　　　　　　　　　　WFB

• Dear Mr. Buckley:

If a liberal calls me a fascist because I am a conservative, what should I do? Should I:

　a) diplomatically ignore the hyperbole;

　b) say: "When I become dictator, you'll go into the camps!"; or

　c) duke him/her out?

I'm inclined toward c), but, being a Midwesterner, I am oblivious to such matters of etiquette. What is the proper response? Any suggestion would be appreciated greatly.

Yours semi-sincerely,
Jeff Tutt
Michigan City, Ind.

Dear Mr. Tutt: You might try, "That's what *all* the communists say about me." Granted, that sort of thing is *tu quoque*. But fascists are famous for that. Cordially,   WFB

• Dear Mr. Buckley:

There is something very intellectual about you, and I like to listen to you on TV as often as possible. To be honest with you, more than half of what you say goes above my head. My rough-neck friends often kid me on this, accusing me of trying to become a snob. But I am the same Pedro as usual, and I think you'll agree with me that there is nothing wrong in trying to improve the cerebral aspects of one's personality.

I used to get irritated by your semi-British accent, but I have gotten used to it now. Even now I wonder how you acquired this kind of accent; I would have considered you an equally effective intellectual even if you had sounded like an Okie.

Hope you will not get offended if I say this: Whenever I watch you on TV, I cannot help feeling that your spasmodic facial twitches are the direct result of hemorrhoidal pain. And for the life of me I can't understand why you should suffer through this when even a sparse application of Preparation H before the show can take full care of it.

Admiringly yours,
Pedro Pacheko
Norman, Okla.

Dear Mr. Pacheko: Concerning the problem of the accent, your quarrel is with my parents, who sent us to schools in London (where my father lived), rather than Oklahoma (where my father didn't live, even though it was nearer to his native Texas). Concerning the other matter, *Firing Line* is proud of its record as a fair-minded forum, and I would never use Preparation H without first offering some to my guests, and the producer, Mr. Steibel, has yet to come up with an appropriate formula for this transaction. Yours cordially,   WFB

• (Excerpt from *The New Yorker;* January 31, 1983, "A Journal—Overdrive" by William F. Buckley, Jr.)

The *Times* called to ask who had taken a photograph of Pat and me on the Orient Express that they will use in the travel section; they want to send the photographer a check (for $75). I tell Frances that the picture in question was taken with my own camera by a waiter, and it would not be feasible to find him. The spread will not be out until next Sunday, and I haven't seen it, but the galleys, corrected over the weekend, amused me, because I had privately gambled that one sentence I wrote would never see the light of day. On learning that the *Times* had, as represented, a strict limit of $500 for any travel piece—a sum that hardly covered my costs—I had written that aboard the Orient Express "the consumption of [drinks from the bar] is encouraged, by the way, and they are cash-and-carry, and there is no nonsense about special rates. A gin-and-tonic is $4, a liqueur $6. These prices, weighed on the scales of the Old Testament, are not prohibitive, unless you are trying to make a living writing for the travel section of the New York *Times.*"

I won—the third sentence did not survive. It's a funny thing about the *Times:* I don't know anybody who works for it who *doesn't* have a sense of humor. (Big exception: John Oakes. But then he retired as editorial-page director several years ago, and is understandably melancholy about having to live in a world whose shape is substantially of his own making.) A. M. Rosenthal, the working head of the newspaper, is one of the funniest men living. Arthur Ochs Sulzberger, the publisher, is wonderfully amusing, and easily amused. And so on. But there is some corporate something that keeps the *Times* from smiling at itself: don't quite know what.

(Telegram addressed to WILLIAM F. BUCKLEY, JR., NATIONAL REVIEW, NEW YORK, *February 2, 1983.)*

YOUR VICIOUS AND TOTALLY UNCALLED-FOR CHARGE THAT THE NEW YORK TIMES HAS NO SENSE OF HUMOR ABOUT ITSELF

WAS SIMPLY ANOTHER EXAMPLE OF THE NATIONWIDE AT-
TACK AGAINST THE FIRST AMENDMENT. WE PLAN TO RESIST
THIS CONSPIRACY DIRECTED AT THE FREE PRESS WITH ALL
OUR MIGHT.

> A. M. ROSENTHAL
> EXECUTIVE EDITOR
> THE NEW YORK TIMES

• Dear Mr. Buckley:
Now that the Catholic bishops have voted for a "nuclear
freeze," would it not be appropriate to call a convocation of
generals and admirals to vote on how Mass should be said?

> Frightfully yours,
> John D. Calhoun
> Colonel, USAF (Retired)
> Ruston, La.

Dear Colonel Calhoun: It would be an improvement on Vatican II. Cordially,   —WFB

• Dear Mr. Buckley:
It's hard to know what to say about an article ["The *New
Republic* Problem," *NR*, April 6] that applauds what *The New
Republic* writes, and then, based on something it has not yet
done, accuses it of bankruptcy, except to say that this must be
as close as *NR* can bring itself to praise a liberal publication like
The New Republic without breaking out in hives. Nonetheless,
as the author of the editorial in question, I will overlook *NR*'s
peculiar allergies, and address the bankruptcy charge.

Assume we endorse Mondale or Hart for President. There's
nothing inconsistent, let alone bankrupt, in doing so while at
the same time pointing out three foreign-policy successes by
the Reagan Administration. For one thing, three policies do
not a Presidency make. In foreign policy, Mr. Reagan has a lot

to answer for, particularly on arms control, and his disastrous misreading of American interests in the Middle East. (Even after Lebanon, Mr. Reagan persists in turning the cheek once again to "moderate" Jordanians and Saudis, who have consistently wrecked every previous Reagan peace initiative.) On domestic policy, the catalogue of sins we believe the President has committed is too long to recapitulate here, but is neatly packed into a terse 2,500-word editorial appearing in the *TNR* issue immediately preceding the one you found so appealing. We venture to guess that even *NR*, if it could suppress its anti-liberal prejudices long enough, could come up with three successes of the Carter Administration. We suggest you start with the Panama Canal Treaty, Camp David, and energy decontrol. Admitting the successes of one's political adversaries is, to us, a sign merely of absent prejudice. It's not an endorsement.

So there is no longer a Jackson wing of the Democratic Party. Perhaps—though your sister publication, *The American Spectator*, writes this very week that *TNR is* the Henry Jackson wing of the Democratic Party—but so what? It sounds peculiar for *NR*, which for so many years could not claim a wing, or even a feather, of the Republican Party, to find fault with *The New Republic* for holding a minority view in its party. *NR* spent 25 years educating its party to the truth; *The New Republic* under Martin Peretz has been at it for only ten. Accordingly, we will use *NR* as the standard: If by 1999 the Democratic Party has not elected a President from the *New Republic* wing of the party, we may just have to rethink our allegiances and turn our attention to educating Republicans on the virtues of social justice.

Sincerely,
Charles Krauthammer
Senior Editor
The New Republic
Washington, D.C.

Dear Mr. Krauthammer: You will understand that we are discouraged that the rightward movement of *The New Republic* coincides almost exactly with the leftward movement of the Democratic Party. In 1999 you can count on us to give you a big party at your baptism/bar mitzvah. Meanwhile, someone will need to see to it that the old republic also survives. It is this that keeps us so busy. Yours cordially, —WFB

• Dear Bill:

You are too complicated for me these days. When I get through reading you I don't know if you are for or against!

Sincerely submitted,
Dottie Nichols
Dewitt, N.Y.

Dear Mrs. Nichols: We are against. Sorry about the ambiguity. Cordially, —WFB

• Dear Mr. Buckley:

I wrote reproachfully to the *New York Times* about Grenada. I think you will be amused by the answer I received from Vice Chairman Sydney Gruson.

Cordially,
Robert V. Harrington
New York, N.Y.

Dear Mr. Harrington:

Mr. Sulzberger is out of the country and your letter has been referred to me.

The rest of the *National Review* article is about as correct as the statement that we "sneer compulsively" at Ronald Reagan for calling the Soviet Union an "evil empire." We editorialized about that particular speech of the President's, but we do not sneer at this or any other President.

I don't think there is profit for anyone in getting into an argument with the *National Review*. The *Times*'s record speaks for itself.

Thank you for writing.

Sincerely,
Sydney Gruson
Vice Chairman
The New York Times Company

Dear Mr. Harrington: I have known Sydney Gruson since 1951 when we were co-boarders in Mexico City at a time when I was serving my country in the CIA while he was playing the horses at the Hipodromo and on the side covering Mexico for the New York *Times*. He is a very wise man. That, you see, is why he knows it is unprofitable to get into an argument with *National Review*. The New York *Times* never sneers at a President, just as *National Review* never sneers at the New York *Times*. And it is true that the *Times*'s record speaks for itself. Ask Castro. Thank you for writing. Cordially,   —WFB

• Dear Wm—

Grammatical Man: Information, Entropy, Language, and Life, by Jeremy Campbell (Simon & Schuster, 1982), gives the "final solution" to the great Willmoore Kendall-Mabel Wood controversy over "which, by the way, why doesn't somebody burn it down?" Campbell notices that Hebrew and other languages regularly use the extra pronoun, and gives examples: "the man that I saw him was your brother," and "I read the book that you read it." He adds that many regional dialects of French work the same way, and conversational constructions in English "contain traces of the Hebrew strategy," as for example: "that's the kind of answer that, when you come to think of it, you find you've forgotten it," and "this is the sort of book that, having once read it, you feel you want to give it to all your friends." These last two are exactly the Willmoore type, instances of anacoluthia caused by a diverting of the attention through the interpolation of a nonqualifying phrase between the relative pronoun and the predicate it goes with.

You were right to have printed Willmoore as was. Mabel was wrong to have kicked up a fuss. Willmoore was right to have said what he said. IS EVERYBODY HAPPY?

Yours ever,
Wm
[W. F. Rickenbacker]
West Boxford, Mass.

Dear Wm: *I* am. Cordially,   Wm

VI
APPRECIATING

1

When We Were Young
and Gray
—Yale, Class of 1950

Three weeks before matriculating at Yale in 1946 I found myself at a little hotel bar in Edgartown with my upcoming college roommate and two of my sisters—the same bar, as it happens, visited rather splashily by Teddy Kennedy the night of Chappaquiddick, when he made certain that he would be seen clocking in. I ordered a beer and was astonished when the waitress asked to see my driver's license. I tried to tell her there was a misprint on it but she said yeah yeah, and did I want a Coke or a 7-Up? I was not twenty-one years old. Given that up until six months earlier I had been in charge of a detachment of approximately a thousand men at Fort Sam Houston, Texas, and that before that I had schooled platoons and even a company or two in infantry practices, and had chaperoned a trainload of 800 reenlistees, including grizzled master sergeants who had landed in Sicily and Normandy, from South Carolina to California, I thought the indignity monstrous, if concededly amusing—but it was good training for someone who in a very little while would find himself a freshman at college.

There were 1,800 of us—double the normal enrollment—

because Yale's contribution to the war effort was to make a comprehensive promise to matriculate every single student it had accepted from the graduating secondary classes during the war, when they got out of the army. Never mind how many we were: somehow Yale would find food, quarters and teachers for them. It is a good thing the war did not go on to Peloponnesian lengths, given that as it was, several hundred freshmen were forced to occupy old Quonset huts, built during the war for service use. The shortage of teachers in certain fields was so acute that in my freshman year I found myself being taught economics by a student socialist from the Law School. But then others suffered at my hands, since the shortage of Spanish teachers converted me into an assistant instructor in my sophomore year (my classroom hours, fit for a postulant, were 8 A.M. Tuesday, Wednesday, Thursday, Friday and Saturday).

So that there was an indistinct class structure, the veterans and the nonveterans. Strictly speaking, the administration pursued egalitarianism in dealing with us, with only the incidental perquisites (veterans got the Old Campus, not the Quonset huts). But in fact, a little winking was done at mannerisms and practices Yale would not, I think, have indulged in seventeen-year-olds. One classmate, a notorious physical slouch who had got through three years in the army only by learning Japanese in Oklahoma (a sedentary way to spend the war), was told matter-of-factly at the compulsory physical exam we were all subjected to that he was expected to leap over a vaulting board. He turned to the athletic examiner and said simply, "You must be joking?" and walked quietly around the obstacle, on to the next, less strenuous exercise. He got away with it.

How do you handle a freshman who—well, there we were, trying out for the Freshman Debate Team, and the turn came for a student I'll call Henry Atterbury. He delivered a fiery oration, and the septuagenarian historian-debate coach said quietly, when meting out his critiques of the speakers, "Mr. Atterbury. You really don't need to speak quite so . . . loudly." He got back from Atterbury, "I'm sorry about that, sir. I got into that habit shouting to my men over the roar of tanks." Roaring Henry Atterbury (as we ever after referred to him), a college freshman, had been a captain in the artillery, and was living now with his *second* wife. I will never forget the handling of Atterbury at the beginning of our sophomore year. He returned to New Haven one week after the semester had begun, and one of the few regulations about which Yale was inflexible was the insistence that all students should be present on the first and the last day of classes. He was accordingly summoned to the office of Dean DeVane, a calm, courteous, scholarly Southerner, who asked why Mr. Atterbury had been late.

"Well sir," said Roaring Henry, "I spent the summer studying the Middle Ages, and I became so engrossed in the subject I completely forgot about the Gregorian calendar change."

The response of Dean DeVane became legendary. "Ah, Mr. Atterbury. In that event, you would have arrived in New Haven one week early." Roaring Henry went into hiding for a while after that one.

My own roommate was not easily trifled with, and he came to an early decision that he needed to do something about the prissy dean of the Engineering School who was an inflexible disciplinarian, requiring attendance at all classes, that being the rule for all students unless, at midterms—which were several months away—they achieved the Honor Roll. When my friend Richie O'Neill slept in one day, he found on the following day a summons to the office of the dean with a name Louis Auchincloss could not have improved upon: Loomis Havemeyer. Richie was six feet two, had fought in the Marines in Okinawa, was all Irish, with a smile like Clark Gable's.

"Why did you miss your class yesterday, Mr. O'Neill?"

"Diarrhea, sir."

He was thereafter immune to summons from that dean.

We weren't an altogether subversive influence on the campus, the veterans. We were three, some four years older than normally matriculating freshmen, and for that reason were in something of a hurry to get on, do some learning, get married, and get started in life. Some even got married during their freshman year, though not many. Money was not much of a problem since the G.I. Bill was paying our way, or substantially paying our way. There was carousing, but not on the order of what one saw in *Animal House*. Those who drank had learned two or three years earlier how to do so and, most of them,

when to stop doing so. A perquisite of the veteran was that he
was permitted to own an automobile on campus, while nonveterans had to wait until junior year to do so. This was primarily a
hypothetical perquisite because, in the fall of 1946, you could
not buy a car unless your uncle was a car dealer or you were
willing to go to the black market. It was eighteen months
before the postwar demand for cars—for any car—was filled.

But somehow there was always transportation, for the week-
ends at Vassar or Smith, or upcountry, skiing. Eighteen hundred bright, individualistic men cultivated a lot of unusual
pursuits. Fernando Valenti was practicing to become the
world's leading harpsichordist. Claes Oldenburg—I must suppose—was dreaming of great workaclay constructions, worrying only that museums would be large enough to house him. I
rounded up a few friends and bought jointly an airplane, and
learned to fly, and learned to crash-land, which I did grandly
one afternoon on the lawn of the Ethel Walker School, hauled
out along with my brother-in-law-to-be by three hundred girls
in high hilarity at the ignominious end of the two fly-happy
Yale freshmen. Friendships were instantly struck up, sometimes under the oddest impulses. I sat for the first lecture in
Physics 10 alongside a young man of grave countenance, with
about one hundred other freshmen, and at the end of the
lecture by the retired naval captain we turned to each other—
strangers—and the extrasensory circuit was instantly completed: We burst out into convulsive, almost hysterical laughter. Because neither one of us had understood a single word
uttered by the instructor. We ended fast friends and copatrons
of a private tutor who barely escorted us through the survivors'
gate of Physics 10. Few of my classmates would then have
predicted that I would emerge the world's leading authority
on the MX missile.

I think most of the freshmen, probably even including
Henry Atterbury, were struck by something we had not, for
some reason, anticipated. The awesome, breath-catching brilliance of some of our teachers. The basic course in philosophy,
a survey course that began with Thales and ended with Whitehead, was taught by a member of the faculty of the Divinity
School whose name was Robert Calhoun (he died recently). A
tall, ruddy-faced man who wore a hearing aid and crew-cut

hair. He spoke in the kind of sentences John Stuart Mill wrote. Never a misplaced accent, qualifier, verb: sentence after sentence of preternatural beauty, formed as if in a magical compositors' shop, by golden artisans. Never pretentious, just plain beautiful. His learning so overwhelmed him that sometimes— and he was a man without affectation of any kind—as he traced a philosopher's thought schematically on the blackboard he would find himself lapsing into Greek, or perhaps Hebrew. Quiet tittering by the students; but he was deaf and didn't hear; and we would struggle to understand. He undertook, at the request of a few of us, to deliver a lecture bemoaning the Soviet coup in Czechoslovakia in 1948, and one cannot believe that Demosthenes ever spoke more movingly. Calhoun, at Yale, was just another professor in a department of philosophy star-studded with learning and brains.

A professor of European history had a lecture course, and each of his lectures—they ran exactly forty-eight minutes— was a forensic tour de force. His description of the Battle of Jutland could have had a long run off Broadway. Pyrotechnics were deemed, at Yale in 1946, a little *infra dig,* so it wasn't thunder and lightning and morning lights that Lewis Curtis gave his students: rather, wit and polish. We could not believe it, and I still wonder at it, that someone can, three times a week, deliver discrete lectures sculpted as lovingly, as finely as a statue. How do they do it? I think the impact of scholarly profundity hit us as freshmen: perhaps even more so the veterans than the younger students, because although here and there we had, in the army and navy, come upon a virtuoso or two at this or that, never on such a scale as at Yale, and never such a congestion of such men. The surprise was therefore greater for the older students, who thought ourselves a pretty cosmopolitan lot. By contrast, at age seventeen one does not know exactly what to expect, and so is less easily surprised.

Another thing that struck us was something I came to think of as a genetic attribute of Yale, and this was a distinctive sense of gentility. We were addressed as adults. And, for the most part, treated as adults by men (I don't remember a woman teacher, but perhaps there were a few) who were so sharply to be distinguished from all those noisy martinets we had experienced at boot camps and later, we had something I would not call less than a vision, of an entirely different kind of social arrangement. A family of scholars. We would eventually learn, though not fully until we read about it in later years, that no petty human vice is neglected in the academy, that fratricide does not stop at academic moats. But students were substantially shielded from such frictions because they were transient, and were not competing for anything. Perhaps our experience was in that sense denatured, but it is an ineffaceable part of the memory of freshman year at Yale for veterans of the World War. We were never quite the same after those four years. Perhaps not better, but different, no question about that.

2

Pope Paul VI, R.I.P.

A BRITISH WAG recently commented that he owned a most valuable copy of Edward Heath's book on sailing—"an uninscribed copy." I never met His Holiness Paul VI, the most accessible pope in history, surely, since Peter left off casting his net for fish to do as much for human souls. But I have memories.

It was about six years ago, in Rome, on a cold, brilliant, windy day in March, at noon in St. Peter's Square; the crowds gathered to hear the pontiff's regular three-minute homily delivered from the venerable balcony. The wind's unruliness caused the papal standard, draped down in front of the balcony, to blow up against Paul's face, repeatedly interfering with his reading of his notes, resisting human efforts to batten it down. The symbolism was providential, even if there was no providential intervention. The Pope, struggling against the turbulence within his own church, working tirelessly, but not with notable success, at once to maintain the deposit of the faith, to invigorate the spiritual impulse in man, and to accept some proposed innovations and reject others, in the attempt of the teacher invested with total spiritual authority by his flock to adapt the Church to irresistible modern changes.

And another memory. Thirteen years ago, the Pope became the second most famous Italian in history to discover America. All New York stopped. In due course, surrounded by cardinals and kings, the Pope entered the cathedral from the main entrance, walking up toward the altar. At first there was utter silence, during which my twelve-year-old son leaned over to whisper to me, "Just think. From here, I could shoot him with a pistol!" As I was recovering from that logistical observation, suddenly the whole assembly burst into applause. In a lifetime, I had never before heard applause in church. It was applause for "the Pope," to be sure; but also it was applause for Paul. The undeniable benevolence, the glint of spirit, the austere seeking after peace and good will and corporal relief.

That night he conducted mass at Yankee Stadium, causing Senator Humphrey a few weeks later at the Al Smith Dinner in New York to comment that the Boston Red Sox were demanding equal time. The spectacle was moving beyond words, as he tendered communion to a half-dozen children of white, black and Hispanic racial background. Again the symbol: Pope Paul was the great ecumenist, the Pope who embraced the Eastern Patriarch and the Archbishop of Canterbury, who received the Prime Minister of Israel, who talked regularly to Marxists, and who died, alas, with no visible signs of having had any impact during his lifetime. The tragic epitaph of Paul's reign is the half-filled American church on Sunday, and the forty thousand priests who put away their collars to take up secular concerns.

Perhaps it would have happened under any pontiff. Perhaps if the great Paul himself, the original Paul, had been the Bishop of Rome, the glacial movement of secularism would have moved as implacably against piety. Was it after all the Pope of Rome who was responsible for the fact that, in his day, the Supreme Court of the United States permitted *Hustler,* but forbade the Lord's Prayer in the public schools?

Concerning at least one matter, the Pope indeed bears responsibility or—according as you look on it—deserves credit. It is not correct to say of him that his hunger for popularity caused him to go to any lengths. He knew, although he did not anticipate the full force of it, that his encyclical reiterating the prohibition of contraceptives would be unpopular, but he did it anyway. His most concrete capitulation, if indeed it was that

—one is not privy to his private preferences in the matter—
was in respect of the Roman liturgy. The liturgy is the common
point of contact between the Catholic communicant and his
Church. It is more than that, as suggested by the phrase *lex
orandi, lex credendi:* How we pray is how we believe. Before
the new liturgy, the mass was constructed around the proposition that one was there to commune with God, with the priest
acting as mediator. After Vatican II, the Church launched into
an orgy of vernacularization which so stresses intracongrega-
tional relations that an alien observer walks away with the
impression that the highlight of the mass comes when the
priest signals the congregation to cohabit with one another. To
pray during the gymnastic exercise of the modern mass,
athwart a vernacular prosody that belong in the Chamber of
Literary Horrors, is an exercise in self-discipline achieved most
easily by the blind and the deaf, to whom, pursuant to the
promises in the Beatitudes, Pope Paul finally brought compensation.

But the stewards of the Lord are expected to do the best
they can, and their judgments are not expected to be infallible,
whatever one concedes in the matter of their sacred pronouncements concerning theological truths. No man ever
tried harder than Pope Paul, or ever earned more convincingly his safe passage from this vale of tears.

3

Martin Luther King Day?

January 23, 1979

WHY NOT? What are the arguments against it? It is true, as Mark Antony told the mob, that the good is often interred with our bones, while only our transgressions survive. Some of Martin Luther King's transgressions survive on magnetic tape, courtesy of the FBI, ordered by Attorney General Robert F. Kennedy. Such transgressions may be relevant when the question is beatification, but not, really, otherwise.

There were other transgressions, other than of the flesh. One would not want to be a citizen of a republic whose constitution incorporated the principles of civil disobedience propounded by Martin Luther King on those occasions when his exhortations slipped into overdrive. Using the King formula, you could go on to say that Sirhan Sirhan's assassination of Robert Kennedy was nothing more than an act of civil disobedience, serving the requirements of an exigent conscience.

Nor would a satisfactory history be written on the universality of Martin Luther King's human concern. When it was black men persecuting white or black men—in the Congo, for instance—he was strangely silent on the subject of human rights. The human rights of Chinese, or of Caucasians living behind the Iron Curtain, never appeared to move him. His thunder was a targeted thunder. When he discovered a concern for others, that concern was ideologically tendentious. He com-

pared Lyndon Johnson's foreign policy in Vietnam to that of
Hitler against the Jews. But it is not being said that Martin
Luther King would have made a great Secretary of State.

It is dimly remembered that in the fall of 1969 President
Nixon was in communication with Mrs. Martin Luther King on
the subject of a suitable federal memorial for her husband.
Mrs. King broke off those communications in a regrettable
way. She said she had detected in the Nixon administration "an
indifferent attitude" toward black and poor people. "We felt
that to get federal support for a memorial would have been a
beautiful thing . . . but President Nixon's attitude, his lack of
real concern, suggests that his administration is motivated by
racist attitudes."

That kind of talk is jarring to the ear. It is as unattractive
when aimed at white people, spoken by blacks, as when aimed
at blacks, spoken by whites. The fact of the matter is that it is
precisely a gesture based on race that brings us now to consider a national holiday to celebrate the birth date of Martin
Luther King.

It is not widely known that the federal government has no
jurisdiction to propose national holidays. What it may do is
propose them for the District of Columbia and for all federal
employees. Almost inevitably, the individual states go along.
There are only two existing federal legal public holidays in
honor of historical figures. They are for Washington and Co-
lumbus. (The other holidays: New Year's, Memorial Day, Independence Day, Labor Day, Veterans' Day, Thanksgiving, and
Christmas.) Lincoln's birthday is not a federal legal holiday. It
can be argued that the man who wrote the Emancipation
Proclamation 116 years ago deserves the federal works. That
he should be passed over in favor of Martin Luther King is a
conciliatory gesture aimed at black Americans and entirely
defensible on those grounds, but that those are the grounds
need not be concealed.

Martin Luther King is the black American who consum-
mated the civil war Abraham Lincoln undertook, largely animated by his belief in metaphysical equality. A gesture of recognition—of King's courage, of the galvanizing quality of a

rhetoric that sought out a reification of the dream of brother-hood—is consistent with the ideals of the country, and a salute to a race of people greatly oppressed during much of U.S. history.

4

Nelson Rockefeller, R.I.P.

February 1, 1979

SOME YEARS AGO (it was during the period of indecision in 1967–68 over whether to contest Richard Nixon for the Republican nomination for the presidency) Henry Kissinger called to advise me that Governor Rockefeller would like to meet me. Meeting me is terribly easy to arrange, so not long after, HK and I rode up the elevator to the Fifth Avenue apartment, and Happy opened the door. What would I like to eat, drink, smoke, etc., and in a few minutes—powerful men, it is my experience, generally let a visitor cool for a moment or two to heighten the suspense, but it was easy to pause there because within eyesight lay several million dollars' worth of nicely distracting art treasures—he strode in. We exchanged pleasantries while I wondered what was the purpose of the meeting. In due course I found myself listening to an hour-long recitation of his early career on the Latin American desk, at the Chapultepec Conference, and at San Francisco, where he had labored continually to counter Soviet machinations. All this was done quietly, in the tones—I gradually perceived—of a postulant. Nelson Rockefeller obviously wished to convince me that he was profoundly anticommunist.

I always believed this true of him, but notwithstanding his consistency on the question—marred by an ambiguity on Vietnam when, briefly, adviser Emmet Hughes prevailed over adviser Henry Kissinger, respectively the dove and the hawk in the inner circle—Nelson Rockefeller permanently alienated the right wing in America. He did this in 1963 when he was induced to denounce in extravagant terms the whole of the conservative movement as if it were a branch of the John Birch Society. His reward was the distasteful episode in San Francisco when delegates who went there grimly determined to nominate Barry Goldwater gave Rockefeller the Bronx cheer —as if to say, "If that is what you think of *us,* this is what we think of *you.*"

But Nelson Rockefeller never gave up. And so now, in 1968, he made a gesture to a representative of the right wing. During the convention itself, against the forlorn possibility that he might actually be nominated over Nixon and Reagan, a special representative of Rockefeller kept me regular company, his mission being to guard against the preemptive denunciation of Rockefeller from certain quarters, which denunciation would have had on Rockefeller's candidacy the same effect that the virtual denunciation of him by the labor leaders had on George McGovern in 1972.

Then, too, there was the image of Rockefeller the Big Spender. He was unquestionably the central figure in the progressive decline of the economy of New York State and New York City. But he came gradually to recognize that there were limits to all of this. And so he quarreled with John Lindsay, who finally joined the Democratic Party, where he had always belonged. And on one occasion, with several dozen persons present, Nelson Rockefeller rose to toast Governor Ronald Reagan: "I feel the urge to confess," said Governor Rockefeller, "that I tried a different approach to state welfare than Governor Reagan. And his has proved more successful than mine."

In 1970 we met to discuss the senatorial race in which my brother James competed, and won. The incumbent Senator Goodell, having been appointed by Governor Rockefeller upon the death of Robert Kennedy, had switched radically to the left, proving an embarrassment to Rockefeller. On that occasion he told me he would give only formalistic support to Goodell, to whom as a fellow Republican he was organizationally committed. "I really am a conservative, you know." And then, winking, "I've got a lot to conserve."

Classically Nelson Rockefeller is an example of the man who, having nothing left to animate him, dies; like Napoleon at Saint Helena, or Robert Taft after Eisenhower's nomination. He was a very strong man, persuasive in conversation, dogged in his pursuit of his goals, unsentimental, yet generous. Henry Kissinger believes he would have been a great President. I think it altogether possible that this is true. He had the strength of character to profit from his own mistakes. If he had been kinder to Nixon during the years of exile, Nixon might have appointed him to replace Agnew. If that had happened, Rockefeller would almost surely have been President last week —in which event, almost surely, he would still be alive.

5

Henry Kissinger

May 30, 1980

(Remarks by WFB at a Testimonial Dinner for Henry
Kissinger, Friars Club, New York, May 3, 1980)

A YEAR AGO, the good news was that we had no hostages in
Iran, and the dollar was worth ten cents more than it is today.
The bad news was that President Carter had *two* more years to
serve. And Henry Kissinger was toying with the idea of running for the Senate, always assuming that Jack Javits elected to
retire. He confided this rumination to me, soliciting my advice,
which is much more valuable than my support. I counseled
him against running for the Senate, pointing out that he might
conceivably win. He was puzzled by my analysis, which
pleased me, since I tend to believe in reciprocity. I explained
to him: You mustn't go to the Senate, I said, because you're the
only other Jackie Kennedy. We need our own Jackie Kennedy,
and, if Senator Javits will forgive me—after all, my brother Jim
may also be listening—it is deglamorizing for a supercelebrity
to go to the Senate. In Henry's case, we considered the alternative, namely having the Senate come to Henry; but Nancy
pointed out the logistical problems, and so he abandoned the
whole idea.

Not so, one supposes, the idea of serving at some future
moment as Secretary of State. After all, Jackie Kennedy could

marry again. It was only Eddie Fisher she was not permitted to marry. It was briefly rumored last week, when Secretary Vance resigned, that Mr. Carter might approach Henry, even as our Joint Chiefs should long since have asked the Israelis kindly to attend to the return of our hostages. But as we know, the call from the White House—which for reasons of protocol, let alone survival, Henry would have had difficulty in rejecting—never came. Instead it went to Senator Muskie, whose last sustained thoughts on foreign policy were his opposition to Henry Kissinger's diplomacy during the Vietnam years. Ah well. When, a generation ago, the dashing mayor of New York, Jimmy Walker, was asked by the press to justify elevating one of his most conspicuously unqualified associates to judge of the Children's Court of Queens, the Mayor answered disarmingly: "The appointment of Judge Hylan means the children can now be tried by their peer." The incumbent Secretary of State may prove excellently qualified to administer the policies of the incumbent President of the United States.

I am delighted to contribute to this nonpartisan celebration of Henry Kissinger, whom I have known for twenty-five years. Curiously, I owe my friendship with our guest of honor to Senator Joseph McCarthy. It was in 1954 that I received a letter, followed by a visit, from the editor of a distinguished academic quarterly, who said he was searching for a literate explanation of the rationale of McCarthyism. I wrote the article, which he never published; from which I am certain Mike Wallace will rejoice to conclude yet again that no literate explanation of McCarthyism is construable, no matter how profound the resources of the sophist. But Henry then invited me to participate in his famous Harvard summer seminars, sensing an obligation to his foreign students to exhibit to them the most exotic specimens in the American political zoo.

What happened, during those years, is something I make bold to say—notwithstanding the shock value of the word, used in such urbane company—what happened—what developed, was: a friendship.

There is no other way to put it, and no other way that I would choose to put it. One reads about our guest of honor all the time, in all the journals—words written by admirers and by critics. On and on they go. They analyze this statement of his, that nuance; they praise or blame him for this policy or that; they assign to him responsibility for this crisis or that démarche. It is comfortable to believe that history will sort it all out, and Henry's next book—as is true of his last one, a modern classic—will of course not begin to end the historical controversies.

What I have come to know over the years is on the other hand unchallengeable. It is, simply stated, that Henry Kissinger is my friend. He has been that for a great many years. That friendship is entirely unaffected by any disagreements we have; unaffected by what I write about his policies, what he does to the world I live in; his opinions, his techniques, with all of which I am frequently in agreement—which does not matter to me, or, I expect, to him. He is, as all of us know, an extraordinary public figure, and I hardly dissociate myself from that chorus which gathers to praise famous men, as the scriptural injunction decrees that we should do. I will go along with that, but when I look at him I am not seeing Caesar. Or Metternich. Or the greatest Secretary of State in American history. A sister of mine, keeping my father company in his last sickness, took an afternoon job with the local radio station, in the little town in South Carolina where my family wintered, writing copy for local advertisers. One day she was approached by an elderly black gentleman of great dignity who presided over a funeral parlor whose services he wished to advertise. My sister asked him what exactly he would like her to say, and he replied, "It doesn't matter, Miss Buckley. Just so it's serene." In the turbulent career of a man of many parts, in the most turbulent and possibly apocalyptic stage in history, one clings to such a serenity as I—and many of you—have found in the friendship of Henry Kissinger.

6

Gary Trudeau

September 15, 1978

(Introduction to *Doonesbury's Greatest Hits* by Gary Trudeau, New York: Holt, Rinehart and Winston, 1978)

IT WAS graduation day at Yale and I flicked through the official program to the page that would give the names of the people fetching honorary degrees. Subconsciously one looks for a Surprise. Marshal Ky would have qualified in 1976. I noticed the name of Trudeau, and uttered a silent prayer of gratitude for Yale's tradition against speeches by endoctored celebrities. It turned out of course to be another Trudeau, one of whom I had not heard; only a year or two older than my graduating son. I assumed he was a local divinity of sorts—indeed, he was so treated; I think I remember rightly that only he received a standing ovation from the graduating class when his name was called out. Perhaps he had invented the neutron bomb? I remembered somebody telling me that all geniuses in the physical sciences discover their fourth dimensions when they are twenty-two years old.

My surprise was genuine, upon hearing the citation, to deduce that he was an artist, or social critic; indeed he was festooned so lavishly by the president of Yale that I wondered how it could be that I had not heard his name before. On

mentioning this later to my astonished son I was made to feel as
though I had not heard of an entire world war. I strained to see,
but from mid-crowd everyone wearing reading glasses and an
academic gown looks pretty much the same—and anyway,
what did it matter? I did not suppose that merely *looking* at
G. B. Trudeau would make me laugh, the way merely looking
at Jack Benny used to make me laugh. I have dug up the
citation read out at New Haven that springy afternoon, and
search it out now for the hyperbole that usually breaks one's
back in the rhetoric of honorary degrees. Listen . . .

> Yale's image, as the hucksters would say, would never be the
> same after what you have done to your classmates and your
> president. Happily, too, your country will never look at itself
> quite as self-seriously, certainly not as self-righteously, thanks to
> your satiric insights into the foibles and pretensions of both the
> notorious and the obscure. For helping keep us sane even when
> the times seem crazed, Yale, with pride and delight, confers
> upon her recent son the degree of Doctor of Humane Letters.

I made a note to look out for what I was informed went out to
the newspapers of the world six times a week under the rubric
"Doonesbury." But since I tend to read only the New York
Times, my resolution flagged; and it was not until receiving this
invitation to review his work that I undertook the assignment
industriously. I think it is in one way unfair to Mr. Trudeau to
have done this to him. Last year a mad musician performed all
thirty-two sonatas of Ludwig van Beethoven without interrup-
tion, and I cannot imagine anyone doing this as a true act of
homage. Yet during the past two weeks every time I have
traveled it has been with a briefcase crammed full of Doonesbury. People of all ages must certainly have thought me re-
verted to infantilism as they saw the comic strips spread about
me. But those who looked me in the eye would have detected
that I share Yale's pride and delight.

What is there to say about Doonesbury, or even about the
comic strip mode? Never having studied a strip before, it is
conceivable that I notice things that are generally unnoticed
by those continuingly familiar with the genre, even as, for
instance, I notice the loud noise at rock concerts. There is, for

instance, the nagging mechanical—and therefore artistic—
problem of reintroducing the reader to the synoptic point at
which he was dropped the day before. In a collection this is
more annoying than if twenty-four hours have gone by since
arriving at the point where the artist left you, and you need a
little nudge. Trudeau handles this very deftly, usually by intro-
ducing into the panel a tilt of some sort that takes the reader
slightly beyond where he was left yesterday, so that he is relieved of that awful sensation of turning wheels without moving forward.

The other problem is the presumptive requirement of the
climax—the gag—at the end of every strip. This cadence no
artist can hope to satisfy, although they must all make the
effort. A collection runs the risk of maximizing the disharmo-
nies. Imagine reading a collection of the last paragraphs of Art
Buchwald's columns. Or, as Zonker would put it, Imagine!
Which digression brings me to note the awful overuse of the
intensifier in Mr. Trudeau's captions. Nothing appears so workaday as to be merely remarkable. Everything is *arresting!* Now
this is in sharp stylistic contrast with the very nearly expres-
sionless faces Mr. Trudeau tends to draw. Nobody ever smiles,
or hardly ever; the effect is wonderful, insofar as it reminds the
reader that no experience, no absurdity, no observation, is
truly new. But nearly everything spoken must be punctuated
with exclamation points and served up in boldface type. I am
as unconvinced that this is necessary as I am persuaded that
Trudeau scores remarkably well in wrenching a climax of sorts
out of almost every one of his strips. There are the anticli-
maxes, but the reader forgives them indulgently; he is well
enough nourished, all the more so since there is all that wonderful assonant humor and derision in midstrip: indeed, not
infrequently the true climaxes come in the penultimate panel,
and the rest is lagniappe.

And then—there is a sense of rhetorical leisure in Trudeau.
What *ever* is the *hurry?* It is very pleasurable, the more so
when one realizes how compressive the form is by nature, like
smoking a cigar on a parachute jump. After reading three
years' worth of Doonesbury I am certain I have read as many
words as are in *War and Peace*. The artist gives off a great air of

authority by this device, rather like those notices in *The New Yorker* in which even the most conventional abbreviations are spurned ("Closed on Sundays and holidays, except for Thanksgiving").

Consider the treatment of an essentially banal exchange. If it were honed less finely, it would not work. One of the characters is watching a television screen, whence the words sound out:

"At the very root of the Big Apple's problems seems to be the endless exodus of the middle class. 'Good Night, New York' is

fortunate to have with us tonight Mr. Jamie Dodd, one such fugitive.

"Jamie, I take it you and your wife have always been anxious to leave New York?"

"Oh no, not at all, Geraldo—in fact, at first the city seemed a marvelous place for an upwardly mobile couple like us! [Note the exclamation point.] But then one day last fall I was promoted to a $45,000 job. That same day my wife was assaulted in the park. The power went off, and the garbage people went on strike . . . And suddenly! Right! Suddenly Darien made *loads* of sense!"

It requires a hypnotic self-assurance to bring off (as Trudeau does) that sequence. As so often, he relies heavily on his meiotic pen to do it.

The longueurs are sometimes almost teasingly didactic. Who else in the funny-paper business would attempt the following? (Again, the action is coming out of the television set.)

"Mr. Finkles, as one of New York's past comptrollers, how were you able to build up such a whopping deficit?"

"Well, Geraldo, we had *many* great tricks. The most common one was selling city bonds on the strength of inflated estimates of anticipated federal funding. This device was very popular among top city money wizards. But let me show you my personal favorite. See Column B here? This is where we charged the final wage period of one fiscal year to the budget of the next! In so doing, we built up a hidden deficit of *two billion dollars!*"

"*Wow!*"

"Now I must caution the folks at home from trying this . . ."

Note the touch of the anticlimax in the last line, inserted in the way that Oliphant permits the kitten or the mouse to pronounce the moral coda. But the unapologetically literate account of the exact character of the financial hanky-panky gives a rollicking sense of reality to the episode.

Note also: "Geraldo." Trudeau likes to identify his characters, and he is quite willing to be personal.

"Good morning. [We see a telephone receptionist.] *New York Daily News* promotion department."

"Yes, hello. I'm about to kill someone and I'd like to talk to somebody about coverage."

"Yes, sir. Would this be an isolated crime of passion, or will you be making a habit of it?"

"Uh, I don't know . . . I'm not sure . . . I mean I don't know my long-range plans yet . . ."

"I'm sorry, sir, but we have to know what sort of story yours is."

"Mine is a story of hopelessness and shattered dreams in the city they call New York."

"Fine. That would be Mr. Breslin. Please hold."

Duke, recalled as ambassador from China, is trying to go back to free-lance journalism, but is in despair.

"Wenner won't even return my calls, so I guess a job at *Rolling Stone* is out."

"Amazing. After all you've been through you'd think he'd at least lend a hand."

"Nope. He needs them both for social climbing."

Duke, by the way, is relieved as chargé in China by Leonard Woodcock.

"Leonard Woodcock! I just can't get over it! What ever could have possessed Carter to pick Woodcock for China?"

"Well, sir [says his Chinese interpreter], maybe it's because Mr. Woodcock's career has been one of great sensitivity to the plight of the working class!"

"Honey, all labor leaders are sensitive to the working class. That's how they avoid belonging to it."

The willingness to criticize the union bureaucracy reminds us with relief that Trudeau, who sprang from the loins of the Vietnam antinomianism, quickly achieved perspective. There is the phone-in radio talk show. The host is talking.

"Was our squalid, cynical mission in Vietnam ever really worth the price? Was it ever worth the . . ."

RING! RING!

"Hello, this is a listener, and I'm sick of your autopsy! Get off it and stop dwelling in the past! It's *over*, hear me?—It's over!"

"Lissen, buddy, the Vietnam debacle rightly occasions a reassessment of our national purposes. We're doin' this gig for the future. We're doin' it for your children!"

"My children? They're in bed."

Indeed, let the co-opters beware (remember Al Capp?). G. B. Trudeau isn't thirty yet, and listen to this indoctrination class in Saigon now that the North Vietnamese have taken over.

"Yes?" [The teacher is responding to a question from a trainee.]

"Excuse me, sir, but I don't think I belong in this class. I already know most of this stuff."

"What's your name? I'll check the print-out."

"Tho. I'm a former commissioned officer."

"Tho? Lou Tho Jr.? You were assigned to this class?"

"Yup."

"That's funny—you were meant to be shot."

"No, that's Dad—Lou, Sr."

Those in search of the meaning of humane letters need go no farther than to Doonesbury.

7

Reflections on Tito

May 8, 1980

In 1970 I visited Belgrade and spent the first morning of my stay there talking with the editor of the weekly journal published by the Communist Party and ostensibly charged with the responsibility of keeping intact the tablets of Marxism-Leninism. I emerged in a state of thorough confusion, inasmuch as the editor had taken economic positions (we did not talk about Tito's political hegemony; nobody talked about Tito's political hegemony in Yugoslavia) with none of which I had any quarrel whatever. He spoke about the value of a vigorous private sector, about regulation by competition, about the virtue—even—of privately owned enterprises.

At that time Yugoslavia's economy was booming, as if responding gratefully to Tito's permissiveness. On my return to the United States, a high U.S. official advised me of a startling bit of intelligence. Tito (the report had it) had confided to Prince Bernhard of the Netherlands, a close friend, that he had come to recognize that applied Marxism was hostile to the material well-being of the common man. However (Tito had allegedly said), having devoted fifty years of his life to the struggle for communism, he did not have the courage to renounce his ideological past. Rather, he would introduce the free market, permitting his people to prosper from the fruits of capitalist enterprise while proceeding ostensibly under the aegis of communism.

But then, in 1971–72, the line abruptly changed. Separatist passions raged, and Tito became once again the marshal, moving to repress those insolent enough to defy him or his orders. He thereupon announced a good old-fashioned purge of the Communist Party, and suddenly he was speaking again in the old, tired accents of the ideologist, plighting his troth to socialism and tightening the bonds he had so recently relaxed. Although there are sharp reminders in Yugoslavia today of a Coca-Colanization—girlie magazines, department stores, traffic jams—and a limited freedom of enterprise (and a freedom to leave the country and return), old soldier Tito redirected his country—or, better stated, his amalgam of countries—toward a general submission, returning to a kind of orthodoxy that made him less conspicuously an enemy of communist centralism.

Tito, in the unforgettable phrase of the political philosopher Karl Wittfogel, suffered from our old friend "the megalomania of the aging despot." He was born in the despotic mode, and although he was prepared to spend cold nights in the trenches with his troops, he was manifestly happier in the caravanserai of the mighty; in the end he lived as sumptuously as the czars whose autocratic hedonism preceded, even if it did not trigger, the great communist revolution of 1917. Tito was a cruel leader, as unforgiving as Fidel Castro, never tiring in his determination to punish even those of his critics who, like Milovan Djilas, had shared his life in the mud and gore of the resistance movement against Hitler during the war. Tito did not execute Djilas when Djilas wrote about that creature that had evolved in the communist world: the new ruling class of totalitarians unmindful of that liberation of the masses which had been understood to be the purpose of communism. He put him in jail, a kinder fate than the execution of Mihajlovich, who had led his own resistance movement against the Nazis but disdained the equally repellent totalitarianism of communism.

Milton Friedman remarked—after his return from a controversial visit to Chile several years ago during which he delivered lectures identical to those he would have delivered in

Chicago, or Washington, or Tel Aviv—that all tyrannies are despicable, but that the tyrannies of the right tend to be less tenacious than those of the left. Dozens of one-party governments in Latin America have evolved into parliaments, often to return to tyranny after bouts with democratic licentiousness. The Greek colonels didn't last so very long; Spain and Portugal are democratic. But left tyrannies have a way of going on and on, subject to revolutionary (or counterrevolutionary) abortion (*vide* Indonesia, Chile). The world is apprehensive about the future of Yugoslavia because the Soviet Union is sitting up there greedily, taking deep draughts of the Brezhnev doctrine. What is not in prospect for the Yugoslavs is personal freedom.

8

Allard Lowenstein, R.I.P.

April 4, 1980

(Remarks at the Memorial Service for Allard Lowenstein, March 18, 1980, by WFB)

POSSIBLY, as a dissenter, my own experience with him was unique, in that we conservatives did not generally endorse his political prescriptions. So that we were, presumptively, opponents of Al Lowenstein, in those straitened chambers in which we spend, and misspend, so much of our lives. It was his genius that so many of those he touched—generally arriving a half hour late—discovered intuitively the underlying communion. He was, in our time, *the* original activist, such was his impatience with the sluggishness of justice; so that his rhythms were more often than not disharmonious with those that govern the practical, banausic councils of this world. His habits were appropriately disarrayed. He was late to breakfast, to his appointments; late in announcing his sequential availability for public service. He was punctual only in registering (though often under age) for service in any army that conceived itself bound to righteousness.

How did he live such a life, so hectic with public concern, while preoccupying himself so fully with individual human beings: whose torments, never mind their singularity, he adopted as his own, with the passion that some give only to the universal? Eleanor Roosevelt, James Burnham once mused, looked on all the world as her personal slum project. Although he was at home with collectivist formulations, one had the impression of Allard Lowenstein that he might be late in aborting a Third World War—because of his absorption with the problems of one sophomore. Oh, they followed him everywhere; because we experienced in him the essence of an entirely personal dedication. Of all the partisans I have known, from the furthest steppes of the spectrum, his was the most undistracted concern, not for humanity—though he was conversant with big-think idiom—but with human beings.

Those of us who dealt with him (often in those narrow passages constrained by time clocks and fire laws and deadlines) think back ruefully on the happy blend of purpose and carelessness with which he arranged his own career and his own schedule. A poet might be tempted to say, "If only the Lord had granted us that Allard should also have arrived late at his own assassination!"

But all his life he was felled by mysteries, dominant among them those most readily understood by more worldly men— namely, that his rhythms were not of this world. His days, foreshortened, lived out the secular dissonances. "Behold, Thou hast made my days as it were a span long: and mine age is even as nothing in respect of Thee; and verily every man living is altogether vanity." The psalmist spoke of Al, on Friday last— "I became dumb, and opened not my mouth; for it was Thy doing." To those not yet dumb, the psalmist also spoke, saying, "The Lord is close to the brokenhearted; and those who are crushed in spirit, He saves." Who was the wit who said that nature abhors a vacuum? Let nature then fill this vacuum. That is the challenge which, bereft, the friends of Allard Lowenstein hurl up to nature, and to nature's God, prayerfully, demandingly, because today, Lord, our loneliness is great.

9

John Lennon, R.I.P.

December 18, 1980

M Y SON (age twenty-eight) said to me the day after, "Imagine how you would have felt if Arturo Toscanini had been killed?" He didn't have to say more, having fingered my own boyhood hero. I can't clearly remember whether, in the thirties, Toscanini was exactly a cult figure. But he was a formidable presence—charismatic, an acknowledged genius, above all a perfectionist. He also liked Broadway music.

My guess is that he would not have been taken by the Beatles. And the general disorder of the Beatles' audience would not have been tolerated by the conductor who, when he played his famous series for NBC, required that the programs be made out of silk, lest he be distracted by the noise of paper flutter. When Toscanini died he was mourned, and they played Verdi's Requiem and broadcast it. But he was old, and Lennon was young; and Toscanini died of a conventional disease of old men, and Lennon died of a bullet wound.

Why was the grief so intense? Those of us who mourned his death without any marked sense of privation (i.e., those of us who did not feel the call of his music or of his words, did not purchase his albums, nor looked to him for sumptuary or moral guidance) mourned for two reasons. The first and obvious being that his killing was one of those grotesqueries so common in this century, about which we can only say in defense of

ourselves that we have not quite got used to them, though this
year alone we have suffered Allard Lowenstein, Sarai Ribicoff,
and Michael Halberstam. Beyond this, our grief is derivative. It
is saddening to experience so deep a sadness in others. It isn't
very often that people gather together in Central Park in order to weep. And one wonders whether it is even seemly to ask
exactly what it was that caused that special bereavement.

I have a notion about this, and it is based on an entire half
day devoted in the winter of 1973 to reading a two-part profile
on John Lennon published in *Rolling Stone*. I cannot remember a worse reading experience. In 1971 John Lennon was a
convinced egomaniac (his word). He could not utter a sentence
without obscenity. His animadversions on his old companions,
in particular Paul McCartney, were quite simply unpleasant
(Paul was jealous of him, the Beatles' music was arid and formalistic). His autobiography was right out of Olympia Press: he
had been stoned "thousands of times." His sex orgies had
cloyed. The fakir in India to whom he had committed himself
turned out to be a commercial old lecher. Everyone was jealous of him. Yoko Ono's least song was better than the best of
the Beatles. At the time, I wrote, "Lennon is greatly talented as
a musician. As a philosopher, he is as interesting as Jelly Roll
Morton, less so, as a matter of fact. He is interesting only to an
anthologist of pieces on 'How I Wrecked My Own Life and Can
Help Wreck Yours.' "

But there followed, not long after, the five years of seclusion.
He is said to have spent most of the time with his wife and son.
And, unless I am deluded by the pervasive sadness, he
achieved something of a nobility of feature. The pictures of
him showed: *gravitas*. No one's face had more aspects than
John Lennon's. He was the mischievous, theatrical, erotic,
iconoclastic playboy.

Then suddenly he seemed to walk tall. And it was in this
posture that he was shot down. And perhaps his own experi-
ences—with drugs, with joyless sex, with enervating solipsism
—shrived him, and the generation that turned out to weep for
him experienced something of that spiritual emancipation that
comes to people who come to see things philosophically. They
find this (I take their word for it) in his music and in his lyrics.

And they found it in him, for reasons no one at Central Park interviewed by the ubiquitous cameras could quite explain, for the best of reasons: namely, that it was unexplainable; is unexplainable. But the grief was real.

10

Harry Elmlark, R.I.P.

January 3, 1981

IT IS NOW a commonplace that often men will die almost
immediately after their retirement, an observation leading to
the psycho-biological hypothesis that men of affairs, plopped
suddenly into retirement—never mind the accompanying
valedictories and gold watches and pensions—suffer a kind of
organic desuetude. Since all those other people out there
whom he used to serve no longer need his services, he has no
services left to offer. Having no particular reason to stay alive,
he somehow contaminates, by his psychological sense of uselessness, his biological self. And then (the theory has it) he
contracts (although one isn't supposed to "contract" such
things, in the sense that one contracts syphilis): heart trouble,
or cancer; whatever.

Harry Elmlark, who died on Christmas Eve, fits tidily as a
datum in the portfolio of the archivists of death-upon-retire-
ment. His official retirement would not begin until the new
year. But he was very unhappy about this undeferrable event.
Harry Elmlark had been something of a legend in the world of
editors and publishers. It is possible that no man of the last
generation knew personally more editors than Harry did, Harry's trade being newspaper syndication of columns and other
features, which for thirty years kept him on the road, hawking
his wares.

He told me (this was at our last meeting, at St. Luke's Hospital in New York) that during the thirties, after he graduated from the University of Virginia, he immediately married his beloved Lillian—whom he promptly retired as a dancer for the Rockettes—assuring her a happy, indeed prodigal life on his weekly salary of $18 (Harry could sell anyone on anything). He confessed to me on his deathbed—from which, fighting that final round, he could not during the last two weeks summon the energy even to turn on the television set—that he had been confident he would realize his dream in the syndicate business, which was to earn $50 a week. "We'd be rich," he recalled, though the words were not readily audible, coming from what was now, by hot pursuit of a most malevolent form of blood and bone cancer, more nearly a rictus than the human face of the aggressive, moody, enthusiastic, childlike, argumentative, devoted agent of his clients' features: the friend and purveyor of James Jackson Kilpatrick, Mary McGrory, the late Bishop Sheen, the Small Society, and, among so many others, me.

We went through the bedside routine . . . the new drug would restore him . . . he'd be home for Christmas . . . there would be plenty to do to keep him busy in the years ahead . . .

His replies, which by temperament would normally have been plucky, were tired. He closed his eyes, and asked simply, "How long will you be away?" I answered: "Just five or six days, Harry." He said, "In case anything happens while you're gone, I'll tell you what I told Helen [his best friend], that I'd rather go at seventy-one having known you for eighteen years, than go at eighty not having known you at all." How does one requite such an expression? The hospital room was dark, so that I could leave him without his seeing any facial betrayals of my verbal assurance that we would meet again on New Year's Eve, at his apartment.

Two days before, Harry's lawyer had called the doctor. "I want to read to you a paragraph from Mr. Elmlark's will," the lawyer had said, and proceeded to read from a California model I had picked up years ago and he had incorporated into his will, to the effect that the testator instructed his doctors not to prolong his life by extravagant and synthetic attentions when the prognosis was reliably negative. The doctor, who had become fond of Harry—as almost everyone became fond of him—privately advised me that the point was moot. The prescriptions were routine; and routinely ineffective over the long term.

But his impending retirement notwithstanding, he did want to live (most people do). True, he was lonely; his Lillian, from whom he had been inseparable, died of cancer in 1973. His only daughter, a few years later. He had a grandson, whose stepmother was kind to him, which dispelled Harry's only official nonprofessional concern. He had contrived the big deal—the syndicate he worked for, sold to the Washington *Star*, then to Time Inc., then to Universal Press: the whole enterprise flourishing under new, young management. The writers he introduced to syndication, notably J. J. Kilpatrick and me (Mary he inherited from the *Star*), were his friends, as were Helen, and June, and Newby and Betty Noyes from the old *Star*.

What to say? I am an executor of his modest estate. My son is a peripheral beneficiary of it. Memorial services are tentative; so that we have sure recourse only to a very private grief, to which this grateful friend gives public expression, notwithstanding that Harry, sitting at his editorial desk across which, for so many years, the copy flowed, would initially have resisted it, but—in the end—let it go; because, even as he loved, however discreetly, he longed also to be loved.

11

Russell Kirk

October 30, 1981

(Remarks by William F. Buckley, Jr., at a testimonial dinner for Russell Kirk at the Mayflower Hotel in Washington on Thursday October 1, 1981. Eight other tributes were heard.)

EXCEPT that we are here to honor Russell Kirk, by this time in the proceedings it would have been, however inappropriate to say, nevertheless true to say—that, really, there is nothing left to say. But a dozen tributes, in the case of Russell Kirk, do not even skirt redundancy, let alone comprehensiveness. The evening was not planned with the exactitude of a *Festschrift*. Given the stochastic proceedings organized by our beloved friend Don Lipsett—around whose image I propose upon retirement to fabricate a necktie, and grow rich from so abundant a documentation of supply-side economics—some of Russell's achievements will several times have been mentioned, the evening having ignored, entirely, many others.

With this in mind, I charged the researchers of *National Review* to go beyond Kirk the renowned historian, Kirk the editor, Kirk the journalist, Kirk the educator, Kirk the family man, Kirk the writer of fiction, Kirk the doyen of important American ghosts. The report of their findings, although not surprising, is testimony to the extraordinary versatility of the man we meet here to honor.

—Did you know, for instance, that Russell Kirk writes most of the lines for Archie Bunker? It is a part of the commercial covenant that Russell must pretend to hate television; indeed, it is probable that he would even go so far as to say he has no idea who Archie Bunker is, even after creating the locus classicus of the ignorant and bigoted American conservative. But, you see, Russell is trained in the dissimulative arts, as witness that:

—It was he, we discover, who installed the tape system in the White House for Richard Nixon. The President did not entrust the exercise to a mere mechanic, insisting instead on a true humanist. For this one, he told Mr. Haldeman, "I need a Renaissance man." And so, in January of 1969, that considerable hiatus at Piety Hill, which resulted in no daughters being born to Mrs. Kirk in October of 1969, was spent by Russell not in delivering the Burke Lectures on the Isle of Man, as advertised; but in the White House where, every morning, dressed as an electrician, Russell first consulted a catalogue to remind himself which was the screwdriver, which the microphone; and, as we all know, the system worked.

—Finally, there are those who do not know what exactly are the concessions that Mr. Allen is agreeing to in the matter of the proposed sale of the AWACS airplanes to Saudi Arabia. It has been touch and go, but only yesterday the President gave the okay. If Israel will agree to permit the Saudis to get the AWACS, Russell Kirk will agree to render instructions on how to fly them in that jargonistic English whose obscurity he has so devastatingly exposed. Thus, the Saudis would get the AWACS, and the Israelis would be assured that they would never get them off the ground . . .

In this room, as it happens, are the only two persons, myself excluded, who have figured regularly in *National Review* throughout the twenty-five years of its existence. The first is the incomparable Erik von Kuehnelt-Leddihn, who two nights ago in my house explained to my astonished guests how history will quite probably regret that we won the First World War. The other is Russell Kirk.

In 1954 I flew to Michigan. I had a single objective, and I greatly feared that I would fail in it. I desired that Professor

Kirk would consent, beginning with the opening issue, to contribute a regular column to *National Review* on doings of the academic world.

I confess I was very nervous. Although Russell was only a few years older, at twenty-eight I felt that an entire world lay between us, and this is so today as, with dismay, I contemplate how very much he knows that I shall never know—that everwidening gulf between his learning and my own. He was then a bachelor, and shortly after I arrived he took me to dinner at a neighborhood restaurant, where he ordered Tom Collinses for both of us. Emboldened by that warm aloofness which is his trademark, I put it to him directly, and his reply was instantaneous: Yes, he would be glad to write a regular column for my prospective magazine. I was so elated by his spontaneous and generous willingness to associate his august name with that of a wizened ex-schoolboy known mostly for an iconoclastic screed directed at his alma mater, that I took to ordering more Tom Collinses, but in every case one for each of us. The evening proceeded toward a pitch of such hilarity that, at midnight, I barely was able to drive the car back to Russell's house. On arriving, he led me to my bedroom, bade me goodnight only a second before I collapsed into my bed, to rise seven hours later and bump into Russell only then emerging from his study. He had, in the interval since dinner, written a chapter of his history of St. Andrews College, and would be catching a little sleep after he served me breakfast.

In twenty-five years he never missed a deadline. At his wedding to what Russell's newspaper column readers resigned themselves finally to acknowledging as "the beauteous Annette," I thought that possibly the most useful gift I might give him would be a honeymoon's-length moratorium from his column, since he was off to Scotland. But, shortly before ascending the altar, when I stammered out the proposal, he responded by reaching into the pocket of his morning coat and coming up with—four columns. Perfectly typed. Perfectly edited. Brilliantly executed. Not many know personally the extraordinary professionalism of Russell Kirk, which matches that of Sam Johnson and G. K. Chesterton. No one, my sister Priscilla apart, knows this better than I, and I salute him for it.

It is of course, as has been suggested, inconceivable to imagine an important, let alone hope for a dominant, conservative movement in America, without his labor. The quantity and quality of it is staggering: that we all know. Reflecting on his formidable work one's mind rests principally, I think, on Russell's knowledge of the critical importance of what came before, of the intellectual treasures of the past. His perspective on the matter is so clear that he recognizes that *every* generation is dependent on what came earlier, to which insight he devoted the epigraph of *A Program for Conservatives,* published by Henry Regnery in 1954. "Long before our time," Cicero wrote in his *De Re Publica,* "the customs of our ancestors molded admirable men, and in turn these eminent men upheld the ways and institutions of their forebears. Our age, however, inherited the Republic like some beautiful painting of bygone days, its colors already fading through great age; and not only has our time neglected to freshen the colors of the picture, but we have failed to preserve its form and outlines."

But, applied to America, that is less true today than it was twenty-five years ago when Russell adduced it, as an epigraph fitting not only for Rome, but prospectively for America. And the difference between then and now is substantially of his own doing. Because, beginning about then, Russell Kirk left the academy—did so notwithstanding his knowledge that academic men are peculiarly unsuited for public life. "Yet though I know these dreadful truths," he wrote in that same book, "and though I am a doctor of letters, and an historian of sorts, in this little book I venture into the dark and bloody ground of political policy, naked unto mine enemies; and I do this not out of foolhardiness, but because the men of affairs who are supposed to be applying the tenets of philosophy to the affairs of nations are doing nothing of the sort—or, at least, when they make such an essay at all, they commonly behave as abstractly and imprudently as if they were so many professors."

But that has changed. In this room are Richard Allen, John East, Martin Anderson, Aram Bakshian, and Bill Casey, men as much at home in the academy as in these other, bloody grounds of which Cicero and Russell spoke. He, as much as anyone, made this possible; and so I take, with pride, the pleasure of telling him publicly that the republic of which Cicero spoke as an evanescent institution in this case survives, owing no debt more heavy, nor recognizing any more gladly, than that—to you.

12

Sadat and the People

October 15, 1981

IT IS SAD to read accounts of the relative indifference of the body of Egyptians to the death of Sadat. No doubt such reports are exaggerated or, more accurately, they are juxtaposed with the kind of hysterical emotional pitches to which the Moslem community is accustomed. The comparison is made with the public grief shown over the death of Nasser. One might add to this the high pitch of enthusiasm shown for Khomeini, and the vituperative mob scenes of which the Shah and the United States were jointly and severally the objects. What one learns about people—Egyptians, Iranians and, one ruefully supposes, Americans under certain kinds of stress—is saddening, and most painfully interesting.

Nasser was a cruel man, a despicable fomenter of hatred. He cared about war and about the destruction of Israel. He thought nothing of wooing Moscow, never mind communism's explicit hostility to any kind of religion. His radio stations blared out the need for a holy war against Israel, in accents not substantially different from those of Qaddafi. He knew, as Qaddafi probably doesn't, how to behave when kings and queens drop in for tea. But he stood for war, for absolute despotism at home, and for the consecration of Mohammed to the cause of anti-Semitism. And when he died, the Egyptian people went mad with grief.

Last week Iranian authorities officially gave out the figure of 1,356 executions since June 1. One reasonably supposes that the figure is greater. These are done under the sponsorship of a man who calls himself a religious leader, and whose represen- tatives cheered the assassination of Anwar Sadat. The mobs in Iran, it is said, are still led emotionally by Khomeini.

One edges, however regretfully, to the conclusion that the meek are unlikely to inherit the earth. Anwar Sadat was not a weak man, though one judges that his meekness was biblical in its sincerity, that his personal radiation of benignity was utterly genuine. True, he had apprenticed under Nasser. But some- how he succeeded in excreting all of Nasser's ways.

He fought honorably but concluded a cease-fire. And then he gave rise to the single most resonant statement of the post- war period, when, standing before the ancient enemy in Jeru- salem, he said, "I renounce my past." He then sought peace with honor.

A few years earlier, recognizing the subversive disposition of his Soviet allies, he booted them out of the country. In the past months he had endured many humiliations at the hands of Mr. Begin, whose sincerity in the matter of autonomy for the West Bank became more and more difficult to aver, but he did so insisting that Begin was a man of honorable intentions, and with that fatalism with which he treated his own life, he treated a historical process which he helped more than any man in the recent history of the region to shape.

At home, he insisted on being the undisputed ruler. But his resolution was not sufficient unto the task, because his leader- ship was disputed. By the left, by the Moslem fundamentalists, by the Israel haters.

There was never any doubt that if challenged publicly he would call out the police, and if necessary the military. And yet when he was killed, the most concentrated aggregation of world leaders came to pay tribute to him since the assassina- tion of John F. Kennedy, President not of a single Near Eastern power, but of the most important and powerful country in the world. Anyone who, particularly in the past six months, has labored over the question whether there is a difference be- tween authoritarian and totalitarian need only consider the differences between Sadat and Qaddafi, or Sadat and Brezhnev, to know instantly the truth.

There remains the people. It is unfair to say of them all that they were unaffected. But it is true that the character of Sadat moved them less than the character of Nasser, and this of course is the reason why, in so large a part of the world, authoritarianism necessarily prevails.

13

Ayn Rand, R.I.P.

March 11, 1982

AYN RAND is dead. So, incidentally, is the philosophy she sought to launch dead; it was, in fact, stillborn. The great public crises in Ayn Rand's career came, in my judgment, when Whittaker Chambers took her on—in December of 1957 when her book *Atlas Shrugged* was dominating the bestseller list, lecturers were beginning to teach something called Randism and students started using such terms as "mysticism of the mind" (religion), and "mysticism of the muscle" (statism). Whittaker Chambers, whose authority with American conservatives was as high as that of any man then living, wrote in *National Review* after a lengthy analysis of the essential aridity of Miss Rand's philosophy, "Out of a lifetime of reading, I can recall no other book in which a tone of overriding arrogance was so implacably sustained. Its shrillness is without reprieve. Its dogmatism is without appeal."

I had met Miss Rand three years before that review was published. Her very first words to me (I do not exaggerate) were: "You ahrr too intelligent to believe in Gott." The critic Wilfrid Sheed once remarked, when I told him the story, "Well, that certainly is an icebreaker." It was; and we conversed, and did so for two or three years. I used to send her postcards in liturgical Latin; but levity with Miss Rand was not an effective weapon. And when I published Whittaker Chambers' review, her resentment was so comprehensive that she regularly inquired of all hosts or toastmasters whether she was being invited to a function at which I was also scheduled to appear, because if that was the case either she would not come or, if so, only after I had left or before I arrived. I fear that I put the lady through a great deal of choreographical pain.

Miss Rand's most memorable personal claim (if you don't count the one about her being the next greatest philosopher after Aristotle) was that since formulating her philosophy of "objectivism" she had never experienced any emotion for which she could not fully account. And then one day, a dozen years ago, she was at a small dinner, the host of which was Henry Hazlitt, the libertarian economist, the other guest being Ludwig von Mises, the grand master of the Austrian school of antistatist economics.

Miss Rand was going on about something or other at which point Mises told her to be quiet, that she was being very foolish. The lady who could account for all her emotions at that point burst out into tears and complained, "You are treating me like a poor, ignorant little Jewish girl!" Mr. Hazlitt, attempting to bring serenity to his table, leaned over and said, "There there, Ayn, that isn't at all what Ludwig was suggesting." But this attempt at conciliation was ruined when Mises jumped up and said, "That iss eggsactly what you ahrr!" Since Mises was himself Jewish, this was not a racist slur. This story was mortal to her reputation as the lady of total self-control.

There were other unpleasantnesses of professional interest, such as her alienation from her principal apostle, Nathaniel Brandon—who was so ungallant as to suggest, in retaliation against her charge that he was trying to swindle her, that the breakup was the result of his rejection of an, er, amatory advance by Miss Rand. Oh goodness, it got ugly.

There were a few who, like Chambers, caught on early. *Atlas Shrugged* was published back before the law of the Obligatory Sex Scene was passed by both houses of Congress and all fifty state legislatures, so that the volume was considered rather risqué, in its day. Russell Kirk, challenged to account for Miss Rand's success if indeed she was merely an exiguous philosophical figure, replied, "Oh, they read her books for the fornicating bits." Unkind. And only partly true.

The Fountainhead, read in a certain way, is a profound assertion of the integrity of art. What did Miss Rand in was her anxiety to theologize her beliefs. She was an eloquent and persuasive antistatist, and if only she had left it at that—but no. She had to declare that God did not exist, that altruism was despicable, that only self-interest is good and noble. She risked, in fact, giving to capitalism that bad name that its enemies have done so well in giving it, and that is a pity. Miss Rand was a talented woman, devoted to her ideals. She came as a refugee from communism to this country as a young woman, and carved out a substantial career. May she rest in peace, and may she experience the demystification of her mind possessed.

14

David Niven, R.I.P.

August 6, 1983

CHÂTEAU-D'OEX, SWITZERLAND—St. Peter's (Anglican) Church is small, so that most of the mourners were outside. In other circumstances one would have said that outside there were the gawkers and voyeurs, except that when David Niven died, everyone mourned him, not least villagers among whom he had lived for thirty winters, who knew him also on the screen. The flowers were Hollywood-grand, but different in arrangement from what the Godfather would have ordered for a prominent member of the family.

The red-bearded English minister intoned, "Mindful of the example shown to us by our dear departed brother David Niven, let us repeat together the prayer of a sixteenth-century pastor, Johann Arndt." It was an absolutely safe bet that David Niven had never heard of Johann Arndt, and there were certainly more movies made by David Niven than sermons listened to by David Niven. Yet it was on the (closed) doors of St. Peter's that he threw himself that midnight in November when his daughter was comatose after a terrible car accident.

"Bestow on me, O Lord, a genial spirit," the minister was reading. On the widow's right sat Prince Rainier, whose own acquaintance with grief had been witnessed by the tens of millions who watched his wife's televised funeral. A genial spirit.

. . . There were four at dinner that night five years earlier, at a restaurant in Monaco, and Rainier was, well, in a grumpy mood. Whatever it is that princes are trained to do to overcome royal distemper was not being done proficiently early on that evening, and this David Niven diagnosed with the speed of an X-ray machine and, like the physician, David Niven knew his duty, and he did it.

It required about twenty minutes for the therapy totally to take hold. It began with a tale of David's initial encounter with a lady of pleasure, when he was fifteen. It traveled through disparate episodes in Hollywood, Bangkok, Camp David; involving Errol Flynn, Tyrone Power, his cook and ski teacher. His own naturally high spirits were engaged, but he was ministering primarily to the needy, and the neediest of all in this world are those who suffer not from hunger but from melancholy. David Niven had only the one fear throughout his working life, which was that he might bore someone, someday. Or that he might fail to stimulate whomever he was talking to. And he had the physician's eye for who, in the room full of people, most needed attention. If ever there was a man who winked at the homely girl, it was Niven.

His friends persuaded him to go to the Mayo Clinic in February 1982. He had been misdiagnosed by half the doctors in Europe, among whom the consensus was that the three or four apparently unrelated things that were happening to him—faintly garbled speech, slight lack of leg coordination, vastly diminished appetite—were owing to a strained nerve dating back to a war injury. In two days the clinic discovered what it was, and told him—much as Colonel C. Aubrey Smith of the Grenadiers would have told Lieutenant Niven that the expedition against the Russians was probably suicidal—that there was no cure, and that he was entering the "galloping" phase of the disease. Two days later, back in Switzerland, he told his friends that he intended to defeat the ridiculous disease, and every day he went for physical therapy.

As his voice control deteriorated, he suffered; but his distinctive exasperation was his relative inability to do his job, which was to be the genial spirit to friends and family.

By the time the next winter came, the last winter, it required concentration to make out what he was saying, but it was still possible, when he spoke slowly. He had, from necessity, become reclusive, but he would go in the afternoons to paint a little on canvases, the last one of which had clouds that, early in February, were pink and white, but by late March had become black and gray, tumultuous even. He was in the hospital before that canvas was completed.

He stepped back one afternoon from his painting. "Do you know, I received a nice letter from a former master at Stowe when he heard I was sick, and I wrote back and said, 'Well, I guess it's just time to pack it in,' and he wrote back,"—by now Niven was beginning to laugh—" 'What do you mean, ready to pack it in. You're only seventy-two. I'm eighty-three and have no intention of packing it in.' " David thought that funny, but then he thought almost everything funny, only now he had to guard against abandoned laughter, because it convulsed him.

The last time, again while painting, he could not control himself. "Ran into someone I hadn't seen for years, in Gstaad, and he shouted out from his car, 'Niven, how the hell are you?' And I shouted back as best I could, 'Well, Sam, you see, I got this bloody dis-ease—' and he interrupted me and said, 'Oh, well, I've got a new bloody car myself!' " Paintbrushes in hand, he doubled over laughing.

Yehudi Menuhin led students in an octet from Mendelssohn, the congregation recited the Lord's Prayer, and the minister closed by giving thanks that "as an actor and as a writer" the deceased "was able to bring happiness to millions of people the world over. Amen." Amen.

15

The Kennedys:
On to Colonus

April 28, 1984

I MET HER, as it happens, before even her husband did, but it was only a casual afternoon outing: I and two college class-mates, she and one of her brothers, afternoon in and out of the swimming pool, that kind of thing. All of this exercised under the watchful eyes of an affectionate but sternly moral mother who would not permit in the house any novel by William Faulkner because he used dirty words. The father was cosmo-politan and not, himself, a Roman Catholic, never mind that a devotion to her faith was his wife's principal extrafamilial en-thusiasm. All the paraphernalia of the leisured class were con-spicuously about, as though a setting for a novel by James Gould Cozzens, or John Cheever.

I never came to know her, though there was a contact or two, and a lot of friends in common. But I watched, as so many others did, and the accumulation of griefs seemed—seems now, with the death of David—very nearly unsupportable. The perspective is necessarily affected by one's own experi-ences. When my father died at seventy-seven he left ten chil-dren, nine of them married, apparently happily so; all of them communicants in the religion in which they had been raised. It would not continue so, but there were those magic moments that froze three decades of happiness in ineffaceable memory.

Ethel Skakel Kennedy's mother and father were then killed

in an airplane crash. The chronology here is not researched, and in any event is irrelevant. In due course her older, dashing brother was killed in another air crash. His widow choked at dinner, while eating chicken, or steak, or whatever. Her brother-in-law, the President of the United States, was assassinated. Five years later her husband was assassinated, leaving her pregnant with her eleventh child. And now her fourth child is dead at twenty-eight, the victim, one is left to gather, of drugs, those spiritually incapacitating killers that—as they used to put it in another context on Sunday mornings—"roam through the world, seeking the destruction of souls."

Senator Edward Kennedy, as he has done since 1968, was immediately on the scene and spoke through an aide to the press. He said that he and his sister-in-law hoped that David would now find, in the company of God, the peace that had eluded him when he lived.

We have all been reminded of the scene in Los Angeles when the thirteen-year-old boy follows on television his father's political triumph in the critical primary, and stays glued to the television set following his father's footsteps to his execution. In the turmoil the child was forgotten for several hours, discovered finally by historian-journalist Theodore White, who could only think to console him by ordering hot chocolate and encouraging him to weep on White's shoulder. What else?

The story of Ethel Kennedy moves one necessarily to thought of the permanent things. How trivially fortune treats us, how heavily it concentrates its spite on some families. But there the examination must never end. What survives in this world also demands our attention: such women as Rose Kennedy, and Jackie, and Ethel.

"History," Whittaker Chambers wrote me (his final letter, a few weeks before his own death), "hit us with a freight train. History has long been doing this to people, monotonously and usually lethally. But we (my general breed) tried . . . to put ourselves together again. . . . But at a price—weariness. People tend to leave Oedipus, shrieking with the blood running down his cheeks—everybody nicely purged by pity and terror, and so home and to bed. But I was about twenty-three when I discovered, rather by chance, that Oedipus went on to

Colonus." Where the blinded, tortured king became finally a source of strength for the country that gave him sanctuary.

So Ethel Kennedy gives strength, as does her family, by proclaiming publicly their faith that God's mysterious ways are to be accepted: wearily, perhaps, but not resentfully. What was it that caused David Kennedy to die? How was Oedipus (finally) taken? The narrator explains to the survivors that suddenly, after conversing with Theseus, Oedipus was gone. "No fiery thunderbolt of the god removed him in that hour, nor any rising of storm from the sea; but either a messenger from the gods, or the world of the dead, the nether adamant, riven for him in love, without pain; for the passing of the man was not with lamentation, or in sickness and suffering, but, above mortals, wonderful. And if to any I seem to speak folly, I would not woo their belief, who count me foolish." It is only in that sense that the departure of David can comfort his mother, and his family, and it is necessary that they be comforted.

16

John Chamberlain

(Introduction to *A Life with the Printed Word* by John Chamberlain, Chicago: Regnery Gateway, 1982)

LATE ONE AFTERNOON in the fall of 1955, on the eve of the appearance of the first issue of *National Review*, something people more loftily situated would have called a "summit conference" was set in New York City, for which purpose a tiny suite in the Commodore Hotel was engaged. Tensions—ideological and personal—had arisen, and the fleeting presence in New York of Whittaker Chambers, who had dangled before us in an altogether self-effacing way the prospect that he might come out of retirement to join the fledgling enterprise, prompted me to bring the principals together for a meeting which had no specific agenda, being designed primarily to reaffirm the common purpose. As I think back on it, two of the five people present at the outset were born troublemakers. To say this about someone is not to dismiss him as merely that: Socrates was a troublemaker, so was Thomas Edison. But troublemaking was not what was primarily needed to distill unity, and so things were not going smoothly, one half hour after the meeting began. And then, when it was nearly six o'clock and I thought I detected in Chambers a look of terminal exasperation, John Chamberlain came in, a briefcase in one hand, a pair of figure skates in the other. He mumbled (he usually mumbles) his apology . . . He had booked the practice time at the ice rink for himself and his daughters . . . The early afternoon editorial meeting had been protracted . . . The traffic difficult . . . No thanks, he didn't want anything to drink— was there any iced tea? He stole a second or two to catch up on Whittaker's family, and then sat back to participate in a conference which had been transformed by his presence at it. When a few days later Chambers wrote, he remarked the sheer "goodness" of John Chamberlain, a quality in him that no man or woman, living or dead, has ever to my knowlege disputed.

At the time a sharp difference had arisen, not between me and John, but between Willi Schlamm and John's wife, Peggy (R.I.P.). Schlamm viewed the projected magazine as a magnetic field with which professional affiliation could no more be denied by the few to whom the call was tendered, than a call to serve as one of the twelve apostles. Poor Peggy would not stand for it: John was serving then as editor of *Barron's* magazine. Before that he had been with *The Freeman,* before that with *Life,* before that *The Wall Street Journal,* before that *Fortune,* before that the New York *Times.* In each of these enterprises he had achieved singularity. He had two daughters not yet grown up. How could anyone reasonably ask that now, in middle age, he detach himself from a secure position to throw in with an enterprise whose working capital would not have seen *Time* magazine through a single issue, or *Barron's* through a dozen, and whose editor-in-chief was not long out of school?

I like to remind myself that I did not figure even indirectly in the protracted negotiation, respecting, as I did, not only the eminence of John Chamberlain but also the altogether understandable desire of his wife for just a little economic security. But Willi was very nearly (nothing ever proved that conclusively shocking to Willi) struck dumb with shock. That was one of the clouds that hung over that late afternoon discussion in which Willmoore Kendall exploited every opportunity to add fuel to the fire, principally by the device of suggesting that for *some* people security means *everything*—the kind of thing John did not wish to hear, among other things because it so inexactly reflected his own priorities: he was concerned not with security, but with domestic peace.

So it went, and in one form or other the tensions continued, though they never proved crippling. John settled the problem by moonlighting, as lead reviewer for *National Review*. But I learned then, during that tense afternoon, the joy of a definitively pacific presence. Ours might have been a meeting to discuss whether to dump the bomb on Hiroshima, and John Chamberlain's presence would have brought to such a meeting, whatever its outcome, a sense of inner peace, manliness, and self-confidence.

There are stories he does not tell, in this engrossing autobiography—stories about himself, and this is characteristic. Bertrand de Jouvenel once told me, in a luncheon devoted to discussing our common friend Willmoore Kendall, that any subject at all is more interesting than oneself. Actually I am not sure that this is so, because some people know no subject thoroughly other than themselves, but with John Chamberlain self-neglect is not an attribute of manners but of personality. When *National Review* started up, he would come in to the office every week (it was then a weekly) and, sitting down in whatever cubicle was empty, type out the lead review, with that quiet confidence exhibited by sea captains when they extricate their huge liners from their hectic municipal slips to begin an ocean voyage. After forty-five minutes or so a definitive book review was done, and he would, quietly, leave, lest he disrupt the office.

In those days "the office" consisted of six or seven cubicles, each one with desk and typewriter. Most of *NR*'s top editorial staffers, from the beginning on, have served only part-time—James Burnham, Willi Schlamm, Willmoore Kendall, Whittaker Chambers, Frank Meyer—so that although they would, week after week, always use the same office, at any given moment at least one cubicle was unoccupied, though seldom the same one. A young graduate of Smith, age twenty-four, four or five months into the magazine's life complained to her classmate, my sister, that the repairman who came once a week to check the typewriters had not once serviced her own. No one was more amused on hearing this than John Chamberlain, the delinquent typewriter repairman, who that week, servicing the typewriter, had written a marvelously illuminating review of the entire fictional work of Mary McCarthy.

I never saw him, during the thirties, slide into his chair at the New York *Times* to write his daily book reviews, many of them masterpieces of the form. Or at *Fortune,* returning from two weeks on the road to write what he here calls a "long piece," which would prove the definitive article on this or that intricate problem of management or labor. Or at *Life,* presiding over the editorial page which was Henry Luce's personal cockpit from which he spoke out, through John, to God and man in authoritative, not to say authoritarian, accents. But I decline to believe that in any of these roles, or in any of the myriad others —as professor at Columbia, as dean at the University of Alabama, as a book writer or columnist—John Chamberlain ever did anything more disruptive than merely to greet whoever stood in the way, and amble over to wherever the nearest typewriter was, there to execute his craft, maintaining standards as high as any set by any critical contemporary. Because John Chamberlain could not ever sing off key. And the combination of a gentle nature and a hard Yankee mind brought forth prose of which this book gives a representative sample. The voice of reason, from an affable man unacquainted with affectation, deeply committed to the cause of his country, which he believes to be coextensive with that of civilization, and certainly with that of his two girls by his first marriage and his son—a budding young poet—by his second, to the enchanting Ernestine, to whom he went soon after Peggy's untimely death.

In this book Chamberlain seeks to bring the reader quietly along, that he might reexperience the author's odyssey. He does this, characteristically, without pushing or shoving; as if to say at any point that if the reader desires to hew to a different turn in the road, why that is all right by Chamberlain; although the probability is that, if the reader will reflect substantially on the data, he will in due course come around.

The data!

We are all familiar with autobiographical accounts of ideological explorations, some of them wonderfully exciting. John Chamberlain's is surely the most soft-throated in the literature.

As a young man who had demonstrated his prowess as a critic (William Lyon Phelps called him the "finest critic of his generation"), as a political thinker manifestly addicted to progress, he wrote his book *A Farewell to Reform,* in which he seemed to give up on organic change, suggesting the advantages of radical alternatives. But his idealism was never superordinated to his intelligence, and in the balance of that decade of the thirties and, following that, of the forties Chamberlain never ceased to look at the data, which carefully he integrated in his productive mind. Along the line (he tells us) he read three books, so to speak at one gulp (how many books has he read, reviewed, during his career? Or better: Has anyone read, and manifestly digested, more books than John Chamberlain?)— and the refractory little tumblers closed, after which he became what is now denominated a "conservative," though Chamberlain prefers the word "voluntarist." The books in question, by the three furies of modern libertarianism—Isabel Paterson, Rose Wilder Lane, Ayn Rand—provided the loose cement. After that, as he shows us here, he ceased to be surprised by evidence now become redundant: evidence that the marketplace really works, really performs social functions, really helps live human beings with live problems.

This book is a story of that journey. Its calmness and lucidity, its acquiescent handling of experience, free of ideological entanglement, provokes in the reader the kind of confidence that John Chamberlain throughout his life has provoked in his friends. That he is that to them—a friend—but that in no circumstances are the claims of friendship so to be put forward as to run any risk of corrupting the purity of his ongoing search— through poetry, fiction, economic texts, corporate reports and, yes, seed catalogues—for just the right formulation of what may be acknowledged as the American proposition, by which an equilibrium of forces breeds the best that can be got out of the jealous, contentious, self-indulgent, uproarious breed of men and women who have made so exciting a world here, giving issue, in one of America's finest moments, to a splendid son, who here has given us his invaluable memoirs.

17

I. Moyer Hunsberger

PASSING ON THE SESQUIPEDALIAN TORCH

December 9, 1978

A GENTLEMAN called I. Moyer Hunsberger, who is by profession a chemist, is also a word lover, and he has brought out a book which he calls *The Quintessential Dictionary,* published by the Hart Publishing Company. Mr. Hunsberger's notion was to put out a book of words which, although not widely known, are quite widely used. He came up with twelve hundred such words, and it is as obvious that a familiarity with them contributes to a richer life as that a familiarity with more books, more poetry, more music, more history, contributes to a richer life.

The distinction Mr. Hunsberger attempts to make is between those words that are infrequently used primarily because the situation is extremely rare in which they are useful—what Dwight Macdonald once termed "words that belong in the zoo section of a dictionary"—and other words, used with good effect, by Mr. Hunsberger's calculations, by a number of contemporary writers, e.g., Meg Greenfield, James J. Kilpatrick, John Leonard, Christopher Porterfield, George Will, Harold Schonberg, R. Z. Sheppard and, well, me.

Now along comes, would you believe it, a librarian, blasting the book in the Tampa *Tribune and Times.* Mr. Joseph Hipp disdains the entire venture in a stretch of unfocused resentment, terminating with the barbarism of the year. "Essentially," he writes, *"The Quintessential Dictionary* is nonessential unless you expect Bill Buckley to tea—and then if that is the case, you will probably find much more to talk about than a dictionary with a snob appeal and nothing else."

In the first place, it is obvious that the dictionary is *nonessential.* So is the Tampa Public Library. But for a librarian to say that an effort to expand one's word knowledge is a venture in snobbery is to undermine the structure of his own profession. To say that a particular word should not be used because it is uncommon is on the order of advising a composer that he may not use a diminished chord in his next symphony. The notion that a thoughtful collection of words is not worth looking into is on the order of telling Mr. Hipp that he ought to close off a section or two of his Library. Such a position encourages the formulation of a new word: *"Hippism:* A Philistine's resentment of a curiosity about the meaning of words. Hippistic, adj.; hippistically, adv."

And I take the opportunity, Mr. Hipp having in this sensitive connection mentioned my name, to disavow a living legend, namely that I am the American fountainhead of recondite words. It is a pity to get in the way of legends that people cherish—Bob Hope, bless him, makes fun of my vocabulary on network TV—and I am opposed to the kind of people who write books saying that John D. Rockefeller wasn't really stingy, and Lizzie Borden didn't really give her mother forty whacks, and technically Socrates *was* guilty. But I have decided to cast off the robes of martyrdom, and I'll tell you what did it. The proximate cause of my declaration is a splendid novel by John Updike called *The Coup.* I read it and here is a list of words in that novel with which *I* am unfamiliar:

Harmattan, dysphoretic, toubab, laterite, suras, euphorbia, extollation, jerboa, coussabe, sareba, bilharzia, pangolins hyraxes, pestles, phloem xylem, eversion, marabout, xerophytic, oleograph, cowries, chrysoprase, henna, scree, riverine, adsorptive, haptic, burnoose.

And so I pass on the sesquipedalian torch. All letters of complaint about unusual words will henceforward be sent on to Mr. Updike. But since he is not as faithful a correspondent as I am, you should not sit up, waiting for a reply. So remember, from now on you won't have Buckley to kick around anymore.

18

Peanut Butter

JUST TO SAY THANKS

March 26, 1981

FOR MANY YEARS I have labored under the burden of an unrequited passion. What have I done for it, in return for all it has done for me? Nothing. But I have wondered what I could use as what the journalists call a "peg."

I have found one. This may strike some of the literal-minded as attenuated, but it goes as follows: This is the centennial year of the Tuskegee Institute, which was founded on the Fourth of July, 1881, by Booker T. Washington. Tuskegee continues to be a remarkable institution, and former Secretary of Defense Donald Rumsfeld is the head of a committee of illustrious men and women who are devoting themselves to raising $20 million to encourage it in its noble work.

What noble work? We have arrived at step two. It was, among other things, the principal academic home of George Washington Carver, and it was G. W. Carver who to all intents and purposes invented the peanut. What he did, more specifically, was document that the cultivation of the peanut despoiled the land far less than the cultivation of cotton, and then he set out to merchandise the peanut in order that there might be a market for it.

He discovered an estimated three hundred uses for it, many of them entirely removed from the peanut's food value. But it is this, of course, that is the wonder of the peanut. The Encyclopedia Britannica informs us that "pound for pound peanuts have more protein, minerals, and vitamins than beef liver, more fat than heavy cream, and more food energy (calories) than sugar." And George Washington Carver discovered— peanut butter.

I have never composed poetry, but if I did, my very first couplet would be:

> *I know that I shall never see*
> *A poem lovely as Skippy's peanut butter.*

When I was first married and made plain to my wife that I expected peanut butter for breakfast every day of my life, including Ash Wednesday, she thought me quite mad (for the wrong reasons). She has not come round, really, and this is a source of great sadness to me because one wants to share one's pleasures.

I was hardened very young to the skeptics. When I was twelve I was packed off to a British boarding school by my father, who dispatched every fortnight a survival package comprising a case of grapefruit and a large jar of peanut butter. I offered to share my tuck with the other boys at my table. They grabbed instinctively for the grapefruit—but one after another actually spit out the peanut butter, which they had never before seen and which only that very year (1938) had become available for sale in London. No wonder they needed American help to win the war.

You can find it now in specialty shops in Europe, but I have yet to see it in anyone's home. And it is outrageously difficult to get even in the typical American hotel. My profession requires me to spend forty or fifty nights on the road every year, and when it comes time to order breakfast over the telephone I summon my resolution—it helps to think about peanut butter when you need moral strength—and add, after the orange juice, coffee, skim milk, and whole-wheat toast, "Do you have any peanut butter?"

Sometimes the room service operator will actually break out laughing when the request is put in, at which point my voice becomes stern and unsmiling. Often the operator will say, "Just a minute," and then she will turn, I suppose to the chef, but I can hear right through the hand she has put over the receiver—"Hey Jack. We got any peanut butter? Room 322 wants some peanut butter!" This furtive philistinism is then regularly followed by giggles all around. One lady recently asked, "How old is your little boy and does he want a peanut butter sandwich?" To which I replied, "My little boy is twenty-eight and is never without peanut butter, because he phones ahead before he confirms hotel reservations."

I introduced Auberon Waugh to cashew butter ten years ago when he first visited America, and although I think it inferior to peanut butter Auberon was quite simply overwhelmed. You can't find it in Great Britain so I sent him a case from the Farmer's Market. It quite changed his writing style: for about ten months he was at peace with the world. I think that was the time he said something pleasant about Harold Wilson. In the eleventh month, it was easy to tell that he had run out. It quite changes your disposition and your view of the world if you cannot have peanut butter every day.

So here is yet another reason for contributing money to the Tuskegee Institute. For all we know, but for it we'd never have tasted peanut butter. There'd be no Planter's, no Jif, no Peter Pan—that terrible thought reminds us of our indebtedness to George Washington Carver.

19

The Harpsichord

(Published in the New York *Time Magazine*, January 2, 1983, under the title "Queen of All Instruments")

January 2, 1983

At NATIONAL REVIEW, we give (of course) a Christmas party. For ten years or so, up until a year ago, the guest performer was Fernando Valenti, once designated (in *Time* magazine) as "the most exciting" recitalist alive, performing on the harpsichord. Then the cancer hit (from which, happily, he is in remission) and, of course, he was making no commitments for the indefinite future. I thought of asking Judith Norell, not only a brilliant musician but also a courageous one, as witness that for a couple of years she consented to be my teacher. But I thought that to present another harpsichordist would skirt insouciance—too much like the King is dead, long live the King. Better something completely different. Michael Sweeley, the president of the Caramoor music center near Katonah, New York, suggested Richard Vogt, Caramoor's choral director, who arrived on a snowy Friday in December at our place in Manhattan with an incredible thirteen performers—singers, a cellist, a harpsichord accompanist and a clarinetist.

Later that night, I measured the reactions of an audience of

about eighty—staff and friends of the magazine. The reaction
to Valenti had always been more than merely courteous. He
weaves his wonders so engagingly that even those who had
never before heard the instrument knew that a magic of sorts
was being brewed. But one simply has to acknowledge that
there are more popular forms of music, and these carried the
day when the happy and talented choristers sang and played,
everything from old English madrigals to "O Little Town of
Bethlehem." The harpsichord is not, in my opinion, a difficult
instrument to listen to, in the sense that one might say of a
bagpipe that an evening with it would prove long. But the pow
is not instantly there in a harpsichord. It requires habituation. I
suppose it is only safe to say it because the experiment is
unlikely, but I warrant that if those children in *The Blue La-
goon* had had a wind-up gramophone that survived the ship-
wreck, along with a record collection one-half harpsichord
music, one-half rock and roll, they'd have learned to prefer the
former to the latter well before they learned to mate. But it
isn't an instrument made for singing along with Mitch, and it
makes sense to acknowledge this going in.

And so we concede that the harpsichord, although there is
no question about the renaissance of early music of which it is
an integral part, continues to be a relatively neglected instrument, in need of a little affirmative action. God knows it was
once worse.

In the winter of 1816, the cold in Paris got most awfully
severe and heating materials scarce. The governors of the
Paris Conservatory met their own crisis with Gallic wit: by
burning, one after another, their abundant supply of harpsichords.

What do you do with a bulky object that has become, quite
simply, useless? Why, dispose of it. If in the course of doing so
you can tease out of it some highly desirable British thermal
units—then why not dispose of it into the fireplaces, rather
than the dustbin?

The act of 1816 is as horrifying as it would be if the Goya
collection in the Prado Museum were burned on the grounds
that Goya was no longer in style. Worse, in a way—because you
cannot any longer "destroy" Goya, whose works are definitively reproduced, even to the point where experts are occa-

sionally needed to authenticate an original. With the burning
of so many Stradivarius-class French harpsichords, a treasury
was depreciated which proved unreplenishable.

Consider. There resides, in the Yale Collection, a Taskin.
There are those who hold that this harpsichord's sound does
not elsewhere, in its singular beauty, exist (so much, by the
way, for the position that sounding boards necessarily deterio-
rate with age). Pascal Taskin the Elder was a harpsichord
maker who made wonderful instruments in the French school
(the others were Italian, Flemish, German, English) during the
third of the three centuries preceding the unconditional victory of the piano. Call that year 1800. The instrument for
which Couperin and Rameau, Soler and Scarlatti, Bach and
Handel had written was, for a very dark age, held to be forever
anachronized. The Western world was entering exuberantly
the age of romance. Schubert was already there, and even
Chopin would soon be born; Keats and Byron were stirring,
Turner and Goya exhibiting, and the artist's vision was of a
pretty girl, just like a melody; even though the girl could be sad
and, in opera, was often expected to commit suicide. The relative austerity of the (relatively astringent) harpsichord was
something people were entirely disposed to discard, in favor of
the mellifluous, sound variable piano.

But it is not really safe to say that the piano was, so to speak,
the evolutionary next step in the development of the harpsichord, as one might say that the DC-4 was the outgrowth of
the DC-3. It is the beginning of knowledge of the harpsichord
to know that it is a different instrument from the piano. A
corollary is that the end of the harpsichord might well have
been dictated, along around 1800, not so much by the realization of the piano, as by the desuetude of Baroque music. The
early sonatas of Beethoven were written for the harpsichord.
His later sonatas could not even be played on a harpsichord
(Beethoven was now absolutely depending, for the communication of his art, on a pedal that sustained notes that had already been struck, by fingers now otherwise occupied; and on
volume differentials from *pianissimo—pp—*to *fortissimo—ff*).
It is more accurate to think in terms, not of a better mouse-
trap's having replaced its predecessor, but of the awakening of

exclusivist artistic appetites appeased only at the expense of totally ignoring what had gone before. There had come a period during which the public *would not listen* to Baroque music, even as, a century and a half later, there came a period during which the public, however briefly, *would not view*, enthusiastically, classical art. In any event the harpsichord, for all intents and purposes, disappeared.

One of several reasons for the unchallengeable supremacy of the modern piano is, of course, its unmatchable versatility. Its tone, however lovely and however interesting, is relatively "white": a clear, neutral voice which can sing any melody without imposing its own personality on its song. A "white" sound might be thought of as a sound unencumbered by extrinsically imposed character. The closer to midpoint between where any string is held down at both ends you pluck or strike it, the "whiter" the sound—i.e., the less affected by the nature of the instrument. Moreover, the highly developed mechanical action of the best grand pianos enables the performer to do almost anything he wishes with this basic, adaptable sound.

Skilled piano builders have even been able to minimize the effect of the piano's only significant limitation (shared with the harpsichord, and with all other keyboard instruments save the organ and certain electronic jazz-rock gizmos): its inability to sustain tones indefinitely at a given volume level (you can toot a horn at a constant level of sound, but a piano key, however hard you hit it, hammers a string whose resonance begins immediately to diminish). The result of all these characteristics is that the modern piano is the willing servant of its master, who may mold an interpretation as he wishes, limited only by his personal musical sensibility and technical skills.

But as Courtenay Caublé, the learned contemporary teacher, harpsichord authority and technician, comments, a fine harpsichord performance is the product of a sort of "musical contract between equal partners." In contrast to the piano, the harpsichord has a distinctive, highly complex tonal personality which substantially limits a performer's interpretation. Moreover, the means by which the sounds are produced imposes severe restrictions on how the performer can express musical textures and lines. And only certain kinds of music lend themselves at all to harpsichord performance.

To the piano-oriented performer, these limitations are fatal. But to the rare performer willing to accept his instrument as a willful rather than a willing partner, the results can be uniquely, stunningly gratifying. A classical attitude about artistic production—illustrated so well, for instance, in many of Igor Stravinsky's neoclassical works, as Caublé points out—is that a work of art gains increasing vigor and beauty as the artist focuses his energies by imposing on himself more and more demanding limitations. Some harpsichord music—for instance, compositions of Rameau and Couperin—is so idiomatic that it is unsuccessful when played on any other instrument, even the versatile piano. Other Baroque compositions—Bach's keyboard works, for instance—though they can be successfully reinterpreted by a modern pianist without doing violence to their inherent musicality, take on, under the fingers of a skilled harpsichordist, a shape and meaning uniquely theirs. Without the use of a sustaining pedal, for instance, and, thus, without dramatic increases or diminutions in volume, the music requires, once again, a *different* shaping. Bach's "Chromatic Fantasy and Fugue" can be played on the clavichord, harpsichord, piano and organ, and is exquisite on all four: But the sound and the shape, and the nature of the excitement, are different in each case. A modern listener can choose which rendering— the piano's or the harpsichord's—is more congenial to his taste. But it remains a fact that, to many listeners, the experience of Caublé's "tripartite marriage of composer, instrument and performer," done by the harpsichord, is not just revelation, but a quite ineffable joy.

During the last years of the century, a music craftsman named Arnold Dolmetsch began to fuss about, repairing old instruments, building new ones, and writing about the lost music of the preceding century. But Dolmetsch came, struggled, and went; and still the harpsichord was rare. But restoration was in the wings, and John Challis, Wanda Landowska and Frank Hubbard were about to happen.

In the fall of 1950, I was freshly graduated from Yale University and living in New Haven. I learned that Ralph Kirkpatrick, who was attached in some vague way to the Yale School of Music, would commemorate the two hundredth anniversary of the death of Johann Sebastian Bach by giving three concerts on successive Tuesdays. He would play the entire "Clavierü-bung," which includes the Six Partitas, the "Goldberg Varia-tions," the "Chromatic Fantasy and Fugue," and four duets.

I had played the piano rather seriously as a boy and young teenager, but always my love and awe of the instrument pur-chased more of my enthusiasm than of my time: which is merciful, because those without serious talent in art are miser-ably misled if deluded into believing they can become serious artists, practicing hours on end to no significant effect. I put-tered. I had an upright piano at Yale (cost, $100), and my attraction to the music of Bach led me to curiosity about the sound and the technique of Baroque instruments.

So I attended these concerts and heard a harpsichord perfor-mance in an auditorium for the first time. During the spring of that year, my father had made me a graduation gift. John Challis received a check for $1,000, and I received a beautiful little clavichord, the drawing-room contemporary of the harp-sichord, back in its golden years. What surprised me was a telephone call, the day after the instrument arrived, from Ralph Kirkpatrick—asking whether he might come to my rooms to try out my clavichord. John Challis had written to say that he had experimented with the instrument's bridge, which lies across the sounding board, dictating the pitch of the strings, and Challis wanted Kirkpatrick's reaction to its effec-tiveness.

In those days (and even today, though to a lesser extent), harpsichord makers and performers made up a tight little fra-ternity, comparable to the computer engineers and builders of twenty and fifteen years ago in California and Boston, though less competitive. The financial stakes, in harpsichord building, are not very high (the artistic stakes are infinite). Someday someone should write "The Soul of the New Machine" around the restoration of the harpsichord, an achievement of the twentieth century.

I remember both the excitement of meeting the illustrious Kirkpatrick, then in his thirties, and the protracted anxiety after he sat down to play. He held a cigarette holder with lit cigarette between his lips. It must have been sadism. Surely it was with malice aforethought that he permitted the ash on his burning cigarette to grow to advanced defumescence, reaching the point where you become furiously certain that the long, dirty ashes would fall into the clavichord's womb, all over your delicate little wooden keys and brass tangents. But then—suddenly—the fingers of one of his hands, theretofore wholly engaged in the nimble articulation of complicated fugues, runs and trills, were unaccountably free. With them he would nonchalantly transport the cigarette holder from his lips to the ashtray at the side of the instrument, tap it, detaching the ash, and return to the keyboard to accompany his other hand, which had never stopped playing.

It was, under the circumstances, with special excitement that I went with my wife to Sprague Hall, filled for the occasion with 500 students, faculty and townfolk. We sat for the beginning of the five hours of the Kirkpatrick-Bach we would hear in the course of the fortnight. The experience was dazzling on several counts. There was the music: unusual, to the inexperienced ear; stringy, controlled, subtle, seductive; engaging, finally. The music, rococo; at times somnolently quiet, lyrical; then gay, turbulent. Finally, overpowering.

And virtuosity. It would be five hours of music profoundly intricate; music that, for the most part, cannot be hummed—because you cannot hum two, let alone three or four melodies at the same time. And so much of the music of the Baroque period is contrapuntal—vertical music, they call it; because, on the page, you see it as a column of melodies, so different from the single-line melody with accompanying chords. The awe would mount.

On the evening after the second concert, Kirkpatrick played the "Goldberg Variations." They are, arguably, the most difficult single keyboard work ever written. I attended a reception for the artist and found myself in conversation, once again, with the gentleman who, a few months earlier, had tried out my Challis. "When," I asked reverently, "did you commit yourself to giving these three concerts?"

"Oh," said Kirkpatrick matter-of-factly (he does not smile easily), "it was last spring, in Italy."

"When," I persevered, "did you *practice* the 'Goldberg'?"

"Oh," said Kirkpatrick, visibly struggling to remember a

detail so inconsequential, "it was on a bus. From Perugia to Rome."

Since I think with the speed of light, I reasoned that Kirkpatrick had spent the entire summer riding buses every day from Rome to Perugia—you know, the kind of thing genius-eccentrics do, when they run out of conventionality—with one of those keyboard simulators on his lap, practicing away for the 300, 400 hours it would take to master the "Goldberg." I asked if he had used such a keyboard? He looked at me, perplexed. "Oh, no," he said. "I *rethought* the 'Goldberg' on that ride."

"Wait a minute," I said sternly, bringing the conversation to attention: "I . . . am . . . asking . . . you: When last did you actually *play* the 'Goldberg'?"

"Oh," he said, ruminatively, "I think it was when I was still at Harvard. I was twenty-one, I think." I wandered away, and have wandered ever since away from such fonts of immortality, awestruck. Although I assume there are complementary talents in the piano world, the impact of that epiphany stayed with me, and I thought for the first time about the infinite complexity of a mind that could recall so formidable a composition as the "Goldberg." I knew then and there that no human achievement I was likely to encounter would ever dwarf, in my estimation, this one. And the harpsichord was his chosen instrument. Kirkpatrick had begun on the piano and switched to the harpsichord as a student at Harvard. That he should have done so was terribly important to me.

During that year and the year or two after, the musical world suddenly found itself in the lap of Wanda Landowska. Although in her seventies, Madame Landowska had just released "The Well-Tempered Clavier." It was rapturously received, which did not surprise her, as I learned in the summer of 1950 when I visited her home in Lakeville, Conn., only five miles from my own home. The first words of the 4-foot-8-inch tiger were: "You ahrr familiar weeth my 'Vell-Temperred' recordings?" I told her I was. She closed her eyes: "Magnificent, no?" I agreed that they were.

It is hard to overestimate the influence of Landowska. For a while, she was virtually alone as a harpsichord performer. Her musicality combined with a sense of theater, concerning

which, in the chaste afteryears of the harpsichord explosion of
the 1950s and 1960s, there has been some reservation. You see,
in the harpsichord you have more than one register, as they are
called. The concert instrument normally has two keyboards.
The lower of these plucks a set of strings at a given point along
their length, producing the "lower-eight-foot" sound. This is
the basic harpsichord sound. But if you depress a note on the
upper keyboard you will hear a slightly different sound, because a different string is being twanged by the plucker (which
is called a plectrum). The plectrum is here positioned under a
different point of that other string, evoking the same pitch, but
of a different quality—more nasal, stringier, muter, whatever.
By depressing a "coupler" you can, by striking only the lower-
keyboard eight-footer, simultaneously depress the same note
in the upper keyboard. It goes without saying that the two
timbres should complement each other, in agreeable har-
mony.

But you have just begun. The lower eight can also be struck,
but this time using the buff stop, whereupon the sound is
damped, giving off a pizzicato sound. This is an either-or situation, but if you wish, you can depress a pure note on the upper
keyboard, using the regular eight-foot, while on the lower keyboard you can depress it in the so-called buff mode. A third
alternative is to shift to the *peau de buffle* (buffalo hide) which
gives you a dreamy-soft version of the regular eight. A third set
of strings is pitched an octave higher than the eight-footers,
and called the four-foot. Much of the time the performer will
simultaneously engage the eight-foot and the four-foot, producing a more solid sound.

Now: Wanda Landowska (and indeed a lot of her immediate
successors, most prominently Kirkpatrick and Valenti) regularly used yet another set of strings, those pitched one octave
below the eight-foot. Now strike a chord and it will sound
almost like an organ roll: the equivalent of three pianists playing with perfect coordination on three octaves. The sound
produced by Landowska was wonderfully varied, with substantial reliance on the 16-foot, using every conceivable combination of register. By the late 1960s the use of a 16-foot
register had become musically unfashionable. Why? For historical, practical and esthetic reasons. Only a few harpsichords,

late in their epoch, had 16-foot registers. To supply the 16-foot, it is required that the instrument be stretched out in length considerably, and that heavy strings be used. The temptation to add the extra effect of the 16-foot tends to overcome many performers' taste, and then the sound of the 16-footer can affect adversely that of the other strings, except where a perfect balance is provided by numinous craftsmen—rare.

The disapproval of the 16-foot register, I barge in to say, is only in part justified. I walked once into the Unitarian Church in Westport, Connecticut, to hear Fernando Valenti record the sonatas of Soler, and he was using the famous Challis on which he had recorded more than fifty long-playing records. It is true that sometimes the sound was that of an organ. It is not true that the sound of a harpsichord working was indistinct. The sound was, well, perfect. I'd have shot anyone who threatened to take away Fernando's 16-footer.

The sound of an individual note of the harpsichord does not, if you are measuring decibels, increase measurably by pounding on it. Dynamic effects are therefore the consequence of balance: of rhythm and timing, of delicate releases, of notes properly held. The pleasure taken from hearing someone with these requisite skills performing on a fine instrument is the pleasure of petit point.

A friend was present at the Frick Collection at what proved to be the last public performance of Landowska. She was playing an obscure sonata by Fisher (J. A., 1744–1806) which my friend happened to have been studying. So that he knew it when what was being played suddenly ceased to be Fisher, becoming Landowska, improvising. My friend was concerned. What was she up to? Memory lapse? But, the work being largely unknown, the audience did not react, and in due course she was back, playing what Fisher wrote.

Next on the program was the famous "Chromatic Fantasy and Fugue." As was her habit, Landowska bowed her head slightly before beginning, bringing her hands—extended—to her lips, as if in prayer. Then the right hand was raised dramatically, as if to strike a hammer blow. Suddenly she stopped, wheeling thoughtfully about to address her audience in her heavily accented, high-pitched voice:

"Ladies and gentlemen, lahst night I had a visitor. It was Poppa Bach. We spoke, of corrse, in Cherrman. He said to me, 'Vanda, haff you ever trried *my* fingerring on the "Chromatic Fantasy"?' 'No,' I said to him, and he said the next time I *must trry.* So tonight, I will use a different fingerring and maybe the result will not be the same azz my *incomparable* recorrding."

Wheel back to the instrument. Hands pressed together, raised to the lips. Right hand up.

And then the "Fantasy." Landowska, having experienced the difficulty with Fisher, evidently did not know whether her memory, suddenly insecure, would sustain her through the "Fantasy" which, unlike the Fisher, is as familiar to Baroque-minded audiences as "Twinkle, Twinkle Little Star," precluding surreptitious improvisation.

No dramatist, given a full year's notice, could have written lines more disarming than those she extemporized. And, of course, no one, in her presence, would profess skepticism about her personal familiarity with Poppa Bach.

By the time she died (1959), musical America was thoroughly exposed to the harpsichord. Frank Hubbard, apprentice to Challis, apprentice to Dolmetsch, put down stakes in Boston. There, with William Dowd, he made instruments. In due course they separated, Hubbard more interested in history and theory, Dowd in making wonderful instruments. And soon there was Eric Herz. And before long Boston became known as the Antwerp of the harpsichord world, Antwerp being where Ruckers, the Flemish master, had captured the attention of the discriminating world of harpsichord listeners. Now there were 100 harpsichord makers, including the mass-production types, mostly out of Germany. W. J. Zuckermann wrote a literate and splendidly illustrated book, *The Modern Harpsichord,* in 1969. "Hardly a day passes in New York," he commented, "in which a recording studio is not using a harpsichord. One musical instrument rental service alone possesses a fleet of 18 harpsichords which it was my lot for many years to tune and service daily. These instruments are used in Muzak for banks and supermarkets, incidental music for Shakespeare dramas, advertising jingles for television, background music for documentary films, Christmas music, children's music, cha-

chas, rock-and-roll. . . . How long this fad (if that is what it is) will last, no one can say, but it still seems to be gathering force."

The answer to that question is that the fad did not last. It is over. But harpsichord devotees, if relatively few in number, can only be said to be beleaguered as, say, Israel is beleaguered. The harpsichord family is confident, proud, serene, and maybe just a little patronizing, like the folks who knew Acapulco before it was famous, or read *Lolita* when the Olympia Press brought it out. Their numbers, measured up against Mr. Zuckermann's graph, are static. This happened in part because the theatricality of the galvanizers of the 1950s became excommunicably unfashionable; in part, because the craze for build-it-yourself harpsichord kits proliferated instruments which, because they were so often inferior, were not up to communicating the singular beauty of the well-crafted machine of the masters. In part, also, because a harpsichord simply will not sound out in the big, standard auditoriums to which people go to hear music performed. O.K. So the true believers listen to the harpsichord through records. This is, for the obvious reason, disappointing to the performing artists, who are hard put to gather together audiences of sufficient size to earn a living by playing. Judith Norell, among the most gifted and versatile artists alive (she has even played Gershwin on the harpsichord), gets critical, not popular, acclaim—but the other day I reached her in Topeka, Kansas, where she was playing chamber music. The legendary Fernando Valenti played 100 Scarlatti sonatas on five consecutive evenings at Carnegie Recital Hall, but never to an audience of more than 100. Bleak stuff.

But it does not matter to *us*, because records are available (and some also own the instrument), so that when the spirit sags and (as Melville put it) we are drawn to the tail end of funeral processions, with only minor exertion over the turntable we can hear the "Goldberg," or Rameau, or the ineffable Scarlatti, and rejoice in communion with the eighteenth century, whose dominant figures, sometimes limited to a mere four octaves, created (some of us maintain) the greatest musical literature extant. Much of music, in all ages, is divine. But *Aïda*, with 100 musicians, 200 choristers, a stage designed by

Zeffirelli costing a million dollars, and three elephants, does not bring more joy than the diffident, gifted Gerald Ranck does, seated alone by that little wooden instrument, using only ten fingers and giving us, at St. George's Episcopal Church in Manhattan, a prelude and a fugue written more than 200 years ago. For the harpsichord.

20

Aloise Steiner Buckley, R.I.P.

April 19, 1985

SHE BORE ten children, nine of whom have written for this journal *[National Review]* or worked for it, or both, and that earns her, I think, this half-acre of space normally devoted to those whose contributions are in the public mode. Hers were not. If ever she wrote a letter to a newspaper, we don't remember it, and if she wrote to a congressman or senator, it was probably to say that she wished him well, notwithstanding his mistaken votes, and would pray for him as she did regularly for her country. If she had lived one day more, she'd have reached her ninetieth birthday. Perhaps somewhere else one woman has walked through so many years charming so many people by her warmth and diffidence and humor and faith. I wish I might have known her.

ASB was born in New Orleans, her ancestors having come there from Switzerland some time before the Civil War. She attended Sophie Newcomb College but left after her second year in order to become a nurse, her intention being to go spiritedly to the front, Over there, Over there. But when the young aspiring nurses were given a test to ascertain whether they could cope with the sight of blood and mayhem, she fainted, and was disqualified. A year later she married a prominent thirty-six-year-old Texas-born attorney who lived and practiced in Mexico City, with which she had had ties because her aunt lived there.

She never lived again in New Orleans, her husband taking her, after his exile from Mexico (for backing an unsuccessful revolution that sought to restore religious liberty), to Europe, where his business led him. They had bought a house in Sharon, Connecticut, and in due course returned there. The great house where she brought us up still stands, condominiums now. But the call of the South was strong, and in the mid-thirties they restored an antebellum house in Camden, South Carolina. There she was wonderfully content, making others happy by her vivacity, her delicate beauty, her habit of seeing the best in everyone, the humorous spark in her eye. She never lost a Southern innocence in which her sisters even more conspicuously shared. One of her daughters was delighted on overhearing an exchange between her and her freshly widowed sister who had for fifty years been married to a New Orleans doctor and was this morning, seated on the porch, completing a medical questionnaire, checking this query, ex-xing the other. She turned to Mother and asked, "Darling, as girls did we have gonorrhea?"

Her cosmopolitanism was unmistakably Made-in-America. She spoke fluent French and Spanish with undiluted inaccuracy. My father, who loved her more even than he loved to tease her, and whose knowledge of Spanish was flawless, once remarked that in forty years she had never once placed a masculine article in front of a masculine noun, or a feminine article in front of a feminine noun, except on one occasion when she accidentally stumbled on the correct sequence, whereupon she stopped—unheard of in her case, so fluently did she aggress against the language—and corrected herself by changing the article: the result being that she spoke, in Spanish, of the latest encyclical of Pius XII, the Potato of Rome ("Pio XII, la Papa de Roma"). She would smile, and laugh compassionately, as though the joke had been at someone else's expense, and perhaps play a little with her pearls, just above the piece of lace she always wore in the V of the soft dresses that covered her diminutive frame.

There were rules she lived by, chief among them those she understood God to have specified, though she outdid Him in her accent on good cheer. And although Father was the un-challenged source of authority at home, she was unchal-lengeably in charge of arrangements in a house crowded with ten children and as many tutors, servants, and assistants. In the very late thirties her children ranged in age from one to twenty-one, and an inbuilt sense of appropriate parietal ar-rangements governed the hour at which each of us should be back from wherever we were—away at the movies, or at a dance, or hearing Frank Sinatra sing in Pawling. The conven-tion was inflexible. On returning, each of us would push, on one of the house's intercoms, the button that said, "ASB." The conversation, whether at ten when she was still awake, or at two when she had been two hours asleep, was always the same: "It's me, Mother." "Good night, darling." If—as hardly ever happened—it became truly late, and her mind had not re-corded the repatriation of all ten of us, she would rise, and walk to the room of the missing child. If there, she would return to sleep, and remonstrate the next day on the forgotten tele-phone call. If not there, she would wait up, and demand an explanation.

Her anxiety to do the will of God was more than ritual. I wrote her once early in 1963. Much of our youth had been spent in South Carolina, and the cultural coordinates of our household were Southern. But the times required that we look Southern conventions like Jim Crow hard in the face, and so I asked her how she could reconcile Christian fraternity with the separation of the races, a convention as natural in the South for a hundred years after the Civil War as women's suffrage became natural after their emancipation, and she wrote, "My darling Bill: This is not an answer to your letter, for I cannot answer it too quickly. It came this morning, and, of course, I went as soon as possible to the Blessed Sacrament in our quiet, beautiful little church here. And, dear Bill, I prayed *so* hard for *humility* and for wisdom and for guidance from the Holy Spirit. I know He will help me to answer your questions as He thinks they should be answered. I must pray longer before I do this."

A few years earlier she had raised her glass on my father's seventy-fifth birthday to say, "Darling, here's to fifteen more years together, and then we'll both go." But my father died

three years later. Her grief was profound, and she emerged
from it through the solvent of prayer, her belief in submission
to a divine order, and her irrepressible delight in her family
and friends. A few years later her daughter Maureen died at
age thirty-one, and she struggled to fight her desolation,
though not with complete success. Her oldest daughter, Aloïse,
died three years later. And then, three months ago, her son
John.

She was by then in a comfortable retirement home, totally
absentminded; she knew us all, but was vague about when last
she had seen us, or where, and was given to making references,
every now and then, to her husband ("Will") and the trip they
planned next week to Paris, or Mexico.

But she sensed what had happened, and instructed her
nurse (she was endearingly under the impression that she
owned the establishment in which she had a suite) to drive her
to the cemetery, and there, unknown to us until later that
afternoon, she saw from her car, at the edge of an assembly of
cars, her oldest son lowered into the earth. He had been visiting her every day, often taking her to a local restaurant for
lunch, and her grief was, by her standards, convulsive; but she
did not break her record—she never broke it—which was
never, ever to complain, because, she explained, she could
never repay God the favors He had done her, no matter what
tribulations she might need to suffer.

Ten years ago, my wife and I arrived in Sharon from New
York much later than we had expected, and Mother had given
up waiting for us, so we went directly up to the guest room.
There was a little slip of blue paper on the bed lamp, another
on the door to the bathroom, a third on the mirror. They were
love notes, on her 3 × 5 notepaper inscribed "Mrs. William F.
Buckley." Little valentines of welcome, as though we were
back from circling the globe. There was no sensation to match
the timbre of her pleasure on hearing from you when you
called her on the telephone, or the vibration of her embrace
when she laid eyes on you. Some things truly are unique.

Five days before she died, one week having gone by without
her having said anything—though she clutched the hands of
her children and grandchildren as they came to visit, came to
say good-bye—the nurse brought her from the bathroom to

the armchair and—inflexible rule—put on her lipstick, and the touch of rouge, and the pearls. Suddenly, and for the first time since the terminal descent had begun a fortnight earlier, she reached out for her mirror. With effort she raised it in front of her face, and then said, a teasing smile on her face as she turned to the nurse, "Isn't it amazing that anyone so old can be so beautiful?" The answer, clearly, was, Yes, it was amazing that anyone could be so beautiful.

INDEX